KṚṢṆA

The Supreme Personality of Godhead

A Summary Study of Śrīla Vyāsadeva's *Śrīmad-Bhāgavatam*, Tenth Canto.

VOLUME III

His Divine Grace
A.C. Bhaktivedanta Swami Prabhupāda
Founder-Ācārya of the International Society for Krishna Consciousness

THE BHAKTIVEDANTA BOOK TRUST

Readers interested in the subject matter of this book are invited by the International Society for Krishna Consciousness to correspond with its Secretary at one of the following addresses:

ISKCON Reader Services
P. O. Box 730
Watford, WD25 8ZE, United Kingdom
Tel: +44 (0)1923 857244
Website: www.iskcon.org.uk

Karuna Bhavan
Bankhouse Road, Lesmahagow
Lanarkshire, ML11 0ES
Scotland, United Kingdom
Tel: +44 (0)1555 894790
Fax: +44 (0)1555 894526
E-mail: karunabhavan@aol.com
Website: www.gouranga.cc

The Bhaktivedanta Book Trust
P. O. Box 380
Riverstone, NSW
Australia 2765
Tel: +61 (0)2 96276306
Fax: +61 (0)2 96276052

The Bhaktivedanta Book Trust
Hare Krishna Land
Juhu, Mumbai 400 049, India
Tel: +91 (0)22 26202921
Fax: +91 (0)22 26200357
E-mail: bbtmumbai@pamho.net
Website: www.bbtindia.net

www.krishna.com

ISBN 0-89213-429-1
ISBN 0-89213-430-5 (30-volume set)

Printed in India

From Apple

Everybody is looking for KṚṢṆA.

Some don't realize that they are, but they are.

KṚṢṆA is GOD, the Source of all that exists, the Cause of all that is, was, or ever will be.

As GOD is unlimited, HE has many Names.

Allah-Buddha-Jehova-Rama: All are KṚṢṆA, all are ONE.

God is not abstract; He has both the impersonal and the personal aspects to His personality which is SUPREME, ETERNAL, BLISSFUL, and full of KNOWLEDGE. As a single drop of water has the same qualities as an ocean of water, so has our consciousness the qualities of GOD'S consciousness . . . but through our identification and attachment with material energy (physical body, sense pleasures, material possessions, ego, etc.) our true TRANSCENDENTAL CONSCIOUSNESS has been polluted, and like a dirty mirror it is unable to reflect a pure image.

With many lives our association with the TEMPORARY has grown. This impermanent body, a bag of bones and flesh, is mistaken for our true self, and we have accepted this temporary condition to be final.

Through all ages, great SAINTS have remained as living proof that this non-temporary, permanent state of GOD CONSCIOUSNESS can be revived in all living Souls. Each soul is potentially divine.

Kṛṣṇa says in *Bhagavad Gita:* "Steady in the Self, being freed from all material contamination, the yogi achieves the highest perfectional stage of happiness in touch with the Supreme Consciousness." (VI, 28)

YOGA (a scientific method for GOD (SELF) realization) is the process by which we purify our consciousness, stop further pollution, and arrive at the state of Perfection, full KNOWLEDGE, full BLISS.

If there's a God, I want to see Him. It's pointless to believe in something without proof, and Kṛṣṇa Consciousness and meditation are methods where you can actually obtain GOD perception. You can actually see God, and hear Him, play with Him. It might sound crazy, but He is actually there, actually with you.

There are many yogic Paths—Raja, Jnana, Hatha, Kriya, Karma, Bhakti—which are *all* acclaimed by the MASTERS of each method.

SWAMI BHAKTIVEDANTA is as his title says, a BHAKTI Yogi following the path of DEVOTION. By serving GOD through each thought, word, and DEED, and by chanting of HIS Holy Names, the devotee quickly develops God-consciousness. By chanting

Hare Kṛṣṇa, Hare Kṛṣṇa
Kṛṣṇa Kṛṣṇa, Hare Hare
Hare Rāma, Hare Rāma
Rāma Rāma, Hare Hare

one inevitably arrives at KṚṢṆA Consciousness. (The proof of the pudding is in the eating!)

I request that you take advantage of this book *KṚṢṆA*, and enter into its understanding. I also request that you make an appointment to meet your God now, through the self liberating process of YOGA (UNION) and GIVE PEACE A CHANCE.

ALL YOU NEED IS LOVE (KRISHNA) HARI BOL

George Harrison 31/3/70

Apple Corps Ltd 3 Savile Row London W1 Gerrard 2772/3993 Telex Apcore London

Introduction

This is a book about Kṛṣṇa, the Supreme Personality of Godhead, by the world's leading authority on this transcendental subject—His Divine Grace A.C. Bhaktivedanta Swami Prabhupāda. In his title to this book, and throughout the work, Śrīla Prabhupāda reminds us that Kṛṣṇa is the Supreme Godhead, the Supreme Being. "Kṛṣṇa is the Godhead," he explains, "because He is all-attractive. From practical experience we can see that one is attractive due to 1) wealth, 2) power, 3) fame, 4) beauty, 5) wisdom, and 6) renunciation. One who is in possession of all six of these opulences at the same time, who possesses them to an unlimited degree, is understood to be the Supreme Personality of Godhead."

Kṛṣṇa is a historical personality who appeared on this earth 5,000 years ago. He stayed on earth for 125 years and played exactly like a human being, but His activities were unparallelled. From the moment of His appearance to the moment of His disappearance, all His activities were extraordinary, and they indicate without a doubt that He is the Supreme Personality of Godhead, the Supreme Lord.

Śrīla Prabhupāda points out the difference between Kṛṣṇa and the modern atheists who try to become God by performing some mystic process. Kṛṣṇa is not the kind of God manufactured in a mystic factory. He never had to do anything to become God because He is God in all circumstances. This book, *Kṛṣṇa,* describes all His activities as a human being. But although Kṛṣṇa plays like a human being, He always maintains His identity as the Supreme Personality of Godhead.

The basis for *Kṛṣṇa* is the Vedic scripture called *Śrīmad-Bhāgavatam,* which is considered the essence of all the Vedic writings, such as the *Vedas* and *Upaniṣads.* It is called the "cream of all Vedic literature."

Śrīmad-Bhāgavatam records the narrations spoken by Śukadeva Gosvāmī to King Parikṣit just before the King's departure from this world. King Parikṣit was the King of the entire world, but he was cursed to die within seven days, and therefore he renounced his throne and went to sit on the bank of the Ganges, fasting until death. At that time he met the great saint Śukadeva Gosvāmī, and he expressed to the Gosvāmī his eagerness to spend his last days hearing about the pastimes of Kṛṣṇa. He assured Śukadeva Gosvāmī, "Hunger and thirst may give trouble to ordinary persons, but the topics of Kṛṣṇa are so nice that one can continue to hear about them without being tired because such hearing situates one in the transcendental position."

When King Parikṣit expressed his untiring desire to hear about Kṛṣṇa, Śukadeva Gosvāmī was very pleased, and he began to speak about Kṛṣṇa's pastimes. He encouraged the King by saying, "Your intelligence is very keen because you are so eager to hear about Kṛṣṇa." He informed the

King that hearing and chanting of the pastimes of Kṛṣṇa are so auspicious that the process purifies the three varieties of men involved; he who recites the transcendental topics of Kṛṣṇa, he who hears such topics, and he who inquires about Kṛṣṇa.

The first volume of *Kṛṣṇa* recounts how Kṛṣṇa appeared as the son of Vasudeva and Devakī, who were imprisoned in the dungeon of the wicked King Kaṁsa. Even from His very appearance Kṛṣṇa showed that He is not an ordinary human being, for He appeared as the majestic four-armed Viṣṇu and then turned Himself into a little baby.

Seeking to protect Him from the envious Kaṁsa, Kṛṣṇa's father escaped from prison and carried his son across the River Yamunā to Gokula, where He became the adopted son of a cowherd man, Nanda Mahārāja, and his wife, Yaśodā.

As the son of Nanda and Yaśodā, Kṛṣṇa performed many pastimes resembling those of an ordinary cowherd boy. Yet He exhibited extraordinary feats demonstrating His power as the Supreme Lord. When Kṛṣṇa was only a few weeks old, a gigantic witch named Pūtanā came to poison the child, but when He sucked Her poisoned breast He also sucked out her life. Similarly, Kṛṣṇa also killed many other demons sent by Kaṁsa. Kṛṣṇa revealed to His mother His identity as God when He showed her all the universes floating within His mouth. He demonstrated His supremacy over all other powerful living entities when He thwarted the wrath of the demigod Indra by lifting Govardhana Hill just as easily as an ordinary child might lift a mushroom. He similarly bewildered the powerful demigod Brahmā. He subdued the poisonous serpent Kāliya by dancing on his many heads, He saved His friends from a raging forest fire, and ultimately He danced with the damsels of Vṛndāvana, the *gopīs*, in the celebrated *rāsa* dance.

Kṛṣṇa then left Vṛndāvana and returned to Mathurā, His birthplace, where He killed the wicked Kaṁsa and released His mother and father. He then constructed the wonderful city of Dvārakā within the sea, married more than 16,000 queens, and expanded Himself into more than 16,000 Kṛṣṇas to live with each queen in her individual palace. This brings us to the beginning of Volume Three.

It may further be noted here that one need not have read Volumes One and Two of *Kṛṣṇa* to appreciate the narration of Volume Three. The pastimes of Kṛṣṇa are fully transcendental. Wherever one begins, one will find that by reading one page after another, an immense treasure of enjoyment and knowledge in art, science, literature, religion and philosophy will surely be revealed, and ultimately, by reading this book, *Kṛṣṇa,* one's love for the Supreme Personality of Godhead will fructify.

Contents

"The Supreme Personality of Godhead is Kṛṣṇa [pronounced KRISHNA]. He has an eternal. blissful, spiritual body. He is the origin of all. He has no other origin, and He is the prime cause of all causes."

Brahma-saṁhitā (5.1)

1 / Lord Kṛṣṇa's Daily Activities

From the Vedic *mantras* we learn that the Supreme Personality of Godhead has nothing to do: *na tasya karyaṁ kranaṁ ca vidyate.* If the Supreme Lord has nothing to do, then how can we speak of the activities of the Supreme Lord? From the previous chapter it is clear that no one can act in the way that Lord Kṛṣṇa does. We should clearly note this fact: the activities of the Lord should be followed, but they cannot be imitated. For example, Kṛṣṇa's ideal life as a householder can be followed, but if one wants to imitate Kṛṣṇa by expanding into many forms, that is not possible. We should always remember, therefore, that Lord Kṛṣṇa, although playing the part of a human being, nevertheless simultaneously maintains the position of the Supreme Personality of Godhead. We can follow Lord Kṛṣṇa's dealing with His wives as an ordinary human being, but His dealing with more than sixteen thousand wives at one time cannot be imitated. The conclusion is that to become ideal householders we should follow in the footsteps of Lord Kṛṣṇa as He displayed His daily activities, but we cannot imitate Him at any stage of our life.

Lord Kṛṣṇa used to lie down with His sixteen thousand wives, but also He would rise up from bed very early in the morning, three hours before sunrise. By nature's arrangement the crowing of the cocks warns of the *brāhma-muhūrta* hour. There is no need of alarm clocks; as soon as the cocks crow early in the morning, it is to be understood that it is time to rise from bed. Hearing that sound, Kṛṣṇa would get up from bed, but His rising early was not very much to the liking of His wives. The wives of Kṛṣṇa were so much attached to Him that they would lie in bed embracing Him, but as soon as the cocks crowed, Kṛṣṇa's wives would be very sorry and would immediately condemn the crowing.

In the garden within the compound of each palace there were *pārijāta* flowers. *Pārijāta* is not an artificial flower. We remember that Kṛṣṇa brought the *pārijāta* trees from heaven and implanted them in all His palaces. Early in the morning, a mild breeze would carry the aroma of the *pārijāta* flower, and Kṛṣṇa would smell it just after rising from bed. Due to this aroma, the honeybees would begin their humming vibration, and the birds also would begin their sweet chirping sounds. All together it would sound like the singing of professional chanters engaged in offering prayers to Kṛṣṇa. Although Śrīmatī Rukmiṇīdevī, the first queen of Lord Kṛṣṇa, knew that *brāhma-muhūrta* is the most auspicious time in the entire day, she would feel disgusted at the appearance of *brāhma-muhūrta* because she was not very happy to have Kṛṣṇa leave her side in bed. Despite Śrīmatī Rukmiṇīdevī's disgust, Lord Kṛṣṇa would immediately get up from bed exactly on the appearance of *brāhma-muhūrta*. An ideal householder should learn from the behavior of Lord Kṛṣṇa how to rise early in the morning, however comfortably he may be lying in bed embraced by his wife.

After rising from bed, Lord Kṛṣṇa would wash His mouth, hands and feet and would immediately sit down and meditate on Himself. This does not mean, however, that we should also sit down and meditate on ourselves. We have to meditate upon Kṛṣṇa, Rādhā-Kṛṣṇa. That is real meditation, Kṛṣṇa is Kṛṣṇa Himself; therefore He was teaching us that *brāhma-muhūrta* should be utilized for meditation on Rādhā-Kṛṣṇa. By doing so, Kṛṣṇa would feel very much satisfied, and similarly we will also feel transcendentally pleased and satisfied if we utilize the *brāhma-muhūrta* period to meditate on Rādhā and Kṛṣṇa and if we think of how Śrī Rukmiṇīdevī and Kṛṣṇa acted as ideal householders to teach the whole human society to rise early in the morning and immediately engage in Kṛṣṇa consciousness. There is no difference between meditating on the eternal forms of Rādhā-Kṛṣṇa and chanting the *mahāmantra*, Hare Kṛṣṇa. As for Kṛṣṇa's meditation, He had no alternative but to meditate on Himself. The object of meditation is Brahman, Paramātmā or the Supreme Personality of Godhead, but Kṛṣṇa Himself is all three: He is the Supreme Personality of Godhead, Bhagavān; the localized Paramātmā is His plenary parcel expansion; and the all-pervading Brahman effulgence is the personal rays of His transcendental body. Therefore Kṛṣṇa is always one, and for Him there is no differentiation. That is the difference between an ordinary living being and Kṛṣṇa. For an ordinary living being there are many distinctions. An ordinary living being is different from his body, and he is different from other species of living entities. A human being is different from other human beings and different from the animals. Even in his own body, there are different bodily limbs. We have our hands and legs, but our hands are different from our legs. The hand cannot act like the leg, nor can the leg act like the hand. The eyes cannot hear like the ears, nor can the ears see like the eyes. All these differences are technically called *svajtiya vijtiya.*

The bodily limitation whereby one part of the body cannot act as another part is totally absent in the Supreme Personality of Godhead. There is no difference between His body and Himself. He is completely spiritual, and therefore there is no material difference between His body and His soul. Similarly, He is not different from His millions of incarnations and plenary expansions. Baladeva is the first expansion of Kṛṣṇa, and from Baladeva expand Saṇkarṣaṇa, Vāsudeva, Pradyumna and Aniruddha. From Saṅkarṣaṇa there is again an expansion of Nārāyaṇa, and from Nārāyaṇa there is a second quadruple expansion of Saṇkarṣaṇa, Vāsudeva, Pradyumna and Aniruddha. Similarly there are innumerable expansions of Kṛṣṇa, but all of them are one. Kṛṣṇa has many incarnations, such as Lord Nṛsiṁha, Lord Boar, Lord Fish and Lord Tortoise, but there is no difference between Kṛṣṇa's original two-handed form, like that of a human being, and these incarnations of gigantic animal forms. Nor is there any difference between the action of one part of His body and that of another. His hands can act as His legs, His eyes can act as His ears, or His nose can act as another part of His body. Kṛṣṇa's smelling and eating and hearing are all the same. We limited living entities have to use a particular part of our body for a particular purpose, but there is no such distinction for Kṛṣṇa. In the *Brahma-saṁhitā* it is said, *aṅgāni yasya sakalendriya-vṛtti*: He can perform the activities of one limb with any other limb. So by analytical study of Kṛṣṇa and His person, it is concluded that He is the complete whole. When He meditates, therefore, He meditates on Himself. The self-meditation by ordinary men, designated in Sanskrit as *so'ham,* is simply imitation. Kṛṣṇa may meditate on Himself because He is the complete whole, but we cannot imitate Him and meditate on ourselves. Our body is a designation; Kṛṣṇa's body is not a designation. Kṛṣṇa's body is also Kṛṣṇa. There is no existence of anything foreign in Kṛṣṇa. Whatever there is in Kṛṣṇa is also Kṛṣṇa. He is therefore the supreme, indestructible complete existence, or the supreme truth.

Kṛṣṇa's existence is not relative existence. Everything else but Kṛṣṇa is a relative truth, but Kṛṣṇa is the Supreme Absolute Truth. Kṛṣṇa does not depend on anything but Himself for His existence. Our existence, however is relative. For example, only when there is the light of the sun, the moon or electricity are we able to see. Our seeing, therefore, is relative, and the light of the sun and moon and electricity is also relative; they are called illuminating only because we see them as such. Dependence and relativity do not exist in Kṛṣṇa. His activities are not dependent on anyone else's appreciation, nor does He depend on anyone else's help. He is beyond the existence of limited time and space, and because He is transcendental to time and space, He cannot be covered by the illusion of *māyā,* whose activities are limited. In the Vedic literature we find that the Supreme Personality of Godhead has multi-potencies. Since all such potencies are emanations from Him, there is no difference between Him and His potencies. Certain philosophers say, however, that when Kṛṣṇa comes He accepts a material body. But even if it is accepted that when He comes to the material world He accepts a material body, it should be concluded also that because the material energy is not different from Him, this body does not act materially. In the *Bhagavad-gītā* it is said, therefore, that He appears by His own internal potency, *ātma-māyā.*

Kṛṣṇa is called the Supreme Brahman because He is the cause of creation, the cause of maintenance and the cause of dissolution. Lord Brahmā, Lord Viṣṇu and Lord Śiva are different expansions of these material qualities. All these material qualities can act upon the conditioned souls, but there is no such action and reaction upon Kṛṣṇa because these qualities are all simultaneously one and different from Him. Kṛṣṇa Himself is simply *sac-cid-ānanda-vigraha,* the eternal form of bliss and knowledge, and because of His inconceivable greatness, He is called the Supreme Brahman. His meditation on Brahman or Paramātmā or Bhagavān is on Himself only and not on anything else beyond Himself. This meditation cannot be imitated by the ordinary living entity.

After His meditation, the Lord would regularly bathe early in the morning with clear sanctified water. Then He would change into fresh clothing, cover Himself with a wrapper and then engage Himself in His daily religious functions. Out of His many religious duties, the first was to offer oblations into the sacrificial fire and silently chant the Gāyatrī *mantra.* Lord Kṛṣṇa, as the ideal householder, executed all the religious functions of a householder without deviation. When the sunrise became visible, the Lord would offer specific prayers to the sun-god. The sun-god and other demigods mentioned in the Vedic scriptures are described as different limbs of the body of Lord Kṛṣṇa, and it is the duty of the householder to offer respects to the demigods and great sages, as well as the forefathers.

As it is said in the *Bhagavad-gītā,* The Lord has no specific duty to perform in this world, and yet He acts just like an ordinary man living an ideal life within this material world. In accordance with Vedic ritualistic principles, the Lord would offer respects to the demigods. The regulative principle by which the demigods and forefathers are worshiped is called *tarpaṇa,* which means pleasing. One's forefathers might have to take a body on another planet, but by performance of this *tarpaṇa* system, they become very happy wherever they may be. It is the duty of the householder to make his family members happy, and by following this *tarpaṇa* system he can make his forefathers happy also. As the perfect exemplary householder, Lord Śrī Kṛṣṇa followed this *tarpaṇa* system and offered respectful obeisances to the elderly superior members of His family.

His next duty was to give cows in charity to the *brāhmaṇas.* Lord Kṛṣṇa used to give as many as 13,084 cows. Each of them was decorated with a silken cover and pearl necklace, their horns were covered with gold plating, and their hooves were silver-plated. All of them were full of milk, due to having their first-born calves with them, and they were very tame and peaceful. When the cows were given in charity to the *brāhmaṇas*, the *brāhmaṇas* also were given nice silken garments, and each was given a deerskin and sufficient quantity of sesame grains. The Lord is generally known as *go-brāhmaṇa-hitāya ca,* which means that His first duty is to see to the welfare of the cows and the *brāhmaṇas.* Thus He used to give cows in charity to the *brāhmaṇas,* with opulent decorations and paraphernalia. Then, wishing for the welfare of all living entities, He would touch auspicious articles such as milk, fire, honey, ghee (clarified butter), gold, jewels and fire. Although the Lord is by nature very beautiful due to the perfect figure of His transcendental body, still He would dress Himself in yellow colored garments and put on His necklace of Kaustubha jewels. He would wear flower garlands, smear His body with the pulp of sandalwood and decorate Himself with other similar cosmetics and ornaments. It is said that the ornaments themselves became beautiful upon being placed on the transcendental body of the Lord. After decorating Himself in this way, the Lord would then look at marble statues of the cow and calf and visit temples of God or demigods like Lord Śiva. There were many *brāhmaṇas* who would come daily to see the Supreme Lord before taking their breakfast; they were anxious to see Him, and He welcomed them.

His next duty was to please all kinds of men belonging to the different castes, both in the city and within the palace compound. He made them happy by fulfilling their different desires, and when the Lord saw them happy He also became very much pleased. The flower garlands, betel nuts, sandalwood pulp and other fragrant cosmetic articles which were offered to the Lord would be distributed by Him, first to the *brāhmaṇas* and elderly members of the family, then to the queens, then to the ministers, and if there were still some balance He would utilize it for His own personal use. By the time the Lord finished all these daily duties and activities,

His charioteer Dāruka would come with His wonderful chariot to stand before the Lord with folded hands, intimating that the chariot was ready, and the Lord would come out of the palace to travel. Then the Lord, accompanied by Uddhava and Sātyaki, would ride on the chariot just as the sun-god rides on his chariot in the morning, appearing with his blazing rays on the surface of the world. When the Lord was about to leave His palaces, all the queens would look at Him with feminine gestures. The Lord would respond to their greetings with smiles, attracting their hearts so much so that they would feel intense separation from the Lord.

Then the Lord would go to the assembly house known as Sudharmā. It may be remembered that the Sudharmā assembly house was taken away from the heavenly planet and was reestablished in the city of Dvārakā. The specific significance of the assembly house was that anyone who entered it would be freed from the six kinds of material pangs, namely hunger, thirst, lamentation, illusion, old age and death. These are the webs of material existence, and as long as one remained in that assembly house of Sudharmā he would not be infected by these six material webs. The Lord would say good-bye in all the sixteen thousand palaces, and again He would become one and enter the Sudharmā assembly house in procession with other members of the Yadu dynasty. After entering the assembly house, He used to sit on the exalted royal throne and would be seen to emanate glaring rays of transcendental effulgence. In the midst of all the great heroes of the Yadu dynasty, Kṛṣṇa resembled the full moon in the sky, surrounded by multi-luminaries. In the assembly house there were professional jokers, dancers, musicians and ballet girls, and as soon as the Lord sat on His throne, they would begin their respective functions in order to please the Lord and put Him in a happy mood. First of all the jokers would talk in such a way that the Lord and His associates would enjoy their humor which would refresh the morning mood. The dramatic actors would then play their parts, and the dancing ballet girls would separately display their artistic movements. All these functions would be accompanied by the beating of *mṛdaṅga* drums and the sounds of the *vīṇā* and flutes and bells, followed by the sound of the *pākhvaj,* another type of drum. Along with these musical vibrations, the auspicious sound of the conchshell would also be added. The professional singers called *sūtas* and *māgadhas* would sing, and others would perform their dancing art. In this way, as devotees, they would offer respectful prayers to the Supreme Personality of Godhead. Sometimes the learned *brāhmaṇas* present in that assembly would chant Vedic hymns and explain them to the audience to their best knowledge, and sometimes some of them would recite old historical accounts of the activities of prominent kings. The Lord, accompanied by His associates, would be very much pleased to hear them.

Once upon a time, a person arrived at the gateway of the assembly house who was unknown to all the members of the assembly, and with the permission of Lord Kṛṣṇa he was admitted into the assembly by the doorkeeper. The doorkeeper was ordered to present him before the Lord, and the man appeared and offered his respectful obeisances unto the Lord with folded hands. It had happened that when King Jarāsandha conquered all other kingdoms many kings did not bow their heads before Jarāsandha, and as a result of this all of them, numbering twenty thousand, were arrested and made his prisoners. The man who was brought before Lord Kṛṣṇa by the doorkeeper was a representative messenger from all these imprisoned kings. Being duly presented before the Lord, the man began to explain the actual situation as follows:

"My dear Lord, You are the eternal form of transcendental bliss and knowledge. As such, You are beyond the reach of the mental speculation or vocal description of any materialistic man within this world. A slight portion of Your glories can be known by persons who are fully surrendered unto Your lotus feet, and by Your grace only such persons become freed from all material anxieties. My dear Lord, I am not one of these surrendered souls; I am still within the duality and illusion of this material existence. I have therefore come to take shelter of Your lotus feet, for I am afraid of the cycle of birth and death. My dear Lord, I think that there are many living entities like me who are eternally entangled in fruitive activities and their resultant reactions. They are never inclined to follow Your instructions by performance of devotional service, although it is pleasing to the heart and most auspicious for one's existence. On the contrary, they are against the path of Kṛṣṇa conscious life, and they are wandering within the three worlds impelled by the illusory energy of material existence.

"My dear Lord, who can estimate Your mercy and Your powerful activities? You are present always as the insurmountable force of eternal time, engaged in baffling the indefatigable desires of the materialists, who are thus repeatedly becoming confused and frustrated. I therefore offer my respectful obeisances unto You in Your form of eternal time. My dear Lord, You are the proprietor of all the worlds, and You have incarnated Yourself along with Your plenary expansion Lord Balarāma. It is said that Your appearance in this incarnation is for the purpose of protecting the faithful and destroying the miscreants. Under the circumstances, how is it possible that miscreants like Jarāsandha can put us into such deplorable conditions of life against Your authority? We are puzzled at the situation and cannot understand how it is possible. It may be that Jarāsandha has been deputed to give us such trouble because of our past misdeeds, but we have heard from revealed scriptures that anyone who surrenders unto Your lotus feet immediately becomes immune to the reactions of sinful life. I have therefore been deputed by all the imprisoned kings to whole-heartedly offer ourselves unto Your shelter, and we hope that Your Lordship will now give us full protection. We have now come to the real conclusion of our lives. Our kingly positions are nothing but the reward of our past pious activities, just as our suffering imprisonment by Jarāsandha is the result of our past impious activities. We realize now that the resultant reactions of both pious and impious activities are temporary and that we can never be happy in this conditioned life. This material body is awarded to us by the modes of material nature, and on account of this we are full of anxieties. The material condition of life simply involves bearing the burden of this dead body. As a result of fruitive activities we have thus been subjected to being beasts of burden for these bodies, and being forced by conditional life, we have given up the pleasing life of Kṛṣṇa consciousness. Now we realize that we are the most foolish persons. We have been entangled in the network of material reaction due to our ignorance. We have therefore come to the shelter of Your lotus feet, which can immediately eradicate all the results of fruitive action and thus free us from the contamination of material pains and pleasures.

"Dear Lord, because we are now surrendered souls at Your lotus feet, You can give us relief from the entrapment of fruitive action made possible by the form of Jarāsandha. Dear Lord, it is known to You that Jarāsandha possesses the power of ten thousand elephants, and with this power he has imprisoned us, just as a lion hypnotizes a flock of sheep. My dear Lord, You have already fought with Jarāsandha eighteen times consecutively, out of which You have defeated him seventeen times by surpassing his extraordinary powerful position. But in Your eighteenth fight, You exhibited Your human behavior, and thus it appeared that You were defeated. My dear Lord, we know very well that Jarāsandha cannot defeat You at any time because Your power, strength, resources and authority are all unlimited. No one can equal You or surpass You. The appearance of defeat by Jarāsandha in the eighteenth engagement is nothing but an exhibition of human behavior. Unfortunately, foolish Jarāsandha could not understand Your tricks, and he has since then become puffed up over his material power and prestige. Specifically, he has arrested us and imprisoned us, knowing fully that as Your devotees, we are subordinate to Your sovereignty.

"Now I have explained our awful position, and Your Lordship can consider and do whatever You like. As the messenger and representative of all those imprisoned kings, I have submitted my words before Your Lordship and presented our prayers to You. All the kings are very anxious to see You so that they can all personally surrender at Your lotus feet. My dear Lord, be merciful upon them and act for their good fortune."

At the very moment the messenger of the imprisoned kings was presenting his appeal before the Lord, the great sage Nārada also arrived. Because he was a great saint, his hair was dazzling like gold, and when he entered the assembly house it appeared that the sun-god was personally present in the midst of the assembly. Lord Kṛṣṇa is the worshipable master of even Lord Brahmā and Lord Śiva, yet as soon as He saw that the sage Nārada had arrived, He immediately stood up along with His ministers and secretaries to receive the great sage and offer His respectful obeisances by bowing His head. The great sage Nārada took a comfortable seat, and Lord Kṛṣṇa worshiped him with all paraphernalia, as required for the regular reception of a saintly person. While He was trying to satisfy Nāradajī, Lord Kṛṣṇa spoke the following words in His sweet and natural voice.

"My dear great sage among the demigods, I think that now everything is well within the three worlds. You are perfectly eligible to travel everywhere in space in the upper, middle and lower planetary systems of this universe. Fortunately, when we meet you we can very easily take information from your holiness of all the news of the three worlds; within this cosmic manifestation of the Supreme Lord, there is nothing concealed from your knowledge. You know everything, and so I wish to question you. Are the Pāṇḍavas doing well, and what is the present plan of King Yudhiṣṭhira? Will you kindly let Me know what they want to do at present?"

The great sage Nārada spoke as follows: "My dear Lord, You have spoken about the cosmic manifestation created by the Supreme Lord, but I know that You are the all-pervading creator. Your energies are so extensive and inconceivable that even powerful personalities like Brahmā, the lord of this particular universe, cannot measure Your inconceivable power. My dear Lord, You are present as the Supersoul in everyone's heart by Your inconceivable potency, exactly like the fire which is present in everyone but which no one can see directly. In conditioned life, every living entity is within the jurisdiction of the three modes of material nature. As such, they are unable to see Your presence everywhere with their material eyes. By Your grace, however, I have seen many times the action of Your inconceivable potency, and therefore when You ask me for news of the Pāṇḍavas, which is not at all unknown to You, I am not surprised at Your inquiry. My dear Lord, by Your inconceivable potencies You create this cosmic manifestation, maintain it and again dissolve it. It is by dint of Your inconceivable potency only that this material world, although a shadow representation of the spiritual world, appears to be factual. No one can understand what You plan to do in the future. Your transcendental position is always inconceivable to everyone. As far as I am concerned, I can simply offer my respectful obeisances unto You again and again. In the bodily concept of knowledge, everyone is driven by material desires, and thus everyone develops new material bodies one after another in the cycle of birth and death. Being absorbed in such a concept of existence, one does not know how to get out of this encagement of the material body. Out of Your causeless mercy, my Lord, You descend to exhibit Your different transcendental pastimes, which are illuminating and full of glory. Therefore I have no alternative but to offer my respectful obeisances unto You. My dear Lord, You are the supreme Parambrahman, and Your pastimes as an ordinary human are another tactical resource, exactly like a play on the stage in which the actor plays parts different from his own identity. You have inquired about Your cousins the Pāṇḍavas in the role of their well-wisher, and therefore I shall let You know about their intentions. Now please hear me. First of all may I inform You that King Yudhiṣṭhira has all material opulences which are possible to achieve in the highest planetary system, Brahmaloka. He has no material opulence for which to aspire, and yet he wants to perform Rājasūya sacrifices only to get Your association and please You.

Nārada informed Lord Kṛṣṇa, "King Yudhiṣṭhira is so opulent that he has attained all the opulences of Brahmaloka even on this earthly planet. He is fully satisfied, and he does not need anything more. He is full in everything, but now he wants to worship You in order to achieve Your causeless mercy, and I beg to request You to fulfill his desires. My dear Lord, in these great sacrificial performances by King Yudhiṣṭhira there will be an assembly of all the demigods and all the famous kings of the world.

"My dear Lord, You are the Supreme Brahman, Personality of Godhead. One who engages himself in Your devotional service by the prescribed methods of hearing, chanting and remembering certainly becomes purified from the contamination of the modes of material nature, and what to speak of those who have the opportunity to see You and touch You directly. My dear Lord, You are the symbol of everything auspicious. Your transcendental name and fame have spread all over the universe, including the higher, middle and lower planetary systems. The transcendental water which washes Your lotus feet is known in the higher planetary system as Mandākinī, in the lower planetary system as Bhogavatī, and in this earthly planetary system as the Ganges. This sacred, transcendental water flows throughout the entire universe, purifying wherever it flows."

Just before the great sage Nārada arrived in the Sudharmā assembly house of Dvārakā, Lord Kṛṣṇa and His ministers and secretaries had been considering how to attack the kingdom of Jarāsandha. Because they were seriously considering this subject, Nārada's proposal that Lord Kṛṣṇa go to Hastināpura for Mahārāja Yudhiṣṭhira's great Rājasūya sacrifice did not much appeal to them. Lord Kṛṣṇa could understand the intentions of his associates because He is the ruler of even Lord Brahmā. Therefore, in order to pacify them, He smilingly said to Uddhava, "My dear Uddhava, you are always my well-wishing confidential friend. I therefore wish to see everything through you because I believe that your counsel is always right. I believe that you understand the whole situation perfectly. Therefore I am asking your opinion. What should I do? I have faith in you, and therefore I shall do whatever you advise." It was known to Uddhava that although Lord Kṛṣṇa was acting like an ordinary man, He knew everything—past, present and future. However, because the Lord was trying to consult with him, Uddhava, in order to render service to the Lord, began to speak.

Thus ends the Bhaktivedanta purport of the Third Volume, First Chapter, of* Kṛṣṇa, *"Lord Kṛṣṇa's Daily Activities."

2 / Lord Kṛṣṇa in Indraprastha City

In the presence of the great sage Nārada and all the other associates of Lord Kṛṣṇa, Uddhava considered the situation and then spoke as follows: "My dear Lord, first of all let me say that the great sage Nārada Muni has requested You to go to Hastināpura to satisfy King Yudhiṣṭhira, your cousin, who is making arrangements to perform the great sacrifice known as Rājasūya. I think, therefore, that Your Lordship should immediately go there to help the King in this great adventure. However, although to accept the invitation offered by the sage Nārada Muni as primary is quite appropriate, at the same time, my Lord, it is Your duty to give protection to the surrendered souls. Both purposes can be served if we understand the whole situation. Unless we are victorious over all the kings, no one can perform this Rājasūya sacrifice. In other words, it is to be understood that King Yudhiṣṭhira cannot perform this great sacrifice without gaining victory over the belligerent King Jarāsandha. The Rājasūya sacrifice can only be performed by one who has gained victory over all directions. Therefore, to execute both purposes, we first of all have to kill Jarāsandha. I think that if we can somehow or other gain victory over Jarāsandha, then automatically all our purposes will be served. The imprisoned kings will be released, and with great pleasure we shall enjoy the spread of Your transcendental fame at having saved the innocent kings whom Jarāsandha has imprisoned.

"But King Jarāsandha is not an ordinary man. He has proved a stumbling block even to great warriors because his bodily strength is equal to the strength of 10,000 elephants. If there is anyone who can conquer this king, he is none other than Bhīmasena because he also possesses the strength of 10,000 elephants. The best thing would be for Bhīmasena to fight alone with him. Then there would be no unnecessary killing of many soldiers. In fact, it will be very difficult to conquer Jarāsandha when he stands with his *akṣauhiṇī* divisions of soldiers. We may therefore adopt a policy more favorable to the situation. We know that King Jarāsandha is very much devoted to the *brāhmaṇas.* He is very charitably disposed towards them; he never refuses any request from a *brāhmaṇa.* I think, therefore, that Bhīmasena should approach Jarāsandha in the dress of a *brāhmaṇa,* beg charity from Him, and then personally engage in fighting Him. And in order to assure Bhīmasena's victory, I think that Your Lordship should also accompany him. If the fighting takes place in Your presence, I am sure Bhīmasena will emerge victorious because simply by Your presence everything impossible is made possible, just as Lord Brahmā creates this universe and Lord Śiva destroys it simply through Your influence.

"Actually, You are creating and destroying the entire cosmic manifestation; Lord Brahmā and Lord Śiva are only the superficially visible causes. Creation and destruction are actually being performed by the invisible time factor, which is Your impersonal representation. Everything is under the control of this time factor. If Your invisible time factor can perform such wonderful acts through Lord Brahmā and Lord Śiva, will not Your personal presence help Bhīmasena to conquer Jarāsandha? My dear Lord, when Jarāsandha is killed, then the queens of all the imprisoned kings will be so joyful at their husbands' being released by Your mercy that they will all begin to sing Ycur glories. They will be as pleased as the *gopīs* were when they were relieved from the hands of Śaṅkhāsura. All the great sages, the King of the elephants, Gajendra, the goddess of fortune, Sītā, and even Your father and mother, were all delivered by Your causeless mercy. We also have been thus delivered, and we are always singing the transcendental glories of Your activities.

"Therefore, I think that if the killing of Jarāsandha is undertaken first, that will automatically solve many other problems. As for the Rājasūya sacrifice arranged in Hastināpura, it will be held, either because of the pious activities of the imprisoned kings or the impious activities of Jarāsandha.

"My Lord, it appears that You are also personally to go to Hastināpura to perform this great sacrifice so that demoniac kings like Jarāsandha and Śiśupāla may be conquered, the pious imprisoned kings released, and at the same time the great Rājasūya sacrifice performed. Considering all these points, I think that Your Lordship should immediately proceed to Hastināpura."

This advice of Uddhava's was appreciated by all who were present in the assembly, and everyone considered that Lord Kṛṣṇa's going to Hastināpura would be beneficial from all points of view. The great sage Nārada, the elderly personalities of the Yadu dynasty, and the Supreme Personality of Godhead Kṛṣṇa Himself all supported the statement of Uddhava. Lord Kṛṣṇa then took permission from His father Vasudeva and grandfather Ugrasena, and He immediately ordered His servants Dāruka and Jaitra to arrange for travel to Hastināpura. When everything was prepared, Lord Kṛṣṇa especially bid farewell to Lord Balarāma and the King of the Yadus, Ugrasena, and after dispatching His queens along with their children and sending their necessary luggage ahead, He mounted His chariot, which bore the flag marked with the symbol of Garuḍa.

Before starting the procession, Lord Kṛṣṇa satisfied the great sage Nārada by offering him different kinds of worshipable articles. Nāradajī wanted to fall at the lotus feet of Kṛṣṇa, but because the Lord was playing the part of a human being, he simply offered his respects within his mind, and fixing the transcendental form of the Lord within his heart, he left the assembly house by the airways. Usually the sage Narada never walks on the surface of the globe, but travels in outer space. After the departure of Nārada, Lord Kṛṣṇa addressed the messenger who had come from the imprisoned kings. He told him that they should not be worried. He would very soon arrange to kill the King of Magadha, Jarāsandha. Thus He wished good fortune to all the imprisoned kings and the messenger. After receiving this assurance from Lord Kṛṣṇa, the messenger returned to the imprisoned kings and informed them of the happy news of the Lord's forthcoming visit. All the kings became joyful at the news and began to wait very anxiously for the Lord's arrival.

The chariot of Lord Kṛṣṇa began to proceed, accompanied by many other chariots, along with elephants, cavalry, infantry and similar royal paraphernalia. Bugles, drums, trumpets, conchshells, horns and coronets all began to produce a loud auspicious sound which vibrated in all directions. The 16,000 queens, headed by the goddess of fortune Rukmiṇīdevī, the ideal wife of Lord Kṛṣṇa, and accompanied by their respective sons, all followed behind Lord Kṛṣṇa. They were dressed in costly garments decorated with ornaments, and their bodies were smeared with sandalwood pulp and garlanded with fragrant flowers. Riding on palanquins which were nicely decorated with silks, flags, and golden lace, they followed their exalted husband, Lord Kṛṣṇa. The infantry soldiers carried shields, swords and lances in their hands and acted as royal bodyguards to the queens. In the rear of the procession were the wives and children of all the other followers, and there were many society girls also following. Many beasts of burden like bulls, buffaloes, mules, and asses carried the camps, bedding and carpets, and the women who were following were seated in separate palanquins on the backs of camels. This panoramic procession was accompanied by the shouts of the people and was full with the display of different colored flags, umbrellas and whisks and different varieties of weapons, dress, ornaments, helmets and armaments. The procession, being reflected in the sunshine, appeared just like an ocean with high waves and sharks.

In this way the procession of Lord Kṛṣṇa's party advanced towards Hastināpura (New Delhi) and gradually passed through the kingdoms of Ānarta (Gujarat Province), Sauvīra (Sauret), the great desert of Rājasthān, and then Kurukṣetra. In between those kingdoms there were many mountains, rivers, towns, villages, pasturing grounds and mining fields. The procession passed through all of these places in its advance. On His way to Hastināpura, the Lord crossed two big rivers, the Dṛṣvatī and the Sarasvatī. Then He crossed the province of Pañchāla and the province of Matsya. In this way, ultimately He arrived at Indraprastha.

The audience of the Supreme Personality of Godhead, Kṛṣṇa, is not very commonplace. Therefore, when King Yudhiṣṭhira heard that Lord Kṛṣṇa had already arrived in his capital city, Hastināpura, he became so joyful that all his hairs stood on end in great ecstasy, and he immediately came out of the city to properly receive Him. He ordered the musical vibration of different instruments and songs, and the learned *brāhmaṇas* of the city began to chant the hymns of the *Vedas* very loudly. Lord Kṛṣṇa is known as Hṛṣīkeśa, the master of the senses, and King Yudhiṣṭhira went forward to receive Him exactly as the senses meet the consciousness of life. King Yudhiṣṭhira was the elderly cousin of Kṛṣṇa. Naturally he had great affection for the Lord, and as soon as he saw Him, his heart became filled with great love and affection. He had not seen the Lord for many days, and therefore he thought himself most fortunate to see Him present before him. The King therefore began to embrace Lord Kṛṣṇa again and again in great affection.

The eternal form of Lord Kṛṣṇa is the everlasting residence of the goddess of fortune. As soon as King Yudhiṣṭhira embraced Him, he became free from all the contamination of material existence. He immediately felt transcendental bliss, and he merged in an ocean of happiness. There were tears in his eyes, and his body shook due to ecstasy. He completely forgot that he was living in this material world. After this, Bhīmasena, the second brother of the Pāṇḍavas, smiled and embraced Lord Kṛṣṇa, thinking of Him as his own maternal cousin, and thus he was merged in great ecstasy. Bhīmasena also was so filled with ecstasy that for the time being he forgot his material existence. Then Lord Śrī Kṛṣṇa Himself embraced the other three Pāṇḍavas, Arjuna, Nakula and Sahadeva. The eyes of all three brothers were inundated with tears, and Arjuna began to embrace Kṛṣṇa again and again because they were intimate friends. The two younger Pāṇḍava brothers, after being embraced by Lord Kṛṣṇa, fell down at His lotus feet to offer their respects. Lord Kṛṣṇa thereafter offered His obeisances to the *brāhmaṇas* present there, as well as to the elderly members of the Kuru dynasty, like Bhīṣma, Droṇa and Dhṛtarāṣṭra. There were many kings of different provinces such as Kuru, Sṛñjaya and Kekaya, and Lord Kṛṣṇa duly reciprocated greetings and respects with them. The professional reciters like the *sūtas, māgadhas,* and *vandinas,* accompanied by the *brāhmaṇas,* began to offer their respectful prayers to the Lord. Artists and musicians like the Gandharvas, as well as the royal jokers, began to play their drums, conchshells, kettledrums, *vīṇās, mṛdaṅgas,* and bugles, and they exhibited their dancing art in order to please the Lord. Thus the all-famous Supreme Personality of Godhead, Lord Kṛṣṇa, entered the great city of Hastināpura, which was opulent in every respect. While Lord Kṛṣṇa was entering the city, everyone was talking amongst themselves about the glories of the Lord, praising His transcendental name, quality, form, etc.

The roads, streets and lanes of Hastināpura were all sprinkled with fragrant water through the trunks of intoxicated elephants. In different places of the city there were colorful festoons and flags decorating the houses and streets. At important road crossings there were gates with golden decorations, and at the two sides of the gates there were golden water jugs. These beautiful decorations glorified the opulence of the city. Participating in this great ceremony, all the citizens of the city gathered here and there, dressed in colorful new clothing, decorated with ornaments, flower garlands, and fragrant scents. Each and every house was illuminated by hundreds and thousands of lamps placed in different corners of the cornices, walls, columns, bases and architraves, and from far away the rays of the lamps resembled the festival of Dīpāvalī (a particular festival observed on the New Year's Day of the Hindu calendar). Within the walls of the houses, fragrant incense was burning, and smoke rose through the windows, making the entire atmosphere very pleasing. On the top of every house flags were flapping, and the gold water pots kept on the roofs shone very brilliantly.

Lord Kṛṣṇa thus entered the city of the Pāṇḍavas, enjoyed the beautiful atmosphere and slowly proceeded ahead. When the young girls in every house heard that Lord Kṛṣṇa, the only object worth seeing, was passing on the road, they became very anxious to see this all-famous personality. Their hair loosened, and their tightened saris became slack due to their hastily rushing to see Him. They gave up their household engagements, and those who were lying in bed with their husbands immediately left them and came directly down onto the street to see Lord Kṛṣṇa.

The procession of elephants, horses, chariots, and infantry was very crowded; some, being unable to see properly in the crowd, got up on the roofs of the houses. They were pleased to see Lord Śrī Kṛṣṇa passing with His thousands of queens. They began to shower flowers on the procession, and they embraced Lord Kṛṣṇa within their minds and gave Him a hearty reception. When they saw Him in the midst of His many queens, like the full moon situated amidst many luminaries, they began to talk amongst themselves.

One girl said to another, "My dear friend, it is very difficult to guess what kind of pious activities these queens might have performed, for they are always enjoying the smiling face and loving glances of Kṛṣṇa." While Lord Kṛṣṇa was thus passing on the road, at intervals some of the opulent citizens, who were all rich, respectable and freed from sinful activities presented auspicious articles to the Lord, just to offer Him a reception to the city. Thus they worshiped Him as humble servitors.

When Lord Kṛṣṇa entered the palace, all the ladies there became overwhelmed with affection just upon seeing Him. They immediately received Lord Kṛṣṇa with glittering eyes expressing their love and affection for Him, and Lord Kṛṣṇa smiled and accepted their feelings and gestures of reception. When Kuntī, the mother of the Pāṇḍavas, saw her nephew Lord Kṛṣṇa, the Supreme Personality of Godhead, she became overpowered with love and affection. She at once got up from her bedstead and appeared before Him with her daughter-in-law, Draupadī, and in maternal love and affection she embraced Him. As he brought Kṛṣṇa within the palace, King Yudhiṣṭhira became so confused in his jubilation that he practically forgot what he was to do at that time in order to receive Kṛṣṇa and worship Him properly. Lord Kṛṣṇa delightfully offered His respects and obeisances to Kuntī and other elderly ladies of the palace. His younger sister, Subhadrā, was also standing there with Draupadī, and both offered their respectful obeisances unto the lotus feet of the Lord. At the indication of her mother-in-law, Draupadī brought clothing, ornaments and garlands, and with this paraphernalia they received the queens Rukmiṇī, Satyabhāmā, Bhadrā, Jāmbavatī, Kālindī, Mitravindā, Lakṣmaṇā and the devoted Satyā. These principal queens of Lord Kṛṣṇa were first received, and then the remaining queens were also offered a proper reception. King Yudhiṣṭhira arranged for Kṛṣṇa's rest and saw that all who came along with Him—namely His queens, His soldiers, His ministers and His secretaries—were comfortably situated. He had arranged that they would experience a new feature of reception everyday while staying as guests of the Pāṇḍavas.

It was during this time that Lord Śrī Kṛṣṇa, with the help of Arjuna, for the satisfaction of the fire-god, Agni, allowed Agni to devour the Khāṇḍava Forest. During the forest fire, Kṛṣṇa saved the demon Mayāsura, who was hiding in the forest. Upon being saved, Mayāsura felt obliged to the Pāṇḍavas and Lord Kṛṣṇa, and he constructed a wonderful assembly house within the city of Hastināpura. In this way, Lord Kṛṣṇa, in order to please King Yudhiṣṭhira, remained in the city of Hastināpura for several months. During His stay, He enjoyed strolling here and there. He used to drive on chariots along with Arjuna, and many warriors and soldiers used to follow them.

Thus ends the Bhaktivedanta purport of the Third Volume, Second Chapter, of Kṛṣṇa, *"Lord Kṛṣṇa in Indraprastha City."*

3 / Liberation of King Jarāsandha

In the great assembly of respectable persons, citizens, friends, relatives, *brāhmaṇas, kṣatriyas* and *vaiśyas,* King Yudhiṣṭhira, in the presence of all, including his brothers, directly addressed Lord Kṛṣṇa as follows: "My dear Lord Kṛṣṇa, the sacrifice known as the Rājasūya *yajña* is to be performed by the emperor, and it is considered to be the king of all sacrifices. By performing this sacrifice, I wish to satisfy all the demigods, who are Your empowered representatives within this material world, and I wish that You will kindly help me in this great adventure so that it may be successfully executed. As far as the Pāṇḍavas are concerned, we have nothing to ask from the demigods. We are personally fully satisfied by being Your devotees. As You say in the *Bhagavad-gītā,* "Persons who are bewildered by material desires worship the demigods," but our purpose is different. I want to perform this Rājasūya sacrifice and invite the demigods to show them that they have no power independent of You. They are all Your servants, and You are the Supreme Personality of Godhead. Foolish persons with a poor fund of knowledge consider Your Lordship an ordinary human being. Sometimes they try to find fault in You, and sometimes they defame You. Therefore I wish to perform this Rājasūya *yajña.* I wish to invite all the demigods, beginning from Lord Brahmā, Lord Śiva and other exalted chiefs of the heavenly planets, and in that great assembly of demigods from all parts of the universe, I want to substantiate that You are the Supreme Personality of Godhead and that everyone is Your servant.

"My dear Lord, those who are constantly in Kṛṣṇa consciousness and who think of Your lotus feet or of Your shoes certainly become free from all contamination of material life. Persons who are engaged in Your service in full Kṛṣṇa consciousness, who meditate upon You only or who offer prayers unto You, are purified souls. Being constantly engaged in Kṛṣṇa conscious service, such persons become freed from the cycle of repeated birth and death. They do not even desire to become freed from this material existence or to enjoy material opulences; their desires are fulfilled by Kṛṣṇa conscious activities. As far as we are concerned, we are fully surrendered unto Your lotus feet, and by Your grace we are so fortunate to see You personally. Therefore, naturally we have no desire for material opulences. The verdict of the Vedic wisdom is that You are the Supreme Personality of Godhead. I want to establish this fact, and I also want to show the world the difference between accepting You as the Supreme Personality of Godhead and accepting You as an ordinary powerful historical person. I wish to show the world that one can attain the highest perfection of life simply by taking shelter at Your lotus feet, exactly as one can satisfy the branches, twigs, leaves and flowers of an entire tree simply by watering the root. Thus, if one takes to Kṛṣṇa consciousness, his life becomes fulfilled both materially and spiritually.

"This does not mean that You are partial to the Kṛṣṇa conscious person and are indifferent to the non-Kṛṣṇa conscious person. You are equal to everyone; that is Your declaration. You cannot be partial to one and not interested in others because You are sitting in everyone's heart as the Supersoul and giving everyone the respective results of his fruitive activities. You give every living entity the chance to enjoy this material world as he desires. As Supersoul, You are sitting in the body along with the living entity, giving him the results of his own actions as well as opportunities to turn toward Your devotional service by developing Kṛṣṇa consciousness. You openly declare that one should surrender unto You, giving up all other engagements, and that You will take charge of him, giving him relief from the reactions of all sins. You are like the desire tree in the heavenly planets, which awards benediction according to one's desires. Everyone is free to achieve the highest perfection, but if one does not so desire, then Your awarding of lesser benedictions is not due to partiality."

On hearing this statement of King Yudhiṣṭhira, Lord Kṛṣṇa replied as follows: "My dear King Yudhiṣṭhira, O killer of enemies, O ideal justice personified, I completely support your decision to perform the Rājasūya sacrifice. By performing this great sacrifice, your good name will remain well established forever in the history of human civilization. My dear King, may I inform you that it is the desire of all great sages, your forefathers, the demigods, and your relatives and friends, including Myself, that you perform this sacrifice, and I think that it will satisfy every living entity. But, because it is necessary, I request that you first of all conquer all the kings of the world and collect all requisite paraphernalia for executing this great sacrifice. My dear King Yudhiṣṭhira, your four brothers are direct representatives of important demigods like Varuṇa, Indra, etc. [It is said that Bhīma was born of the demigod Varuṇa, and Arjuna was born of the demigod Indra, whereas King Yudhiṣṭhira himself was born of the demigod Yamarāja.] Your brothers are great heroes, and you are the most pious and self-controlled king and are therefore known as Dharmarāja. All of you are so qualified in devotional service unto Me that automatically I have become rivalled by you."

Lord Kṛṣṇa told King Yudhiṣṭhira that He becomes conquered by the love of one who has conquered his senses. One who has not conquered his senses cannot conquer the Supreme Personality of Godhead. This is the secret of devotional service. To conquer the senses means to engage them constantly in the service of the Lord. The specific qualification of all the Pāṇḍava brothers was that they always engaged their senses in the service of the Lord. One who thus engages his senses becomes purified, and with purified senses one can actually render service to the Lord. The Lord can thus be conquered by the devotee by loving transcendental service.

Lord Kṛṣṇa continued: "There is no one in the three worlds of the universe, including the powerful demigods, who can surpass My devotees in any of the six opulences, namely, wealth, strength, reputation, beauty, knowledge and renunciation. Therefore, if you want to conquer the worldly kings, there is no possibility of their emerging victorious."

When Lord Kṛṣṇa thus encouraged King Yudhiṣṭhira, the King's face brightened like a blossoming flower because of transcendental happiness, and thus he ordered his younger brothers to conquer all the worldly kings in all directions. Lord Kṛṣṇa empowered the Pāṇḍavas to execute His great mission of chastising the infidel miscreants of the world and giving protection to His faithful devotees. In His Viṣṇu form, the Lord therefore carries four kinds of weapons in His four hands. He carries a lotus flower and a conchshell in two hands, and in the other two hands He carries a club and a disc. The club and disc are meant for the nondevotees, but because the Lord is the Supreme Absolute, the resultant action of all His weapons is one and the same. With the club and the disc He chastises the miscreants so that they may come to their senses and know that they are not all in all. Over them there is the Supreme Lord. And by bugling with the conchshell and by offering blessings with the lotus flower, He always assures the devotees that no one can vanquish them, even in the greatest calamity. King Yudhiṣṭhira, being thus assured by the indication of Lord Kṛṣṇa, ordered his youngest brother, Sahadeva, accompanied by soldiers of the Sṛñjaya tribe, to conquer the southern countries. Similarly, he ordered Nakula, accompanied by the soldiers of Matsyadeśa, to conquer the kings of the western side. He sent Arjuna, accompanied by the soldiers of Kekayadeśa, to conquer the kings of the northern side, and Bhīmasena, accompanied by the soldiers of Madradeśa (Madras), was ordered to conquer the kings on the eastern side.

It may be noted that by dispatching his younger brothers to conquer in different directions, King Yudhiṣṭhira did not actually intend that they declare war with the kings. Actually, the brothers started for different directions to inform the respective kings about King Yudhiṣṭhira's intention to perform the Rājasūya sacrifice. The kings were thus informed that they were required to pay taxes for the execution of the sacrifice. This payment of taxes to Emperor Yudhiṣṭhira meant that the king accepted his subjugation before him. In case of a king's refusal to act accordingly, there was certainly a fight. Thus by their influence and strength, the brothers conquered all the kings in different directions, and they were able to bring in sufficient taxes and presentations. These were brought before King Yudhiṣṭhira by his brothers.

King Yudhiṣṭhira was very anxious, however, when he heard that King Jarāsandha of Magadha did not accept his sovereignty. Seeing King Yudhiṣṭhira's anxiety, Lord Kṛṣṇa informed him of the plan explained by Uddhava for conquering King Jarāsandha. Bhīmasena, Arjuna and Lord Kṛṣṇa then started together for Girivraja, the capital city of Jarāsandha, dressing themselves in the garb of *brāhmaṇas.* This was the plan devised by Uddhava before Lord Kṛṣṇa started for Hastināpura, and now it was given practical application.

King Jarāsandha was a very dutiful householder, and he had great respect for the *brāhmaṇas.* He was a great fighter, a *kṣatriya* king, but he was never neglectful of the Vedic injunctions. According to Vedic injunctions, the *brāhmaṇas* are considered to be the spiritual masters of all other castes. Lord Kṛṣṇa, Arjuna and Bhīmasena were actually *kṣatriyas,* but they dressed themselves as *brāhmaṇas,* and at the time when King Jarāsandha was to give charity to the *brāhmaṇas* and receive them as guests, they approached him.

Lord Kṛṣṇa, in the dress of a *brāhmaṇa,* said to the King: "We wish all glories to your majesty. We are three guests at your royal palace, and we are coming from a great distance. We have come to ask you for charity, and we hope that you will kindly bestow upon us whatever we ask from you. We know about your good qualities. A person who is tolerant is always prepared to tolerate everything, even though distressful. Just as a criminal can perform the most abominable acts, so a greatly charitable person like you can give anything and everything he is asked for. For a great personality like you, there is no distinction between relatives and outsiders. A famous man lives forever, even after his death; therefore, any person who is completely fit and able to execute acts which will perpetuate his good name and fame and yet does not do so becomes abominable in the eyes of great persons. Such a person cannot be condemned enough, and his refusal to give charity is lamentable throughout his whole life. Your majesty must have heard the glorious names of charitable personalities such as Hariścandra, Rantideva and Mudgala, who used to live only on grains picked up from the paddy field, and the great Mahārāja Śibi, who saved the life of a pigeon by supplying flesh from his own body. These great personalities have attained immortal fame simply by sacrificing this temporary and perishable body." Lord Kṛṣṇa, in the garb of a *brāhmaṇa,* thus informed Jarāsandha that fame is imperishable, but the body is perishable. If one can attain imperishable name and fame by sacrificing his perishable body, he becomes a very respectable figure in the history of human civilization.

While Lord Kṛṣṇa was speaking in the garb of a *brāhmaṇa* along with Arjuna and Bhīma, Jarāsandha marked that the three of them did not appear to be actual *brāhmaṇas.* There were signs on their bodies by which Jarāsandha could understand that they were *kṣatriyas.* Their shoulders were marked with an impression due to carrying bows; they had beautiful bodily structure, and their voices were grave and commanding. Thus he definitely concluded that they were not *brāhmaṇas,* but *kṣatriyas.* He was also thinking that he had seen them somewhere before. Although these three persons were *kṣatriyas,* they had come to his door begging alms like *brāhmaṇas.* Therefore he decided that he would fulfill their desires, in spite of their being *kṣatriyas.* He thought in this way because their position had already been diminished by their appearing before him as beggars. "Under the circumstances," he thought, "I am prepared to give them anything. Even if they ask for my body, I shall not hesitate to offer it to them." In this regard, he began to think of Bali Mahārāja. Lord Viṣṇu in the dress of a *brāhmaṇa* appeared as a beggar before Bali, and in that way He snatched away all of his opulence and kingdom. He did this for the benefit of Indra, who, having been defeated by Bali Mahārāja, was bereft of his kingdom. Although Bali Mahārāja was cheated, his reputation as a great devotee who was able to give anything and everything in charity is still glorified throughout the three worlds. Bali Mahārāja could guess that the *brāhmaṇa* was Lord Viṣṇu Himself and that He had come to him just to take away his opulent kingdom on behalf of Indra. Bali's spiritual master and family priest, Śukrācārya, repeatedly warned him about this, and yet Bali did not hesitate to give in charity whatever the *brāhmaṇa* wanted, and at last he gave up everything to that *brāhmaṇa.* "It is my strong determination," thought Jarāsandha, "that if I can achieve immortal reputation by sacrificing this perishable body, I must act for that purpose; the life of a *kṣatriya* who does not live for the benefit of the *brāhmaṇa* is certainly condemned."

Actually King Jarāsandha was very liberal in giving charity to the *brāhmaṇas,* and thus he informed Lord Kṛṣṇa, Bhīma and Arjuna: "My dear *brāhmaṇas,* you can ask from me whatever you like. If you so desire, you can take my head also. I am prepared to give it."

After this, Lord Kṛṣṇa addressed Jarāsandha as follows: "My dear King, please note that we are not actually *brāhmaṇas,* nor have we come to ask for foodstuffs or grains. We are all *kṣatriyas,* and we have come to beg a duel with you. We hope that you will agree to this proposal. You may note that here is the second son of King Pāṇḍu, Bhīmasena, and the third son of Pāṇḍu, Arjuna. As for Myself, you may know that I am your old enemy, Kṛṣṇa, the cousin of the Pāṇḍavas."

When Lord Kṛṣṇa disclosed their disguise, King Jarāsandha began to laugh very loudly, and then in great anger and in a grave voice he exclaimed, "You fools! If you want to fight with me, I immediately grant your request. But, Kṛṣṇa, I know that You are a coward. I refuse to fight with You because You become very confused when You face me in fighting. Out of fear of me You left Your own city, Mathurā, and now You have taken shelter within the sea; therefore I must refuse to fight with You. As far as Arjuna is concerned, I know that he is younger than me and is not an equal fighter. I refuse to fight with him because he is not in any way an equal competitor. But as far as Bhīmasena is concerned, I think he is a suitable competitor to fight with me." After speaking in this way, King Jarāsandha immediately handed a very heavy club to Bhīmasena, and he himself took another, and thus all of them went outside the city walls to fight.

Bhīmasena and King Jarāsandha engaged themselves in fighting, and with their respective clubs, which were as strong as thunderbolts, they began to strike one another very severely, both of them being eager to fight. They were both expert fighters with clubs, and their techniques of striking one another were so beautiful that they appeared to be two dramatic artists dancing on a stage. When the clubs of Jarāsandha and Bhīmasena loudly collided, they sounded like the impact of the big tusks of two fighting elephants or like a thunderbolt in a flashing electrical storm. When two elephants fight together in a sugarcane field, each of them snatches a stick of sugarcane and, by catching it tightly in its trunk, strikes the other. Each elephant heavily strikes his enemy's shoulders, arms, collarbones, chest, thighs, waist, and legs, and in this way the sticks of sugarcane are smashed. Similarly, all the clubs used by Jarāsandha and Bhīmasena were broken, and so the two enemies prepared to fight with their strong-fisted hands. Both Jarāsandha and Bhīmasena were very angry, and they began to smash each other with their fists. The striking of their fists sounded like the striking of iron bars or like the sound of thunderbolts, and they appeared to be like two elephants fighting. Unfortunately, however, neither was able to defeat the other because both were very expert in fighting, both were of equal strength, and their fighting techniques were equal also. Neither Jarāsandha nor Bhīmasena became fatigued or defeated in the fighting, although they struck each other continually. At the end of a day's fighting, both lived at night as friends in Jarāsandha's palace, and the next day they fought again. In this way they passed twenty-seven days in fighting.

On the twenty-eighth day, Bhīmasena told Kṛṣṇa, "My dear Kṛṣṇa, I must frankly admit that I cannot conquer Jarāsandha." Lord Kṛṣṇa, however, knew the mystery of the birth of Jarāsandha. Jarāsandha was born in two different parts from two different mothers. When his father saw that the baby was useless, he threw the two parts in the forest, where they were later found by a black-hearted witch named Jarā. She managed to join the two parts of the baby from top to bottom. Knowing this, Lord Kṛṣṇa therefore also knew how to kill him. He gave hints to Bhīmasena that since Jarāsandha was brought to life by the joining of the two parts of his body, he could be killed by the separation of these two parts. Thus Lord Kṛṣṇa transferred His power into the body of Bhīmasena and informed him of the device by which Jarāsandha could be killed. Lord Kṛṣṇa immediately picked up a twig from a tree and, taking it in His hand, bifurcated it. In this way He hinted to Bhīmasena how Jarāsandha could be killed. Lord Kṛṣṇa, the Supreme Personality of Godhead, is omnipotent, and if He wants to kill someone, no one can save that person. Similarly, if He wants to save someone, no one can kill him.

Informed by the hints of Lord Kṛṣṇa, Bhīmasena immediately took hold of the legs of Jarāsandha and threw him to the ground. When Jarāsandha fell to the ground, Bhīmasena immediately pressed one of Jarāsandha's legs to the ground and took hold of the other leg with his two hands. Catching Jarāsandha in this way, he tore his body in two, beginning from the anus up to the head. As an elephant breaks the branches of a tree in two, so Bhīmasena separated the body of Jarāsandha. The audience standing nearby saw that the body of Jarāsandha was now divided into two halves, so that each half had one leg, one thigh, one testicle, one breast, half a backbone, half a chest, one collarbone, one arm, one eye, one ear, and half a face.

As soon as the news of Jarāsandha's death was announced, all the citizens of Magadha began to cry, "Alas, alas," while Lord Kṛṣṇa and Arjuna embraced Bhīmasena to congratulate him. Although Jarāsandha was killed, neither Kṛṣṇa nor the two Pāṇḍava brothers made a claim to the throne. Their purpose in killing Jarāsandha was to stop him from creating a disturbance against the proper discharge of world peace. A demon always creates disturbances, whereas a demigod always tries to keep peace in the world. The mission of Lord Kṛṣṇa is to give protection to the righteous persons and to kill the demons who disturb a peaceful situation. Therefore Lord Kṛṣṇa immediately called for the son of Jarāsandha, whose name was Sahadeva, and with due ritualistic ceremonies He asked him to occupy the seat of his father and reign over the kingdom peacefully. Lord Kṛṣṇa is the master of the whole cosmic creation, and He wants everyone to live peacefully and execute Kṛṣṇa consciousness. After installing Sahadeva on the throne, He released all the kings and princes who had been imprisoned unnecessarily by Jarāsandha.

Thus ends the Bhaktivedanta purport of the Third Volume, Third Chapter, of* Kṛṣṇa, *"Liberation of King Jarāsandha."

4 / Lord Kṛṣṇa Returns to the City of Hastināpura

The kings and the princes released by Lord Kṛṣṇa after the death of Jarāsandha were rulers of different parts of the world. Jarāsandha was so powerful in military strength that he had conquered all these princes and kings, numbering 20,800. They were all incarcerated within a mountain cave especially constructed as a fort, and for a long time they were kept in that situation. When they were released by the grace of Lord Kṛṣṇa, they all looked very unhappy, their garments were niggardly, and their faces were almost dried up for want of proper bodily care. They were very weak due to hunger, and their faces had lost all beauty and luster. Because of the kings' long imprisonment, every part of their bodies had become slackened and invalid. But although suffering in that miserable condition of life, they had the opportunity to think about the Supreme Personality of Godhead, Viṣṇu.

Now before them they saw the color of the transcendental body of Lord Kṛṣṇa, exactly like the hue of a newly arrived cloud in the sky. He appeared before them nicely covered by yellow colored silken garments, with four hands like Viṣṇu, and carrying the different symbols of the club, the conchshell, the disc and the lotus flower. There were marks of golden lines on His chest, and the nipples of His breast appeared to be like the whorl of a lotus flower. His eyes appeared to be spread like the petals of a lotus flower, and His smiling face exhibited the symbol of eternal peace and prosperity. His glittering earrings were set beautifully, and His helmet was bedecked with valuable jewels. The Lord's necklace of pearls and the bangles and bracelets nicely situated on His body all shone with a transcendental beauty. The Kaustubha jewel hanging on His chest glittered with great luster, and the Lord wore a beautiful flower garland. After so much distress, when the kings and princes saw Lord Kṛṣṇa, with His beautiful transcendental features, they looked upon Him to their hearts' content, as if they were drinking nectar through their eyes, licking His body with their tongues, smelling the aroma of His body with their noses, and embracing Him with their arms. Just by dint of their being in front of the Supreme Personality of Godhead, all reactions to their sinful activities were washed away. Therefore, without reservation, they surrendered themselves at the lotus feet of the Lord. It is stated in the *Bhagavad-gītā* that unless one is freed from all kinds of sinful reactions, one cannot fully surrender unto the lotus feet of the Lord. All the princes who saw Lord Kṛṣṇa forgot all their past tribulations. With folded hands and with great devotion, they began to offer prayers to Lord Kṛṣṇa, as follows.

"Dear Lord, O Supreme Personality of Godhead, master of all demigods, You can immediately remove all Your devotees' pangs because Your devotees are fully surrendered unto You. O dear Lord Kṛṣṇa, O eternal Deity of transcendental bliss and knowledge, You are imperishable, and we offer our respectful obeisances unto Your lotus feet. It is by Your causeless mercy that we have been released from the imprisonment of Jarāsandha, but now we pray unto You to release us from the imprisonment with the illusory energy of this material existence. Please, therefore, stop our continuous cycle of birth and death. We now have sufficient experience of the miserable material condition of life in which we are fully absorbed, and having tasted its bitterness, we have come to take shelter under Your lotus feet. Dear Lord, O killer of the demon Madhu, we can now clearly see that Jarāsandha was not at fault in the least; it is actually by Your causeless mercy that we were bereft of our kingdoms because we were very proud of calling ourselves rulers and kings. Any ruler or king who becomes too puffed up with false prestige and power does not get the opportunity to understand his real constitutional position and eternal life. Such foolish so-called rulers and kings become falsely proud of their position under the influence of Your illusory energy; they are just like a foolish person who considers a mirage in the desert to be a reservoir of water. Foolish persons think that their material possessions will give them protection, and those who are engaged in sense gratification falsely accept this material world as a place of eternal enjoyment. O Lord, O Supreme Personality of Godhead, we must admit that, before this, we were puffed up with our material opulences. Because we were all envious of each other and wanted to conquer one another, we all engaged in fighting for supremacy, even at the cost of sacrificing the lives of many citizens."

This is the disease of political power. As soon as a king or a nation becomes rich in material opulences, it wants to dominate other nations by military aggression. Similarly, mercantile men want to monopolize a certain type of business and control other mercantile groups. Degraded by false prestige and infatuated by material opulences, human society, instead of striving for Kṛṣṇa consciousness, creates havoc and disrupts peaceful living. Thus men naturally forget the real purpose of life: to attain the favor of Lord Viṣṇu, the Supreme Personality of Godhead.

The kings continued: "O Lord, we were simply engaged in the abominable task of killing citizens and alluring them to be unnecessarily killed, just to satisfy our political whims. We did not consider that Your Lordship is always present before us in the form of cruel death. We were so fooled that we became the cause of death for others, forgetting our own impending death. But, dear Lord, the retaliation of the time element, which is Your representative, is certainly insurmountable. The time element is so strong that no one can escape its influence; therefore we have received the reactions of our atrocious activities, and we are now bereft of all opulences and stand before You like street beggars. We consider our position to be Your causeless, unalloyed mercy upon us because now we can understand that we were falsely proud and that our material opulences could be withdrawn from us within a second by Your will. By Your causeless mercy only, we are now able to think of Your lotus feet. This is our greatest gain. Dear Lord, it is known to everyone that the body is a breeding ground of diseases. Now we are sufficiently aged, and instead of being proud of our bodily strength, we are getting weaker day by day. We are no longer interested in sense gratification or the false happiness derived through the material body. By Your grace, we have now come to the conclusion that hankering after such material happiness is just like searching for water in a desert mirage. We are no longer interested in the results of our pious activities, such as performing great sacrifices in order to be elevated to the heavenly planets. We now understand that such elevation to a higher material standard of life in the heavenly planets may sound very relishable, but actually there cannot be any happiness within this material world. We pray for Your Lordship to favor us by instructing us how to engage in the transcendental loving service of Your lotus feet so that we may never forget our eternal relationship with Your Lordship. We do not want liberation from the entanglement of material existence. By Your will we may take birth in any species of life; it does not matter. We simply pray that we may never forget Your lotus feet under any circumstances. Dear Lord, we now surrender unto Your lotus feet by offering our respectful obeisances unto You because You are the Supreme Lord, the Personality of Godhead, Kṛṣṇa, the son of Vasudeva. You are the Supersoul in everyone's heart, and You are Lord Hari, who can take away all miserable conditions of material existence. Dear Lord, Your name is Govinda, the reservoir of all pleasure. One who is engaged in satisfying Your senses automatically satisfies his own senses also, and therefore You are known as Govinda. Dear Lord, You are ever famous, for You can put an end to all the miseries of Your devotees. Please, therefore, accept us as Your surrendered servants."

After hearing the prayers of the kings released from the prison of Jarāsandha, Lord Kṛṣṇa, who is always the protector of surrendered souls and the ocean of mercy for the devotees, replied to them as follows in His sweetly transcendental voice, which was grave and full of meaning. "My dear kings," He said, "I bestow upon you My blessings. From this day forth you will be attached to My devotional service without fail. I give you this benediction, as you have desired. You may know from Me that I am always sitting within your hearts as Supersoul, and because you have now turned your faces towards Me, I, as master of everyone, shall always give you good counsel so that you may never forget Me and so that gradually you will come back home, back to Godhead. My dear kings, your decision to give up all conceptions of material enjoyment and turn instead toward My devotional service is factually the symptom of your good fortune. Henceforward you will always be blessed with blissful life. I confirm that all you have spoken about Me in your prayers is factual. It is a fact that the materially opulent position of one who is not fully Kṛṣṇa conscious is the cause of his downfall and of his becoming a victim of the illusory energy. In the past, there were many rebellious kings, such as Haihaya, Nahuṣa, Vena, Rāvaṇa and Narakāsura. Some of them were demigods, and some of them were demons, but because of their false perception of their positions, they fell from their exalted posts, and thus they no longer remained the kings of their respective kingdoms.

"While lost in the violence of conditional life, every one of you must understand that anything material has its starting point, growth, expansion, deterioration, and, finally, disappearance. All material bodies are subjected to these six conditions, and any relative acquisitions which are accumulated by this body are definitely subject to final destruction. Therefore, no one should be attached to perishable things. As long as one is within this material body, he should be very cautious in worldly dealings. The most perfect way of life in this material world is simply to be devoted to My transcendental loving service and to honestly execute the prescribed duties of one's particular position of life. As far as you are concerned, you all belong to *kṣatriya* families. Therefore, you should live honestly, according to the prescribed duties befitting the royal order, and you should make your citizens happy in all respects. Keep to the standard of *kṣatriya* life. Do not beget children out of sense gratification, but simply take charge of the welfare of the people in general. Everyone takes birth in this material world because of the contaminated desires of his previous life, and thus he is subjected to the stringent laws of nature, such as birth and death, distress and happiness, profit and loss. One should not be disturbed by duality, but should always be fixed in My service and thus remain balanced in mind and satisfied in all circumstances, considering all things to be given by Me, and one should remain undeviated from engagement in devotional service. Thus one can live a very happy and peaceful life, even within this material condition. In other words, one should actually be callous to this material body and its by-products and should remain unaffected by them. He should remain fully satisfied in the interests of the spirit soul and be engaged in the service of the Supersoul. One should engage his mind only on Me, one should simply become My devotee, one should simply worship Me, and one should offer his respectful obeisances unto Me alone. In this way, one can cross over this ocean of nescience very easily and at the end come back to Me. In conclusion, your lives should constantly be engaged in My service."

After delivering His instructions to the kings and princes, Lord Kṛṣṇa immediately arranged for their comfort and asked many servants and maidservants to take care of them. Lord Kṛṣṇa requested Sahadeva, the son of King Jarāsandha, to supply all necessities to the kings and also asked him to show them all respect and honor. In pursuance of the order of Lord Kṛṣṇa, Sahadeva offered them all honor, and presented them with ornaments, garments, garlands, and other paraphernalia. After taking their baths and dressing very nicely, the kings appeared happy and gentle. Then they were supplied nice foodstuffs. Lord Kṛṣṇa supplied everything for their comfort, as was befitting their royal positions. Since the kings were so mercifully treated by Lord Kṛṣṇa, they felt great happiness, and all their bright faces appeared just like the stars in the sky after the end of the rainy season. They were all nicely dressed and ornamented, and their earrings glittered. Each one was then seated on a chariot bedecked with gold and jewels and drawn by decorated horses. After seeing that each was taken care of, Lord Kṛṣṇa, in a sweet voice, asked them to return to their respective kingdoms. By His very liberal behavior, unparalleled in the history of the world, Lord Kṛṣṇa released all the kings who had been in the clutches of Jarāsandha, and being fully satisfied, the kings began to engage in chanting His holy name, thinking of His holy form, and glorifying His transcendental pastimes as the Supreme Personality of Godhead. So engaged, they returned to their respective kingdoms. The citizens of their kingdoms were very greatly pleased to see them return, and when they heard of the kind dealings of Lord Kṛṣṇa, they all became very happy. The kings began to manage the affairs of their kingdoms in accordance with the instructions of Lord Kṛṣṇa, and all those kings and their subjects passed their days very happily. This is the vivid example of the Kṛṣṇa conscious society. If the people of the world divide the whole society, in terms of their respective material qualities, into four orders for material and spiritual progress, centering around Kṛṣṇa and following the instructions of Kṛṣṇa as stated in *Bhagavad-gītā,* the entire human society will undoubtedly be happy. This is the lesson that we have to take from this incident.

After thus causing the annihilation of Jarāsandha by Bhīmasena and after being properly honored by Sahadeva, the son of Jarāsandha, Lord Kṛṣṇa, accompanied by Bhīmasena and Arjuna, returned to the city of Hastināpura. When they reached the precincts of Hastināpura, they blew their respective conchshells, and by hearing the sound vibrations and understanding who was arriving, everyone immediately became cheerful. But upon hearing the conchshells, the enemies of Kṛṣṇa became very sorry. The citizens of Indraprastha felt their hearts become joyful simply by hearing the vibration of Kṛṣṇa's conchshell because they could understand that Jarāsandha had been killed. Now the performance of the Rājasūya sacrifice by King Yudhiṣṭhira was almost certain. Bhīmasena, Arjuna, and Kṛṣṇa, the Supreme Personality of Godhead, arrived before King Yudhiṣṭhira and offered their respects to the King. King Yudhiṣṭhira attentively heard the narration of the killing of Jarāsandha and the setting free of the kings. He also heard of the tactics which were adopted by Kṛṣṇa to kill Jarāsandha. The king was naturally affectionate toward Kṛṣṇa, but after hearing the story, he became even more bound in love for Kṛṣṇa; tears of ecstasy glided from his eyes, and he became so stunned that he was almost unable to speak.

Thus ends the Bhaktivedanta purport of the Third Volume, Fourth Chapter, of Kṛṣṇa, *"Lord Kṛṣṇa Returns to the City of Hastināpura."*

5 / The Deliverance of Śiśupāla

King Yudhiṣṭhira became very happy after hearing the details of the Jarāsandha episode, and he spoke as follows: "My dear Kṛṣṇa, O eternal form of bliss and knowledge, all the exalted directors of the affairs of this material world, including Lord Brahmā, Lord Śiva and King Indra, are always anxious to receive and carry out orders from You, and whenever they are fortunate enough to receive such orders, they immediately take them and keep them in their hearts. O Kṛṣṇa, You are unlimited, and although we sometimes think of ourselves as royal kings and rulers of the world and become puffed up over our paltry positions, we are very poor in heart. Actually, we are fit to be punished by You, but the wonder is that instead of punishing us, You so kindly and mercifully accept our orders and carry them out properly. Others are very surprised that Your Lordship can play the part of an ordinary human, but we can understand that You are performing these activities just like a dramatic artist. Your real position is always exalted, exactly like that of the sun, which always remains at the same temperature both during the time of its rising and the time of its setting. Although we feel the difference in temperature between the rising and the setting sun, the temperature of the sun never changes. You are always transcendentally equipoised, and thus You are neither pleased nor disturbed by any condition of material affairs. You are the Supreme Brahman, the Personality of Godhead, and for You there are no relativities. My dear Mādhava, You are never defeated by anyone. Material distinctions—'This is me.' 'This is you.' 'This is mine.' 'This is yours.'—are all conspicuous by dint of their absence in You. Such distinctions are visible in the lives of everyone, even the animals, but those who are pure devotees are freed from these false distinctions. Since these distinctions are absent in Your devotees, they cannot possibly be present in You."

After satisfying Kṛṣṇa in this way, King Yudhiṣṭhira arranged to perform the Rājasūya sacrifice. He invited all the qualified *brāhmaṇas* and sages to take part and appointed them to different positions as priests in charge of the sacrificial arena. He invited the most expert *brāhmaṇas* and sages, whose names are as follows: Kṛṣṇa-dvaipāyana Vyāsadeva, Bharadvāja, Sumantu, Gautama, Asita, Vasiṣṭha, Cyavana, Kaṇva, Maitreya, Kavaṣa, Trita, Viśvāmitra, Vāmadeva, Sumati, Jaimini, Kratu, Paila, Parāśara, Garga, Vaiśampāyana, Atharvā, Kaśyapa, Dhaumya, Paraśurāma, Śukrācārya, Āsuri, Vītihotra, Madhucchandā, Vīrasena, and Akṛtavraṇa. Besides all these *brāhmaṇas* and sages, he invited such respectful old men as Droṇācārya, Bhīṣma, the grandfather of the Kurus, Kṛpācārya, and Dhṛtarāṣṭra. He also invited all the sons of Dhṛtarāṣṭra, headed by Duryodhana, and the great devotee Vidura was also invited. Kings from different parts of the world, along with their ministers and secretaries, were also invited to see the great sacrifice performed by King Yudhiṣṭhira, and the citizens, comprising learned *brāhmaṇas,* chivalrous *kṣatriyas,* well-to-do *vaiśyas,* and faithful *śūdras,* all visited the ceremony.

The *brāhmaṇa* priests and sages in charge of the sacrificial ceremony constructed the sacrificial arena as usual with a plow of gold, and they initiated King Yudhiṣṭhira as the performer of the great sacrifice, in accordance with Vedic rituals. Long years ago, when Varuṇa performed a similar sacrifice, all the sacrificial utensils were made of gold. Similarly, in the Rājasūya sacrifice of King Yudhiṣṭhira, all the utensils required for the sacrifice were golden.

In order to participate in the great sacrifice performed by King Yudhiṣṭhira, all the exalted demigods like Lord Brahmā, Lord Śiva, and Indra the King of heaven, accompanied by their associates, as well as the predominating deities of higher planetary systems like Gandharvaloka, Siddhaloka, Janaloka, Tapoloka, Nāgaloka, Yakṣaloka, Rākṣasaloka, Pakṣiloka and Cāraṇaloka, as well as famous kings and their queens, were all present by the invitation of King Yudhiṣṭhira. All the respectable sages, kings and demigods who assembled there unanimously agreed that King Yudhiṣṭhira was quite competent to take the responsibility of performing the Rājasūya sacrifice; no one was in disagreement on this fact. All of them knew thoroughly the position of King Yudhiṣṭhira; because he was a great devotee of Lord Kṛṣṇa, no accomplishment was extraordinary for him. The learned *brāhmaṇas* and priests saw to it that the sacrifice by Mahārāja Yudhiṣṭhira was performed in exactly the same way as in bygone ages by the demigod Varuṇa. According to the Vedic system, whenever there is an arrangement for sacrifice, the members participating in the sacrifice are offered the juice of the *soma* plant. The juice of the *soma* plant is a kind of life-giving beverage. On the day of extracting the *soma* juice, King Yudhiṣṭhira very respectfully received the special priest who had been engaged to detect any mistake in the formalities of sacrificial procedures. The idea is that the Vedic *mantras* must be enuciated perfectly and chanted with the proper accent; if the priests who are engaged in this business commit any mistake, the checker or referee priest immediately corrects the procedure, and thus the ritualistic performances are perfectly executed. Unless it is perfectly executed, a sacrifice cannot yield the desired result. In this age of Kali there is no such learned *brāhmaṇa* or priest available; therefore, all such sacrifices are forbidden. The only sacrifice recommended in the *śāstras* is the chanting of the Hare Kṛṣṇa *mantra.*

Another important procedure is that the most exalted personality in the assembly of such a sacrificial ceremony is first offered worship. After all arrangements were made for Yudhiṣṭhira's sacrifice, the next consideration was who should be worshiped first in the ceremony. This particular ceremony is called Agrapūjā. *Agra* means first, and *pūjā* means worship. This Agrapūjā is similar to election of the president. In the sacrificial assembly, all the members were very exalted. Some proposed to elect one person as the perfect candidate for accepting Agrapūjā, and others proposed someone else.

When the matter remained undecided, Sahadeva began to speak in favor of Lord Kṛṣṇa. He said, "Lord Kṛṣṇa, the best amongst the members of the Yadu dynasty and the protector of His devotees, is the most exalted personality in this assembly. Therefore I think that He should without any objection be offered the honor of being worshiped first. Although demigods such as Lord Brahmā, Lord Śiva, Indra, the King of heavenly planets, and many other exalted personalities are present in this assembly, no one can be equal to or greater than Kṛṣṇa in terms of time, space, riches, strength, reputation, wisdom, renunciation or any other consideration. Anything which is considered opulent is present originally in Kṛṣṇa. As an individual soul is the basic principle of the growth of his material body, similarly Kṛṣṇa is the Supersoul of this cosmic manifestation. All kinds of Vedic ritualistic ceremonies, such as the performance of sacrifices, the offering of oblations in the fire, the chanting of the Vedic hymns and the practice of mystic *yoga*—all are meant for realizing Kṛṣṇa. Whether one follows the path of fruitive activities or the path of philosophical speculation, the ultimate destination is Kṛṣṇa; all bona fide methods of self-realization are meant for understanding Kṛṣṇa. Ladies and gentlemen, it is superfluous to speak about Kṛṣṇa, because every one of you exalted personalities know the Supreme Brahman, Lord Kṛṣṇa, for whom there are no material differences between body and soul, between energy and the energetic, or between one part of the body and another. Since everyone is a part and parcel of Kṛṣṇa, there is no qualitative difference between Kṛṣṇa and all living entities. Everything is an emanation of Kṛṣṇa's energies, the material and spiritual energies. Kṛṣṇa's energies are like the heat and light of the fire; there is no difference between the quality of heat and light and the fire itself.

"Also, Kṛṣṇa can do anything He likes with any part of His body. We can execute a particular action with the help of a particular part of our body, but He can do anything and everything with any part of His body. And because His transcendental body is full of knowledge and bliss in eternity, He doesn't undergo the six kinds of material changes–birth, existence, growth, fruitive action, dwindling and vanishing. Unforced by any external energy, He is the supreme cause of the creation, maintenance and dissolution of everything that be. By the grace of Kṛṣṇa only, everyone is engaged in the practice of religiousness, the development of economic conditions, the satisfaction of the senses and, ultimately, the achievement of liberation from material bondage. These four principles of progressive life can be executed by the mercy of Kṛṣṇa only. He should therefore be offered the first worship of this great sacrifice, and no one should disagree. As by watering the root, the watering of the branches, twigs, leaves and flowers is automatically accomplished, or as by supplying food to the stomach, the nutrition and metabolism of all parts of the body are automatically established, so by offering the first worship to Kṛṣṇa, everyone present in this meeting–including the great demigods–will be satisfied. If anyone is charitably disposed, it will be very good for him to give in charity only to Kṛṣṇa, who is the Supersoul of everyone, regardless of his particular body or individual personality. Kṛṣṇa is present as the Supersoul in every living being, and if we can satisfy Him, then automatically every living being becomes satisfied."

Sahadeva was fortunate to know of the glories of Kṛṣṇa, and after describing them in brief, he stopped speaking. After this speech was delivered, all the members present in that great sacrificial assembly applauded, confirming his words continuously by saying, "Everything that you have said is completely perfect. Everything that you have said is completely perfect." King Yudhiṣṭhira, after hearing the confirmation of all present, especially of the *brāhmaṇas* and learned sages, worshiped Lord Kṛṣṇa according to the regulative principles of the Vedic injunctions. First of all, King Yudhiṣṭhira–along with his brothers, wives, children, other relatives and ministers–washed the lotus feet of Lord Kṛṣṇa and sprinkled the water on their heads. After this, Lord Kṛṣṇa was offered various kinds of silken garments of yellow color, and heaps of jewelry and ornaments were presented before Him for His use.

King Yudhiṣṭhira felt such ecstasy by honoring Kṛṣṇa, who was his only lovable object, that tears glided down from his eyes, and although He wanted to, he could not see Lord Kṛṣṇa very well. Lord Kṛṣṇa was thus worshiped by King Yudhiṣṭhira. At that time all the members present in that assembly stood up with folded hands and began to chant, *"Jaya! Jaya! Namaḥ! Namaḥ!"* When all joined together to offer their respectful obeisances to Kṛṣṇa, there were showers of flowers from the sky.

In that meeting, King Śiśupāla was also present. He was an avowed enemy of Kṛṣṇa for many reasons, especially because of Kṛṣṇa's having stolen Rukmiṇī from the marriage ceremony; therefore, he could not tolerate such honor to Kṛṣṇa and glorification of His qualities. Instead of being happy to hear the glories of the Lord, he became very angry. When everyone offered respect to Kṛṣṇa by standing up, Śiśupāla remained in his seat, but when he became angry at Kṛṣṇa's being honored, Śiśupāla stood up suddenly, and, raising his hand, began to speak very strongly and fearlessly against Lord Kṛṣṇa. He spoke in such a way that Lord Kṛṣṇa could hear him very distinctly.

"Ladies and gentlemen, I can appreciate now the statement of the *Vedas* that, after all, time is the predominating factor. In spite of all endeavors to the contrary, the time element executes its own plan without opposition. For example, one may try his best to live, but when the time for death comes, no one can check it. I see here that although there are many stalwart personalities present in this assembly, the influence of time is so strong that they have been misled by the statement of a boy who has foolishly spoken about Kṛṣṇa. There are many learned sages and elderly persons present, but still they have accepted the statement of a foolish boy. This means that by the influence of time, even the intelligence of such honored persons as are present in this meeting can be misdirected. I fully agree with the respectable persons present here that they are competent enough to select the personality who can be first worshiped, but I cannot agree with the statement of a boy like Sahadeva, who has spoken so highly about Kṛṣṇa and has recommended that Kṛṣṇa is fit to accept the first worship in the sacrifice. I can see that in this meeting there are many personalities who have undergone great austerities, who are highly learned and who have performed many penances. By their knowledge and direction, they can deliver many persons who are suffering from the pangs of material existence. There are great *ṛṣis* here whose knowledge has no bounds, as well as many self-realized persons and *brāhmaṇas* also, and therefore I think that any one of them could have been selected for the first worship because they are worshipable even by the great demigods, kings and emperors. I cannot understand how you could have selected this cowherd boy, Kṛṣṇa, and have left aside all these other great personalities. I think Kṛṣṇa to be no better than a crow—how can He be fit to accept the first worship in this great sacrifice?

"We cannot even ascertain as yet to which caste this Kṛṣṇa belongs or what His actual occupational duty is." Actually, Kṛṣṇa does not belong to any caste, nor does He have to perform any occupational duty. It is stated in the *Vedas* that the Supreme Lord has nothing to do as His prescribed duty. Whatever has to be done on His behalf is executed by His different energies.

Śiśupāla continued: "Kṛṣṇa does not belong to a high family. He is so independent that no one knows His principles of religious life. It appears that He is outside the jurisdiction of all religious principles. He always acts independently, not caring for the Vedic injunctions and regulative principles. Therefore He is devoid of all good qualities." Śiśupāla indirectly praised Kṛṣṇa by saying that He is not within the jurisdiction of Vedic injunction. This is true because He is the Supreme Personality of Godhead. That He has no qualities means that Kṛṣṇa has no material qualities, and because He is the Supreme Personality of Godhead, He acts independently, not caring for conventions or social or religious principles.

Siśupāla continued: "Under these circumstances, how can He be fit to accept the first worship in the sacrifice? Kṛṣṇa is so foolish that He has left Mathurā, which is inhabited by highly elevated persons following the Vedic culture, and He has taken shelter in the ocean, where there is not even talk of the *Vedas*. Instead of living openly, He has constructed a fort within the water and is living in an atmosphere where there is no discussion of Vedic knowledge. And whenever He comes out of the fort, He simply harasses the citizens like a dacoit, thief or rogue."

Śiśupāla went crazy because of Kṛṣṇa's being elected the supreme first-worshiped person in that meeting, and he spoke so irresponsibly that it appeared that he had lost all his good fortune. Being overcast with misfortune, Śiśupāla continued to insult Kṛṣṇa further, and Lord Kṛṣṇa patiently heard him without protest. Just as a lion does not care when a flock of jackals howl, Lord Kṛṣṇa remained silent and unprovoked. Kṛṣṇa did not reply to even a single accusation made by Śiśupāla, but all the members present in the meeting, except a few who agreed with Śiśupāla, became very agitated because it is the duty of any respectable person not to tolerate blasphemy against God or His devotee. Some of them, who thought that they could not properly take action against Śiśupāla, left the assembly in protest, covering their ears with their hands in order not to hear further accusations. Thus they left the meeting condemning the action of Śiśupāla. It is the Vedic injunction that whenever there is blasphemy of the Supreme Personality of Godhead, one must immediately leave. If he does not do so, he becomes bereft of his pious activities and is degraded to the lower condition of life.

All the kings present, belonging to the Kuru dynasty, Matsya dynasty, Kekaya dynasty and Sṛñjaya dynasty, became very angry and immediately took up their swords and shields to kill Śiśupāla. Śiśupāla was so foolish that he did not become even slightly agitated, although all the kings present were ready to kill him. He did not care to think of the pros and cons of his foolish talking, and when he saw that all the kings were ready to kill him, instead of stopping, he stood to fight with them and took up his sword and shield. When Lord Kṛṣṇa saw that they were going to engage in fighting in the arena of the auspicious Rājāsūya *yajña,* He personally pacified them. Out of His causeless mercy He Himself decided to kill Śiśupāla. When Śiśupāla was abusing the kings who were about to attack him, Lord Kṛṣṇa took up His disc, which was as sharp as the blade of a razor, and immediately separated the head of Śiśupāla from his body.

When Śiśupāla was thus killed, a great roar and howl went up from the crowd of that assembly. Taking advantage of that disturbance, the few kings who were supporters of Śiśupāla quickly left the assembly out of fear for their lives. But despite all this, the fortunate Śiśupāla's spirit soul immediately merged into the body of Lord Kṛṣṇa in the presence of all members, exactly as a burning meteor falls to the surface of the globe. Śiśupāla's soul's merging into the transcendental body of Kṛṣṇa reminds us of the story of Jaya and Vijaya, who fell to the material world from the Vaikuṇṭha planets upon being cursed by the four Kumāras. For their return to the Vaikuṇṭha world, it was arranged that both Jaya and Vijaya for three consecutive births would act as deadly enemies of the Lord, and at the end of these lives they would again return to the Vaikuṇṭha world and serve the Lord as His associates.

Although Śiśupāla acted as the enemy of Kṛṣṇa, he was not for a single moment out of Kṛṣṇa consciousness. He was always absorbed in thought of Kṛṣṇa, and thus he got first the salvation of *sāyujya-mukti,* merging into the existence of the Supreme, and finally became reinstated in his original position of personal service. The *Bhagavad-gītā* corroborates the fact that if one is absorbed in the thought of the Supreme Lord at the time of death, he immediately enters the kingdom of God after quitting his material body. After the salvation of Śiśupāla, King Yudhiṣṭhira rewarded all the members present in the sacrificial assembly. He sufficiently remunerated the priests and the learned sages for their engagement in the execution of the sacrifice, and after performing all this routine work, he took his bath. This bath at the end of the sacrifice is also technical. It is called the *avabhṛtha* bath.

Lord Kṛṣṇa thus enabled the performance of the Rājasūya *yajña* arranged by King Yudhiṣṭhira to be successfully completed, and, being requested by His cousins and relatives, He remained in Hastināpura for a few months more. Although King Yudhiṣṭhira and his brothers were not willing to have Lord Kṛṣṇa leave Hastināpura, Kṛṣṇa arranged to take permission from the King to return to Dvārakā, and thus He returned home along with His queens and ministers.

The story of the fall of Jaya and Vijaya from the Vaikuṇṭha planets to the material world is described in the Seventh Canto of *Śrīmad-Bhāgavatam.* The killing of Śiśupāla has a direct link with that narration of Jaya and Vijaya, but the most important instruction that we get from this incident is that the Supreme Personality of Godhead, being absolute, can give salvation to everyone, whether one acts as His enemy or as His friend. It is therefore a misconception that the Lord acts with someone in the relationship of a friend and with someone else in the relationship of an enemy. His being an enemy or friend is always on the absolute platform. There is no material distinction.

After King Yudhiṣṭhira took his bath after the sacrifice and stood in the midst of all the learned sages and *brāhmaṇas,* he seemed exactly like the King of heaven and thus looked very beautiful. King Yudhiṣṭhira sufficiently rewarded all the demigods who participated in the *yajña,* and being greatly satisfied, all of them left praising the King's activities and glorifying Lord Kṛṣṇa.

When Śukadeva Gosvāmī was narrating these incidents of Kṛṣṇa's killing Śiśupāla and describing the successful execution of the Rājasūya *yajña* by Mahārāja Yudhiṣṭhira, he pointed out also that after the successful termination of the *yajña* there was only one person who was not happy. He was Duryodhana. Duryodhana by nature was very envious because of his sinful life, and he appeared in the dynasty of the Kurus as a chronic disease personified in order to destroy the whole family.

Śukadeva Gosvāmī assured Mahārāja Parīkṣit that the pastimes of Lord Kṛṣṇa—the killing of Śiśupāla and Jarāsandha and the releasing of the imprisoned kings—are all transcendental vibrations, and anyone who hears these narrations from the authorized persons will be immediately freed from all the reactions of the sinful activities of his life.

Thus ends the Bhaktivedanta purport of the Third Volume, Fifth Chapter, of* Kṛṣṇa, *"The Deliverance of Śiśupāla."

6 / Why Duryodhana Felt Insulted at the End of the Rājasūya Sacrifice

King Yudhiṣṭhira was known as *ajātaśatru,* or a person who has no enemy. Therefore, when all men, all demigods, all kings, sages and saints saw the successful termination of the Rājasūya *yajña* performed by King Yudhiṣṭhira, they became very happy That Duryodhana alone was not happy was astonishing to Mahārāja Parīkṣit, and therefore he requested Śukadeva Gosvāmī to explain this.

Śukadeva Gosvāmī said, "My dear King Parīkṣit, your grandfather, King Yudhiṣṭhira, was a great soul. His congenial disposition attracted everyone as his friend, and therefore he was known as *ajātaśatru,* one who never created an enemy. He engaged all the members of the Kuru dynasty in taking charge of different departments for the management of the Rājasūya sacrifice. For example, Bhīmasena was put in charge of the kitchen department, Duryodhana in charge of the treasury department, Sahadeva in charge of the reception department, Nakula in charge of the store department, and Arjuna was engaged in looking after the comforts of the elderly persons. The most astonishing feature was that Kṛṣṇa, the Supreme Personality of Godhead, took charge of washing the feet of all the incoming guests. The Queen, the goddess of fortune Draupadī, was in charge of administering the distribution of food, and because Karṇa was famous for giving charity, he was put in charge of the charity department. In this way Sātyaki, Vikarṇa, Hārdikya, Vidura, Bhūriśravā, and Santardana, the son of Bāhlīka, were all engaged in different departments for managing the affairs of the Rājasūya sacrifice. They were all so bound in loving affection for King Yudhiṣṭhira that they simply wanted to please him.

After Śiśupāla had died by the mercy of Lord Kṛṣṇa and had become merged in the spiritual existence, and after the end of the Rājasūya *yajña,* when all friends, guests and well-wishers had been sufficiently honored and rewarded, King Yudhiṣṭhira went to bathe in the Ganges. The city of

Hastināpura is today standing on the bank of the Yamunā, and the statement of *Śrīmad-Bhāgavatam* that King Yudhiṣṭhira went to bathe in the Ganges indicates, therefore, that during the time of the Pāṇḍavas, the River Yamunā was also known as the Ganges. While the King was taking the *avabhṛtha* bath, different musical instruments, such as *mṛdaṅgas*, conchshells, drums, kettledrums and bugles, vibrated. In addition, the ankle bells of the dancing girls jingled. Many groups of professional singers played *vīṇās*, flutes, gongs and cymbals, and thus a tumultuous sound vibrated in the sky. The princely guests from many kingdoms, like Sṛñjaya, Kāmboja, Kuru, Kekaya and Kośala, were present with their different flags and gorgeously decorated elephants, chariots, horses and soldiers. All were passing in a procession, and King Yudhiṣṭhira was in the forefront. The executive members, such as the priests, religious ministers and *brāhmaṇas*, were performing a sacrifice, and all were loudly chanting the Vedic hymns. The demigods, the inhabitants of the Pitṛloka and Gandharvaloka, as well as many sages, showered flowers from the sky. The men and women of Hastināpura, Indraprastha, their bodies smeared with scents and floral oils, were nicely dressed in colorful garments and decorated with garlands, jewels and ornaments. They were all enjoying the ceremony, and they threw on each other liquid substances like water, oil, milk, butter and yogurt. Some even smeared these on each other's bodies. In this way, they were enjoying the occasion. The professional prostitutes were also engaged by jubilantly smearing these liquid substances on the bodies of the men, and the men reciprocated in the same way. All the liquid substances had been mixed with turmeric and saffron, and their color was a lustrous yellow.

In order to observe the great ceremony, many wives of the demigods had come in different airplanes, and they were visible in the sky. Similarly, the queens of the royal family arrived gorgeously decorated and surrounded by bodyguards on the surface on different palanquins. During this time, Lord Kṛṣṇa, the maternal cousin of the Pāṇḍavas, and His special friend Arjuna, were both throwing the liquid substances on the bodies of the queens. The queens became bashful, but at the same time their beautiful smiling brightened their faces. Because of the liquid substances thrown on their bodies, the saris covering them became completely wet. The different parts of their beautiful bodies, particularly their breasts and their waists, became partially visible because of the wet cloth. The queens also brought in buckets of liquid substances and sprinkled them on the bodies of their brothers-in-law. As they engaged in such jubilant activities, their hair fell loose, and the flowers decorating their bodies began to fall. When Lord

Kṛṣṇa, Arjuna and the queens were thus engaged in these jubilant activities, persons who were not clean in heart became agitated by lustful desires. In other words, such behavior between pure males and females is enjoyable, but persons who are materially contaminated become lustful.

King Yudhiṣṭhira, in a gorgeous chariot yoked by excellent horses, was present with his queens, including Draupadī and others. The festivities of the sacrifice were so beautiful that it appeared as if Rājasūya was standing there in person with the functions of the sacrifice.

Following the Rājasūya sacrifice, there was the Vedic ritualistic duty known as *patnīsaṁyāja.* This sacrifice was performed along with one's wife, and it was also duly performed by the priests of King Yudhiṣṭhira. When Queen Draupadī and King Yudhiṣṭhira were taking their *avabhṛtha* bath, the citizens of Hastināpura as well as the demigods began to beat on drums and blow trumpets out of feelings of happiness, and there was a shower of flowers from the sky. When the King and the Queen finished their bath in the Ganges, all the other citizens, consisting of all the *varṇas* or castes—the *brāhmaṇas,* the *kṣatriyas,* the *vaiśyas,* and the *śūdras*—took their baths in the Ganges. Bathing in the Ganges is recommended in the Vedic literatures because by such bathing one becomes freed from all sinful reactions. This is still current in India, especially at particularly auspicious moments. At such times, millions of people bathe in the Ganges.

After taking his bath, King Yudhiṣṭhira dressed in a new silken cloth and wrapper and decorated himself with valuable jewelry. The King not only dressed himself and decorated himself, but he also gave clothing and ornaments to all the priests and to the others who had participated in the *yajñas.* In this way, they were all worshiped by King Yudhiṣṭhira. He constantly worshiped his friends, his family members, his relatives, his well-wishers and everyone present, and because he was a great devotee of Lord Nārāyaṇa, or because he was a Vaiṣṇava, he therefore knew how to treat everyone well. The Māyāvadi philosophers' endeavor to see everyone as God is an artificial way towards oneness, but a Vaiṣṇava or a devotee of Lord Nārāyaṇa sees every living entity as part and parcel of the Supreme Lord. Therefore, a Vaiṣṇava's treatment of other living entities is on the absolute platform. Since one cannot treat one part of his body differently from another part because they all belong to the same body, so a Vaiṣṇava does not see a human being as distinct from an animal because in both of them he sees the soul and the Supersoul seated simultaneously.

When everyone was refreshed after bathing and was dressed in silken clothing with jeweled earrings, flower garlands, turbans, long wrappers and pearl necklaces, they looked, altogether, like the demigods from heaven.

This was especially true of the women, who were very nicely dressed. Each wore a golden belt around the waist. They were all smiling. Spots of *tilaka* and curling hair were scattered here and there. This combination was very attractive.

Persons who had participated in the Rājasūya sacrifice–including the most cultured priests, the *brāhmaṇas* who had assisted in the performance of the sacrifice, the citizens of all *varṇas,* kings, demigods, sages, saints and citizens of the Pitṛloka–were all very much satisfied by the dealings of King Yudhiṣṭhira, and at the end they happily departed for their residences. While returning to their homes, they talked of the dealings of King Yudhiṣṭhira, and even after continuous talk of his greatness they were not satiated, just as one may drink nectar over and over again and never be satisfied. After the departure of all others, Mahārāja Yudhiṣṭhira restrained the inner circle of his friends, including Lord Kṛṣṇa, by not allowing them to leave. Lord Kṛṣṇa could not refuse the request of the King. He therefore sent back all the heroes of the Yadu dynasty, like Sāmba and others. All of them returned to Dvārakā, and Lord Kṛṣṇa personally remained in order to give pleasure to the King.

In the material world, everyone has a particular type of desire to be fulfilled, but one is never able to fulfill his desires to his full satisfaction. But King Yudhiṣṭhira, because of his unflinching devotion to Kṛṣṇa, could fulfill all his desires successfully by the performance of the Rājasūya *yajña.* From the description of the execution of the Rājasūya *yajña,* it appears that such a function is a great ocean of opulent desires. It is not possible for an ordinary man to cross over such an ocean; nevertheless, by the grace of Lord Kṛṣṇa, King Yudhiṣṭhira was able to cross over it very easily, and thus he became freed from all anxieties.

When Duryodhana saw that Mahārāja Yudhiṣṭhira had become very famous after performance of the Rājasūya *yajña* and was fully satisfied in every respect, he began to burn with the fire of envy because his mind was always poisonous. For one thing, he envied the imperial palace which had been constructed by the demon Maya for the Pāṇḍavas. The palace was excellent in its puzzling artistic workmanship and was befitting the position of great princes, kings or leaders of the demons. In that great palace, the Pāṇḍavas were living with their family members, and Queen Draupadī was serving her husbands very peacefully. And because in those days Lord Kṛṣṇa was also there, the palace was also decorated by His thousands of queens. When the queens, with their heavy breasts and thin waists, moved within the palace, and their ankle bells rang very melodiously with their movement, the whole palace appeared to be more opulent than the heavenly kingdoms. Because a portion of their breasts was sprinkled with saffron powder, the pearl necklaces on their breasts appeared to be reddish. With their full earrings and flowing hair, the queens appeared very beautiful. After looking at such beauties in the palace of King Yudhiṣṭhira, Duryodhana became envious. He became especially envious and lustful upon seeing the beauty of Draupadī because he had cherished a special attraction for her from the very beginning of her marriage with the Pāṇḍavas. In the marriage selection assembly of Draupadī, Duryodhana had also been present, and with other princes he had been very much captivated by the beauty of Draupadī, but had failed to achieve her.

Once upon a time, King Yudhiṣṭhira was sitting on the golden throne in the palace constructed by the demon Maya. His four brothers and other relatives, as well as his great well-wisher, the Supreme Personality of Godhead, Kṛṣṇa, were present and the material opulence of King Yudhiṣṭhira seemed no less than that of Lord Brahmā. When he was sitting on the throne surrounded by his friends, and the reciters were offering prayers to him in the form of nice songs, Duryodhana, with his younger brother, came to the palace. Duryodhana was decorated with a helmet, and he carried a sword in his hand. He was always in an envious and angry mood, and therefore, on a slight provocation, he spoke sharply with the doorkeepers and became angry. He was irritated because he failed to distinguish between water and land. By the craftmanship of the demon Maya, the palace was so decorated in different places that one who did not know the tricks would consider water to be land and land to be water. Duryodhana was also illusioned by this craftmanship, and when he was crossing water thinking it to be land, he fell down. When Duryodhana, out of his foolishness, had thus fallen, the queens enjoyed the incident by laughing. King Yudhiṣṭhira, could understand the feelings of Duryodhana, and he tried to restrain the queens from laughing, but Lord Kṛṣṇa indicated that King Yudhiṣṭhira should not restrain them from enjoying the incident. Kṛṣṇa desired that Duryodhana might be fooled in that way and that all of them might enjoy his foolish behavior. When everyone laughed, Duryodhana felt very insulted, and his hair stood up in anger. Being thus insulted, he immediately left the palace, bowing his head. He was silent and did not protest. When Duryodhana left in such an angry mood, everyone regretted the incident, and King Yudhiṣṭhira also became very sorry. But despite all occurrences, Kṛṣṇa was silent. He did not say anything against or in favor of the incident. It appeared that Duryodhana had been put into illusion by the supreme will of Lord Kṛṣṇa, and this was the beginning of the enmity between the two sects of the Kuru dynasty. It appeared that it was a part of Kṛṣṇa's plan in His mission to decrease the burden of the world.

King Parīkṣit had inquired from Śukadeva Gosvāmī as to why Duryodhana was not satisfied after the termination of the great Rājasūya sacrifice, and thus it was explained by Śukadeva Gosvāmī.

Thus ends the Bhaktivedanta purport of the Third Volume, Sixth Chapter, of Kṛṣṇa, *"Why Duryodhana Felt Insulted at the End of the Rājasūya Sacrifice."*

7 / The Battle Between Śālva and the Members of the Yadu Dynasty

While Śukadeva Gosvāmī was narrating various activities of Lord Kṛṣṇa in playing the role of an ordinary human being, he also narrated the history of the battle between the dynasty of Yadu and a demon of the name Śālva, who had managed to possess a wonderful airship named Saubha. King Śālva was a great friend of Śiśupāla's. When Śiśupala went to marry Rukmiṇī, Śālva was one of the members of the bridegroom's party. When there was a fight between the soldiers of the Yadu dynasty and the kings of the opposite side, Śālva was defeated by the soldiers of the Yadu dynasty. But, despite his defeat, he made a promise before all the kings that he would in the future rid the whole world of all the members of the Yadu dynasty. Since his defeat in the fight during the marriage of Rukmiṇī, he had maintained within himself an unforgettable envy of Lord Kṛṣṇa, and he was, in fact, a fool, because he had promised to kill Kṛṣṇa.

Usually such foolish demons take shelter of a demigod like Lord Śiva to execute their ulterior plans, and so Śālva, in order to get strength, took shelter of the lotus feet of Lord Śiva. He underwent a severe type of austerity during which he would eat no more than a handful of ashes daily. Lord Śiva, the husband of Pārvatī, is generally very merciful, and he becomes very quickly satisfied if someone undertakes severe austerities in order to please him. So after continued austerities by Śālva for one year, Lord Śiva became pleased with him and asked him to beg for the fulfillment of his desire.

Śālva begged from Lord Śiva the gift of an airplane which would be so strong that it could not be destroyed by any demigod, demon, human being, Gandharva, Nāga, or even by any Rākṣasa. Moreover, he desired that the airplane be able to fly anywhere and everywhere he would like to pilot it, and be specifically very dangerous and fearful to the dynasty of the Yadus. Lord Śiva immediately agreed to give him the benediction, and

Śālva took the help of the demon Maya to manufacture this iron airplane, which was so strong and formidable that no one could crash it. It was a very big machine, almost like a big city, and it could fly so high and at such a great speed that it was almost impossible to see where it was, and so there was no question of attacking it. Although it might be dark outside, the pilot could fly it anywhere and everywhere. Having acquired such a wonderful airplane, Śālva flew it to the city of Dvārakā, because his main purpose in obtaining the airplane was to attack the city of the Yadus, toward whom he maintained a continual feeling of animosity.

Śālva thus not only attacked the city of Dvārakā from the sky, but he also surrounded the city by a large number of infantry. The soldiers on the surface began to attack the beautiful spots of the city.They began to destroy the baths, the city gates, the palaces and the skyscraper houses, the high walls around the city and the beautiful spots where people would gather for recreation. While the soldiers were attacking on the surface, the airplane began to drop big slabs of stone, tree trunks, thunderbolts, poisonous snakes and many other dangerous things. Śālva also managed to create such a strong whirlwind within the city that all of Dvārakā became dark because of the dust that covered the sky. The airplane occupied by Śālva put the entire city of Dvārakā into distress equal to that caused on the earth long, long ago by the disturbing activities of Tripurāsura. The inhabitants of Dvārakā Purī became so harassed that they were not in a peaceful condition for even a moment.

The great heroes of Dvārakā City, headed by commanders such as Pradyumna, counterattacked the soldiers and the airplane of Śālva. When he saw the extreme distress of the citizens, Pradyumna immediately arranged his soldiers and personally got upon a chariot, encouraging the citizens by assuring safety. Following his command, many warriors like Sātyaki, Cārudeṣṇa and Sāmba, all young brothers of Pradyumna, as well as Akrūra, Kṛtavarmā, Bhānuvinda, Gada, Śuka and Sāraṇa—all came out of the city to fight with Śālva. All of them were great fighters; each one could fight with thousands of men. All were fully equipped with necessary weapons and assisted by hundreds and thousands of charioteers, elephants, horses and infantry soldiers. Fierce fighting began between the two parties, exactly as was formerly carried on between the demigods and the demons. The fighting was very severe, and whoever observed the fierce nature of the fight felt his hairs stand on end.

Pradyumna immediately counteracted the mystic demonstration occasioned by the airplane of Śālva, the King of Saubha. By the mystic power of the airplane, Śālva had created a darkness as dense as night, but Pradyumna all of a sudden appeared like the rising sun. As with the rising of the sun the darkness of night is immediately dissipated, so with the appearance of Pradyumna the power exhibited by Śālva became null and void. Each and every one of Pradyumna's arrows had a golden feather at the end, and the shaft was fitted with a sharp iron edge. By releasing twenty-five such arrows, Pradyumna severely injured Śālva's commander-in-chief. He then released another one hundred arrows toward the body of Śālva. After this, he pierced each and every soldier by releasing one arrow, and he killed the chariot drivers by firing ten arrows at each one of them. The carriers like the horses and elephants were killed by the release of three arrows directed toward each one of them. When everyone present on the battlefield saw this wonderful feat of Pradyumna, the great fighters on both the sides began to praise his acts of chivalry.

But still the airplane occupied by Śālva was very mysterious. It was so extraordinary that sometimes there would appear to be many airplanes in the sky, and sometimes it would be seen that there was none. Sometimes it was visible, and sometimes it was not visible, and the warriors of the Yadu dynasty became puzzled about the whereabouts of the peculiar airplane. Sometimes they would see the airplane on the ground, and sometimes they would see it flying in the sky. Sometimes they would see the airplane resting on the peak of a hill, and sometimes it was seen floating on the water. The wonderful airplane was flying in the sky like a firefly in the wind—it was not steady even for a moment. But despite the mysterious maneuvering of the airplane, the commanders and the soldiers of the Yadu dynasty would immediately rush toward Śālva wherever he was present with his airplane and soldiers. The arrows released by the dynasty of the Yadus were as brilliant as the sun and as dangerous as the tongues of serpents. All the soldiers fighting on behalf of Śālva became soon distressed by the incessant release of arrows upon them by the heroes of the Yadu dynasty, and Śālva himself became unconscious from the attack of these arrows.

The soldiers and the fighters fighting on behalf of Śālva were also very strong, and the release of their arrows also harassed the heroes of the Yadu dynasty. But still the Yadus were so strong and determined that they did not move from their strategic positions. The heroes of the Yadu dynasty were determined to either die in the battlefield or gain victory. They were confident of the fact that if they would die in the fighting they would attain a heavenly planet, and if they would come out victorious they would enjoy the world. The name of Śālva's commander-in-chief was Dyumān. He was very powerful, and although bitten by twenty-five of Pradyumna's arrows, he suddenly attacked Pradyumna with his fierce club and struck him so strongly that Pradyumna became unconscious. Immediately there was a roaring, "Now he is dead! Now he is dead!" The force of the club on the chest of Pradyumna was very severe, enough to tear asunder the chest of an ordinary man.

Pradyumna's chariot was being driven by the son of Dāruka. According to Vedic military principles, the chariot driver and the hero on the chariot have to cooperate during the fighting. As such, it was the duty of the chariot driver to take care of the hero on the chariot during the dangerous and precarious fighting on the battlefield. Thus Dāruka removed the body of Pradyumna from the battlefield. Two hours later, in a quiet place, Pradyumna regained his consciousness, and when he saw that he was in a place other than the battlefield he addressed the charioteer and condemned him:

"Oh, you have done the most abominable act! Why have you moved me from the battlefield? My dear charioteer, I have never heard that anyone in our family was ever removed from the battlefield. None of them left the battlefield while fighting. By this removal you have overburdened me with a great defamation. It will be said that I left the battlefield while fighting was going on. My dear charioteer, I must accuse you—you are a coward and emasculator! Tell me, how can I go before my uncle Balarāma and before my father Kṛṣṇa, and what shall I say before them? Everyone will talk about me and say that I fled from the fighting place, and if they inquire from me about this, what will be my reply? My sisters-in-law will play jokes upon me with sarcastic words: 'My dear hero, how have you become such a coward? How have you become a eunuch? How have you become so low in the eyes of the fighters who opposed you?' I think, my dear charioteer, that you have committed a great offense by removing me from the battlefield."

The charioteer of Pradyumna replied, "My dear sir, I wish a long life for you. I think I did not do anything wrong, as it is the duty of the charioteer to help the fighter in the chariot when he is in a precarious condition. My dear sir, you are completely competent in the battlefield activities. It is the mutual duty of the charioteer and the warrior to give protection to each other in a precarious condition. I was completely aware of the regulative principles of fighting, and I did my duty. The enemy all of a sudden struck you with his club so severely that you lost consciousness. You were in a dangerous position, surrounded by your enemies. Therefore I was obliged to act as I did."

Thus ends the Bhaktivedanta purport of the Third Volume, Seventh Chapter, of* Kṛṣṇa, *"The Battle Between Śālva and the Yadu Dynasty."

8 / The Deliverance of Śālva

After talking with his charioteer, the son of Dāruka, Pradyumna could understand the real circumstances, and therefore he refreshed himself by washing his mouth and hands. Arming himself properly with bows and arrows, he asked his charioteer to take him near the place where Śālva's commander-in-chief was standing. During the short absence of Pradyumna from the battlefield, Dyumān, Śālva's commander-in-chief, had been taking over the position of the soldiers of the Yadu dynasty. By appearing in the battlefield, Pradyumna immediately stopped him and struck him with eight arrows. With four arrows he killed his four horses, with one arrow he killed his chariot driver and with another arrow he cut his bow in two; with another arrow, he cut his flag into pieces, and with another he severed his head from his body.

On the other fronts, heroes like Gada, Sātyaki and Sāmba were engaged in killing the soldiers of Śālva. The soldiers who were staying with Śālva in the airplane were also killed in the fighting, and they fell into the ocean. Each party began to strike the opposite party very severely. The battle was fierce and dangerous and continued for twenty-seven days without stop. While the fight was going on in the city of Dvārakā, Kṛṣṇa was staying at Indraprastha along with the Pāṇḍavas and King Yudhiṣṭhira. This fighting with Śālva took place after the Rājasūya *yajña* had been performed by King Yudhiṣṭhira and after the killing of Śiśupāla. When Lord Kṛṣṇa understood that there was great danger in the city of Dvārakā, He took permission from the elderly members of the Pāṇḍava family, especially from his aunt Kuntīdevī, and started immediately for Dvārakā.

Lord Kṛṣṇa began to think that while He was arriving in Hastināpura with Balarāma after the killing of Śiśupāla, Śiśupāla's men must have attacked Dvārakā. On reaching Dvārakā, Lord Kṛṣṇa saw that the whole city was greatly endangered. He placed Balarāmajī in a strategic position for the protection of the city, and He Himself asked His charioteer Dāruka to prepare to start. He said, "Dāruka, please immediately take Me to where Śālva is staying. You may know that this Śālva is a very powerful, mysterious man. Don't fear him in the least." As soon as he got his orders from Lord Kṛṣṇa, Dāruka had Him seated on the chariot and drove very quickly toward Śālva.

The chariot of Lord Kṛṣṇa was marked with the flag bearing the insignia of Garuḍa, and as soon as the soldiers and warriors of the Yadu dynasty saw the flag, they could understand that Lord Kṛṣṇa was on the battlefield. By this time, almost all the soldiers of Śālva had been killed, but when Śālva saw that Kṛṣṇa had come to the battlefield, he released a great, powerful weapon which flew through the sky with a roaring sound like a great meteor. It was so bright that the whole sky lit up by its presence. But as soon as Lord Kṛṣṇa appeared, He tore the great weapon into hundreds and thousands of pieces by releasing His own arrow.

Lord Kṛṣṇa struck Śālva with sixteen arrows, and with showers of arrows He overpowered the airplane, just as the sun in a clear sky overpowers the whole sky by an unlimited number of molecules of sunshine. Śālva struck a severe blow to Kṛṣṇa's left side, where the Lord was carrying His bow, Śārṅga, and as a result the Śārṅga bow fell from Lord Kṛṣṇa's hand. This dropping of the bow was indeed wonderful. Great personalities and demigods who were observing the fighting between Śālva and Kṛṣṇa became most perturbed by this, and they began to exclaim, "Alas! Alas!"

Śālva thought that he had become victorious, and with a roaring sound began to address Lord Kṛṣṇa as follows: "You rascal, Kṛṣṇa! You kidnapped Rukmiṇī forcibly, even in our presence. You baffled my friend Śiśupāla and married Rukmiṇī Yourself. And in the great assembly at King Yudhiṣṭhira's Rājasūya *yajña,* while my friend Śiśupāla was a little absent-minded, You took an opportunity to kill him. Everyone thinks that You are a great fighter and that no one can conquer You. So now You'll have to prove Your strength. I think that if You stand before me any longer, with my sharpened arrows I shall send You to a place wherefrom You will never return." "

To this Lord Kṛṣṇa replied, "Foolish Śālva, you are talking nonsensically. You do not know that the moment of death is already upon your head. Those who are actually heroes do not talk much. They prove their prowess by practical exhibition of chivalrous activities." After saying this, Lord Kṛṣṇa, in great anger, struck Śālva on the collarbone with His club so severely that he began to bleed internally and tremble as if he were going to collapse from severe cold. Before Kṛṣṇa was able to strike him again, however, Śālva became invisible by his mystic power.

Within a few moments, a mysterious unknown man came before Lord Kṛṣṇa. Crying loudly, he bowed down at the Lord's lotus feet and said to Him, "Since You are the most beloved son of Your father Vasudeva, Your mother Devakī has sent me to inform You of the unfortunate news that Your father has been arrested by Śālva and taken away by force. He took him just as a butcher mercilessly takes away an animal." When Lord Kṛṣṇa heard this unfortunate news from the unknown man, He at first became most perturbed, just like an ordinary human being. His face showed signs of grief, and He began to cry in a pitious tone, "How could that happen? My brother Lord Balarāma is there, and it is impossible for anyone to conquer Balarāmajī. He is in charge of Dvārakā City, and I know He is always alert. How could Śālva possibly enter the city and arrest My father in that way? Whatever he may be, Śālva's power is limited, so how could it be possible that he has conquered the strength of Balarāmajī and taken away My father, arresting him as described by this man? Alas! Destiny is, after all, very powerful."

While Śrī Kṛṣṇa was thinking like this, Śālva brought before Him in custody a man exactly resembling Vasudeva, His father. These were all creations of the mystic power of Śālva.

Śālva began to address Kṛṣṇa, "You rascal, Kṛṣṇa! Look. This is Your father who has begotten You and by whose mercy You are still living. Now just see how I kill Your father. If You have any strength, try to save him." The mystic juggler, Śālva, speaking in this way before Lord Kṛṣṇa, immediately cut off the head of the false Vasudeva. Without hesitation he took away the dead body and got into his airplane. Lord Kṛṣṇa is the self-sufficient Supreme Personality of Godhead, yet because He was playing the role of a human being, He became very depressed for a moment, as if He had actually lost His father. But at the next moment He could understand that the arrest and killing of His father were demonstrations of the mystic powers which Śālva had learned from the demon Maya. Coming to His right consciousness, He could see that there was no messenger and no head of His father, but that only Śālva had left in his airplane, which was flying in the sky. He then began to think of slaying Śālva.

Kṛṣṇa's reaction is a controversial point among great authorities and saintly persons. How could Kṛṣṇa, the Supreme Personality of Godhead, the reservoir of all power and knowledge, be bewildered in such a way? Lamentation, aggrievement and bewilderment are characteristics of persons who are conditioned souls, but how can such things affect the person of the Supreme, who is full of knowledge, power and all opulence? Actually, it is not at all possible that Lord Kṛṣṇa was misled by the mystic jugglery of Śālva. He was displaying His pastime in playing the role of a human being. Great saintly persons and sages who are engaged in the devotional service of the lotus feet of Lord Kṛṣṇa and who have thus achieved the greatest perfection of self-realization have transcended the bewilderments of the bodily concept of life. Lord Kṛṣṇa is the ultimate goal of life for such saintly persons. How then could Kṛṣṇa have been bewildered by the mystic jugglery of Śālva? The conclusion is that Lord Kṛṣṇa's bewilderment was another opulence of His supreme personality.

When Śālva thought that Kṛṣṇa had been bewildered by his mystic representations, he became encouraged and began to attack the Lord with greater strength and energy by showering volumes of arrows upon Him. But the enthusiasm of Śālva can be compared to the speedy march of flies into a fire. Lord Kṛṣṇa, by hurling His arrows with unfathomable strength, injured Śālva, whose armor, bow and jewelled helmet all scattered into pieces. With a crashing blow from Kṛṣṇa's club, Śālva's wonderful airplane burst into pieces and fell into the sea. Śālva was very careful, and instead of crashing with the airplane, he managed to jump onto the land. He again rushed towards Lord Kṛṣṇa. When Śālva ran swiftly to attack Kṛṣṇa with His club, Lord Kṛṣṇa cut off his hand, which fell to the ground with the club. Finally deciding to kill him, the Lord took up His wonderful disc, which was shining like the brilliant sun at the time of the dissolution of the material creation. When Lord Śrī Kṛṣṇa stood up with His disc to kill Śālva, He appeared just like the red sun rising over a mountain. Lord Kṛṣṇa then cut off his head, and the head, with its earrings and helmet, fell on the ground. Śālva was thus killed in the same way as Vṛtrāsura was killed by Indra, the King of heaven.

When Śālva was killed, all his soldiers and followers began to cry, "Alas! Alas!" While Śālva's men were thus crying, the demigods from the heavenly planets showered flowers on Kṛṣṇa and announced the victory by beating on drums and blowing bugles. At this very moment, other friends of Śiśupāla, such as Dantavakra, appeared on the scene to fight with Kṛṣṇa in order to avenge the death of Śiśupāla. When Dantavakra appeared before Lord Kṛṣṇa, he was extremely angry.

Thus ends the Bhaktivedanta purport of the Third Volume, Eighth Chapter, of Kṛṣṇa, *"The Deliverance of Śālva."*

9 / The Killing of Dantavakra, Vidūratha and Romaharṣaṇa

After the demise of Śiśupāla, Śālva and Pauṇḍra, another foolish demoniac king of the name Dantavakra wanted to kill Kṛṣṇa in order to avenge the death of his friend Śālva. He became so agitated that he personally appeared on the battlefield without the proper arms and ammunition and without even a chariot. His only weapon was his great anger, which was red-hot. He carried only a club in his hand, but he was so powerful that when he moved, everyone felt the earth tremble. When Lord Kṛṣṇa saw him approaching in a very heroic mood, He immediately got down from His chariot, for it was a rule of military etiquette that fighting should take place only between equals. Knowing that Dantavakra was alone and armed with only a club, Lord Kṛṣṇa responded similarly and prepared Himself by taking His club in His hand. When Kṛṣṇa appeared before him, Dantavakra's heroic march was immediately stopped just as the great, furious waves of the ocean are stopped by the beach.

At that time, Dantavakra, who was the King of Karūṣa, stood up firmly with his club and spoke to Lord Kṛṣṇa as follows: "It is a great pleasure and fortunate opportunity, Kṛṣṇa, that we are facing each other eye to eye. My dear Kṛṣṇa, after all, You are my eternal cousin, and I should not kill You in this way, butunfortunately You have committed a great mistake by killing my friend Śālva. Moreover, You are not satisfied by killing my friend, but I know that You want to kill me also. Because of Your determination, I must kill You by tearing You into pieces with my club. Kṛṣṇa, although You are my relative, You are foolish. You are our greatest enemy, so I must kill You today just as a person removes a boil on his body by a surgical operation. I am always very much obliged to my friends, and I therefore consider myself indebted to my dear friend Śālva. I can only liquidate my indebtedness to him by killing You."

As the caretaker of an elephant tries to control the animal by striking it with his trident, so Dantavakra tried to control Kṛṣṇa simply by speaking strong words. After finishing his vituperation, he struck Kṛṣṇa on the head with his club and made a roaring sound like a lion. Although struck strongly by the club of Dantavakra, Kṛṣṇa did not move even an inch, nor did He feel any pain. Taking His Kaumodakī club and moving very skillfully, Kṛṣṇa struck the chest of Dantavakra so fiercely that the heart of Dantavakra split in twain. As a result, Dantavakra began to vomit blood, his hairs became scattered, and he fell to the ground, spreading his hands and legs. Within only a few minutes all that remained of Dantavakra was a dead body on the ground. After the death of Dantavakra, just as at the time of Śiśupāla's death, in the presence of all persons standing there, a small particle of spiritual effulgence came out of the demon's body and very wonderfully merged into the body of Lord Kṛṣṇa.

Dantavakra had a brother named Vidūratha who became overwhelmed with grief at the death of Dantavakra. Out of grief and anger, Vidūratha was breathing very heavily, and just to avenge the death of his brother he also appeared before Lord Kṛṣṇa with a sword and a shield in his hands. He wanted to kill Kṛṣṇa immediately. When Lord Kṛṣṇa understood that Vidūratha was looking for the opportunity to strike Him with his sword, He employed His Sudarśana cakra, His disc, which was as sharp as a razor, and without delay he cut off the head of Vidūratha, with its helmet and earrings.

In this way, after killing Śālva and destroying his wonderful airplane and then killing Dantavakra and Vidūratha, Lord Kṛṣṇa at last entered His city, Dvārakā. It would not have been possible for anyone but Kṛṣṇa to kill these great heroes, and therefore all the demigods from heaven and the human beings on the surface of the globe were glorifying Him. Great sages and ascetics, the denizens of the Siddha and Gandharva planets, the denizens known as Vidyādharas, Vāsuki and the Mahānāgas, the beautiful angels, the inhabitants of Pitṛloka, the Yakṣas, the Kinnaras and the Cāraṇas all began to shower flowers upon Him and sing the songs of His victory in great jubilation. Decorating the entire city very festively, the citizens of Dvārakā held a great celebration, and when Lord Kṛṣṇa passed through the city all the members of the Vṛṣṇi dynasty and the heroes of the Yadu dynasty followed Him with great respect. These are some of the transcendental pastimes of Lord Kṛṣṇa, who is the master of all mystic power and the Lord of all cosmic manifestations. Those who are fools, who are like animals, sometimes think that Kṛṣṇa is defeated, but factually He is the Supreme Personality of Godhead, and no one can defeat Him. He always remains victorious over everyone. He is the only one God, and all others are His subservient order carriers.

Once upon a time, Lord Balarāma heard that there was an arrangement being made for a fight between the two rival parties in the Kuru dynasty, one headed by Duryodhana and the other by the Pāṇḍavas. He did not like the idea that He was to be only a mediator to stop the fighting. Finding it unbearable not to take an active part on behalf of either of the parties, He left Dvārakā on the plea of visiting various holy places of pilgrimage. He first of all visited the place of pilgrimage known as Prabhāsakṣetra. He took His bath there, and He pacified the local *brāhmaṇas* and offered oblations to the demigods, *pitās,* great sages and people in general, in accordance with Vedic ritualistic ceremonies. That is the Vedic method of visiting holy places. After this, accompanied by some respectable *brāhmaṇas,* He decided to visit different places on the bank of the River Sarasvatī. He gradually visited such places as Pṛthūdaka, Bindusara, Tritakūpa, Sudarśanatīrtha, Viśālatīrtha, Brahmatīrtha and Cakratīrtha. Besides these, He also visited all the holy places on the bank of Sarasvatī River running toward the east. After this He visited all the principal holy places on the bank of the Yamunā and on the bank of the Ganges. Thus He gradually came to the holy place known as Naimiṣāraṇya.

This holy place, Naimiṣāraṇya, is still existing in India, and in ancient times it was especially used for the meetings of great sages and saintly persons with the aim of understanding spiritual life and self-realization. When Lord Balarāma visited that place there was a great sacrifice being performed by a great assembly of transcendentalists. Such meetings were planned to last thousands of years. When Lord Balarāma arrived, all the participants of the meeting–great sages, ascetics, *brāhmaṇas* and learned scholars–immediately arose from their seats and welcomed Him with great honor and respect. Some offered Him respectful obeisances, and those who were elderly great sages and *brāhmaṇas* offered Him blessings by standing up. After this formality, Lord Balarāma was offered a suitable seat, and everyone present worshiped Him. Everyone in the assembly stood up in the presence of Balarāma because they knew Him to be the Supreme Personality of Godhead. Education or learning means to understand the Supreme Personality of Godhead; therefore, although Lord Balarāma appeared on the earth as a *kṣatriya,* all the *brāhmaṇas* and sages stood up because they knew who Lord Balarāma was.

Unfortunately, after being worshiped and seated at His place, Lord Balarāma saw Romaharṣaṇa, the disciple of Vyāsadeva (the literary incarnation of Godhead), still sitting on the Vyāsāsana. He had neither gotten up from his seat nor offered Him respects. Because he was seated on the Vyāsāsana, he foolishly thought himself greater than the Lord; therefore he did not get down from his seat or bow down before the Lord. Lord

Balarāma then considered the history of Romaharṣaṇa: he was born in a *sūta* family or a mixed family, born of a *brāhmaṇa* woman and *kṣatriya* man. Therefore although Romaharṣaṇa considered Balarāma a *kṣatriya,* he should not have remained sitting on a higher seat. Lord Balarāma considered that Romaharṣaṇa, according to his position by birth, should not have accepted the higher sitting position, because there were many learned *brāhmaṇas* and sages present. He also observed that Romaharṣaṇa not only did not come down from his exalted seat, but he did not even stand up and offer his respects when Balarāmajī entered the assembly. Lord Balarāma did not like the audacity of Romaharṣaṇa, and he became very angry with him.

When a person is seated on the Vyāsāsana, he does not generally have to stand up to receive a particular person entering the assembly, but in this case the situation was different because Lord Baladeva is not an ordinary human being. Therefore, although Romaharṣaṇa Sūta was voted to the Vyāsāsana by all the *brāhmaṇas,* he should have followed the behavior of other learned sages and *brāhmaṇas* who were present and should have known that Lord Balarāma is the Supreme Personality of Godhead. Respects are always due to Him, even though such respects can be avoided in the case of an ordinary man. The appearances of Kṛṣṇa and Balarāma are especially meant for reestablishment of the religious principles. As stated in the *Bhagavad-gītā,* the highest religious principle is to surrender unto the Supreme Personality of Godhead. It is also confirmed in the *Śrīmad-Bhagavatam* that the topmost perfection of religiousness is to be engaged in the devotional service of the Lord.

When Lord Balarāma saw that Romaharṣaṇa Sūta did not understand the highest principle of religiousness in spite of having studied all the *Vedas,* He certainly could not support his position. Romaharṣaṇa Sūta had been given a chance to become a perfect *brāhmaṇa,* but because of his ill behavior in his relationship with the Supreme Personality of Godhead, his low birth was immediately remembered. Romaharṣaṇa Sūta had been given the position of a *brāhmaṇa,* but he had not been born in the family of a *brāhmaṇa;* he had been born in a *pratiloma* family. According to the Vedic concept, there are two kinds of mixed family heritage. They are called *anuloma* and *pratiloma.* When a male is united with a female of a lower caste, the offspring is called *anuloma;* but when a male unites with a woman of a higher caste, the offspring is called *pratiloma.* Romaharṣaṇa Sūta belonged to the *pratiloma* family because his father was a *kṣatriya* and his mother a *brāhmaṇa.* Because Romaharṣaṇa's transcendental realization was not perfect, Lord Balarāma remembered his *pratiloma* heritage. The idea is that any man can be given the chance to become a *brāhmaṇa,* but if he improperly uses the position of a *brāhmaṇa* without actual realization, then his elevation to the brahminical position is not valid.

After seeing the deficiency of realization in Romaharṣaṇa Sūta, Lord Balarāma decided to chastise him for being puffed up. Lord Balarāma therefore said, "This man is liable to be awarded the death punishment because, although he has the good qualification of being a disciple of Lord Vyāsadeva and although he has studied all the Vedic literature from this exalted personality, he was not submissive in the presence of the Supreme Personality of Godhead." As stated in the *Bhagavad-gītā,* a person who is actually a *brāhmaṇa* and is very learned must automatically become very gentle also. In the case of Romaharṣaṇa Sūta, although he was very learned and had been given the chance to become a *brāhmaṇa*, he had not become gentle. From this we can understand that when one is puffed up by material acquisition, he cannot acquire the gentle behavior befitting a *brāhmaṇa.* The learning of such a person is as good as a valuable jewel decorating the hood of a serpent. Despite the valuable jewel on the hood, a serpent is still a serpent and is as fearful as an ordinary serpent. If a person does not become meek and humble, all his studies of the *Vedas* and *Purāṇas* and his vast knowledge in the *śāstras* become simply outward dress, like the costume of a theatrical artist dancing on the stage. Lord Balarāma began to consider thus: "I have appeared in order to chastise false persons who are internally impure but externally pose themselves to be very learned and religious. My killing of such persons is proper to check them from further sinful activity."

Lord Balarāma had avoided taking part in the Battle of Kurukṣetra, and yet because of His position, the reestablishment of religious principles was his prime duty. Considering these points, He killed Romaharṣaṇa Sūta simply by striking him with a *kuśa* straw, which was nothing but a blade of grass. If someone questions how Lord Balarāma could kill Romaharṣaṇa Sūta simply by striking him with a blade of *kuśa* grass, the answer is given in the *Śrīmad-Bhāgavatam* by the use of the word *prabhu* (master). The Lord's position is always transcendental, and because He is omnipotent He can act as He likes without being obliged to the material laws and principles. Thus it was possible for Him to kill Romaharṣaṇa Sūta simply by striking him with a blade of *kuśa* grass.

At the death of Romaharṣaṇa Sūta, everyone present became much aggrieved, and there was roaring and crying. Although all the *brāhmaṇas* and sages present there knew Lord Balarāma to be the Supreme Personality of Godhead, they did not hesitate to protest the Lord's action, and they humbly submitted, "Our dear Lord, we think that Your action is not in line with the religious principles. Dear Lord Yadunandana, we may inform You that we *brāhmaṇas* posted Romaharṣaṇa Sūta on that exalted position for the duration of this great sacrifice. He was seated on the Vyāsāsana by our election, and when one is seated on the Vyāsāsana, it is improper for him to stand up to receive a person. Moreover, we awarded Romaharṣaṇa Sūta an undisturbed duration of life. Under the circumstances, since Your Lordship has killed him without knowing all these facts, we think that Your action has been equal to that of killing a *brāhmaṇa.* Dear Lord, deliverer of all fallen souls, we know certainly that You are the knower of all Vedic principles. You are the master of all mystic powers; therefore ordinarily the Vedic injunctions cannot be applied to Your personality. But we request that You show Your causeless mercy upon others by kindly atoning for this killing of Romaharṣaṇa Sūta. We do not, however, suggest what kind of act You should perform to atone for killing him; we simply suggest that some method of atonement be adopted by You so that others may follow Your action. What is done by a great personality is followed by the ordinary man."

The Lord replied, "Yes, I must atone for this action, which may have been proper for Me, but is improper for others; therefore, I think it is My duty to execute a suitable act of atonement enjoined in the authorized scriptures. Simultaneously I can also give this Romaharṣaṇa Sūta life again, with a span of long duration, sufficient strength, and full power of the senses. Not only this, if you desire, I shall be glad to award him anything else which you may ask. I shall be very glad to grant all these boons in order to fulfill your desires."

This statement of Lord Balarāma definitely confirms that the Supreme Personality of Godhead is free to act in any way. Although it may be considered that His killing of Romaharṣaṇa Sūta was improper, He could immediately counteract the action with greater profit to all. Therefore, one should not imitate the actions of the Supreme Personality of Godhead; one should simply follow the instructions of the Lord. All the great learned sages present realized that although they considered the action of Lord Balarāma to be improper, the Lord was able to immediately compensate with greater profits. Not wanting to detract from the mission of the Lord in killing Romaharṣaṇa Sūta, all of them prayed, "Our dear Lord, the uncommon use of Your *kuśa* weapon to kill Romaharṣaṇa Sūta may remain as it is; because of Your desire to kill him, he should not be brought to life again. At the same time Your Lordship may remember that we sages and *brāhmaṇas* voluntarily gave him long life; therefore, such a benediction should not be nullified." Thus the request of all the learned *brāhmaṇas* in the assembly was ambiguous because they wanted to keep intact the benediction given by them that Romaharṣaṇa Sūta would continue to live until the end of the great sacrifice, but at the same time they did not want to nullify Balarāma's killing him.

The Supreme Personality of Godhead therefore solved the problem in a manner befitting His exalted position, and said, "Because the son is produced from the body of the father, it is the injunction of the *Vedas* that the son is the father's representative. Therefore I say that Ugraśravā Sūta, the son of Romaharṣaṇa Sūta, should henceforth take his father's position and continue the discourses on the *Purāṇas,* and because you wanted Romaharṣaṇa to have a long duration of life, this benediction will be transferred to his son. The son, Ugraśravā, will therefore have all the facilities you offered–long duration of life in a good and healthy body, without any disturbances and full strength of all the senses.

Lord Balarāma then implored all the sages and *brāhmaṇas* that aside from the benediction offered to the son of Romaharṣaṇa, they should ask from Him any other benediction, and He would be prepared to fulfill it immediately. The Lord thus placed Himself in the position of an ordinary *kṣatriya* and informed the sages that He did not know in what way He could atone for His killing of Romaharṣaṇa, but whatever they would suggest He would be glad to accept.

The *brāhmaṇas* could understand the purpose of the Lord, and thus, they suggested that He atone for His action in a manner which would be beneficial for them. They said, "Our dear Lord, there is a demon of the name Balvala. He is the son of Ilvala, but he is a very powerful demon, and he visits this sacred place of sacrifice every fortnight on the full moon and moonless days and creates a great disturbance to the discharge of our duties in the sacrifice. O descendant of the Daśārha family, we all request You to kill this demon. We think that if You kindly kill him, that will be Your atonement on our behalf. The demon occasionally comes here and profusely throws upon us contaminated, impure things like puss, blood, stool, urine and wine, and he pollutes this sacred place by showering such filth upon us. After killing Balvala, You may continue touring all these sacred places of pilgrimage for twelve months, and in that way You will be completely freed from all contamination. That is our prescription."

Thus ends the Bhaktivedanta purport of the Third Volume, Ninth Chapter, of* Kṛṣṇa, *"The Killing of Dantavakra, Vidūratha and Romaharṣaṇa."

10/ The Liberation of Balvala, and Lord Balarāma's Touring the Sacred Places

Lord Balarāma prepared Himself to meet the demon Balvala. At the time when the demon usually attacked the sacred place, there appeared a great hailstorm, the whole sky became covered with dust and the atmosphere became surcharged with a filthy smell. Just after this, the mischievous demon Balvala began to shower torrents of stool and urine and other impure substances on the arena of sacrifice. After this onslaught, the demon himself appeared with a great trident in his hand. He was a gigantic person, and his black body was like a huge mass of carbon. His hair, his beard and his moustache appeared reddish, like copper, and because of his great beard and moustache, his mouth appeared to be very dangerous and fierce. As soon as He saw the demon, Lord Balarāma prepared to attack him. He first began to consider how He could smash the great demon to pieces. Lord Balarāma called for His plow and club, and they immediately appeared before Him. The demon Balvala was flying in the sky, and at the first opportunity Lord Balarāma dragged him down with His plow and angrily smashed the demon's head with His club. By Balarāma's striking, the forehead of the demon became fractured. There was a profuse flow of blood from his forehead, and he began to scream loudly. In this way the demon, who had been such a great disturbance to the pious *brāhmaṇas,* fell to the ground. His falling was like a great mountain with a red oxide peak being struck by a thunderbolt and smashed to the ground.

The inhabitants of Naimiṣāraṇya, learned sages and *brāhmaṇas,* became most pleased by seeing this, and they offered their respectful prayers to Lord Balarāma. They offered their heartfelt blessings upon the Lord, and all agreed that Lord Balarāma's attempt to do anything would never be a failure. The sages and *brāhmaṇas* then performed a ceremonial bathing of Lord Balarāma, just as King Indra is bathed by the demigods when he is victorious over the demons. The *brāhmaṇas* and sages honored Lord

Balarāma by presenting Him first-class new clothing and ornaments and the lotus flower garland of victory, the reservoir of all beauty, which was never to be dried up, being in everlasting existence.

After this incidence, Lord Balarāma took permission from the *brāhmaṇas* assembled at Naimiṣāraṇya and, accompanied by other *brāhmaṇas,* went to the bank of the River Kauṣikī. After taking His bath in this holy place, He proceeded toward the River Sarayū and visited the source of the river. He began to travel on the bank of the Sarayū River, and He gradually reached Prayāga, where there is a confluence of three rivers, the Ganges, Yamunā and Sarasvatī. Here also He regularly took His bath, worshiped the local temples of God and, as it is enjoined in the Vedic literature, offered oblations to the forefathers and sages. He gradually reached the *āśrama* of the sage Pulaha and from there went to Gaṇḍakī on the River Gomatī. After this He took His bath in the River Vipāśā. Then gradually He came to the bank of the Śoṇa River. (The Śoṇa River is still running as one of the big rivers in the Behar Province.) He also took His bath there and performed the Vedic ritualistic ceremonies. He continued His travels and gradually came to the pilgrimage city of Gayā where there is a celebrated Viṣṇu temple. According to the advice of His father Vasudeva, He offered oblations to the forefathers in this Viṣṇu temple. From here He traveled to the delta of the Ganges, where the sacred River Ganges mixes with the Bay of Bengal. This sacred place is called Gaṅgāsāgara, and at the end of January every year there is still a great assembly of saintly persons and pious men, just as there is an assembly of saintly persons in Prayāga every year which is called the Magh Mela Fair.

After finishing His bathing and ritualistic ceremonies at Gaṅgāsāgara, Lord Balarāma proceeded toward the mountain known as Mahendra Parvata. At this place He met Paraśurāma, the incarnation of Lord Kṛṣṇa, and He offered him respect by bowing down before him. After this He gradually turned toward southern India and visited the banks of the River Godāvarī. After taking His bath in the River Godāvarī and performing the necessary ritualistic ceremonies, He gradually visited the other rivers—the Veṇā, Pampā and Bhīmarathī. On the bank of the River Bhīmarathī there is the deity called Svāmī Kārttikeya. After visiting Kārttikeya Lord Balarāma gradually proceeded to Śailapura, a pilgrimage city in the province of Mahārāṣṭra. Śailapura is one of the biggest districts in Mahārāṣṭra Province. He then gradually proceeded towards the Draviḍadeśa. Southern India is divided into five parts, called Pañcadraviḍa. Northern India is also divided into five parts, called Pañcagaura. All the important *ācāryas* of the modern age, namely Śaṅkarācārya, Rāmānujācārya,

Madhvācārya, Viṣṇusvāmī, and Nimbārka, advented themselves in these Draviḍa Provinces. Lord Caitanya appeared in Bengal, which is part of the five Gauradeśas.

The most important place of pilgrimage in southern India, or Draviḍa, is Veṅkaṭācala, commonly known as Bālajī. After visiting this place Lord Balarāma proceeded toward Viṣṇukāñcī, and from there He proceeded on the bank of the Kāverī. He took His bath in the River Kāverī; then He gradually reached Raṅgakṣetra. The biggest temple in the world is in Raṅgakṣetra, and the Viṣṇu deity there is celebrated as Raṅganātha. A similar temple of Raṅganātha is in Vṛndāvana, although it is not as big as the temple in Raṅgakṣetra.

While going to Viṣṇukāñcī, Lord Balarāma also visited Śivakāñcī. After visiting Raṅgakṣetra, He gradually proceeded toward Mathurā, commonly known as the Mathurā of southern India. After visiting this place, He gradually proceeded toward Setubandha. Setubandha is the place where Lord Rāmacandra constructed the stone bridge from India to Laṅkā (Ceylon). In this particularly holy place, Lord Balarāma distributed ten thousand cows to the local *brāhmaṇa* priests. It is the Vedic custom that when a rich visitor goes to any place of pilgrimage he gives in charity to the local priests gifts of horses, cows, ornaments and garments. This system of visiting places of pilgrimage and providing the local *brāhmaṇa* priests with all necessities of life has greatly deteriorated in this age of Kali. The richer section of the population, because of its degradation in Vedic culture, is no longer attracted by these places of pilgrimage, and the *brāhmaṇa* priests who depended on such visitors have also deteriorated in their professional duty of helping the visitors. These *brāhmaṇa* priests in the places of pilgrimage are called *paṇḍa* or *paṇḍit*. This means that they formerly were very learned *brāhmaṇas* and used to guide the visitors in all details of the purpose of coming there, and thus both the visitors and the priests were benefited by mutual cooperation.

It is clear from the description of *Śrīmad-Bhāgavatam* that when Lord Balarāma was visiting the different places of pilgrimage, He properly followed the Vedic system. After distributing cows at Setubandha, Lord Balarāma proceeded toward the Kṛtamālā and Tāmraparṇī Rivers. These two rivers are celebrated as sacred, and Lord Balarāma bathed in both. He then proceeded toward Malaya Hill. This Malaya Hill is very great, and it is said that it is one of seven peaks called the Malaya Hills. The great sage Agastya used to live there, and Lord Balarāma visited him and offered His respects by bowing down before him. After taking the sage's blessings, Lord Balarāma, with the sage's permission, proceeded toward the Indian Ocean.

At the point of the cape there is a big temple of the goddess Durgā where she is known as Kanyākumārī. This temple of Kanyākumārī was also visited by Lord Rāmacandra, and therefore it is to be understood that the temple has been existing for millions of years. From there, Lord Balarāma went on to visit the pilgrimage city known as Phālgunatīrtha, which is on the shore of the Indian Ocean, or the Southern Ocean. Phālgunatīrtha is celebrated because Lord Viṣṇu in His incarnation of Ananta is lying there. From Phālgunatīrtha, Lord Balarāma went on to visit another pilgrimage spot known as Pañcāpsarasa. There also He bathed according to the regulative principles and observed the ritualistic ceremonies. This site is also celebrated as a shrine of Lord Viṣṇu; therefore Lord Balarāma distributed ten thousand cows to the local *brāhmaṇa* priests.

From Cape Comarin Lord Balarāma turned toward Kerala. The country of Kerala is still existing in southern India under the name of South Kerala. After visiting this place, He came to Gokarṇatīrtha, where Lord Śiva is constantly worshiped. Balarāma then visited the temple of Āryādevī, which is completely surrounded by water. From that island, He went on to a place known as Śūrpāraka. After this He bathed in the rivers known as Tāpī, Payoṣṇī, and Nirvindhyā, and He came to the forest known as Daṇḍakāraṇya. This is the same Daṇḍakāraṇya Forest where Lord Rāmacandra lived while He was in exile. Lord Balarāma next came to the bank of the River Narmadā, the biggest river in central India. On the bank of this sacred Narmadā there is a pilgrimage spot known as Māhiṣmati Purī. After bathing there, according to regulative principles, Lord Balarāma returned to Prabhāsatīrtha, wherefrom He had begun His journey.

When Lord Balarāma returned to Prabhāsatīrtha He heard from the *brāhmaṇas* that most of the *kṣatriyas* in the Battle of Kurukṣetra had been killed. Balarāma felt relieved to hear that the burden of the world had been reduced. Lord Kṛṣṇa and Balarāma appeared on this earth to lessen the burden of military strength created by the ambitious *kṣatriya* kings. This is the way of materialistic life: not being satisfied by the absolute necessities of life, people ambitiously create extra demands, and their illegal desires are checked by the laws of nature or by laws of God, appearing as famine, war, pestilence and similar catastrophes. Lord Balarāma heard that although most of the *kṣatriyas* had been killed, the Kurus were still engaged in fighting. Therefore He returned to the battlefield just on the day Bhīmasena and Duryodhana were engaged in a personal duel As well-wisher of both of them, Lord Balarāma wanted to stop them, but they would not stop.

When Lord Balarāma appeared on the scene, King Yudhiṣṭhira and his young brothers, Nakula, Sahadeva, Lord Kṛṣṇa and Arjuna, immediately offered Him their respectful obeisances, but they did not speak at all. The reason they were silent was that Lord Balarāma was somewhat affectionate toward Duryodhana, and Duryodhana had learned from Balarāmajī the art of fighting with a club. Thus, when the fighting was going on, King Yudhiṣṭhira and others thought that Balarāma might come there to say something in favor of Duryodhana, and they therefore remained silent. Both Duryodhana and Bhīmasena were very enthusiastic in fighting with clubs, and in the midst of large audiences, each was very skillfully trying to strike the other, and while attempting to do so they appeared to be dancing. But although they appeared to be dancing, it was clear that both of them were very angry.

Lord Balarāma, wanting to stop the fighting, said, "My dear King Duryodhana and Bhīmasena, I know that both of you are great fighters and are well known in the world as great heroes, but still I think that Bhīmasena is superior to Duryodhana in bodily strength. On the other hand, Duryodhana is superior in the art of fighting with a club. Taking this into consideration, My opinion is that neither of you is inferior to the other in fighting. Under the circumstances, there is very little chance of one of you being defeated by the other. Therefore I request you not to waste your time in fighting in this way. I wish you to stop this unnecessary fight."

The good instruction given by Lord Balarāma to both Bhīmasena and Duryodhana was intended for the equal benefit of both of them. But they were so enwrapped in anger against each other that they could only remember their long-lasting personal enmity. Each thought only of killing the other, and they did not give much importance to the instruction of Lord Balarāma. Both of them then became like madmen in remembering the strong accusations and ill behavior they had exchanged with one another. Lord Balarāma, being able to understand the destiny which was awaiting them, was not eager to go further in the matter. Therefore, instead of staying, He decided to return to the city of Dvārakā.

When He returned to Dvārakā, He was received with great jubilation by relatives and friends, headed by King Ugrasena and other elderly persons; all of them came forward to welcome Lord Balarāma. After this, He again went to the holy place of pilgrimage at Naimiṣāraṇya, and the sages, saintly persons and *brāhmaṇas* all received Him standing. They understood that Lord Balarāma, although a *kṣatriya,* was now retired from the fighting business. The *brāhmanas* and the sages, who were always for peace and tranquility, were very pleased at this. All of them embraced Balarāma with great affection and induced Him to perform various kinds of sacrifices in that sacred spot of Naimiṣāraṇya. Actually Lord Balarāma had no business performing the sacrifices recommended for ordinary human beings; He is the Supreme Personality of Godhead, and therefore He Himself is the enjoyer of all such sacrifices. As such, His exemplary action in performing sacrifices was only to give a lesson to the common man to show how one should abide by the injunction of the *Vedas*.

The Supreme Personality of Godhead Balarāma instructed the sages and saintly persons at Naimiṣāranya on the subject matter of the living entities' relationship with this cosmic manifestation, on how one should accept this whole universe and on how one should relate with the cosmos in order to achieve the highest goal of perfection, the understanding that the whole cosmic manifestation is resting on the Supreme Personality of Godhead and that the Supreme Personality of Godhead is also all-pervading, even within the minutest atom, by the function of His Paramātmā feature.

Lord Balarāma then took the *avabhṛtha* bath which is accepted after finishing sacrificial performances. After taking His bath, He dressed Himself in new silken garments and decorated Himself with beautiful jewelry amidst His relatives and friends. He appeared to be a shining full moon amidst the luminaries in the sky. Lord Balarāma is the Personality of Godhead Ananta Himself; therefore He is beyond the scope of understanding by mind, intelligence or body. He descended exactly like a human being and behaved in that way for His own purpose; we can only explain His activities as the Lord's pastimes. No one can even estimate the extent of the unlimited demonstrations of His pastimes because He is all-powerful. Lord Balarāma is the original Viṣṇu; therefore anyone remembering these pastimes of Lord Balarāma in the morning and evening, will certainly become a great devotee of the Supreme Personality of Godhead, and thus his life will become successful in all respects.

Thus ends the Bhaktivedanta purport of the Third Volume, Tenth Chapter, of Kṛṣṇa, *"The Liberation of Balvala, and Lord Balarāma's Touring the Sacred Places."*

11/ Meeting of Lord Kṛṣṇa with Sudāmā Brāhmaṇa

King Parīkṣit was hearing the narrations of the pastimes of Lord Kṛṣṇa and Lord Balarāma from Śukadeva Gosvāmī. These pastimes are all transcendentally pleasurable to hear, and Mahārāja Parīkṣit addressed Śukadeva Gosvāmī as follows: "My dear Lord, the Supreme Personality of Godhead Kṛṣṇa is the bestower of both liberation and love of God simultaneously. Anyone who becomes a devotee of the Lord automatically attains liberation without having to make a separate attempt. The Lord is unlimited, and as such, His pastimes and activities for creating, maintaining and destroying the whole cosmic manifestation are unlimited. I therefore wish to hear about His other pastimes of which you may not have spoken as yet. My dear master, the conditioned souls within this material world have been frustrated by searching out the pleasure of happiness derived from sense gratification. Such desires for material enjoyment are always piercing the heart of conditioned souls. But I am actually experiencing how the transcendental topics of Lord Kṛṣṇa's pastimes can relieve one from the state of being affected by such sense gratificatory material activities. I think that no intelligent person can reject this method of hearing the transcendental pastimes of the Lord again and again; simply by hearing, one can remain always steeped in transcendental pleasure. Thus one will not be attracted by material sense gratification."

In this statement, Mahārāja Parīkṣit has used two important words: *viṣaṇṇaḥ* and *viśeṣajñaḥ: viṣaṇṇaḥ* means "morose." The materialistic persons are inventing many ways and means to become fully satisfied, but actually they remain morose. The point may be raised that sometimes those who are transcendentalists also remain morose. Parīkṣit Mahārāja has used, however, the word *viśeṣajñaḥ*. There are two kinds of transcendentalists, namely the impersonalists and the personalists. *Viśeṣajñaḥ* refers to the personalists, who are interested in transcendental variegatedness. The devotees become jubilant by hearing the descriptions of the personal activities of the Supreme Lord, whereas the impersonalists, who are actually more attracted by the impersonal feature of the Lord, are only superficially attracted by the personal activities of the Lord. As such, in spite of coming in contact with the pastimes of the Lord, the impersonalists do not fully realize the benefit to be derived, and thus they remain in exactly the same morose position, due to fruitive activity, with the materialists.

King Parīkṣit continued: "The capacity for talking can be perfected only by describing the transcendental qualities of the Lord. The capacity for working with one's hands can be successful only when one engages himself in the service of the Lord with those hands. Similarly, one's mind can be pacified only when he simply thinks of Kṛṣṇa in full Kṛṣṇa consciousness. This does not mean that one has to be very thoughtful, but one simply has to understand that Kṛṣṇa, the Absolute Truth, is all-pervasive, by His localized aspect as Paramātmā. If only one can think that Kṛṣṇa, as Paramātmā, is everywhere, even within the atom, then one can perfect the thinking, feeling and willing function of his mind. The perfect devotee does not see the material world as it appears to material eyes, but he sees everywhere the presence of his worshipable Lord in His Paramātmā feature."

Mahārāja Parīkṣit continued to say that the function of the ear can be perfected simply by engagement in hearing the transcendental activities of the Lord. He said further that the function of the head can be fully utilized when the head is engaged in bowing down before the Lord and His representative. That the Lord is represented in everyone's heart is a fact, and therefore the highly advanced devotee offers his respects to every living entity, considering that the body is the temple of the Lord. But it is not possible for all men to come to that stage of life immediately, because that stage is for the first-class devotee. The second-class devotee can consider the Vaiṣṇavas, or the devotees of the Lord, to be representatives of Kṛṣṇa, and the devotee who is just beginning, the neophyte or third-class devotee, can bow his head before the Deity in the temple and before the spiritual master, who is the direct manifestation of the Supreme Personality of Godhead. In the neophyte stage, in the intermediate stage, or in the fully advanced perfected stage, one can make the function of the head perfect by bowing down before the Lord or His representative. Similarly, he can perfect the function of the eyes by seeing the Lord and His representative. In this way, everyone can elevate the functions of the different parts of his body to the highest perfectional stage simply by engaging them in the service of the Lord or His representative. If one is able to do nothing more, he can simply bow down before the Lord and His representative and drink the *caraṇāmṛta,* the water which has washed the lotus feet of the Lord or His devotee.

On hearing these statements of Mahārāja Parīkṣit, Śukadeva Gosvāmī became overwhelmed with devotional ecstasy because of King Parīkṣit's advanced understanding of the Vaiṣṇava philosophy. Śukadeva Gosvāmī was already engaged in describing the activities of the Lord, and when he was asked by Mahārāja Parīkṣit to describe them further, he continued with great pleasure to narrate *Śrīmad-Bhāgavatam.*

There was a very nice *brāhmaṇa* friend of Lord Kṛṣṇa. As a perfect *brāhmaṇa,* he was very elevated in transcendental knowledge, and because of his advanced knowledge, he was not at all attached to material enjoyment. Therefore he was very peaceful and had achieved supreme control over his senses. This means that the *brāhmaṇa* was a perfect devotee because unless one is a perfect devotee, he cannot achieve the highest standard of knowledge. It is stated in the *Bhagavad-gītā* that a person who has come to the point of perfection of knowledge surrenders unto the Supreme Personality of Godhead. In other words, any person who has surrendered his life for the service of the Supreme Personality of Godhead has come to the point of perfect knowledge. The result of perfect knowledge is that one becomes detached from the materialistic way of life. This detachment means complete control of the senses, which are always attracted by material enjoyment. The senses of the devotee become purified, and in that stage the senses are engaged in the service of the Lord. That is the complete field of devotional service.

Although the *brāhmaṇa* friend of Lord Kṛṣṇa was a householder, he was not busy accumulating wealth for very comfortable living; therefore he was satisfied by the income which automatically came to him according to his destiny. This is the sign of perfect knowledge. A man who is in perfect knowledge knows that one cannot be happier than he is destined to be. In this material world, everyone is destined to suffer a certain amount of distress and to enjoy a certain amount of happiness. The amount of happiness and distress is already predestined for every living entity. No one can increase or decrease the happiness of the materialistic way of life. The *brāhmaṇa,* therefore, did not exert himself for more material happiness, but he used his time for advancement of Kṛṣṇa consciousness. Externally he appeared to be very poor because he had no rich dress and could not provide a very rich dress for his wife, and because their material condition was not very opulent they were not even eating sufficiently, and thus both he and his wife appeared to be very thin. The wife was not very anxious for her personal comfort, but she felt very concerned for her husband, who was such a pious *brāhmaṇa.* She was trembling due to her weak health, and although she did not like to dictate to her husband, she spoke as follows:

"My dear lord, I know that Lord Kṛṣṇa, who is the husband of the goddess of fortune, is your personal friend. You are also a devotee of Lord Kṛṣṇa, and He is always ready to help His devotee. Even if you think that you are not rendering any devotional service to the Lord, still you are surrendered to Him, and the Lord is the protector of the surrendered soul. Moreover, I know that Lord Kṛṣṇa is the ideal personality of Vedic culture. He is always in favor of brahminical culture and is very kind to the qualified *brāhmaṇas.* You are the most fortunate person because you have as your friend the Supreme Personality of Godhead. Lord Kṛṣṇa is the only shelter for personalities like you because you are fully surrendered unto Him. You are saintly, learned and fully in control of your senses. Under the circumstances, Lord Kṛṣṇa is your only shelter. Please, therefore, go to Him. I am sure that He will immediately understand your impoverished position. You are also a householder; therefore without any money you are in a distressed condition. But as soon as He understands your position, He will certainly give you sufficient riches so that you can live very comfortably. Lord Kṛṣṇa is now the King of the Bhoja, Vṛṣṇi and Andhaka dynasties, and I have heard that He never leaves His capital city, Dvārakā. He is living there without outside engagements. He is so kind and liberal that He immediately gives everything, even His personal self, to any person who surrenders unto Him. When He is prepared to give Himself personally to His devotee, then there is nothing wonderful in giving some material riches. Of course, He does not give much material wealth to His devotee if the devotee is not very fixed, but I think in your case He knows perfectly well how much you are fixed in devotional service. Therefore He will not hesitate to award you some material benefit for the bare necessities of life."

In this way, the wife of the *brāhmaṇa* again and again requested, in great humility and submission, that he go to Lord Kṛṣṇa. The *brāhmaṇa* thought that there was no need to ask any material benefit from Lord Śrī Kṛṣṇa, but he was induced by the repeated requests of his wife. Moreover, he thought, "If I go there I shall be able to see the Lord personally. That will be a great opportunity, even if I don't ask any material benefit from Him." When he had decided to go to Kṛṣṇa, he asked his wife if she had anything in the home that he could offer to Kṛṣṇa, because he must take some presentation for his friend. The wife immediately collected four palmsful of chipped rice from her neighboring friends and tied it in a small cloth, like a handkerchief, and gave it to her husband to present to Kṛṣṇa. Without waiting any longer, the *brāhmaṇa* took the presentation and began to proceed toward Dvārakā to see his Lord. While he was proceeding toward Dvārakā he was absorbed in the thought of how he could be able to see Lord Kṛṣṇa. He had no thought within his heart other than Kṛṣṇa.

It was of course very difficult to reach the palaces of the kings of the Yadu dynasty, but *brāhmaṇas* were allowed to visit, and when the *brāhmaṇa* friend of Lord Kṛṣṇa went there, he, along with other *brāhmaṇas,* had to pass through three military encampments. In each camp there were very big gates, and he also had to pass through them. After the gates and the camps, there were sixteen thousand big palaces, the residential quarters of the sixteen thousand queens of Lord Kṛṣṇa. The *brāhmaṇa* entered one palace which was very gorgeously decorated. When he entered this beautiful palace, he felt that he was swimming in the ocean of transcendental pleasure. He felt himself constantly diving and surfacing in that transcendental ocean.

At that time, Lord Kṛṣṇa was sitting on the bedstead of Queen Rukmiṇī. Even from a considerable distance He could see the *brāhmaṇa* coming to His home, and He could recognize him as His friend. Lord Kṛṣṇa immediately left His seat and came forward to receive His *brāhmaṇa* friend and, upon reaching him, embraced the *brāhmaṇa* with His two arms. Lord Kṛṣṇa is the reservoir of all transcendental pleasure, and yet He Himself felt great pleasure upon embracing the poor *brāhmaṇa* because He was meeting His very dear friend. Lord Kṛṣṇa had him seated on His own bedstead and personally brought him all kinds of fruits and drinks to offer him, as is proper in receiving a worshipable guest. Lord Śrī Kṛṣṇa is the supreme pure, but because He was playing the role of an ordinary human being, He immediately washed the *brāhmaṇa's* feet and, for His own purification, sprinkled the water onto His head. After this the Lord smeared the body of the *brāhmaṇa* with different kinds of scented pulp, such as sandalwood, *aguru* and saffron. He immediately burned several kinds of scented incense, and, as is usual, He offered him *ārātrika* with burning lamps. After thus offering him an adequate welcome and after the *brāhmaṇa* had taken food and drink, Lord Kṛṣṇa said, "My dear friend, it is a great fortune that you have come here."

The *brāhmaṇa,* being very poor, was not dressed nicely; his clothing was torn and dirty, and his body was also very lean and thin. He appeared not to be very clean, and because of his weak body, his bones were distinctly visible. The goddess of fortune Rukmiṇīdevī personally began to fan him with the *cāmara* fan, but the other women in the palace became astonished at Lord Kṛṣṇa's behavior in receiving the *brāhmaṇa* in that way. They were surprised to see how eager Lord Kṛṣṇa was to welcome this particular *brāhmaṇa.* They began to wonder how Lord Kṛṣṇa could personally receive a *brāhmaṇa* who was poor, not very neat or clean, and poorly dressed; but at the same time they could realize that the *brāhmaṇa* was not an ordinary living being. They knew that he must have performed great pious activities; otherwise why was Lord Kṛṣṇa, the husband of the goddess of fortune, taking so much care for him? They were still more surprised to see that the *brāhmaṇa* was seated on the bedstead of Lord Kṛṣṇa. They were especially surprised to see that Lord Kṛṣṇa had embraced him exactly as He embraced His elder brother, Balarāmaji, because Lord Kṛṣṇa used to embrace only Rukmiṇī or Balarāma, and no one else.

After receiving the *brāhmaṇa* nicely, and seating him on His own cushioned bed, Lord Kṛṣṇa said, "My dear *brāhmaṇa* friend, you are a most intelligent personality, and you know very well the principles of religious life. I believe that after you finished your education at the house of our teacher and after you sufficiently remunerated him, you must have gone back to your home and accepted a suitable wife. I know very well that from the beginning you were not at all attached to the materialistic way of life, nor did you desire to be very opulent materially, and therefore you are in need of money. In this material world, persons who are not attached to material opulence are very rarely found. Such unattached persons haven't the least desire to accumulate wealth and prosperity for sense gratification, but sometimes they are found to collect money just to exhibit the exemplary life of a householder. They show how by proper distribution of wealth one can become an ideal householder and at the same time become a great devotee. Such ideal householders are to be considered followers of My footsteps. I hope, My dear *brāhmaṇa* friend, you remember all those days of our school life when both you and I were living together at the boarding house. Actually, whatever knowledge both you and I received in our life was accumulated in our student life.

"If a man is sufficiently educated in student life under the guidance of a proper teacher, then his life becomes successful in the future. He can very easily cross over the ocean of nescience, and he is not subjected to the influence of illusory energy. My dear friend, everyone should consider his father to be his first teacher because by the mercy of one's father one gets this body. The father is therefore the natural spiritual master. Our next spiritual master is he who initiates us into transcendental knowledge, and he is to be worshiped as much as I am. The spiritual master may be more than one. The spiritual master who instructs the disciples about spiritual matters is called *śikṣa-guru,* and the spiritual master who initiates the disciple is called *dīksā-guru.* Both of them are My representatives. There may be many spiritual masters who instruct, but the initiator spiritual master is one. A human being who takes advantage of these spiritual masters and, receiving proper knowledge from them, crosses the ocean of material existence, is to be understood as having properly utilized his human form of life. He has practical knowledge that the ultimate interest of life, which is to be gained only in this human form, is to achieve spiritual perfection and thus be transferred back home, back to Godhead.

"My dear friend, I am Paramātmā, the Supersoul present in everyone's heart, and it is My direct order that human society must follow the principles of *varṇa* and *āśrama.* As I have stated in the *Bhagavad-gītā,* the human society should be divided, according to quality and action, into four *varṇas.* Similarly, everyone should divide his life into four parts. One should utilize the first part of life in becoming a bona fide student, receiving adequate knowledge and keeping oneself in the vow of *brahmacarya,* so that one may completely devote his life for the service of the spiritual master without indulging in sense gratification. A *brahmacārī* is meant to lead a life of austerities and penance. The householder is meant to live a regulated life of sense gratification, but no one should remain a householder for the third stage of life. In that stage, one has to return to the austerities and penances formerly practiced in *brahmacārī* life and thus relieve himself of the attachment to household life. After being relieved of his attachments to the materialistic way of life, one may accept the order of *sannyāsa.*

"As the Supersoul of the living entities, sitting in everyone's heart, I observe everyone's activity in every stage and order of life. Regardless of which stage one is in, when I see that one is engaged seriously and sincerely in discharging the duties ordered by the spiritual master, and is thus dedicating his life to the service of the spiritual master, that person becomes most dear to Me. As far as the life of *brahmacarya* is concerned, if one can continue the life of a *brahmacārī* under the direction of a spiritual master, that is extremely good; but if in *brahmacārī* life one feels sex impulses, then he should take leave of his spiritual master, satisfying him according to the *guru's* desire. According to the Vedic system, a gift is offered to the spiritual master, which is called *guru-dakṣiṇā.* Then the disciple should take to householder life and accept a wife according to religious rites."

These instructions given by Lord Kṛṣṇa while talking with His friend the learned *brāhmaṇa* are very good for the guidance of human society. A system of human civilization that does not promote *varṇa* and *āśrama* is nothing but polished animal society. Indulgence in sex life by a man or woman living single is never acceptable in human society. A man should either strictly follow the principles of *brahmacārī* life or, with the permission of the spiritual master, should get married. Single life with illicit sex is animal life. For the animals there is no marriage institution.

Modern society does not aim at fulfilling the mission of human life. The mission of human life is to go back home, back to Godhead. To fulfill this mission, the system of *varṇa* and *āśrama* must be followed. When the system is followed rigidly and consciously, it fulfills this mission of life. When it is followed indirectly, without guidance of superior order, then it simply creates a disturbing condition in human society, and there is no peace and prosperity.

Kṛṣṇa continued to talk with His *brāhmaṇa* friend: "My dear friend, I think you remember our activities during the days when we were living as students. You may remember that once we went to collect fuel from the forest on the order of the *guru's* wife. While we were collecting the dried wood, we by chance entered the dense forest and became lost. There was an unexpected dust storm and then clouds and lightning in the sky and the explosive sound of thunder. Then sunset came, and we were lost in the dark jungle. After this, there was severe rainfall; the whole ground was overflooded with water, and we could not trace out the way to return to our *guru's āśrama.* You may remember that heavy rainfall—it was not actually rainfall but a sort of devastation. On account of the dust storm and the heavy rain, we began to feel greatly pained, and in whichever direction we turned we were bewildered. In that distressed condition, we took each other's hand and tried to find our way out. We passed the whole night in that way, and early in the morning when our absence became known to our *gurudeva,* he sent his other disciples to search us out. He also came with them, and when they reached us in the jungle they found us to be very distressed.

"With great compassion our *gurudeva* said, 'My dear boys, it is very wonderful that you have suffered so much trouble for me. Everyone likes to take care of his body as the first consideration, but you are so good and faithful to your *guru* that without caring for bodily comforts you have taken so much trouble for me. I am also glad to see that bona fide students like you will undergo any kind of trouble for the satisfaction of the spiritual master. That is the way for a bona fide disciple to become free from his debt to the spiritual master. It is the duty of the disciple to dedicate his life to the service of the spiritual master. My dear best of the twice-born, I am greatly pleased by your action, and I bless you: May all your desires and ambitions be fulfilled. May the understanding of the *Vedas* which you have learned from me always continue to remain within your memory, so that at every moment you can remember the teachings of the *Vedas* and quote their instructions without difficulty. Thus you will never be disappointed in this life or in the next.'"

Kṛṣṇa continued: "My dear friend, you may remember that many such incidents occurred while we were in the *āśrama* of our spiritual master. Both of us can realize that without the blessings of the spiritual master no one can be happy. By the mercy of the spiritual master and by his blessings, one can achieve peace and prosperity and be able to fulfill the mission of human life."

On hearing this, the learned *brāhmaṇa* replied, "My dear Kṛṣṇa, You are the Supreme Lord and the supreme spiritual master of everyone, and since I was fortunate enough to live with You in the house of our *guru,* I think I have nothing more to do in the matter of prescribed Vedic duties. My dear Lord, the Vedic hymns, ritualistic ceremonies, religious activities, and all other necessities for the perfection of human life, including economic development, sense gratification and liberation, are all derived from one source: Your supreme personality. All the different processes of life are ultimately meant for the understanding of Your personality. In other words, they are the different parts of Your transcendental form. And yet You played the role of a student and lived with us in the house of the *guru.* This means that You adopted all these pastimes for Your pleasure only; otherwise there was no need for Your playing the role of a human being."

Thus ends the Bhaktivedanta purport of the Third Volume, Eleventh Chapter, of* Kṛṣṇa, *"Meeting of Lord Kṛṣṇa with Sudāmā Brāhmaṇa."

12 / The Brāhmaṇa Sudāmā Benedicted by Lord Kṛṣṇa

Lord Kṛṣṇa, the Supreme Personality of Godhead, the Supersoul of all living entities, knows very well everyone's heart. He is especially inclined to the *brāhmaṇa* devotees. Lord Kṛṣṇa is also called *brahmaṇyadeva,* which means that He is worshiped by the *brāhmaṇas.* Therefore it is understood that a devotee who is fully surrendered unto the Supreme Personality of Godhead has already acquired the position of a *brāhmaṇa.* Without becoming a *brāhmaṇa,* one cannot approach the Supreme Brahman, Lord Kṛṣṇa. Kṛṣṇa is especially concerned with vanquishing the distress of His devotees, and He is the only shelter of pure devotees.

Lord Kṛṣṇa was engaged for a long time in talking with Sudāmā Vipra about their past association. Then, just to enjoy the company of an old friend, Lord Kṛṣṇa began to smile, and asked, "My dear friend, what have you brought for Me? Has your wife given you some nice eatable for Me?" While He was addressing His friend, Lord Kṛṣṇa was looking upon him and smiling with great love. He continued: "My dear friend, you must have brought some presentation for Me from your home."

Lord Kṛṣṇa knew that Sudāmā was hesitating to present Him the paltry chipped rice which was actually unfit for His eating, and understanding the mind of Sudāmā Vipra the Lord said, "My dear friend, certainly I am not in need of anything, but if My devotee gives Me something as an offering of love, even though it may be very insignificant, I accept it with great pleasure. On the other hand, if a person is not a devotee, even though he may offer Me very valuable things, I do not like to accept them. I actually accept only things which are offered to Me in devotion and love; otherwise, however valuable the thing may be, I do not accept it. If My pure devotee offers Me even the most insignificant things—a little flower, a little piece of leaf, a little water—but saturates the offering in devotional love, then I not only gladly accept such an offering, but I eat it with great pleasure."

Lord Kṛṣṇa assured Sudāmā Vipra that He would be very glad to accept the chipped rice which he had brought from home, yet out of great shyness, Sudāmā Vipra hesitated to present it to the Lord. He was thinking, "How can I offer such insignificant things to Kṛṣṇa?" and he simply bowed his head.

Lord Kṛṣṇa, the Supersoul, knows everything in everyone's heart. He knows everyone's determination and everyone's want. He knew, therefore, the reason for Sudāmā Vipra's coming to Him. He knew that, driven by extreme poverty, he had come there at the request of his wife. Thinking of Sudāmā as His very dear class friend, He knew that Sudāmā's love for Him as a friend was never tainted by any desire for material benefit. Kṛṣṇa thought, "Sudāmā has not come asking anything from Me, but being obliged by the request of his wife, he has come to see Me just to please her." Lord Kṛṣṇa therefore decided that He would give more material opulence to Sudāmā Vipra than could be imagined even by the King of heaven.

He then snatched the bundel of chipped rice which was hanging on the shoulder of the poor *brāhmaṇa,* packed in one corner of his wrapper, and said, "What is this? My dear friend, you have brought Me nice, palatable chipped rice!" He encouraged Sudāmā Vipra, saying, "I consider that this quantity of chipped rice will not only satisfy Me, but will satisfy the whole creation." It is understood from this statement that Kṛṣṇa, being the original source of everything, is the root of the entire creation. As watering the root of a tree immediately distributes water to every part of the tree, so an offering made to Kṛṣṇa, or any action done for Kṛṣṇa, is to be considered the highest welfare work for everyone, because the benefit of such an offering is distributed throughout the creation. Love for Kṛṣṇa becomes distributed to all living entities.

While Lord Kṛṣṇa was speaking to Sudāmā Vipra, He ate one morsel of chipped rice from his bundle, and when He attempted to eat a second morsel, Rukmiṇīdevī, who is the goddess of fortune herself, checked the Lord by catching hold of His hand. After touching the hand of Kṛṣṇa, Rukmiṇī said, "My dear Lord, this one morsel of chipped rice is sufficient to cause him who offered it to become very opulent in this life and to continue his opulence in the next life. My Lord, You are so kind to Your devotee that even this one morsel of chipped rice pleases You very greatly, and Your pleasure assures the devotee opulence both in this life and in the next." This indicates that when food is offered to Lord Kṛṣṇa with love and devotion and He is pleased and accepts it from the devotee, Rukmiṇīdevī, the goddess of fortune, becomes so greatly obliged to the devotee that she has to personally go to the devotee's home to turn it into the most opulent home in the world. If one feeds Nārāyaṇa sumptuously, the goddess of fortune, Lakṣmī, automatically becomes a guest in one's house, which means that one's home becomes opulent. The learned *brāhmaṇa* Sudāmā passed that night at the house of Lord Kṛṣṇa, and while he was there he felt as if he were living in the Vaikuṇṭha planet. Actually he was living in Vaikuṇṭha, because wherever Lord Kṛṣṇa, the original Nārāyaṇa, and Rukmiṇīdevī, the goddess of fortune, live is not different from the spiritual planet, Vaikuṇṭhaloka.

The learned *brāhmaṇa* Sudāmā did not appear to have received anything substantial from Lord Kṛṣṇa while he was at His place, and yet he did not ask anything from the Lord. The next morning he started for his home, thinking always about his reception by Kṛṣṇa, and thus he became merged in transcendental bliss. All the way home he was simply remembering the dealings of Lord Kṛṣṇa, and he was feeling very happy to have seen the Lord.

The *brāhmaṇa* began to think as follows: "It is most pleasurable to see Lord Kṛṣṇa, who is most devoted to the *brāhmaṇas.* How great a lover He is of the brahminical culture! He is the Supreme *Brahman* Himself, yet He reciprocates with the *brāhmaṇas.* He also respects the *brāhmaṇas* so much that He embraced to His chest a poor *brāhmaṇa* like me, although He never embraces anyone to His chest except the goddess of fortune. How can there be any comparison between me, a poor, sinful *brāhmaṇa,* and the Supreme Lord Kṛṣṇa, who is the only shelter of the goddess of fortune? And yet, considering me as a *brāhmaṇa,* He embraced me with heartfelt pleasure in His two transcendental arms. Lord Kṛṣṇa was so kind to me that He allowed me to sit down on the same bedstead where the goddess of fortune lies down. He considered me to be His real brother. How can I appreciate my obligation to Him? When I was tired, Śrīmatī Rukmiṇīdevī, the goddess of fortune, began to fan me, holding the *cāmara* whisk in her own hand. She never considered her exalted position as the first queen of Lord Kṛṣṇa. I was rendered service by the Supreme Personality of Godhead because of His high regard for the *brāhmaṇas,* and by massaging my legs and feeding me with His own hand, He practically worshiped me! Aspiring for elevation to the heavenly planets, or liberation or all kinds of material opulences, or perfection in the mystic *yoga* powers, everyone throughout the universe worships the lotus feet of Lord Kṛṣṇa. Yet the Lord was so kind to me that He did not give me even a farthing, knowing very well that I am a poverty-stricken man who, if I got some money, might become puffed up and mad after material opulence and so forget Him."

The statement of the *brāhmaṇa* Sudāmā is correct. An ordinary man who is very poor and prays to the Lord for benediction in material opulence, and who somehow or other becomes richer in material opulence, immediately forgets his obligation to the Lord. Therefore, the Lord does not offer opulences to His devotee unless the devotee is thoroughly destitute. Rather, if a neophyte devotee serves the Lord very sincerely and at the same time wants material opulence, the Lord keeps him from obtaining it.

Thinking in this way, the learned *brāhmaṇa* gradually reached his own home. But on reaching there he saw that everything was wonderfully changed. He saw that in place of his cottage there were big palaces made of valuable stones and jewels, glittering like the sun, moon and rays of fire. Not only were there big palaces, but at intervals there were beautifully decorated parks, in which many beautiful men and women were strolling. In those parks there were nice lakes full of lotus flowers and beautiful lilies, and there were flocks of multicolored birds. Seeing the wonderful conversion of his native place, the *brāhmaṇa* began to think to himself, "How am I seeing all these changes? Does this place belong to me, or to someone else? If it is the same place where I used to live, then how has it so wonderfully changed?"

While the learned *brāhmaṇa* was considering this, a group of beautiful men and women with features resembling those of the demigods, accompanied by musical chanters, approached to welcome him. All were singing auspicious songs. The wife of the *brāhmaṇa* became very glad on hearing the tidings of her husband's arrival, and with great haste she also came out of the palace. The *brāhmaṇa's* wife appeared so beautiful that it seemed as if the goddess of fortune herself had come to receive him. As soon as she saw her husband present before her, tears of joy began to fall from her eyes, and her voice became so choked up that she could not even address her husband. She simply closed her eyes in ecstasy. But with great love and affection she bowed down before her husband, and within herself she thought of embracing him. She was fully decorated with a gold necklace and ornaments, and while standing among the maidservants she appeared like the wife of a demigod just alighting from an airplane. The *brāhmaṇa* was surprised to see his wife so beautiful, and in great affection and without saying a word he entered the palace with his wife.

When the *brāhmaṇa* entered his personal apartment in the palace, he saw that it was not an apartment, but the residence of the King of heaven. The palace was surrounded by many columns of jewels. The couches and the bedsteads were made of ivory, bedecked with gold and jewels, and the bedding was as white as the foam of milk and as soft as a lotus flower. There were many whisks hanging from golden rods, and many golden thrones with sitting cushions as soft as the lotus flower. In various places there were velvet and silken canopies with laces of pearls hanging all around. The structure of the building was standing on first-class transparent marble, with engravings made of emerald stones. All the women in the palace were carrying lamps made of valuable jewels. The flames and the jewels combined to produce a wonderfully brilliant light. When the *brāhmaṇa* saw his position suddenly changed to one of opulence, and when he could not determine the cause for such a sudden change, he began to consider very gravely how it had happened.

He thus began to think, "From the beginning of my life I have been extremely poverty-stricken, so what could be the cause of such great and sudden opulence? I do not find any cause other than the all-merciful glance of my friend Lord Kṛṣṇa, the chief of the Yadu dynasty. Certainly these are gifts of Lord Kṛṣṇa's causeless mercy. The Lord is self-sufficient, the husband of the goddess of fortune, and thus He is always full with six opulences. He can understand the mind of His devotee, and He sumptuously fulfills the devotee's desires. All these are acts of my friend, Lord Kṛṣṇa. My beautiful dark friend Kṛṣṇa is far more liberal than the cloud which can fill up the great ocean with water. Without disturbing the cultivator with rain during the day, the cloud brings liberal rain at night just to satisfy him. And yet when the cultivator wakes up in the morning, he considers that it has not rained enough. Similarly, the Lord fulfills the desire of everyone according to his position, and yet one who is not in Kṛṣṇa consciousness considers all the gifts of the Lord to be less than his desire. On the other hand, when the Lord receives a little thing in love and affection from His devotee, He considers it a great and valuable gift. The vivid example is myself. I simply offered Him a morsel of chipped rice, and in exchange He has given me opulences greater than the opulence of the King of heaven."

What the devotee actually offers to the Lord is not needed by the Lord. He is self-sufficient. If the devotee offers something to the Lord, it acts for his own interest because whatever a devotee offers to the Lord comes back in a quantity a million times greater than what was offered. One does not become a loser by giving to the Lord, but he becomes a gainer by millions of times.

The *brāhmaṇa*, feeling great obligation to Kṛṣṇa, thought, "I pray to have the friendship of Lord Kṛṣṇa and to engage in His service, and to surrender fully unto Him in love and affection, life after life. I do not want any opulence. I only desire not to forget His service. I simply wish to be associated with His pure devotees. May my mind and activities be always engaged in His service. The unborn Supreme Personality of Godhead Kṛṣṇa knows that many great personalities have fallen from their positions because of extravagant opulence. Therefore, even when His devotee asks for some opulence from Him, the Lord sometimes does not give it. He is very cautious about His devotees. Because a devotee in an immature position of devotional service may, if offered great opulence, fall from his position due to being in the material world, the Lord does not offer opulence to him. This is another manifestation of the causeless mercy of the Lord upon His devotee. His first interest is that the devotee may not fall. He is exactly like a well-wishing father who does not give much wealth into the hand of his immature son, but who, when the son is grown up and knows how to spend money, gives him the whole treasury house."

The learned *brāhmaṇa* thus concluded that whatever opulences he had received from the Lord should not be used for his extravagant sense gratification, but for the service of the Lord. The *brāhmaṇa* accepted his newly-acquired opulence, but he did so in a spirit of renunciation, unattached to sense gratification, and thus he lived very peacefully with his wife, enjoying all the facilities of opulence as *prasādam* of the Lord. He enjoyed varieties of foodstuff by offering it to the Lord and then taking it as *prasādam.* Similarly, if by the grace of the Lord we get such opulences as material wealth, fame, power, education and beauty, it is our duty to consider that they are all gifts of the Lord and must be used for His service, not for our sense enjoyment. The learned *brāhmaṇa* remained in that position, and instead of deteriorating due to great opulence, his love and affection for Lord Kṛṣṇa increased day after day. Material opulence can be the cause of degradation and also the cause of elevation, according to the purposes for which it is used. If opulence is used for sense gratification, it is the cause of degradation, and if it is used for the service of the Lord, it is the cause of elevation.

It is evident from Lord Kṛṣṇa's dealings with Sudāmā Vipra that the Supreme Personality of Godhead is very, very pleased with a person who is possessed of brahminical qualities. A qualified *brāhmaṇa* like Sudāmā Vipra is naturally a devotee of Lord Kṛṣṇa. Therefore it is said, *brāhmaṇo vaiṣṇavaḥ:* a *brāhmaṇa* is a *Vaiṣṇava.* Or sometimes it is said, *brāhmaṇaḥ paṇḍitaḥ. Paṇḍita* means a highly learned person. A *brāhmaṇa* cannot be foolish or uneducated. Therefore there are two divisions of *brāhmaṇas,* namely *Vaiṣṇavas* and *paṇḍitas.* Those who are simply learned are *paṇḍits,* but not yet devotees of the Lord, or *Vaiṣṇavas.* Lord Kṛṣṇa is not especially pleased with them. Simply the qualification of being a learned *brāhmaṇa* is not sufficient to attract the Supreme Personality of Godhead. A *brāhmaṇa* must not only be well qualified according to the requirements stated in scriptures such as *Śrīmad Bhagavad-gītā* and *Śrīmad-Bhāgavatam,* but at the same time he must be a devotee of Lord Kṛṣṇa. The vivid example is Sudāmā Vipra. He was a qualified *brāhmaṇa,* unattached to all sorts of material sense enjoyment, and at the same time a great devotee of Lord Kṛṣṇa. Lord Kṛṣṇa, the enjoyer of all sacrifices and penances, is very fond of a *brāhmaṇa* like Sudāmā Vipra, and we have seen by the actual behavior of Lord Kṛṣṇa how much He adores such a *brāhmaṇa.* Therefore, the ideal stage of human perfection is to become a *brāhmaṇa-vaiṣṇava* like Sudāmā Vipra.

Sudāmā Vipra realized that although Lord Kṛṣṇa is unconquerable, He nevertheless agrees to be conquered by His devotees. He realized how kind Lord Kṛṣṇa was to him, and he was always in trance, constantly thinking of Kṛṣṇa. By such constant association with Lord Kṛṣṇa, whatever darkness of material contamination was remaining within his heart was completely cleared away, and very shortly he was transferred to the spiritual kingdom, which is the goal of all saintly persons in the perfectional stage of life. Śukadeva Gosvāmī has stated that all persons who hear this history of Sudāmā Vipra and Lord Kṛṣṇa will know how affectionate Lord Kṛṣṇa is to the *brāhmaṇa* devotees like Sudāmā. Therefore anyone who hears this history gradually becomes as qualified as Sudāmā Vipra, and he is thus transferred to the spiritual kingdom of Lord Kṛṣṇa.

Thus ends the Bhaktivedanta purport of the Third Volume, Twelfth Chapter, of* Kṛṣṇa, *"The Brāhmaṇa Sudāmā Benedicted by Lord Kṛṣṇa."

13/ Lord Kṛṣṇa and Balarāma Meet the Inhabitants of Vṛndāvana

Once upon a time while Lord Kṛṣṇa and Balarāma were living peacefully in Their great city of Dvārakā, there was the rare occasion of a full solar eclipse, such as takes place at the end of every *kalpa,* or day of Brahmā. At the end of every *kalpa* the sun is covered by a great cloud, and incessant rain covers the lower planetary systems up to Svargaloka. By astronomical calculation, people were informed about this great eclipse prior to its taking place, and therefore everyone, both men and women, decided to assemble at the holy place in Kurukṣetra known as Samanta-pañcaka.

The Samanta-pañcaka pilgrimage site is celebrated because Lord Paraśurāma performed great sacrifices there after having killed all the *kṣatriyas* in the world twenty-one times. Lord Paraśurāma killed all the *kṣatriyas,* and their accumulated blood flowed like a stream. Lord Paraśurāma dug five big lakes at Samanta-pañcaka, and filled them with this blood. Lord Paraśurāma is *Viṣṇu-tattva.* As stated in the *Īśopaniṣad, Viṣṇu-tattva* cannot be contaminated by any sinful activity. Yet although Lord Paraśurāma is fully powerful and uncontaminated, in order to exhibit ideal character, He performed great sacrifices at Samanta-pañcaka to atone for His so-called sinful killing of the *kṣatriyas.* By His example, Lord Paraśurāma established that the killing art, although sometimes necessary, is not good. Lord Paraśurāma considered Himself culpable for the sinful killing of the *kṣatriyas;* therefore, how much more are we culpable for such abominable unsanctioned acts. Thus, killing of living entities is prohibited from time immemorial all over the world.

Taking advantage of the occasion of the solar eclipse, all important persons visited the holy place of pilgrimage. Some of the important personalities are mentioned as follows. Among the elderly persons there were Akrūra, Vasudeva and Ugrasena; among the younger generation there were Gada, Pradyumna, Sāmba, and many other members of the Yadu dynasty who had come there with a view to atone for sinful activities accrued in the course of discharging their respective duties. Because almost all the members of the Yadu dynasty went to Kurukṣetra, some important personalities, like Aniruddha, the son of Pradyumna, and Kṛtavarmā, the commander-in-chief of the Yadu dynasty, along with Sucandra, Śuka and Sāraṇa remained in Dvārakā to protect the city.

All the members of the Yadu dynasty were naturally very beautiful, and yet on this occasion, when they appeared duly decorated with gold necklaces and flower garlands, dressed in valuable clothing and properly armed with their respective weapons, their natural beauty and personalities were a hundred times enhanced. The members of the Yadu dynasty came to Kurukṣetra in their gorgeously decorated chariots resembling the airplanes of the demigods, pulled by big horses that moved like the waves of the ocean, and some of them rode on sturdy, stalwart elephants that moved like the clouds in the sky. Their wives were carried on beautiful palanquins by beautiful men whose features resembled those of the Vidyādharas. The entire assembly looked as beautiful as an assembly of the demigods of heaven.

After arriving in Kurukṣetra, the members of the Yadu dynasty took their baths ceremoniously, with self-control, as enjoined in the *śāstras,* and they observed fasting for the whole period of the eclipse in order to nullify the reactions of their sinful activities. Since it is a Vedic custom to give in charity as much as possible during the hours of the eclipse, the members of the Yadu dynasty distributed many hundreds of cows in charity to the *brāhmaṇas.* All those cows were fully decorated with nice dress and ornaments. The special feature of these cows was that they had golden ankle bells and flower garlands on their necks.

All the members of the Yadu dynasty again took their baths in the lakes created by Lord Paraśurāma. After this they sumptuously fed the *brāhmaṇas* with first-class cooked food, all prepared in butter. According to the Vedic system, there are two classes of food. One is called raw food, and the other is called cooked food. Raw food does not include raw vegetables and raw grains, but food boiled in water; whereas cooked food is made in ghee. *Capatis, dahl,* rice and ordinary vegetables are called raw foods, as are fruits and salads. But *puris, kacuri, saṅgosas,* sweet balls, etc., are called cooked foods. All the *brāhmaṇas* invited on that occasion by the members of the Yadu dynasty were fed sumptuously with cooked food.

The ceremonial functions performed by the members of the Yadu dynasty externally resembled the ritualistic performances performed by the *karmīs.* When a *karmī* performs some ritualistic ceremony, his ambition is sense gratification--good position, good wife, good house, good children or good wealth; but the ambition of the members of the Yadu dynasty was different. Their ambition was to offer perpetual faith and devotion to Kṛṣṇa. All the members of the Yadu dynasty were great devotees. As such, after many births of accumulated pious activities, they were given the chance to associate with Lord Kṛṣṇa. In going to take their baths in the place of pilgrimage at Kurukṣetra or observing the regulative principles during the solar eclipse or feeding the *brāhmaṇas*—in all their activities—they simply thought of devotion to Kṛṣṇa. Their ideal worshipable Lord was Kṛṣṇa, and no one else.

After feeding the *brāhmaṇas,* it is the custom for the host, with their permission, to accept *prasādam.* Thus, with the permission of the *brāhmaṇas,* all the members of the Yadu dynasty took lunch. Then they selected resting places underneath big, shadowy trees, and when they had taken sufficient rest, they prepared to receive visitors, among whom there were relatives and friends, as well as many subordinate kings and rulers. There were the rulers of the Matsya Province, Uśīnara Province, Kośala Province, Vidarbha Province, Kuru Province, Sṛñjaya Province, Kāmboja Province, Kekaya Province and many other countries and provinces. Some of the rulers belonged to opposing parties, and some were friends. But above all, the visitors from Vṛndāvana were most prominent. The residents of Vṛndāvana, headed by Nanda Mahārāja, had been living in great anxiety because of separation from Kṛṣṇa and Balarāma. Taking advantage of the solar eclipse, they all came to see their life and soul, Kṛṣṇa and Balarāma.

The inhabitants of Vṛndāvana were well-wishers and intimate friends of the Yadu dynasty. This meeting of the two parties after long separation was a very touching incident. Both the Yadus and the residents of Vṛndāvana felt such great pleasure in meeting and talking together that it was a unique scene. Meeting after long separation, they were all jubilant; their hearts were throbbing, and their faces appeared like freshly bloomed lotus flowers. There were drops of tears falling from their eyes, the hair on their bodies stood on end, and because of their extreme ecstasy, they were temporarily speechless. In other words, they began to dive in the ocean of happiness.

While the men were meeting in that way, the women were also meeting one another in the same manner. They were embracing each other in great friendship, smiling very mildly, and looking at one another with much affection. When they were embracing each other in their arms, the saffron and *kuṅkuma* spread on their breasts was exchanged from one person to another, and they all felt heavenly ecstasy. Due to such heart-to-heart embracing, torrents of tears glided down their cheeks. The juniors were offering obeisances to the elders, and the elders were offering their blessings to the juniors. They were thus welcoming one another and asking after each other's welfare. Ultimately, however, all their talk was only of Kṛṣṇa. All the neighbors and relatives were connected with Lord Kṛṣṇa's pastimes in this world, and as such Kṛṣṇa was the center of all their activities. Whatever activities they performed—social, political, religious, or conventional—were transcendental.

The real elevation of human life rests on knowledge and renunciation. As stated in the *Śrīmad-Bhāgavatam,* in the First Canto, devotional service rendered to Kṛṣṇa automatically produces perfect knowledge and renunciation. The family members of the Yadu dynasty and the cowherd men of Vṛndāvana had their minds fixed on Kṛṣṇa. That is the symptom of all knowledge, and because their minds were always engaged in Kṛṣṇa, they were automatically freed from all material activities. This stage of life is called *yukta-vairāgya* as enunciated by Śrīla Rūpa Gosvāmī. Knowledge and renunciation, therefore, do not mean dry speculation and renunciation of activities. Rather, one must start speaking and acting only in relationship with Kṛṣṇa.

In this meeting at Kurukṣetra, Kuntīdevī and Vasudeva, who were sister and brother, met after a long period of separation, along with their respective sons and daughters-in-law, wives, children and other family members. By talking among themselves, they soon forgot all their past miseries. Kuntīdevī especially addressed her brother Vasudeva as follows: "My dear brother, I am very unfortunate, because not one of my desires has ever been fulfilled; otherwise how could it happen that although I have such a saintly brother as you, perfect in all respects, you did not inquire from me as to how I was passing my days in a distressed condition of life." It appears that Kuntīdevī was remembering the miserable days when she had been banished along with her sons through the mischievous plans of Dhṛtarāṣṭra and Duryodhana. She continued; "My dear brother, I can understand that when providence goes against someone, even one's nearest relatives also forget him. In such a condition, even one's father, one's mother or one's own children will forget him. Therefore, my dear brother, I do not accuse you."

Vasudeva replied to his sister: "My dear sister, do not be sorry, and do not blame me in that way. We should always remember that we all are only toys in the hands of providence. Everyone is under the control of the Supreme Personality of Godhead. It is under His control only that all kinds of fruitive actions and the resultant reactions take place. My dear sister, you know that we were very much harassed by King Kaṁsa, and by his persecutions we were scattered here and there. We were always full of anxieties. Only in the last few days have we returned to our own places, by the grace of God."

After this conversation, Vasudeva and Ugrasena received the kings who came to see them, and they sufficiently welcomed them all. Seeing Lord Kṛṣṇa present on the spot, all the visitors felt transcendental pleasure and became very peaceful. Some of the prominent visitors were as follows: Bhīṣmadeva, Droṇācārya, Dhṛtarāṣṭra, Duryodhana, and Gāndhārī along with her sons; King Yudhiṣṭhira along with his wife, and the Pāṇḍavas along with Kuntī; Sṛñjaya, Vidura, Kṛpācārya, Kuntibhoja, Virāṭa, King Nagnajit, Purujit, Drupada, Śalya, Dhṛṣṭaketu, the King of Kāśī, Damaghoṣa, Viśālākṣa, the King of Mithilā, the King of Madras (formerly known as Madra), the King of Kekaya, Yudhāmanyu, Suśarmā, Bāhlīka along with his sons, and many other rulers who were subordinate to King Yudhiṣṭhira.

When they saw Lord Kṛṣṇa with His thousands of queens, they became fully satisfied at the sight of such beauty and transcendental opulence. All who were there personally visited Lord Balarāma and Kṛṣṇa, and being properly welcomed by the Lord they began to glorify the members of the Yadu dynasty, especially Kṛṣṇa and Balarāma. Because he was the King of the Bhojas, Ugrasena was considered the chief Yadu, and therefore the visitors specifically addressed him: "Your majesty Ugrasena, King of the Bhojas, factually the Yadus are the only persons within this world who are perfect in all respects. All glories unto you! All glories unto you! The specific condition of your perfection is that you are always seeing Lord Kṛṣṇa, who is sought after by many mystic *yogīs* undergoing severe austerities and penances for great numbers of years. All of you are in direct touch with Lord Kṛṣṇa at every moment.

"All the Vedic hymns are glorifying the Supreme Personality of Godhead, Kṛṣṇa. The Ganges water is considered sanctified because of its being the water used to wash the lotus feet of Lord Kṛṣṇa. The Vedic literatures are nothing but the injunctions of Lord Kṛṣṇa. The purpose of the study of all the *Vedas* is to know Kṛṣṇa; therefore, the words of Kṛṣṇa and the message of His pastimes are always purifying. By the influence of time and circumstances, all the opulences of this world had become almost completely wiped out, but since Kṛṣṇa has appeared on this planet, all auspicious features have again appeared due to the touch of His lotus feet. Because of His presence, all our ambitions and desires are gradually being fulfilled. Your majesty, King of the Bhojas, you are related with the Yadu dynasty by matrimonial relationship, and by blood relationship also. As a result, you are constantly in touch with Lord Kṛṣṇa, and you have no difficulty in seeing Him at any time. Lord Kṛṣṇa moves with you, talks with you, sits with you, rests with you, and dines with you. The Yadus appear to be always engaged in worldly affairs which are considered to lead to the royal road to hell, but due to the presence of Lord Kṛṣṇa, the original Personality of Godhead in the Viṣṇu category, who is omniscient, omnipresent and omnipotent, all of you are factually relieved from all material contamination, and are situated in the transcendental position of liberation and Brahman existence."

When they had heard that Kṛṣṇa would be present in Kurukṣetra because of the solar eclipse, the residents of Vṛndāvana, headed by Mahārāja Nanda, had also decided to go there, and therefore all the members of the Yadu dynasty were attending. King Nanda, accompanied by his cowherd men, had loaded all their necessary paraphernalia on bullock carts, and all of the Vṛndāvana residents had come to Kurukṣetra to see their beloved sons Lord Balarāma and Lord Kṛṣṇa. When the cowherd men of Vṛndāvana arrived in Kurukṣetra, all the members of the Yadu dynasty became most pleased. As soon as they saw the residents of Vṛndāvana, they stood up to welcome them, and it appeared that they had again regained their life. Both had been very eager to meet, and when they actually came forward and met, they embraced one another to their heart's satisfaction and remained in embrace for a considerable time.

As soon as Vasudeva saw Nanda Mahārāja, he jumped and ran over to him and embraced him very affectionately. Vasudeva began to narrate his past history—how he had been imprisoned by King Kaṁsa, how his babies had been killed, and how immediately after Kṛṣṇa's birth he had carried Him to the place of Nanda Mahārāja, and how Kṛṣṇa and Balarāma had been raised by Nanda Mahārāja and his queen, Yaśodā, as their own children. Similarly, Lord Balarāma and Kṛṣṇa also embraced King Nanda and mother Yaśodā and then offered Their respect unto their lotus feet by bowing down. Because of Their filial affection for Nanda and Yaśodā, both Lord Kṛṣṇa and Balarāma became choked up, and for a few seconds They could not speak. The most fortunate King Nanda and mother Yaśodā placed their sons on their laps and began to embrace Them to their full satisfaction. Because of separation from Kṛṣṇa and Balarāma, both King Nanda and Yaśodā had been merged in great distress for a very long time. Now, after meeting Them and embracing Them, all their sufferings were mitigated.

After this, Kṛṣṇa's mother, Devakī, and Balarāma's mother, Rohiṇī, both embraced mother Yaśodā. They said, "Dear Queen Yaśodādevī, both you and Nanda Mahārāja have been great friends to us, and when we remember you we are immediately overwhelmed by the thought of your friendly activities. We are so indebted to you that even if we were to return your benediction by giving you the opulence of the King of heaven, it would not be enough to repay you for your friendly behavior. We shall never forget your kindly behavior toward us. When both Kṛṣṇa and Balarāma were born, before they even saw Their real father and mother, They were entrusted to your care, and you raised Them as your own children, fostering Them as birds take care of their offspring in the nest. You have nicely fed, nourished and loved Them and have performed many auspicious religious ceremonies for Their benefit.

"Actually They are not our sons; They belong to you. Nanda Mahārāja and yourself are the real father and mother of Kṛṣṇa and Balarāma. As long as They were under your care They had not even a pinch of difficulty. Under your protection, They were completely out of the way of all kinds of fear. This most affectionate care which you have taken for Them is completely befitting your elevated position. The most noble personalities do not discriminate between their own sons and the sons of others, and there cannot be any personalities more noble than Nanda Mahārāja and yourself."

As far as the *gopīs* of Vṛndāvana were concerned, from the very beginning of their lives, they did not know anything beyond Kṛṣṇa. Kṛṣṇa and Balarāma were their life and soul. The *gopīs* were so attached to Kṛṣṇa that they could not even tolerate not seeing Him momentarily when their eyelids blinked and impeded their vision. They condemned Brahmā, the creator of the body, because he foolishly made eyelids which blinked and checked their seeing Kṛṣṇa. Because they had been separated from Kṛṣṇa for so many years, the *gopīs,* having come along with Nanda Mahārāja and mother Yaśodā, felt intense ecstasy in seeing Kṛṣṇa. No one can even imagine how anxious the *gopīs* were to see Kṛṣṇa again. As soon as Kṛṣṇa became visible to them, they took Him inside their hearts through their eyes and embraced Him to their full satisfaction. Even though they were embracing Kṛṣṇa only mentally, they became so ecstatic and overwhelmed with joy that for the time being they completely forgot themselves. The ecstatic trance which they achieved simply by mentally embracing Kṛṣṇa is impossible to achieve even for great *yogīs* constantly engaged in meditation on the Supreme Personality of Godhead. Kṛṣṇa could understand that the *gopīs* were rapt in ecstasy by embracing Him in their minds, and therefore, since He is present in everyone's heart, He also reciprocated the embracing from within.

Kṛṣṇa was sitting with mother Yaśodā and His other mothers, Devakī and Rohiṇī, but when the mothers engaged in talking, He took the opportunity and went to a secluded place to meet the *gopīs.* As soon as He approached the *gopīs,* the Lord began to smile, and after embracing them and inquiring about their welfare, He began to encourage them, saying, "My dear friends, you know that both Lord Balarāma and Myself left Vṛndāvana just to please Our relatives and family members. Thus We were long engaged in fighting with Our enemies and were obliged to forget you, who were so much attached to Me in love and affection. I can understand that by this action I have been ungrateful to you, but still I know you are faithful to Me. May I inquire if you have been thinking of Us although We had to leave you behind? My dear *gopīs,* do you now dislike remembering Me, considering Me to have been ungrateful to you? Do you take My misbehavior with you very seriously?

"After all, you should know it was not My intention to leave you; our separation was ordained by providence, who after all is the supreme controller and does as he desires. He causes the intermingling of different persons, and again disperses them as he desires. Sometimes we see that due to the presence of clouds and strong wind, atomic particles of dust and broken pieces of cotton are intermingled together, and after the strong wind subsides, all the particles of dust and cotton are again separated, scattered in different places. Similarly, the Supreme Lord is the creator of everything. The objects which we see are different manifestations of His energy. By His supreme will we are sometimes united and sometimes separated. We can therefore conclude that ultimately we are absolutely dependent on His will.

"Fortunately, you have developed loving affection for Me, which is the only way to achieve the transcendental position of association with Me. Any living entity who develops such unalloyed devotional affection for Me certainly at the end goes back to home, back to Godhead. In other words, unalloyed devotional service and affection for Me are the cause of supreme liberation.

"My dear *gopī* friends, you may know from Me that it is My energies only which are acting everywhere. Take, for example, an earthen pot. It is nothing but a combination of earth, water, air, fire and sky. It is always of the same physical composites, whether in its beginning, during its existence or after its annihilation. When it is created, the earthen pot is made of earth, water, fire, air and sky; while it remains, it is the same in composition; and when it is broken and annihilated, its different ingredients are conserved in different parts of the material energy. Similarly, at the creation of this cosmic manifestation, during its maintenance, and after its dissolution, everything is but a different manifestation of My energy. And because the energy is not separate from Me, it is to be concluded that I am existing in everything.

"In the same way, the body of a living being is nothing but a composition of the five elements, and the living entity embodied in the material condition is also part and parcel of Me. The living entity is imprisoned in the material condition on account of his false conception of himself as the supreme enjoyer. This false ego of the living entity is the cause of his imprisonment in material existence. As the Supreme Absolute Truth, I am transcendental to the living entity, as well as to his material embodiment. The two energies, material and spiritual, are both acting under My supreme control. My dear *gopīs,* I request that instead of being so afflicted, you try to accept everything with a philosophical attitude. Then you will understand that you are always with Me and that there is no cause of lamentation in our being separated from one another."

This important instruction of Lord Kṛṣṇa's to the *gopīs* can be utilized by all devotees engaged in Kṛṣṇa consciousness. The whole philosophy is considered on the basis of inconceivable, simultaneous oneness and difference. In *Bhagavad-gītā* the Lord says that He is present everywhere in His impersonal feature. Everything is existing in Him, but still He is not personally present everywhere. The cosmic manifestation is nothing but a display of Kṛṣṇa's energy, and because the energy is not different from the energetic, nothing is different from Kṛṣṇa. When this absolute consciousness, Kṛṣṇa consciousness, is absent, we are separated from Kṛṣṇa; but fortunately, if this Kṛṣṇa consciousness is present, then we are not separated from Kṛṣṇa. The process of devotional service is the revival of Kṛṣṇa consciousness, and if the devotee is fortunate enough to understand that the material energy is not separated from Kṛṣṇa, then he can utilize the material energy and its products in the service of the Lord. But in the absence of Kṛṣṇa consciousness, the forgetful living entity, although part and parcel of Kṛṣṇa, falsely puts himself in the position of enjoyer of the material world and, being thus implicated in material entanglement, is forced by the material energy to continue his material existence. This is also confirmed in the *Bhagavad-gītā.* Although a living entity is forced to act by the material energy, he falsely thinks that he is the all-in-all and the supreme enjoyer.

If the devotee knows perfectly that the *arcā-vigraha,* or Deity form of Lord Kṛṣṇa in the temple, is exactly the same *sac-cid-ānanda-vigraha* as Kṛṣṇa Himself, then his service to the temple Deity becomes direct service to the Supreme Personality of Godhead. Similarly, the temple itself, the temple paraphernalia and the food offered to the Deity are also not separate from Kṛṣṇa. One has to follow the rules and regulations prescribed by the *ācāryas,* and thus, under superior guidance, Kṛṣṇa-realization is fully possible, even in this material existence.

The *gopīs,* having been instructed by Kṛṣṇa in this philosophy of simultaneous oneness and difference, remained always in Kṛṣṇa consciousness and thus became liberated from all material contamination. The consciousness of the living entity who falsely presents himself as the enjoyer of the material world is called *jīva-kośa,* which means imprisonment by the false ego. Not only the *gopīs* but anyone who follows these instructions of Kṛṣṇa becomes immediately freed from the *jīva-kośa* imprisonment. A person in full Kṛṣṇa consciousness is always liberated from false egoism; he utilizes everything for Kṛṣṇa's service and is not at any time separated from Kṛṣṇa.

The *gopīs* therefore prayed to Kṛṣṇa, "Dear Kṛṣṇa, from Your navel emanated the original lotus flower which is the birthsite of Brahmā, the creator. No one can estimate Your glories or Your opulence, which therefore remain always a mystery even to the highest thoughtful men, the masters of all yogic power. The conditioned soul fallen in the dark well of this material existence can very easily, however, take shelter of the lotus feet of Lord Kṛṣṇa. Thus his deliverance is guaranteed." The *gopīs* continued: "Dear Kṛṣṇa, we are always busy in our family affairs. We therefore request that You remain within our hearts as the rising sun, and that will be Your greatest benediction."

The *gopīs* are always liberated souls, because they are fully in Kṛṣṇa consciousness. They only pretended to be entangled in household affairs in Vṛndāvana. In spite of their long separation, the inhabitants of Vṛndāvana, the *gopīs,* were not interested in the idea of going with Kṛṣṇa to His capital city, Dvārakā. They wanted to remain busy in Vṛndāvana and thus feel the presence of Kṛṣṇa in every step of their lives. They immediately invited Kṛṣṇa to come back to Vṛndāvana. This transcendental emotional existence of the *gopīs* is the basic principle of Lord Caitanya's teaching. The *Ratha-yātrā* Festival observed by Lord Caitanya is the emotional process of taking Kṛṣṇa back to Vṛndāvana. Śrīmatī Rādhārāṇī refused to go with Kṛṣṇa to Dvārakā to enjoy His company in the atmosphere of royal opulence, but wanted to enjoy His company in the original Vṛndāvana atmosphere. Lord Kṛṣṇa, being profoundly attached to the *gopīs,* never goes away from Vṛndāvana, and the *gopīs* and other residents of Vṛndāvana remain fully satisfied in Kṛṣṇa consciousness.

Thus ends the Bhaktivedanta purport of the Third Volume, Thirteenth Chapter, of* Kṛṣṇa, *"Lord Kṛṣṇa and Balarāma Meet the Inhabitants of Vṛndāvana."

14 / Draupadī Meets the Queens of Kṛṣṇa

There were many visitors who came to see Kṛṣṇa, and among them were the Pāṇḍavas, headed by King Yudhiṣṭhira. After talking with the *gopīs* and bestowing upon them the greatest benediction, Lord Kṛṣṇa came to welcome King Yudhiṣṭhira and other relatives who had come to see Him. He first of all inquired from them whether their situation was auspicious. Actually, there is no question of ill fortune for anyone who sees the lotus feet of Lord Kṛṣṇa, yet when Lord Kṛṣṇa, as a matter of etiquette, inquired from King Yudhiṣṭhira about his welfare, the King became very happy by such a reception and began to address the Lord thus: "My dear Lord Kṛṣṇa, great personalities and devotees in full Kṛṣṇa consciousness always think of Your lotus feet and remain fully satisfied by drinking the nectar of transcendental bliss. The nectar which they constantly drink sometimes comes out of their mouths and is sprinkled on others as the narration of Your transcendental activities. This nectar coming from the mouth of a devotee is so powerful that if one is fortunate enough to have the opportunity to drink it, he immediately becomes freed from the continuous journey of birth and death. Our material existence is caused by our forgetfulness of Your personality, but fortunately, the darkness of forgetfulness is immediately dissipated if one is privileged to hear about Your glories. Therefore, my dear Lord, where is the possibility of ill fortune for one who is constantly engaged in hearing Your glorious activities?

"Since we are fully surrendered unto You and have no other shelter than Your lotus feet, we are always confident of our good fortune. My dear Lord, You are the ocean of unlimited knowledge and transcendental bliss. The result of the action of mental concoction is to exist in the three temporary phases of material life—wakefulness, sleep and deep sleep. But these conditions cannot exist in Kṛṣṇa consciousness. All such reactions are invalidated by practice of Kṛṣṇa consciousness. You are the ultimate destination of all liberated persons. Out of Your independent will only, You have descended on this earth by the use of Your own internal potency, *yogamāyā*, and in order to reestablish the Vedic principles of life, You have appeared just like an ordinary human being. Since You are the Supreme Person, there cannot, therefore, be any ill luck for one who has fully surrendered unto You."

When Lord Kṛṣṇa was busy meeting various kinds of visitors and while they were engaged in offering prayers to the Lord, the female members of the Kuru dynasty and the Yadu dynasty took the opportunity of meeting with one another and engaging in talk of Lord Kṛṣṇa's transcendental pastimes. The first inquiry was made by Draupadī to the wives of Lord Kṛṣṇa. She addressed them: "My dear Rukmiṇī, Bhadrā, Jāmbavatī, Satyā, Satyabhāmā, Kālindī, Śaibyā, Lakṣmaṇā, Rohiṇī and all other wives of Lord Kṛṣṇa, will you please let us know how Lord Kṛṣṇa, the Supreme Personality of Godhead, accepted you as His wives and married you in pursuance of the marriage ceremonies of ordinary human beings?

To this question, the chief of the queens, Rukminīdevī, replied, "My dear Draupadī, it was practically a settled fact that princes like Jarāsandha and others wanted me to marry King Śiśupāla, and, as is usual, all the princes present during the marriage ceremony were prepared with their armor and weapons to fight with any rival who dared to stop the marriage. But the Supreme Personality of Godhead kidnapped me the way a lion takes away a lamb from the flock. This was not, however, a very wondrous act for Lord Kṛṣṇa, because anyone who claims to be a very great hero or king within this world is subordinate to the lotus feet of the Lord. All the kings touch their helmets to the lotus feet of Lord Kṛṣṇa. My dear Draupadī, it is my eternal desire that life after life I may be engaged in the service of Lord Kṛṣṇa, who is the reservoir of all pleasure and beauty. This is my only desire and ambition in life."

After this, Satyabhāmā began to speak. She said, "My dear Draupadī, my father was very much afflicted on the death of his brother, Prasena, and he falsely accused Lord Kṛṣṇa of killing his brother and stealing the Syamantaka jewel, which had actually been taken by Jāmbavān. Lord Kṛṣṇa, in order to establish His pure character, fought with Jāmbavān and rescued the Syamantaka jewel, which was later delivered to my father. My father was very much ashamed and sorry for accusing Lord Kṛṣṇa of his brother's death. After getting back the Syamantaka jewel, he thought it wise to rectify his mistake, so although he had promised others my hand in marriage, he submitted the jewel and myself at the lotus feet of Kṛṣṇa, and thus I was accepted as His maidservant and wife."

After this, Jāmbavatī replied to Draupadī's question. She said, "My dear Draupadī, when Lord Kṛṣṇa attacked my father Jāmbavān, the King of the *ṛkṣas,* my father did not know that Lord Kṛṣṇa was his former master, Lord Rāmacandra, the husband of Sītā. Not knowing the identity of Lord Kṛṣṇa, my father remained continually engaged in fighting with Him for twenty-seven days. After this period, when he became very tired and fatigued, he could understand that since no one but Lord Rāmacandra could defeat him, his opponent, Lord Kṛṣṇa, must be the same Lord Rāmacandra. He thus came to his senses and not only immediately returned the Syamantaka jewel, but in order to satisfy the Lord, he presented me to Him to become His wife. In this way I was married to the Lord, and thus my desire to remain life after life as a servitor of Kṛṣṇa was fulfilled."

After this, Kālindī said, "My dear Draupadī, I was engaged in great austerities and penances in order to get Lord Kṛṣṇa as my husband. When Lord Kṛṣṇa became aware of this fact, He very kindly came to me along with His friend Arjuna and accepted me as His wife. Lord Kṛṣṇa then took me away from the bank of Yamunā, and since then I have been engaged in the house of Lord Kṛṣṇa as a sweeper. And the Lord is treating me as His wife."

After this, Mitravindā said, "My dear Draupadī, there was a great assembly of princes at my *svayaṁvara* ceremony. Lord Kṛṣṇa was also present in that meeting, and He accepted me as His maidservant by defeating all the princes present there. He immediately took me away to Dvārakā, exactly as a lion takes a deer from a pack of dogs. When I was thus taken away by Lord Kṛṣṇa, my brothers wanted to fight with Him, and later on they were defeated. Thus my desire to become the maidservant of Kṛṣṇa life after life was fulfilled."

After this, Satyā addressed Draupadī in this way: "My dear Draupadī, my father arranged for an assembly for my *svayaṁvara* [the personal selection of a husband], and in order to test the strength and heroism of the prospective bridegrooms, my father stipulated that they each fight with his seven ferocious bulls, which had long, serpentine horns. Many heroic prospective bridegrooms tried to defeat the bulls, but unfortunately they were all severely struck, and they returned to their homes as defeated invalids. When Lord Śrī Kṛṣṇa came and fought with the bulls, they were just like playthings for Him. He captured the bulls and roped each one of them by their nostrils. Thus they came under His control, just like a goat's small kids come very easily under the control of children.

My father became very pleased and married me with Lord Kṛṣṇa in great pomp, giving as my dowry many divisions of soldiers, horses, chariots and elephants, along with hundreds of maidservants. Thus Lord Kṛṣṇa brought me to His capital city, Dvārakā. On the way back, He was also assaulted by many princes, but Lord Kṛṣṇa defeated all of them, and thus I have the privilege of serving His lotus feet as a maidservant."

After this, Bhadrā began to speak. She said, "My dear Draupadī, Lord Kṛṣṇa is the son of my maternal uncle. Fortunately, I became attracted to His lotus feet. When my father understood these feelings of mine, he personally arranged for my marriage, inviting Lord Kṛṣṇa to marry me and giving Him in dowry one *akṣauhiṇī,* or division of armed forces, along with many maidservants and other royal paraphernalia. I do not know whether I shall be able to have the shelter of Lord Kṛṣṇa life after life, but still I pray to the Lord that wherever I may take my birth I may not forget my relationship with His lotus feet."

Then Lakṣmaṇā said, "My dear Queen, many times I have heard the great sage Nārada glorifying the pastimes of Lord Kṛṣṇa. I became attracted to the lotus feet of Kṛṣṇa when I heard Nārada say that the goddess of fortune, Lakṣmī, was also attracted to His lotus feet. Since then I have always been thinking of Him, and thus my attraction for Him has increased. My dear Queen, my father was very affectionate toward me. When he understood that I was attracted to Kṛṣṇa, he devised a plan. His plan was like that devised by your father; during the *svayaṁvara,* the prospective bridegrooms had to pierce the eyes of a fish with their arrows. The difference between the competition in your *svayaṁvara* and mine was that in your case the fish was hanging openly on the ceiling, in clear view, but in my case the fish was covered with a cloth and could only be seen by the reflection of the cloth in a pot of water. That was the special feature of my *svayaṁvara.*

"The news of this device was spread all over the world, and when the princes heard of it, they arrived at my father's capital city from all directions, fully equipped with armor and guided by their military instructors. Each one of them desired to win me as his wife, and one after another they raised the bow and arrow which was left there for piercing the fish. Many could not even join the bowstring to the two ends of the bow, and without attempting to pierce the fish, they simply left the bow as it was and went away. Some with great difficulty drew the string from one end to the other, and being unable to tie the other end, they were suddenly knocked down by the spring-like bow. My dear Queen, you will be surprised to know that at my *svayaṁvara* meeting there were many famous kings and heroes present. Heroes like Jarāsandha, Ambaṣṭha, Śiśupāla, Bhīmasena, Duryodhana and Karṇa were, of course, able to string the bow, but they could not pierce the fish, because it was covered, and they could not trace it out from the reflection. The celebrated hero of the Pāṇḍavas, Arjuna, was able to see the reflection of the fish on the water, but although with great caution he traced out the location of the fish and shot an arrow, he did not pierce the fish in the right spot. His arrow at least touched the fish, and so he proved himself better than all other princes.

"All the princes who had tried to pierce the target were disappointed, being baffled in their attempts, and some candidates had even left the place without making an attempt, but when at last Lord Kṛṣṇa took up the bow, He was able to tie the bowstring very easily, just as a child plays with a toy. He placed the arrow, and looking only once at the reflection of the fish in the water, He shot the arrow, and the pierced fish immediately fell down. This victory of Lord Kṛṣṇa was accomplished at noon, during the moment called *abhijit,* which is astronomically calculated as auspicious. At that time the vibration of *'Jaya! Jaya!'* was heard all over the world, and from the sky came sounds of drums beat by the denizens of heaven. Great demigods were overwhelmed with joy and began to shower flowers on the earth.

"At that time, I entered the arena of competition, and the ankle bells on my legs were sounding very melodiously as I walked. I was nicely dressed with new silken garments, flowers were decorating my hair, and because of Lord Kṛṣṇa's victory, I was in ecstatic joy and smiling very pleasingly. I was carrying in my hands a golden necklace bedecked with jewels, which was glittered at intervals. My curling hair encircled my face, which was shining with a bright luster due to the reflection of my various rings. My eyes blinking, I first of all observed all the princes present, and when I reached my Lord I very slowly placed the golden necklace on His neck. As I have already informed you, from the very beginning my mind had been attracted by Lord Kṛṣṇa, and thus I considered the garlanding of the Lord to be my great victory. As soon as I placed my garland on the neck of the Lord, there sounded immediately the combined vibration of *mṛdaṅgas, paṭahas,* conchshells, drums, kettledrums and other instruments, causing a tumultuous sound, and while the music played, expert male and female dancers began to dance, and singers began to sing sweetly.

"My dear Draupadī, when I accepted Lord Kṛṣṇa as my worshipable husband, and He also accepted me as His maidservant, there was a tumultuous roaring among the disappointed princes. All of them became very agitated because of their lusty desires, but without caring for them, my husband, in His form as the four-handed Nārāyaṇa, immediately took me on His chariot, which was drawn by four excellent horses. Expecting opposition from the princes, He armored Himself and took up His bow named Śārṅga, but our celebrated driver, Dāruka, drove the beautiful chariot without a moment's delay toward the city of Dvārakā. Thus, in the presence of all the princes, I was carried away very quickly, exactly as a deer is carried away from the flock by a lion. Some of the princes, however, wanted to check our progress, and thus, equipped with proper weapons, they opposed us, just as dogs try to oppose the progressive march of a lion. At that time, due to the arrows released by the Śārṅga bow of Lord Kṛṣṇa, some of the princes were cut on their left hands, some of them lost their legs, and some lost their heads and their lives, and others fled from the battlefield.

"The Supreme Personality of Godhead then entered the most celebrated city of the universe, Dvārakā, and as He entered the city, He appeared like the shining sun. The whole city of Dvārakā was profusely decorated on that occasion. There were so many flags and festoons and gates all over Dvārakā that the sunshine could not even enter the city. I have already told you that my father was very much affectionate to me, so when he saw that my desire was fulfilled by getting Lord Kṛṣṇa as my husband, in great happiness he began to distribute to friends and relatives various kinds of gifts, such as valuable dresses, ornaments, bedsteads and sitting carpets. Lord Kṛṣṇa is always self-sufficient, yet my father, out of his own accord, offered my husband a dowry consisting of riches, soldiers, elephants, chariots, horses and many rare and valuable weapons. He presented all these to the Lord with great enthusiasm. My dear Queen, at that time I could guess that in my previous life I must have performed some wonderfully pious activity, and as a result I can in this life be one of the maidservants in the house of the Supreme Personality of Godhead."

When all the principal queens of Lord Kṛṣṇa had finished their statements, Rohiṇī, as the representative of the other sixteen thousand queens, began to narrate the incident of their becoming wives of Kṛṣṇa.

"My dear Queen, when Bhaumāsura was conquering all the world, he collected wherever possible all the beautiful daughters of the kings and kept us arrested within his palace. When news of our imprisonment reached Lord Kṛṣṇa, He fought with Bhaumāsura and released us. Lord Kṛṣṇa killed Bhaumāsura and all his soldiers, and although He had no need to accept even one wife, He nevertheless, by our request, married all sixteen thousand of us. My dear Queen, our only qualification was that we were always thinking of the lotus feet of Lord Kṛṣṇa, which is the way to release oneself from the bondage of repeated birth and death. My dear Queen Draupadī, please take it from us that we are not after any opulence such as kingdom, empire, or a position of heavenly enjoyment. We do not want to enjoy such material opulences, nor do we desire to achieve the yogic perfections, nor the exalted post of Lord Brahmā. Nor do we want any of the different kinds of liberation—*sālokya, sārṣṭi, sāmīpya* or *sāyujya.* We are not at all attracted by any of these opulences. Our only ambition is to bear on our heads life after life the dust particles attached to the lotus feet of Lord Kṛṣṇa. The goddess of fortune also desired to keep that dust on her breast along with the fragrant saffron. We simply desire this dust, which accumulates underneath the lotus feet of Kṛṣṇa as He travels on the land of Vṛndāvana as a cowherd boy. The *gopīs* especially, and also the cowherd men and the aborigine tribeswomen, always desire to become the grass and straw on the street of Vṛndāvana, to be trampled on by the lotus feet of Kṛṣṇa. My dear Queen, we wish to remain as such life after life, without any other desire."

Thus ends the Bhaktivedanta purport of the Third Volume, Fourteenth Chapter, of* Kṛṣṇa, *"Draupadī Meets the Queens of Kṛṣṇa."

15 / Sacrificial Ceremonies Performed by Vasudeva

Among the women present at Kurukṣetra during the solar eclipse were Kuntī, Gāndhārī, Draupadī, Subhadrā and the queens of many other kings, as well as the *gopīs* from Vṛndāvana. When the different queens of Lord Kṛṣṇa were submitting their statements as to how they were married and accepted by Lord Kṛṣṇa as His wives, all the female members of the Kuru dynasty were struck with wonder. They were filled with admiration at how all the queens of Kṛṣṇa were attached to Him with love and affection. When they heard about the queens' intensity of love and affection for Kṛṣṇa, they could not check their eyes from filling up with tears.

While the women were engaged in conversations among themselves and the men were similarly engaged in conversation, there arrived almost all the important sages and ascetics from all directions, who had come for the purpose of seeing Lord Kṛṣṇa and Balarāma. Chief among the sages were Kṛṣṇa-dvaipāyana Vyāsa, the great sage Nārada, Cyavana, Devala, Asita, Viśvāmitra, Śatānanda, Bharadvāja, Gautama, and Lord Paraśurāma along with his disciples; Vasiṣṭha, Gālava, Bhṛgu, Pulastya, Kaśyapa, Atri, Mārkaṇḍeya, Bṛhaspati, Dvita, Trita, Ekata; the four Kumāra sons of Brahmā, Sanaka, Sanandana, Sanātana and Sanatkumāra; Aṅgira and Agastya, Yājñavalkya and Vāmadeva.

As soon as the sages and ascetics arrived, all the kings, including Mahārāja Yudhiṣṭhira and the Pāṇḍavas and Lord Kṛṣṇa and Balarāma, immediately got up from their seats and offered their respects by bowing down to the universally respected sages. After this, the sages were properly welcomed by being offered seats and water for washing their feet. Palatable fruits, garlands of flowers, incense, and sandalwood pulp were presented, and all the kings, led by Kṛṣṇa and Balarāma, worshiped the sages according to the Vedic rules and regulations. When all the sages were comfortably seated, Lord Kṛṣṇa, who descended for the protection of religion, began to address them on behalf of all the kings. When Kṛṣṇa began to speak, all became silent, being eager to hear and understand His welcoming words to the sages.

Lord Kṛṣṇa spoke thus: "All glories to the assembled sages and ascetics! Today we are all feeling that our lives have become successful. Today we have achieved the desired goal of life, because we are now seeing face to face all the exalted liberated sages and ascetics whom even the great demigods in the heavens desire to see. Persons who are neophytes in devotional service and who simply offer their respectful obeisances to the Deity in the temple but cannot realize that the Lord is situated in everyone's heart, and those who simply worship different demigods for fulfillment of their own lusty desires, are unable to understand the importance of these sages. They cannot take advantage of receiving these sages by seeing them with their eyes, by touching their lotus feet, by inquiring about their welfare or by diligently worshiping them."

Neophyte devotees or religionists cannot understand the importance of great *mahātmās.* They go to the temple as a matter of formality and pay their respectful obeisances unto the Deity. When one is promoted to the next platform of trance consciousness, one can understand the importance of *mahātmās* and devotees, and in that stage the devotee tries to please them. Therefore, Lord Kṛṣṇa said that the neophyte cannot understand the importance of great sages, devotees or ascetics.

Kṛṣṇa continued, "One cannot purify himself by traveling to holy places of pilgrimage and taking bath there or by seeing the Deities in the temples. But if one happens to meet a great devotee, a *mahātmā* who is representative of the Personality of Godhead, one becomes immediately purified. In order to become purified, there is the injunction to worship the fire, the sun, the moon, the earth, the water, the air, the sky and the mind. By worshiping all the elements and their predominating deities, one can become free from the influence of envy, but all the sins of an envious person can be nullified immediately simply by serving a great soul. My dear revered sages and respectable kings, you can take it from Me that a person who accepts this material body made of three elements—mucus, bile and air—as his own self, who considers his family and relatives as his own, and who accepts material things as worshipable, or who visits holy places of pilgrimage just to take a bath there, but never associates with great personalities, sages and *mahātmās*—such a person, even in the form of a human being, is nothing but an animal, like an ass."

When the supreme authority, Lord Kṛṣṇa, was thus speaking with great gravity, all the sages and ascetics remained in dead silence. They became amazed upon hearing Him speaking the absolute philosophy of life in such a concise way. Unless one is very much advanced in knowledge, one thinks his body to be his self, his family members to be his kith and kin, and the land of his birth to be worshipable. From this concept of life, the modern ideology of nationalism has sprung up. Lord Kṛṣṇa condemned such ideas, and He also condemned persons who take the trouble to go to holy places of pilgrimage just to take a bath and come back without taking the opportunity to associate with the great devotees and *mahātmās* living there. Such persons are compared to the most foolish animal, the ass. All those who heard considered the speech of Lord Kṛṣṇa for some time, and they concluded that Lord Kṛṣṇa was actually the Supreme Personality of Godhead, playing the role of an ordinary human being who is forced to take a certain type of body as a result of the reactions of his past deeds. He was assuming this pastime as an ordinary human simply to teach the people in general how they should live for perfection of the human mission.

Having concluded that Kṛṣṇa was the Supreme Personality of Godhead, the sages began to address Him thus: "Dear Lord, we, the leaders of human society, are supposed to possess the proper philosophy of life, and yet we are becoming bewildered by the spell of Your external energy. We are surprised to see Your behavior, which is just like that of an ordinary human being and which conceals Your real identity as the Supreme Personality of Godhead, and we therefore consider Your pastimes to be all-wonderful.

"Our dear Lord, by Your own energy You are creating, maintaining and annihilating the whole cosmic manifestation of different names and forms, in the same way as the earth creates many forms of stone, trees and other varieties of names and forms and yet remains the same. Although You are creating varieties of manifestation through Your energy, You are unaffected by all those actions. Our dear Lord, we remain simply stunned by seeing Your wonderful actions. Although You are transcendental to this entire material creation and are the Supreme Lord and the Supersoul of all living entities, You nevertheless appear on this earth by Your internal potency to protect Your devotees and destroy the miscreants. By such appearance You reestablish the principles of eternal religion, which the human society forgets by long association with the material energy. Our dear Lord, You are the creator of the social orders and spiritual statuses of the human society according to quality and work, and when these orders are misguided by unscrupulous persons, You appear and set them right.

"Dear Lord, the Vedic knowledge is the representation of Your pure heart. Austerities, study of the *Vedas*, and meditative trances lead to different realizations of Your Self in Your manifested and nonmanifested aspects. The entire phenomenal world is a manifestation of Your impersonal energy, but You Yourself, as the original Personality of Godhead, are nonmanifested there. You are the Supreme Soul, the Supreme Brahman. Persons who are situated in brahminical culture, therefore, can understand the truth about Your transcendental form. Thus You always hold the *brāhmaṇas* in respect, and thus You are considered to be the topmost of all followers of brahminical culture. You are therefore known as *brahmaṇya-deva.* Our dear Lord, You are the last word in good fortune and the last resort of all saintly persons; therefore we all consider that we have achieved the perfection of our life, education, austerity and acquisition of transcendental knowledge by meeting You. Factually, You are the ultimate goal of all transcendental achievements.

"Our dear Lord, there is no end to Your unlimited knowledge. Your form is transcendental, eternally existing in full bliss and knowledge. You are the Supreme Personality of Godhead, the Supreme Brahman, the Supreme Soul. Being covered by the spell of Your internal potency, *yogamāyā,* You are now temporarily concealing Your unlimited potencies, but still we can understand Your exalted position, and therefore all of us offer You our respectful obeisances. Dear Lord, You are enjoying Your pastimes in the role of a human being, concealing Your real character of transcendental opulence; therefore, all the kings who are present here, even the members of the Yadu dynasty who are constantly mingling with You, eating with You, and sitting with You, cannot understand that You are the original cause of all causes, the soul of everyone, the original cause of all creation.

"When a person dreams at night, hallucinatory figures created by the dream are accepted as real, and the imaginary dream body is accepted as one's real body. For the time being one forgets that besides the body created in hallucination, there is another, real body in his awakened state. Similarly, in the awakened state also, the bewildered conditioned soul considers sense enjoyment to be real happiness.

"By the process of enjoyment of the senses of the material body, the spirit soul is covered, and his consciousness becomes materially contaminated. It is due to material consciousness that one cannot understand the Supreme Personality of Godhead, Kṛṣṇa. All great mystic *yogīs* endeavor to revive their Kṛṣṇa consciousness by mature practice of the *yoga* system and thus understand Your lotus feet and meditate upon Your transcendental form. In this way the accumulated result of sinful activities is counteracted. It is said that the water of the Ganges can vanquish volumes of a person's sinful actions, but the Ganges water is glorious only due to

His Divine Grace A. C. Bhaktivedanta Swami Prabhupāda
Founder-*Ācārya* of the International Society for Krishna Consciousness

Catching Jarāsandha in this way, Bhīmasena tore his body in two. *(p. 25)*

Śiśupāla continued to insult Kṛṣṇa, and Kṛṣṇa patiently heard him without protest. *(p. 38)*

They were all enjoying the occasion by throwing liquid substances on each other. *(p. 42)*

Kṛṣṇa cut off Śālva's head, and the head, with earrings and helmet, fell on the ground. *(p. 54)*

Balarāma killed Romaharṣaṇa simply by striking him with a blade of grass. *(p. 59)*

At the first opportunity Balarāma dragged the demon down with His plow. *(p. 62)*

The women in the palace were surprised to see that the poor *brāhmaṇa* was seated on the bedstead of Lord Kṛṣṇa. *(p. 73)*

All the members of the Yadu dynasty again took their baths in the lakes created by Lord Paraśurāma. *(p. 85)*

"Dear Kṛṣṇa, from Your navel emanated the original lotus flower which is the birthsite of Brahmā, the creator." *(p. 93)*

Arjuna was simply looking over the beautiful Subhadrā, who was very enchanting even to the great heroes and kings. *(p. 122)*

The Lord would sprinkle water on the bodies of the queens with a syringelike instrument. *(p. 236)*

Your lotus feet. The Ganges water is flowing as perspiration from the lotus feet of Your Lordship. And we are all so fortunate that today we have been able to directly see Your lotus feet. Dear Lord, we are all surrendered souls, devotees of Your Lordship; therefore, please be kind and bestow Your causeless mercy upon us. We know well that persons who have become liberated by constant engagement in Your devotional service are no longer contaminated by the material modes of nature; thus they have become eligible to be promoted to the kingdom of God in the spiritual world."

After first offering prayers to Lord Kṛṣṇa, the assembled sages wanted to take permission from King Dhṛtarāṣṭra and King Yudhiṣṭhira and then depart for their respective *āśramas.* At that time, however, Vasudeva, the father of Lord Kṛṣṇa and the most celebrated of all pious men, approached the sages and with great humility offered his respects by falling down at their feet. Vasudeva said, "My dear great sages, you are more respected than the demigods. I therefore offer my respectful obeisances unto you. I wish that you will accept my one request, if you so desire. I shall consider it a great blessing if you kindly explain the supreme fruitive activity by which one can counteract the reactions of all other activities."

The great sage Nārada was the leader of all the sages present there. Therefore he began to speak. "My dear sages," he said, "it is not very difficult to understand that because of his great goodness and simplicity, Vasudeva, who has become the father of the Personality of Godhead by accepting Kṛṣṇa as his son, is inclined to ask us about his welfare. It is said that familiarity breeds contempt. As such, Vasudeva, having Kṛṣṇa as his son, does not regard Kṛṣṇa with awe and veneration. Sometimes it is seen that persons who are living on the bank of the Ganges do not consider the Ganges to be very important, and they go far away in order to take their baths at a place of pilgrimage. Being that Lord Kṛṣṇa, whose knowledge is never second in any circumstances, is personally present, there is no need of Vasudeva's asking us for instruction.

"Lord Kṛṣṇa is not affected by the process of creation, maintenance and annihilation; His knowledge is never influenced by any agency beyond Himself. He is not agitated by the interaction of the material qualities, which changes things in the modes of time. His transcendental form is full of knowledge which never becomes agitated by ignorance, pride, attachment, envy or sense enjoyment. His knowledge is never subjected to the laws of *karma* regarding pious or impious activities; nor is it influenced by the three modes of material energy. No one is greater than or equal to Him, because He is the supreme authority, the Personality of Godhead.

"The ordinary conditioned human being may think the conditioned soul, who is covered by his materialistic senses, mind and intelligence, to be equal to Kṛṣṇa, but Lord Kṛṣṇa is just like the sun, which, although it sometimes may appear to be so, is never covered by the cloud, snow or fog or by other planets. When the eyes of less intelligent men are covered by such influences, they think the sun to be invisible. Similarly, persons influenced by the senses and addicted to material enjoyment cannot have a clear vision of the Supreme Personality of Godhead."

The sages present then began to address Vasudeva in the presence of Lord Kṛṣṇa, Balarāma and many other kings, and, as requested by him, they gave their instructions: "To counteract the reaction of *karma,* or desires impelling one to fruitive activities, one must execute the prescribed sacrifices which are meant for worshiping Lord Viṣṇu with faith and devotion. Lord Viṣṇu is the beneficiary of the results of all sacrificial performances. Great personalities and sages who are sufficiently experienced to possess vision of the three phases of the time element, namely past, present and future, and those who are able to see everything clearly through the eyes of revealed scriptures, have unanimously recommended that to purify the dust of material contamination accumulated in the heart and to clear the path of liberation and thereby achieve transcendental bliss, one must please Lord Viṣṇu. For everyone in the different social orders *(brāhmaṇa, kṣatriya* and *vaiśya)* who are living as householders, this worship of the Supreme Personality of Godhead Lord Viṣṇu, who is known as Puruṣottama, the original person, is recommended as the only auspicious path.

"All conditioned souls within this material world have deep-rooted desires to lord it over the resources of material nature. Everyone wants to accumulate riches, everyone wants to enjoy life to the greatest extent, everyone wants a wife, home and children, and everyone wants to become happy in this world and be elevated to the heavenly planets in the next life. But these desires are the causes of one's material bondage. Therefore, to get liberation from this bondage, one has to sacrifice his honestly earned riches for the satisfaction of Lord Viṣṇu.

"The only process to counteract all sorts of material desire is to engage oneself in the devotional service of Lord Viṣṇu. In this way a self-controlled person, even while remaining in householder life, should give up the three kinds of material desires, namely desire for the acquisition of material opulences, the enjoyment of wife and children, and elevation to higher planets. Eventually he may give up householder life and accept the renounced order of life, engaging himself completely in the devotional service of the Lord. Everyone, even if born in a higher status of life as *brāhmaṇa, kṣatriya,* or *vaiśya,* is certainly indebted to the demigods, to the sages, to the forefathers, to living entities and so on, and in order to liquidate all these debts, one has to perform sacrifices, study the Vedic literature, and generate children in religious householder life. If somehow one accepts the renounced order of life without fulfilling this debt, certainly he falls down from his position. Today you have already liquidated your debts to your forefathers and the sages. Now, by performing sacrifices, you can free yourself from indebtedness to the demigods and thus take complete shelter of the Supreme Personality of Godhead. My dear Vasudeva, certainly you have already performed many pious activities in your previous lives. Otherwise, how could you be the father of Kṛṣṇa and Balarāma, the Supreme Personality of Godhead?"

Saintly Vasudeva, after hearing all the sages, offered his respectful obeisances unto their lotus feet. In this way he pleased the sages, and then he elected for them to perform the *yajñas.* When the sages were elected as priests of the sacrifices, they also in their turn induced Vasudeva to collect the required paraphernalia for executing the *yajñas* in that place of pilgrimage. Thus Vasudeva was persuaded to start to perform the *yajñas,* and all the members of the Yadu dynasty took their baths, dressed themselves very nicely, and decorated themselves beautifully and garlanded themselves with lotus flowers. Vasudeva's wives, dressed with nice garments and ornaments and golden necklaces, approached the arena of sacrifice carrying in their hands the required articles to offer in the sacrifice.

When everything was complete, there was heard the vibration of *mṛdaṅgas,* conchshells, kettledrums and other musical instruments. Professional dancers, both male and female, began to dance. The *sūtas* and *māgadhas,* who were professional singers, began to offer prayers by singing. The Gandharvas and their wives, whose voices were very sweet, began to sing many auspicious songs. Vasudeva anointed his eyes with collyrium, smeared butter over his body, and then, along with his eighteen wives, headed by Devakī, sat before the priests to be purified by the *abhiṣeka* ceremony. All such ceremonies were observed strictly according to the principles of scriptures, as was done formerly in the case of the moon with the stars. Vasudeva, because he was being initiated for the sacrifice, was dressed in deerskin, but all his wives were dressed with very nice saris, bangles, necklaces, ankle bells, earrings and many other ornaments. Vasudeva looked very beautiful surrounded by his wives, exactly like the King of heaven when he performs such sacrifices.

At that time, when Lord Kṛṣṇa and Lord Balarāma, along with Their wives, children and relatives, sat down in that great sacrificial arena, it appeared that the Supreme Personality of Godhead was present along with all His part and parcel living entities and multi-energies. We have heard from the *śāstras* that Lord Kṛṣṇa has multi-energies and parts and parcels, but now in that sacrificial arena all could actually experience how the Supreme Personality of Godhead eternally exists along with His different energies. At that time, Lord Kṛṣṇa appeared as Lord Nārāyaṇa, and Lord Balarāma appeared as Saṅkarṣaṇa, the reservoir of all living entities.

Vasudeva satisfied Lord Viṣṇu by performing different kinds of sacrifices, such as *jyotiṣṭoma, darṣa* and *pūrṇamāsa.* Some of these *yajñas* are called *prākṛta,* and some of them are known as *sauryasatra* or *vaikṛta.* Thereafter, the other sacrifices, known as *agnihotra,* were also performed, and the prescribed articles were offered in the proper way. In this way Lord Viṣṇu became pleased. The ultimate purpose of offering oblations in sacrifice is to please Lord Viṣṇu. But in this age of Kali it is very difficult to collect the different articles required for offering sacrifices. People have neither the means to collect the required paraphernalia nor the necessary knowledge or tendency to offer such sacrifices. Therefore, in this age of Kali, when people are mostly unfortunate, full of anxieties and disturbed by various kinds of calamities, the only sacrifice recommended is the performance of *saṅkīrtana-yajña.* Worshiping Lord Caitanya by this *saṅkīrtana-yajña* is the only recommended process in this age.

After the performance of the different sacrifices, Vasudeva offered ample riches, clothing, ornaments, cows, land and maidservants to the priests. Thereafter, all the wives of Vasudeva took their *avabhṛtha* baths and performed the part of the sacrificial duties known as *patnīsaṁyāja.* After finishing the offering with all the required paraphernalia, they all took their baths together in the lakes constructed by Paraśurāma, which are known as the Rāma-hrada. After Vasudeva and his wives took their baths, all the garments and ornaments which they wore were distributed to the subordinate persons who were engaged in singing, dancing and similar activities. We may note that the performance of sacrifice necessitates the profuse distribution of riches. Charity is offered to the priests and the *brāhmaṇas* in the beginning, and used garments and ornaments are offered in charity to the subordinate assistants after the performance of the sacrifice.

After offering the used articles to the singers and reciters, Vasudeva and his wives, dressed with new ornaments and dresses, fed everyone very sumptuously, beginning from the *brāhmaṇas* down to the dogs. After this, all the friends, family members, wives and children of Vasudeva, along with all the kings and members of the Vidarbha, Kośala, Kuru, Kāśī, Kekaya and Sṛñjaya dynasties, assembled together. The priests, the demigods, the people in general, the forefathers, the ghosts and the *Cāraṇas* were all sufficiently remunerated by being offered ample gifts and respectful honor. Then all the persons assembled there took permission from Lord Kṛṣṇa, the husband of the goddess of fortune, and while glorifying the perfection of the sacrifice made by Vasudeva, they departed to their respective homes.

At that time, when King Dhṛtarāṣṭra, Vidura, Yudhiṣṭhira, Bhīma, Arjuna, Bhīṣmadeva, Droṇācārya, Kuntī, Nakula, Sahadeva, Nārada, Lord Vyāsadeva and many other relatives and kinsmen were about to part, they felt separation and therefore embraced each and every member of the Yadu dynasty with great feeling. Many others who were assembled in that sacrificial arena also departed. After this, Lord Kṛṣṇa and Lord Balarāma, along with King Ugrasena, satisfied the inhabitants of Vṛndāvana, headed by Mahārāja Nanda and the cowherd men, by profusely offering all kinds of gifts in order to worship them and please them. Out of their great feelings of friendship, the inhabitants of Vṛndāvana remained there for a considerable time along with the members of the Yadu dynasty.

After performing this sacrifice, Vasudeva felt so satisfied that there was no limit to his happiness. All the members of his family were with him, and in their presence he caught hold of the hands of Nanda Mahārāja and addressed him thus: "My dear brother, the Supreme Personality of Godhead has created a great tie of bondage which is known as the bondage of love and affection. I think it is a very difficult job for even the great sages and saintly persons to cut such a tie of love. My dear brother, you have exhibited feelings of love for me, which I was not able to return. I think, therefore, that I am ungrateful. You have behaved exactly as is characteristic of saintly persons, but I shall never be able to repay you. I have no means to repay you for your friendly dealings. Nevertheless I am confident that our tie of love will never break. Our relationship of friendship must ever continue, in spite of my inability to repay you. I hope you will excuse me for this inability.

"My dear brother, in the beginning, due to my being imprisoned, I could never serve you as a friend, and although at the present moment I am very opulent, because of my material prosperity I have become blind. I therefore cannot satisfy you properly even at this time. My dear brother, you are so nice and gentle that you offer all respect to others, but you don't care for any respect for yourself. A person seeking for auspicious progress in life must not possess too much material opulence with which to become blind and puffed up, but he should take care of his friends and relatives."

When Vasudeva was speaking to Nanda Mahārāja in this way, he was influenced by a great feeling for the friendship of Nanda Mahārāja and the beneficial activities executed by King Nanda on his behalf. As such, his eyes filled with tears, and he began to cry. Desiring to please his friend Vasudeva and being affectionately bound with love for Lord Kṛṣṇa and Balarāma, Nanda Mahārāja passed three months in their association. At the end of this time, all the members of the Yadu dynasty tried to please the inhabitants of Vrndāvana to their hearts' content. The members of the Yadu dynasty tried to satisfy Nanda Mahārāja and his associates by offering them clothing, ornaments, and many other valuable articles, and they all became fully satisfied. Vasudeva, Ugrasena, Lord Kṛṣṇa, Lord Balarāma, Uddhava and all other members of the Yadu dynasty presented their individual gifts to Nanda Mahārāja and his associates. After Nanda Mahārāja received these farewell presentations, he, along with his associates, started for Vrajabhūmi, Vṛndāvana. The minds of the inhabitants of Vṛndāvana remained, however, with Kṛṣṇa and Balarāma, and therefore all of them started for Vṛndāvana without their minds.

When the members of the Vṛṣṇi family saw all their friends and visitors departing, they observed that the rainy season was approaching, and thus they decided to return to Dvārakā. They were fully satisfied, for they regarded Kṛṣṇa as everything. When they returned to Dvārakā, they began with great satisfaction to describe the sacrifice performed by Vasudeva, their meeting with various friends and well-wishers, and various other incidences which occurred during their travels in the places of pilgrimage.

Thus ends the Bhaktivedanta purport of the Third Volume, Fifteenth Chapter, of* Kṛṣṇa, *"Sacrificial Ceremonies Performed by Vasudeva."

16/ Spiritual Instruction for Vasudeva and Return of the Six Dead Sons of Devakī by Lord Kṛṣṇa

It is a Vedic custom that the junior members of the family should offer respects to the elderly persons every morning. The children or the disciples especially should offer their respects to the parents or the spiritual master in the morning. In pursuance of this Vedic principle, Lord Kṛṣṇa and Balarāma used to offer Their obeisances to Their father, Vasudeva, along with his wives. One day, after having returned from the sacrificial performances at Kurukṣetra, when Lord Kṛṣṇa and Balarāma went to offer Their respect to Vasudeva, Vasudeva took the opportunity of appreciating the exalted position of his two sons. Vasudeva had the opportunity to understand the position of Kṛṣṇa and Balarāma from the great sages who had assembled in the arena of the sacrifice. He not only heard from the sages, but on many occasions he actually experienced that Kṛṣṇa and Balarāma were not ordinary human beings, but were very extraordinary. Thus he believed the words of the sages that his sons Kṛṣṇa and Balarāma were the Supreme Personality of Godhead.

With firm faith in his sons, he addressed them thus: "My dear Kṛṣṇa, You are the *sac-cid-ānanda-vigraha* Supreme Personality of Godhead, and my dear Balarāma, You are Saṅkarṣaṇa, the master of all mystic powers. I have now understood that You are eternal. Both of You are transcendental to this material manifestation and to its cause, the Supreme Person Mahā-Viṣṇu. You are the original controller of all. You are the rest of this cosmic manifestation. You are its creator, and You are also its creative ingredients. You are the master of this cosmic manifestation, and actually this manifestation is created for Your pastimes only.

"The different material phases from the beginning to the end of the cosmos manifest under different time formulas are also Yourself, because You are both the cause and effect of this manifestation. The two features of this material world, the predominator and the predominated, are also

You, and You are the supreme transcendental controller who stands above them. Therefore, You are beyond the perception of our senses. You are the supreme soul, unborn and unchanging. You are not affected by the six kinds of transformations which occur in the material body. The wonderful varieties of this material world are also created by You, and You have entered as the Supersoul into each living entity and even into the atom. You are the maintainer of everything.

"The vital force which is acting as the life principle in everything and the creative force derived from it are not acting independently, but are dependent upon You, the Supreme Person behind these forces. Without Your will, they cannot work. Material energy has no cognizance. It cannot act independently without being agitated by You. Because the material nature is dependent upon You, the living entities can only attempt to act. But without Your sanction and will they cannot perform anything or achieve the result they desire.

"The original energy is only an emanation from You. My dear Lord, the shining of the moon, the heat of the fire, the rays of the sun, the glittering of the stars, and the electric lightning which is manifested as very powerful, as well as the gravity of the mountains, the energy of the earth and the quality of its flavor—all are different manifestations of You. The pure taste of water and the vital force which maintains all life are also features of Your Lordship. The water and its taste are also Yourself.

"My dear Lord, although the forces of the senses, the mental power of thinking, willing and feeling, and the strength, movement and growth of the body appear to be performed by different movements of the airs within the body, they are all ultimately manifestations of Your energy. The vast expanse of outer space rests in Yourself. The vibration of the sky, its thunder, the supreme sound *omkāra* and the arrangement of different words to distinguish one thing from the other are symbolic representations of Yourself. Everything is Yourself. The senses, the controllers of the senses, the demigods, and the acquisition of knowledge which is the purpose of the senses, as well as the subject matter of knowledge—all are Yourself. The resolution of intelligence and the sharp memory of the living entity are also Yourself. You are the egotistic principle in ignorance which is the cause of this material world, the egotistic principle of passion which is the cause of the senses, and the egotistic principle of goodness which is the origin of the different controlling deities of this material world. The illusory energy, or *māyā,* which is the cause of the conditioned soul's perpetual transmigration from one form to another, is Yourself.

"My dear Supreme Personality of Godhead, You are the original cause of all causes, exactly as the earth is the original cause of different kinds of trees, plants and similar varieties of manifestation. As the earth is represented in everything, so You are present throughout this material manifestation as Supersoul. You are the supreme cause of all causes, the eternal principle. Everything is, in fact, a manifestation of Your one energy. The three qualities of material nature—*sattva, rajas* and *tamas*—and the result of their interaction, are linked up with You by Your agency of *yogamāyā.* They are supposed to be independent, but actually the total material energy is resting upon You, the Supersoul. Since You are the supreme cause of everything, the interactions of material manifestation—birth, existence, growth, transformation, deterioration and annihilation—are all absent in Yourself. Your supreme energy, *yogamāyā,* is acting in variegated manifestations, but because *yogamāyā* is Your energy, You are therefore present in everything."

In the *Bhagavad-gītā,* this fact is very nicely explained in the Ninth Chapter, wherein the Lord says, "In My impersonal form I am spread all over the material energy; everything is resting in Me, but I am not there." This very statement is also given by Vasudeva. To say He is not present everywhere means that He is aloof from everything, although His energy is acting everywhere. This can be understood by a crude example: In a big establishment, the energy, or the organization of the supreme boss, is working in every nook and corner of the business, but that does not mean that the original proprietor is present there, although in every department and every atmosphere the presence of the proprietor is felt by the worker. The physical presence of the proprietor in every department is formality only. Actually his energy is working everywhere. Similarly, the omnipresence of the Supreme Personality of Godhead is felt in the action of His energies. Therefore the philosophy of inconceivable simultaneous oneness with and difference from the Supreme Lord is confirmed everywhere. The Lord is one, but His energies are diverse.

Vasudeva said, "This material world is like a great flowing river, and its waves are the three material modes of nature—goodness, passion and ignorance. This material body, as well as the senses, the faculties of thinking, feeling and willing and the stages of distress, happiness, attachment and lust—all are different products of these three qualities of nature. The foolish person who cannot realize Your transcendental identity above all this material reaction continues to remain in the entanglement of fruitive activity and is subjected to the continuous process of birth and death without a chance of being freed."

This is also confirmed in a different way by the Lord in the Fourth

Chapter of *Bhagavad-gītā*. There it is said that anyone who knows the appearance and activities of the Supreme Lord Kṛṣṇa becomes freed from the clutches of material nature and goes back home, back to Godhead. Therefore Kṛṣṇa's transcendental name, form, activities and qualities are not products of this material nature.

"My dear Lord," Vasudeva continued, "despite all these defects of the conditioned soul, if someone somehow or other comes in contact with devotional service, he achieves this civilized human form of body with developed consciousness and thereby becomes capable of executing further progress in devotional service. And yet, illusioned by the external energy, people generally do not utilize this advantage of the human form of life. Thus they miss the chance of eternal freedom and unnecessarily spoil the progress they have made after thousands of births.

"In the bodily concept of life, one is attached to the offspring of the body, due to false egotism, and everyone in conditioned life is entrapped by false relationships and false affection. The whole world is moving under this false impression of material bondage. I know that neither of You are my sons; You are the original chief and progenitor, the Personalities of Godhead, known as Pradhāna and Puruṣa. But You have appeared on the surface of this globe in order to minimize the burden of the world by killing the *kṣatriya* kings who are unnecessarily increasing their military strength. You have already informed me about this in the past. My dear Lord, You are the shelter of the surrendered soul, the supreme well-wisher of the meek and humble. I am therefore taking shelter of Your lotus feet, which alone can give one liberation from the entanglement of material existence.

"For a long time I have simply considered this body to be myself, and although You are the Supreme Personality of Godhead, I considered You to be my son. My dear Lord, at the very moment when You first appeared in Kaṁsa's prison house, I was informed that You were the Supreme Personality of Godhead and that You had descended for the protection of the principles of religion as well as the destruction of the unfaithful. Although unborn, You descend in every millennium to execute Your mission. My dear Lord, as in the sky there are many forms appearing and disappearing, so You also appear and disappear in many eternal forms. Who, therefore, can understand Your pastimes or the mystery of Your appearance and disappearance? Our only business should be to glorify Your supreme greatness."

When Vasudeva was addressing his divine sons in that way, Lord Kṛṣṇa and Balarāma were smiling. Because They are very affectionate to Their devotees, They accepted all the appreciation of Vasudeva with a kindly smiling attitude. Kṛṣṇa then began to confirm all Vasudeva's statements as follows: "My dear father, whatever you may say, We are, after all, your sons. What you have said about us is certainly a highly philosophical understanding of spiritual knowledge. I accept it in total without exception."

Vasudeva was in the complete perfection of life in considering Lord Kṛṣṇa and Balarāma to be his sons, but because the sages assembled in the place of pilgrimage at Kurukṣetra had spoken about the Lord as the supreme cause of everything, Vasudeva simply repeated it out of his love for Kṛṣṇa and Balarāma. Lord Kṛṣṇa did not wish to detract from His relationship with Vasudeva as father and son; therefore in the very beginning of His reply He accepted the fact that He is the eternal son of Vasudeva and that Vasudeva is the eternal father of Kṛṣṇa. After this, Lord Kṛṣṇa informed His father of the spiritual identity of all living entities. He continued, "My dear father, everyone, including Myself and My brother Balarāma, as well as all the inhabitants of the city of Dvārakā and the whole cosmic manifestation, is exactly as you have already explained, but all of us are also qualitatively one."

Lord Kṛṣṇa intended for Vasudeva to see everything in the vision of a *mahābhāgavata,* a first-class devotee. A first-class devotee sees that all living entities are part and parcel of the Supreme Lord and that the Supreme Lord is situated in everyone's heart. In fact, every living entity has spiritual identity, but in contact with material existence he becomes influenced by the material modes of nature. He becomes covered by the concept of bodily life, forgetting that his spirit soul is of the same quality as the Supreme Personality of Godhead. One mistakenly considers one individual to be different from another simply because of their material bodily coverings. Because of differences between bodies, the spirit soul appears before us differently.

Lord Kṛṣṇa then gave a nice example in terms of the five material elements. The total material elements, namely, the sky, the air, the fire, the water and the earth, are present in everything in the material world, whether in an earthen pot or in a mountain or in the trees or in an earring. These five elements are present in everything, in different proportions and quantities. A mountain is a gigantic form of the combination of these five elements, and a small earthen pot is of the same elements, but in a smaller quantity. Therefore all material items, although in different shapes or different quantities, are of the same ingredients. Similarly, the living entities–beginning from Lord Kṛṣṇa and including the *Viṣṇu-tattva* and millions of Viṣṇu forms, and then the living entities in different forms, beginning from Lord Brahmā down to the small ant—are all of the same quality in spirit. Some are great in quantity, and some are small, but qualitatively they are of the same nature. It is therefore confirmed in the *Upaniṣads* that Kṛṣṇa, or the Supreme Lord, is the chief among all living entities, and He maintains them and supplies them with all necessities of life. Anyone who knows this philosophy is in perfect knowledge. The Vedic version *tat tvam asi,* "Thou art the same," does not mean that everyone is God, but everyone is qualitatively of the same nature as that of God.

After hearing Kṛṣṇa speak the entire philosophy of spiritual life in an abbreviated summation, Vasudeva was exceedingly pleased with his son. Being thus elated, he could not speak, but remained silent. In the meantime, Devakī, the mother of Lord Kṛṣṇa, sat by the side of her husband. Previously she had heard that both Kṛṣṇa and Balarāma were so kind upon Their teacher that They had brought back the teacher's dead sons from the clutches of the superintendent of death, Yamarāja. Since she had heard this incident, she had been also thinking of her own sons who were killed by Kaṁsa, and while remembering them she became overwhelmed with grief.

In compassion for her dead sons, Devakī began to appeal to Lord Kṛṣṇa and Balarāma thus: "My dear Balarāma, Your very name suggests that You give all pleasure and all strength to everyone. Your unlimited potency is beyond the reach of our minds and words, and my dear Kṛṣṇa, You are the master of all mystic *yogīs.* I also know that You are the master of the Prajāpatis like Brahmā and his assistants, and You are the original Personality of Godhead, Nārāyaṇa. I also know for certain that You have descended to annihilate all kinds of miscreants who have been misled in the course of time. They have lost control of their minds and senses, fallen from the quality of goodness, and have deliberately neglected the direction of the revealed scriptures by living a life of extravagancy and impudency. You have descended on the earth to minimize the burden of the world by killing such miscreant rulers. My dear Kṛṣṇa, I know that Mahā-Viṣṇu, who is lying in the causal ocean of the cosmic manifestation and who is the source of this whole creation, is simply an expansion of Your plenary portion. Creation, maintenance and annihilation of this cosmic manifestation are being effected only by Your plenary portion. I am, therefore, taking shelter of You without any reservation. I have heard that when You wanted to reward Your teacher, Sāndīpani Muni, and he asked You to bring back his dead son, You and Balarāma immediately brought him from the custody of Yamarāja, although he had been dead for a very long time. By this act I understand You to be the supreme master of all mystic *yogīs*. I am, therefore, asking You to fulfill my desire in the same way. In other words, I am asking You to bring back all my sons who were killed by Kaṁsa; upon Your bringing them back, my heart will be content, and it will be a great pleasure for me just to see them once."

After hearing Their mother speak in this way, Lord Balarāma and Kṛṣṇa immediately called for the assistance of *yogamāyā* and started for the lower planetary system known as Sutala. Formerly, in His incarnation of Vāmana, the Supreme Personality of Godhead was satisfied by the king of the demons, Bali Mahārāja, who donated to Him everything he had. Bali Mahārāja was then given the whole of Sutala for his residence and kingdom. Now when this great devotee, Bali Mahārāja, saw that Lord Balarāma and Kṛṣṇa had come to his planet, he immediately merged in the ocean of happiness. As soon as he saw Lord Kṛṣṇa and Balarāma in his presence, he and all his family members stood up from their seats and bowed down at the lotus feet of the Lord. Bali Mahārāja offered Lord Kṛṣṇa and Balarāma the best seat he had in his possession, and when both Lords were seated comfortably, he began to wash Their lotus feet. He then sprinkled the water on his head and on the heads of his family members. The water used to wash the lotus feet of Kṛṣṇa and Balarāma can purify even the greatest demigods, such as Lord Brahmā.

After this, Bali Mahārāja brought valuable garments, ornaments, sandalwood pulp, betel nuts, lamps and various nectarean foodstuffs, and along with his family members he worshiped the Lord according to the regulative principles and offered his riches and body unto the lotus feet of the Lord. King Bali was feeling such transcendental pleasure that he repeatedly grabbed the lotus feet of the Lord and kept them on his chest; and sometimes he put them on the top of his head, and in this way he was feeling transcendental bliss. Tears of love and affection began to flow down from his eyes, and all his hairs stood on end. He began to offer prayers to the Lords in a voice which choked up intermittently.

"My Lord Balarāma, You are the original Anantadeva. You are so great that Anantadeva Śeṣa and other transcendental forms have originally emanated from You and Lord Kṛṣṇa. You are the original Personality of Godhead, and Your eternal form is all-blissful and full of complete knowledge. You are the creator of the whole world. You are the original initiator and propounder of the systems of *jñāna-yoga* and *bhakti-yoga*. You are the Supreme Brahman, the original Personality of Godhead. I therefore with all respect offer my obeisances unto both of You. My dear Lords, it is very difficult for the living entities to get to see You, yet when You are merciful upon Your devotees it becomes easy for them to see You. As such, only out of Your causeless mercy have You agreed to come here and be visible to us, who are generally influenced by the qualities of ignorance and passion.

"My dear Lord, we belong to the *daitya* or demon category. The demons or demonic persons—the Gandharvas, the Siddhas, the Vidyādharas, the Cāraṇas, the Yakṣas, the Rākṣasas, the Piśācas, the ghosts and the hobgoblins—are incapable, by nature, of worshiping You or becoming Your devotees. Instead of becoming Your devotees, they simply become impediments on the path of devotion. But, opposed to them, You are the Supreme Personality of Godhead, representing all the *Vedas* and situated in the mode of uncontaminated goodness. Your position is always transcendental. For this reason, some of us, although born of the modes of passion and ignorance, have taken shelter of Your lotus feet and become devotees. Some of us are actually pure devotees, and some of us have taken shelter of Your lotus feet, desiring to gain something from devotion.

"By Your causeless mercy only we demons are in direct contact with Your personality. This contact is not possible even for the great demigods. No one knows how You act through Your *yogamāyā* potency. Even demigods cannot calculate the expanse of the activities of Your internal potency, so how is it possible for us to know it? I therefore place my humble prayers before You: please be kind to me, who am fully surrendered unto You, and favor me with Your causeless mercy so that I may simply remember Your lotus feet birth after birth. My only ambition is that I may live alone just like the *paramahaṁsas* who, traveling alone here and there in great peace of mind, depend simply upon Your lotus feet. I also desire that if I have to associate with anyone, they may be only Your pure devotees and no one else, because Your pure devotees are always well-wishers of all living entities.

"My dear Lord, You are the supreme master and director of the whole world. Please, therefore, engage me in Your service and let me thus become freed from all material contaminations. You can purify me in that way because if someone engages himself in the loving service of Your Lordship, he immediately becomes free from all kinds of regulative principles enjoined in the *Vedas*."

The word *paramahaṁsa* mentioned here means the supreme swan. It is said that the swan can draw milk out from a reservoir of water; it can take only the milk portion and reject the watery portion. Similarly, a person who can draw out the spiritual portion from this material world and who can live alone, depending only on the Supreme Spirit, not on the material world, is called *paramahaṁsa.* When one achieves the *paramahaṁsa* platform, he is no longer under the regulative principles of the Vedic injunctions. A *paramahaṁsa* accepts only the association of pure devotees and rejects others who are too materially addicted. In other words, those who are materially addicted cannot understand the value of the *paramahaṁsa,* but those who are fortunately advanced in spiritual sense take shelter of the *paramahaṁsa* and thus successfully complete the mission of human life.

After Lord Kṛṣṇa heard the prayers of Bali Mahārāja, He spoke as follows: "My dear King of the demons, in the millennium of the Svāyambhuva Manu, the Prajāpati known as Marīci begot six sons, all demigods, in the womb of his wife, Ūrṇā. Once upon a time, Lord Brahmā became captivated by the beauty of his daughter and was following her, impelled by sex desire. At that time, these six demigods looked at the action of Lord Brahmā with abhorrence. This criticism of Brahmā's action by the demigods constituted a great offense on their part, and for this reason they were condemned to take birth as the sons of the demon Hiraṇyakaśipu. These sons of Hiraṇyakaśipu were thereafter put in the womb of mother Devakī, and as soon as they took their birth, Kaṁsa killed them one after another. My dear King of the demons, again, mother Devakī is very anxious to see these six dead sons again, and she is very much aggrieved on account of their early death at the hand of Kaṁsa. I know that all of them are living with you. I have decided to take them with Me in order to pacify My mother Devakī. After seeing My mother, all these six conditioned souls will be liberated, and thus in great pleasure they will be transferred to their original planet. The names of these six conditioned souls are as follows: Smara, Udgītha, Pariṣvaṅga, Pataṅga, Kṣudrabhṛt and Ghṛṇī. They will be again reinstated in their former position as demigods."

After thus informing the King of the demons, Kṛṣṇa stopped speaking, and Bali Mahārāja understood the Lord's purpose. He worshiped Him sufficiently, and thereafter Lord Kṛṣṇa and Lord Balarāma took away the six conditioned souls and returned to the city of Dvārakā, where He presented them as little babies before His mother, Devakī. Mother Devakī became overwhelmed with joy and was so ecstatic in motherly feeling that immediately milk began to flow from her breasts, and she fed the babies with great satisfaction. She began to take them on her lap again and again, smelling their heads and thinking, "He has gotten my lost children back!" For the time being she became overpowered by the energy of Viṣṇu, and in great motherly affection she began to enjoy the company of her lost children.

The milk from the breast of Devakī was transcendental nectar because the same milk had been sucked by Lord Kṛṣṇa. As such, the babies who sucked the breast of Devakījī, which had touched the body of Lord Kṛṣṇa, immediately became self-realized persons. The babies therefore began to offer their obeisances unto Lord Kṛṣṇa, Balarāma, their father Vasudeva, and mother Devakī. After this, they were immediately transferred to their respective heavenly planets.

After they departed, Devakī became stunned with wonder that her dead children had come back and had again been transferred to their respective planets. She could adjust the events only by thinking of Lord Kṛṣṇa's pastimes, in which, because Lord Kṛṣṇa's potencies are all inconceivable, anything wonderful can be performed. Without accepting the inconceivable, unlimited potencies of the Lord, one cannot understand that Lord Kṛṣṇa is the Supreme Soul. By His unlimited potencies, He performs unlimited pastimes also, and no one can describe them in full nor can anyone know them all. Sūta Gosvāmī, speaking *Śrīmad-Bhāgavatam* before the sages of Naimiṣāraṇya, headed by Śaunaka Ṛṣi, gave his verdict in this connection as follows.

"Great sages, please understand that the transcendental pastimes of Lord Kṛṣṇa are all eternal. They are not ordinary narrations of historical incidences. Such narrations are identical with the Supreme Personality of Godhead Himself. Anyone, therefore, who hears such narrations of the Lord's pastimes becomes immediately freed from the contamination of material existence. And those who are pure devotees enjoy these narrations as nectar entering into their ears." Such narrations were described by Śukadeva Gosvāmī, the exalted son of Vyāsadeva, and anyone who hears them, as well as anyone who describes them for the hearing of others, becomes Kṛṣṇa conscious. And it is only the Kṛṣṇa conscious persons who become eligible for going back home, back to Godhead.

Thus ends the Bhaktivedanta purport of the Third Volume, Sixteenth Chapter, of Kṛṣṇa, *"Spiritual Instruction for Vasudeva and Return of the Six Dead Sons of Devakī by Lord Kṛṣṇa."*

17 / The Kidnapping of Subhadrā and Lord Kṛṣṇa's Visiting Śrutadeva and Bahulāśva

After hearing this incident, King Parīkṣit became more inquisitive to hear about Kṛṣṇa and His pastimes, and thus he inquired from Śukadeva Gosvāmī how his grandmother Subhadrā was kidnapped by his grandfather Arjuna at the instigation of Lord Kṛṣṇa. King Parīkṣit was very much eager to learn about his grandfather's kidnapping and marriage of his grandmother.

Thus Śukadeva Gosvāmī began to narrate the story as follows: "Once upon a time, your grandfather Arjuna, the great hero, was visiting several holy places of pilgrimage, and while he was thus traveling all over he happened to come to the Prabhāsakṣetra. In the Prabhāsakṣetra he heard the news that Lord Balarāma was negotiating the marriage of Subhadrā, the daughter of Arjuna's maternal uncle, Vasudeva. Although her father, Vasudeva, and her brother, Kṛṣṇa, were not in agreement with Him, Balarāma was in favor of marrying Subhadrā to Duryodhana. Arjuna, however, desired to gain the hand of Subhadrā."

As he thought of Subhadrā and her beauty, Arjuna became more and more captivated with the idea of marrying her, and with a plan in mind he dressed himself like a Vaiṣṇava *sannyāsī,* carrying a *tridaṇḍa* in his hand. The Māyāvādī *sannyāsīs* take one *daṇḍa,* or one rod, whereas the Vaiṣṇava *sannyāsīs* take three *daṇḍa,* or three rods. The three rods, or *tridaṇḍa,* indicate that a Vaiṣṇava *sannyāsī* vows to render service to the Supreme Personality of Godhead by his body, mind and words. The system of *tridaṇḍa-sannyāsa* has been in existence for a long time, and the Vaiṣṇava *sannyāsīs* are called *tridaṇḍīs,* or sometimes *tridaṇḍi-svāmīs* or *tridaṇḍi-gosvāmīs.*

Sannyāsīs are generally meant to travel all over the country for preaching work, but during the four months of the rainy season in India, from September through December, they do not travel, but take shelter in one place and remain there without moving. This non-movement of the *sannyāsī* is called *Cāturmāsya-vrata.* When a *sannyāsī* stays in a place for four months, the local inhabitants of that place take advantage of his presence to become spiritually advanced. Arjuna, in the dress of a *tridaṇḍi-sannyāsī,* remained in the city of Dvārakā for four months, devising a plan whereby he could get Subhadrā as his wife. The inhabitants of Dvārakā as well as Lord Balarāma could not recognize the *sannyāsī* to be Arjuna; therefore all of them offered their respect and obeisances to the *sannyāsī* without knowing the actual situation.

One day Lord Balarāma invited this particular *sannyāsī* to lunch at His home. Balarāmajī very respectfully offered him all kinds of palatable dishes, and the so-called *sannyāsī* was eating sumptuously. While eating at the home of Balarāmajī, Arjuna was simply looking over beautiful Subhadrā, who was very enchanting even to the great heroes and kings. Out of love for her, Arjuna's eyes brightened, and he began to see her with glittering eyes. Arjuna decided that somehow or other he would achieve Subhadrā as his wife, and his mind became agitated on account of this strong desire.

Arjuna, the grandfather of Mahārāja Parīkṣit, was himself extraordinarily beautiful, and his bodily structure was very much attractive to Subhadrā. Subhadrā also decided within her mind that she would accept only Arjuna as her husband. As a simple girl, she was smiling with great pleasure, looking at Arjuna. Thus Arjuna also became more and more attracted by her. In this way, Subhadrā dedicated herself to Arjuna, and he resolved to marry her by any means. He then became absorbed twenty-four hours a day in the thought of how he could get Subhadrā as his wife. He was afflicted with the thought of getting Subhadrā, and had not a moment's peace of mind.

Once upon a time, Subhadrā, seated on a chariot, came out of the palace fort to see the gods in the temple. Arjuna took this opportunity, and with the permission of Vasudeva and Devakī, he kidnapped her. After getting on Subhadrā's chariot, he prepared himself for a fight. Taking up his bow and holding off with his arrows the soldiers ordered to check him, Arjuna took Subhadrā away. While Subhadrā was being thus kidnapped by Arjuna, her relatives and family members began to cry, but still he took her, just as a lion takes his share and departs. When it was disclosed to Lord Balarāma that the so-called *sannyāsī* was Arjuna and that he had planned such a device simply to take away Subhadrā and that he had actually taken her, He became very angry. Just as the waves of the ocean become agitated on a full moon day, Lord Balarāma became greatly disturbed.

Lord Kṛṣṇa was in favor of Arjuna; therefore, along with other members of the family, He tried to pacify Balarāma by falling at His feet and begging Him to pardon Arjuna. Lord Balarāma was then convinced that Subhadrā was attached to Arjuna, and He became pleased to know that she wanted Arjuna as her husband. The matter was settled, and in order to please the newly married couple, Lord Balarāma arranged to send a dowry, consisting of an abundance of riches, elephants, chariots, horses, servants and maidservants.

Mahārāja Parīkṣit was very anxious to hear more about Kṛṣṇa, and so, after finishing the narration of Arjuna's kidnapping Subhadrā, Śukadeva Gosvāmī began to narrate another story, as follows.

There was a householder *brāhmaṇa* in the city of Mithilā, the capital of the kingdom of Videha. This *brāhmaṇa,* whose name was Śrutadeva, was a great devotee of Lord Kṛṣṇa. Due to his being fully Kṛṣṇa conscious and always engaged in the service of the Lord, he was completely peaceful in mind and detached from all material attraction. He was very learned and had no other desire than to be fully situated in Kṛṣṇa consciousness. Although in the order of householder life, he never took great pains to earn anything for his livelihood; he was satisfied with whatever he could achieve without much endeavor, and somehow or other he lived in that way. Every day he would get necessities for life in just the quantity required, and not more. That was his destiny. The *brāhmaṇa* had no desire to get more than what he needed, and thus he was peacefully executing the regulative principles of a *brāhmaṇa's* life, as enjoined in the revealed scriptures.

Fortunately, the King of Mithilā was as good a devotee as the *brāhmaṇa.* The name of this famous King was Bahulāśva. He was very well established in his reputation as a good king, and he was not at all ambitious to extend his kingdom for the sake of sense gratification. As such, both the *brāhmaṇa* and King Bahulāśva remained pure devotees of Lord Kṛṣṇa in Mithilā.

Since Lord Kṛṣṇa was very merciful upon these two devotees, King Bahulāśva and the *brāhmaṇa,* Śrutadeva, He one day asked His driver, Dāruka, to take His chariot into the capital city of Mithilā. Lord Kṛṣṇa was accompanied by the great sages Nārada, Vāmadeva, Atri, Vyāsadeva, Paraśurāma, Asita, Aruṇi, Bṛhaspati, Kaṇva, Maitreya, Cyavana and others. Lord Kṛṣṇa and the sages were passing through many villages and towns, and everywhere the citizens would receive them with great respect and offer them articles in worship. When the citizens came to see the Lord and all of them assembled together in one place, it seemed that the sun was present along with his various satellite planets. In that journey, Lord Kṛṣṇa and the sages passed through the kingdoms of Ānarta, Dhanva,

Kurujāṅgala, Kaṅka, Matsya, Pāñcāla, Kunti, Madhu, Kekaya, Kośala and Arṇa, and thus all the citizens of these places, both men and women, could see Lord Kṛṣṇa eye to eye. In this way they enjoyed celestial happiness, with open hearts full of love and affection for the Lord, and when they saw the face of the Lord, it seemed to them that they were drinking nectar through their eyes. When they saw Kṛṣṇa, all the ignorant misconceptions of their lives dissipated. When the Lord passed through the various countries and the people came to visit Him, simply by glancing over them the Lord would bestow all good fortune upon them and liberate them from all kinds of ignorance. In some places, the demigods also would join with the human beings, and their glorification of the Lord would cleanse all directions of all inauspicious things. In this way, Lord Kṛṣṇa slowly and gradually reached the kingdom of Videha.

When the news of the Lord's arrival was received by the citizens, they all felt unlimited happiness and came to welcome Him, taking gifts in their hands to offer. As soon as they saw Lord Kṛṣṇa, their hearts immediately blossomed in transcendental bliss, just as a lotus flower blooms on the rising of the sun. Previously they had simply heard the names of the great sages, but had never seen them. Now, by the mercy of Lord Kṛṣṇa, they had the opportunity of seeing both the great sages and the Lord Himself.

King Bahulāśva, as well as the *brāhmaṇa,* Śrutadeva, knowing well that the Lord had come there just to grace them with favor, immediately fell at the Lord's lotus feet and offered their respects. With folded hands, the King and the *brāhmaṇa* each simultaneously invited Lord Kṛṣṇa and all the sages to his home. In order to please both of them, Lord Kṛṣṇa expanded Himself into two and went to the houses of each one of them; yet neither the King nor the *brāhmaṇa* could understand that the Lord had gone to the house of the other. Both thought that the Lord had gone only to his own house. That He and His companions were present in both houses, although both the *brāhmaṇa* and the King thought He was present in his house only, is another opulence of the Supreme Personality of Godhead. This opulence is described in the revealed scriptures as *vaibhava-prakāśa.* Similarly, when Lord Kṛṣṇa married sixteen thousand wives, He also expanded Himself into sixteen thousand forms, each one of them as powerful as He Himself. Similarly, in Vṛndāvana, when Brahmā stole away Kṛṣṇa's cows, calves and cowherd boys, Kṛṣṇa expanded Himself into many new cows, calves and cowherd boys.

Bahulāśva, the King of Videha, was very intelligent and was a perfect gentleman. He was astonished that so many great sages, along with the

Supreme Personality of Godhead, were personally present in his home. He knew perfectly well that the conditioned soul, especially when engaged in worldly affairs, cannot be a hundred percent pure, whereas the Supreme Personality of Godhead and His pure devotees are always transcendental to worldly contamination. Therefore, when he found that the Supreme Personality of Godhead Kṛṣṇa and all the great sages were at his home, he was astonished, and he began to thank Lord Kṛṣṇa for His causeless mercy.

Feeling very much obliged and wanting to receive his guests to the best of his capacity, he called for nice chairs and cushions, and Lord Kṛṣṇa, along with all the sages, sat down very comfortably. At that time, King Bahulāśva's mind was very restless, not because of any problems, but because of great ecstasy of love and devotion. His heart was filled with love and affection for the Lord and His associates, and his eyes were filled with tears of ecstasy. He arranged to wash the feet of his divine guests, and after washing them he and his family members sprinkled the water on their own heads. After this, he offered to the guests nice flower garlands, sandalwood pulp, incense, new garments, ornaments, lamps, cows and bulls. In a manner just befitting his royal position, he worshiped each one of them in this way. When all had been fed sumptuously and were sitting very comfortably, Bahulāśva came before Lord Kṛṣṇa and caught His lotus feet. He placed them on his lap and, while massaging the feet with his hands, began to speak about the glories of the Lord in a sweet voice.

"My dear Lord, You are the Supersoul of all living entities and as witness within the heart are cognizant of everyone's activities. As such, being duty-bound, we always think of Your lotus feet so that we can remain in a secure position without deviating from Your eternal service. As a result of our continuous remembrance of Your lotus feet, You have kindly visited my place personally to favor me with Your causeless mercy. We have heard, my dear Lord, that by Your various statements You confirm Your pure devotees to be more dear to You than Lord Balarāma or Your constant servitor the goddess of fortune. Your devotees are dearer to You than Your first son, Lord Brahmā, and I am sure that You have so kindly visited my place in order to prove Your divine statement. I cannot imagine how people can be godless and demoniac even after knowing of Your causeless mercy and affection for Your devotees who are constantly engaged in Kṛṣṇa consciousness. How can they forget Your lotus feet?

"My dear Lord, it is known to us that You are so kind and liberal that when a person leaves everything just to engage in Kṛṣṇa consciousness, You sometimes give Yourself in exchange for that unalloyed service. You have appeared in the Yadu dynasty to fulfill Your mission of reclaiming all conditioned souls rotting in the sinful activities of material existence, and this appearance is already famous all over the world. My dear Lord, You are the ocean of unlimited mercy, love and affection. Your transcendental form is full of bliss, knowledge and eternity. You can attract everyone's heart by Your beautiful form as Śyāmasundara, Kṛṣṇa. Your knowledge is unlimited, and to teach all people how to execute devotional service You have sent Your incarnation Nara-Nārāyaṇa, who is engaged in severe austerities and penances at Badarīnārāyaṇa. Kindly, therefore, accept my humble obeisances at Your lotus feet. My dear Lord, I beg to request You and Your companions, the great sages and *brāhmaṇas,* to remain at my place so that this family of the famous King Nimi may be sanctified by the dust of Your lotus feet at least for a few days." Lord Kṛṣṇa could not refuse the request of His devotee, and thus He remained there for a few days along with the sages in order to sanctify the city of Mithilā and all its citizens.

Meanwhile, the *brāhmaṇa,* simultaneously receiving Lord Kṛṣṇa and His associates at his home, became transcendentally overwhelmed with joy. After offering his guests nice sitting places, the *brāhmaṇa* began to dance, throwing his wrap around his body. Śrutadeva, being not at all rich, offered only mattresses, wooden planks, straw carpets, etc., to his distinguished guests, Lord Kṛṣṇa and the sages, but he welcomed them to his best capacity. He began to speak very highly of the Lord and the sages, and he and his wife washed the feet of each one of them. After this, he took the water and sprinkled it over all the members of his family, and although it appeared that the *brāhmaṇa* was very poor, he was at that time most fortunate. While Śrutadeva was welcoming Lord Kṛṣṇa and His associates, he simply forgot himself in transcendental joy. After welcoming the Lord and His companions, according to his capacity he brought fruits, incense, scented water, scented clay, *tulasī* leaves, *kuśa* straw and lotus flowers. They were not very costly items and could be secured very easily, but because they were offered with devotional love, Lord Kṛṣṇa and His associates accepted them very gladly. The *brāhmaṇa's* wife cooked very simple foods like rice and dahl, and Lord Kṛṣṇa and His followers were very pleased to accept them because they were offered in devotional love. When Lord Kṛṣṇa and His associates were fed in this way, the *brāhmaṇa* Śrutadeva was thinking thus: "I am fallen into the deep, dark well of householder life and am the most unfortunate person. How has it become possible that Lord Kṛṣṇa, who is the Supreme Personality of Godhead, and His associates, the great sages, whose very presence makes a place as sanctified as a pilgrimage site, have agreed to come to my place?" While the *brāhmaṇa* was thinking in this way, the guests finished their lunch and sat back very comfortably. At that time, the *brāhmaṇa,* Śrutadeva, and his wife, children and other relatives, appeared there to render service to the distinguished guests. While touching the lotus feet of Lord Kṛṣṇa, the *brāhmaṇa* began to speak.

"My dear Lord," he said, "You are the Supreme Person, Puruṣottama, situated transcendentally to the manifested and unmanifested material creation. The activities of this material world and of the conditioned souls have nothing to do with Your position. We can appreciate that it is not that only today You have given me Your audience. You are associating with all the living entities as Paramātmā since the beginning of creation."

This statement of the *brāhmaṇa* is very instructive. It is a fact that the Supreme Lord Personality of Godhead in His Paramātmā feature entered the creation of this material world as Mahā-Viṣṇu, Garbhodakaśāyī Viṣṇu and Kṣīrodakaśāyī Viṣṇu, and in a very friendly attitude the Lord is sitting along with the conditioned soul in the body. Therefore, every living entity has the Lord with him from the very beginning, but due to his mistaken consciousness of life, the living entity cannot understand this. When his consciousness is, however, changed into Kṛṣṇa consciousness, he can immediately understand how Kṛṣṇa is trying to assist the conditioned souls to get out of the material entanglement.

Śrutadeva continued, "My dear Lord, You have entered this material world as if in a sleeping condition. A conditioned soul, while sleeping, creates false or temporary worlds; he becomes busy in many illusory activities–sometimes becoming a king, sometimes being murdered or sometimes going to an unknown city–and all these are simply temporary affairs. Similarly, Your Lordship, apparently also in a sleeping condition, enters this material world to create a temporary manifestation, not for Your personal necessities, but for the conditioned soul who wants to imitate Your Lordship as enjoyer. The conditioned soul's enjoyment in the material world is temporary and illusory. And yet the conditioned soul is by himself unable to create such a temporary situation for his illusory enjoyment. In order to fulfill his desires, although they are temporary and illusory, You enter in this temporary manifestation to help him. Thus, from the beginning of the conditioned soul's entering into the material world, You are his constant companion. When, therefore, the conditioned soul comes in contact with a pure devotee and takes to devotional service, beginning from the process of hearing Your transcendental pastimes, glorifying Your transcendental activities, worshiping Your eternal form in the temple, offering prayers to You and engaging in discussion to understand Your transcendental position, he then gradually becomes freed from the contamination of material existence. His heart becomes cleansed of all material dust, and thus gradually You become visible in the heart of the devotee. Although You are constantly with the conditioned soul, only when he becomes purified by devotional service do You become revealed to him. Others, who are bewildered by fruitive activities, either by Vedic injunction or customary dealings, and who do not take to devotional service, become captivated by the external happiness of the bodily concept of life. You are not revealed to such persons. Rather, You remain far, far away from them. But for one who, being engaged in Your devotional service, has purified his heart by constant chanting of Your holy name, You become very easily understood as his eternal constant companion.

"It is said that Your Lordship, sitting in the heart of a devotee, gives him direction by which he can very quickly come back to home, back to You. This direct dictation by You reveals Your existence within the heart of the devotee. Only a devotee can immediately appreciate Your existence within his heart, whereas for a person who has only a bodily concept of life and is engaged in sense gratification You always remain covered by the curtain of *yogamāyā*. Such a person cannot realize that You are very near, sitting within his heart. For a nondevotee, You are appreciated only as ultimate death. The difference is like the difference between a cat's carrying its kittens in its mouth and a cat's carrying a rat in its mouth. In the mouth of the cat, the rat feels its death, whereas the kittens in the mouth of the cat feel motherly affection. Similarly, You are present to everyone, but the nondevotee feels You as ultimate cruel death, whereas for a devotee You are the supreme instructor and philosopher. The atheist, therefore, understands the presence of God as death, but the devotee understands the presence of God always within his heart, takes dictation from You, and lives transcendentally, not being affected by the contamination of the material world.

"You are the supreme controller and superintendent of the material nature's activities. The atheistic class of men simply observe the activities of material nature, but cannot find You as the original background. A devotee, however, can immediately see Your hand in every movement of material nature. The curtain of *yogamāyā* cannot cover the eyes of the devotee of Your Lordship, but it can cover the eyes of the nondevotee. The nondevotee is unable to see You eye to eye, just as a person whose eyes are interrupted by the covering of a cloud cannot see the sun, although persons who are flying above the cloud can see the sunshine brilliantly, as it is. My dear Lord, I offer my respectful obeisances unto You. My dear self-effulgent Lord, I am Your eternal servitor. Therefore, kindly order me —what can I do for You? The conditioned soul feels the pangs of material contamination as threefold miseries as long as You are not visible to him. And as soon as You are visible by development of Kṛṣṇa consciousness, all miseries of material existence simultaneously become vanquished."

The Supreme Personality of Godhead Kṛṣṇa is naturally very much affectionately inclined to His devotees. When He heard Śrutadeva's prayers of pure devotion, He was very much pleased and immediately caught his hands and began to address Him thus: "My dear Śrutadeva, all these great sages and saintly persons have been very kind to you by personally coming here to see you. You should consider this opportunity to be a great fortune for you. They are so kind that they are traveling with Me, and wherever they go they immediately make the whole atmosphere as pure as transcendence simply by the touch of the dust of their feet. People are accustomed to go to the temples of God. They also visit holy places of pilgrimage, and after prolonged association with such activities, for many days by touch and by worship, gradually they become purified. But the influence of great sages and saintly persons is so great that by seeing them one immediately becomes completely purified.

"Moreover, the very purifying potency of pilgrimages or worship of different demigods is also achieved by the grace of saintly persons. A pilgrimage site becomes a holy place because of the presence of the saintly persons there. My dear Śrutadeva, when a person is born as a *brāhmaṇa,* he immediately becomes the best of all human beings. And if such a brāhmaṇa, remaining self-satisfied, practices austerities, studies the *Vedas* and engages in My devotional service, as is the duty of the *brāhmaṇa* —or in other words, if a *brāhmaṇa* becomes a Vaiṣṇava—how wonderful is his greatness! My feature of four-handed Nārāyaṇa is not so pleasing or dear to Me as is a *brāhmaṇa* Vaiṣṇava. *Brāhmaṇa* means 'one well conversant with Vedic knowledge'; a *brāhmaṇa* is the insignia of perfect knowledge, and I am the full-fledged manifestation of all gods. The less intelligent class of men do not understand Me as the highest knowledge, nor do they understand the influence of the *brāhmaṇa* Vaiṣṇava. They are influenced by the three modes of material nature and thus dare to criticize Me and My pure devotees. A *brāhmaṇa* Vaiṣṇava, or a devotee already on the brahminical platform, can realize Me within his heart, and therefore he definitely concludes that the whole cosmic manifestation and its different features are effects of different energies of the Lord. Thus he has a clear conception of the whole material nature and the total material energy, and in every action such a devotee sees Me only, and nothing else.

"My dear Śrutadeva, you may therefore accept all these great saintly persons, *brāhmaṇas* and sages as My bona fide representatives. By worshiping them faithfully, you will be worshiping Me more diligently. I consider worship of My devotees to be better than direct worship of Me. If someone attempts to worship Me directly without worshiping My devotees, I do not accept such worship, even though it may be presented with great opulence."

In this way both the *brāhmaṇa,* Śrutadeva, and the King of Mithilā, under the direction of the Lord, worshiped both Kṛṣṇa and His followers, the great sages and saintly *brāhmaṇas,* on an equal level of spiritual importance. Both *brāhmaṇa* and King ultimately achieved the supreme goal of being transferred to the spiritual world. The devotee does not know anyone except Lord Kṛṣṇa, and Kṛṣṇa is most affectionate to His devotee. Lord Kṛṣṇa remained in Mithilā both at the house of the *brāhmaṇa* Śrutadeva and at the palace of King Bahulāśva. And after favoring them lavishly by His transcendental instructions, He went back to His capital city, Dvārakā.

The instruction we receive from this incident is that King Bahulāśva and Śrutadeva the *brāhmaṇa* were accepted by the Lord on the same level because both were pure devotees. This is the real qualification for being recognized by the Supreme Personality of Godhead. Because it has become the fashion of this age to become falsely proud of having taken birth in the family of a *kṣatriya* or of a *brāhmaṇa,* we see persons without any qualification other than birth claiming to be *brāhmaṇa* or *kṣatriya* or *vaiśya.* But as it is stated in the scriptures, *kalau śūdra-sambhava:* "In this age of Kali, everyone is a *śūdra.*" This is because there is no performance of the purificatory processes known as *saṁskāras,* which begin from the time of the mother's pregnancy and continue up to the point of the individual's death. No one can be classified as a member of a particular caste, especially of a higher caste—*brāhmaṇa, kṣatriya* or *vaiśya*—simply by birthright. If one is not purified by the process of the seed-giving ceremony, or *Garbhādhāna-saṁskāra*, he is immediately classified amongst the *śūdras,* because only the *śūdras* do not undergo this purificatory process. Sex life without the purificatory process of Kṛṣṇa consciousness is merely the seed-giving process of the *śūdras* or the animals. But Kṛṣṇa consciousness is the highest perfection, by which everyone can come to the platform of a Vaiṣṇava. This includes having all the qualifications of a *brāhmaṇa.* The Vaiṣṇavas are trained to become freed from the four kinds of sinful activities—illicit sex, indulgence in intoxicants, gambling, and eating animal foodstuffs. No one can be on the brahminical platform without having these preliminary qualifications, and without becoming a qualified *brāhmaṇa,* one cannot become a pure devotee.

Thus ends the Bhaktivedanta purport of the Third Volume, Seventeenth Chapter, of Kṛṣṇa, *"The Kidnapping of Subhadrā and Lord Kṛṣṇa's Visiting Śrutadeva and Bahulāśva."*

18 / Prayers by the Personified Vedas

King Parīkṣit inquired from Śukadeva Gosvāmī about a very important topic in understanding transcendental subject matter. His question was, "Since Vedic knowledge generally deals with the subject matter of the three qualities of the material world, how then can it approach the subject matter of transcendence, which is beyond the approach of the three material modes? Since the mind is material and the vibration of words is a material sound, how can the Vedic knowledge, expressing by material sound the thoughts of the mind, approach transcendence? Description of a subject matter necessitates describing its source of emanation, its qualities and its activities. Such description can be possible only by thinking with the material mind and by vibrating material words. Although Brahman, or the Absolute Truth, has no material qualities, our power of speaking does not go beyond the material qualities. How then can Brahman, the Absolute Truth, be described by your words? I do not see how it is possible to understand transcendence from such expressions of material sound."

The purpose of King Parīkṣit's inquiring was to ascertain from Śukadeva Gosvāmī whether the *Vedas* ultimately describe the Absolute Truth as impersonal or as personal. Understanding of the Absolute Truth progresses in three features–impersonal Brahman, Paramātmā localized in everyone's heart and, at last, the Supreme Personality of Godhead Kṛṣṇa.

The *Vedas* deal with three departments of activities. One is called *karma-kāṇḍa,* or activities under Vedic injunction which gradually purify one to understand his real position; the next is *jñāna-kāṇḍa,* the process of understanding the Absolute Truth by speculative methods; and the third is *upāsanā-kāṇḍa,* or worship of the Supreme Personality of Godhead and sometimes of the demigods also. The worship of the demigods recommended in the *Vedas* is ordered with the understanding of the demigods' relationship to the Personality of Godhead. The Supreme Personality of Godhead has many parts and parcels; some are called ***svāṁśas,*** or His personal expansions, and some are called ***vibhinnāṁśas,*** the living entities. All such expansions, both ***svāṁśas*** and ***vibhinnāṁśas,*** are emanations from the original Personality of Godhead. ***Svāṁśa*** expansions are called *Viṣṇu-tattva,* whereas the ***vibhinnāṁśa*** expansions are called *jīva-tattva.* The different demigods are *jīva-tattva.* The conditioned souls are generally put into the activities of the material world for sense gratification; therefore, as stated in the *Bhagavad-gītā,* to regulate those who are very much addicted to different kinds of sense gratification the worship of demigods is sometimes recommended. For example, for persons who are very much addicted to meat-eating, the Vedic injunction recommends that after worshiping the form of the goddess Kālī and sacrificing a goat (not any other animal) under *karma-kāṇḍa* regulation, the worshipers may be allowed to eat meat. The idea is not to encourage one to eat meat, but to allow one who is persistent to eat meat under certain restricted conditions. Therefore, worship of the demigods is not worship of the Absolute Truth, but by worshiping the demigods one gradually comes to accept the Supreme Personality of Godhead in an indirect way. This indirect acceptance is described in the *Bhagavad-gītā* as *avidhi. Avidhi* means not bona fide. Since demigod worship is not bona fide, the impersonalists stress concentration on the impersonal feature of the Absolute Truth. King Parīkṣit's question was, which is the ultimate target of Vedic knowledge—this concentration on the impersonal feature of the Absolute Truth or concentration on the personal feature? After all, both the impersonal and personal features of the Supreme Lord are beyond our material conception. The impersonal feature of the Absolute, the Brahman effulgence, is but the rays of the personal body of Kṛṣṇa. These rays of the personal body of Kṛṣṇa are cast all over the creation of the Lord, and the portion of the effulgence which is covered by the material cloud is called the created cosmos of the three material qualities—*sattva, rajas* and *tamas.* How can persons who are within this clouded portion called the material world conceive of the Absolute Truth by the speculative method?

In answering King Parīkṣit's question, Śukadeva Gosvāmī replied that the Supreme Personality of Godhead has created the mind, senses and living force for the purpose of sense gratification in transmigration from one kind of body to another, as well as for the purpose of allowing liberation from the material conditions. In other words, the senses, mind and living force can be utilized for sense gratification and transmigration from one body to another or for the matter of liberation. The Vedic injunctions are there just to give the conditioned souls the chance for sense gratification under regulative principles, and thereby also give them the chance for promotion to the higher conditions of life; ultimately, if the consciousness is purified, one comes to his original position and goes back home, back to Godhead.

The living force is intelligent. One therefore has to utilize his intelligence over the mind and the senses. When the mind and senses are purified by the proper use of intelligence, then the conditioned soul is liberated; otherwise, if the intelligence is not properly utilized in controlling the senses and mind, the conditioned soul continues to transmigrate from one kind of body to another simply for sense gratification. Another point clearly stated in the answer of Śukadeva Gosvāmī is that the Lord created the mind, senses and intelligence of the individual living force. It is not stated that the living entities themselves were ever created. Just as the shining particles of the sun's rays are always existing along with the sun, the living entities exist eternally as parts and parcels of the Supreme Personality of Godhead. The conditioned souls, although eternally existing as part of the Supreme Lord, are sometimes put within the cloud of the material concept of life, in the darkness of ignorance. The whole Vedic process is to alleviate that darkened condition. Ultimately, when the senses and mind of the conditioned being become fully purified, he then comes to the original position, called Kṛṣṇa consciousness, and that is liberation.

In the *Vedānta-sūtra,* the first *sūtra,* or code, questions about the Absolute Truth. *Athāto brahma-jijñāsā:* What is the nature of the Absolute Truth? The next *sūtra* answers that the nature of the Absolute Truth is that He is the origin of everything. Whatever we experience, even in this material condition of life, is but an emanation from Him. The Absolute Truth created the mind and senses and intelligence. This means that the Absolute Truth is not without mind, intelligence and senses. In other words, He is not impersonal. The very word "created" means that He has transcendental intelligence. For example, when the father begets a child, the child has senses because the father also has senses. The child is born with hands and legs because the father also has hands and legs. Sometimes it is said, therefore, that man is made after the image of God. The Absolute Truth is therefore the Supreme Personality, with transcendental mind, senses and intelligence. When one's mind, intelligence and senses are purified of material contamination, one can understand the original feature of the Absolute Truth as a person.

The Vedic process is to gradually promote the conditioned soul from the mode of ignorance to the mode of passion and from the mode of passion to the mode of goodness. In the mode of goodness there is sufficient light for understanding things as they are. For example, from earth a tree grows, and from the wood of the tree, fire is ignited. In that igniting process we first of all find the smoke, and the next stage is heat, and then fire. When there is actually fire, we can utilize it for various purposes; therefore, fire is the ultimate goal. Similarly, in the gross material stage of life the quality of ignorance is very much prominent. Dissipation of this ignorance takes place in the gradual progress of civilization from the barbarian stage to civilized life, and when one comes to the form of civilized life, he is said to be in the mode of passion. In the barbarian stage, or in the mode of ignorance, the senses are gratified in a very crude way, whereas in the mode of passion or in the civilized stage of life, the senses are gratified in a polished manner. But when one is promoted to the mode of goodness, one can understand that the senses and the mind are only engaged in material activities due to being covered by perverted consciousness. When this perverted consciousness is gradually transformed into Kṛṣṇa consciousness, then the path of liberation is opened. So it is not that one is unable to approach the Absolute Truth by the senses and the mind. The conclusion is, rather, that the senses, mind and intelligence in the gross stage of contamination cannot appreciate the nature of the Absolute Truth, but, when purified, the senses, mind and intelligence can understand what the Absolute Truth is. This purifying process is called devotional service, or Kṛṣṇa consciousness.

In the *Bhagavad-gītā* it is clearly stated that the purpose of Vedic knowledge is to understand Kṛṣṇa, and Kṛṣṇa is understood by devotional service, beginning with the process of surrender. As stated in the *Bhagavad-gītā,* one has to think of Kṛṣṇa always. One has to render loving service to Kṛṣṇa always, and one has to always worship and bow down before Kṛṣṇa. By this process only can one enter into the kingdom of God without any doubt.

When one is enlightened in the mode of goodness by the process of devotional service, he is freed from the modes of ignorance and passion. The word *ātmane* indicates the stage of brahminical qualification in which one is allowed to study the Vedic literatures known as the *Upaniṣads.* The *Upaniṣads* describe in different ways the transcendental qualities of the Supreme Lord. The Absolute Truth, the Supreme Lord, is called *nirguṇa.* That does not mean that He has no qualities. It is only because He has qualities that the conditioned living entities can have qualities. The purpose of studying the *Upaniṣads* is to understand the transcendental quality of the Absolute Truth, as opposed to the material qualities of ignorance, passion and goodness. That is the way of Vedic understanding. Great sages like the four Kumāras, headed by Sanaka, followed these principles of Vedic knowledge and came gradually from impersonal understanding to the platform of personal worship of the Supreme Lord. It is therefore recommended that we must follow the great personalities. Śukadeva Gosvāmī is also one of the great personalities, and his answer to the inquiry of Mahārāja Parikṣit is authorized. One who follows in the footsteps of such great personalities surely walks very easily on the path of liberation and ultimately goes back to home, back to Godhead. That is the way of perfecting this human form of life.

Śukadeva Gosvāmī continued to speak to Parīkṣit Mahārāja. "My dear King," he said, "I will narrate in this regard a nice story. This story is important because it is in connection with Nārāyaṇa, the Supreme Personality of Godhead. This narration is a conversation between Nārāyaṇa Ṛṣi and the great sage Nārada. Nārāyaṇa Ṛṣi still resides in Badarīkāśrama in the Himalayan hills and is accepted as an incarnation of Nārāyaṇa. Once when Nārada, the great devotee and ascetic amongst the demigods, was traveling in different planets, he desired to personally meet the ascetic Nārāyaṇa in Badarīkāśrama and offer him his respects. This great sage incarnation of Godhead, Nārāyaṇa Ṛṣi, has been undergoing great penances and austerities from the very beginning of the creation in order to teach the inhabitants of Bhāratavarṣa how to attain the highest perfectional stage of going back to Godhead. His austerities and penances are exemplary practices for the human being."

Badarīkāśrama is situated in the northernmost part of the Himalayan Mountains and is always covered with snow. Religious Indians still go to visit this place during the summer season, when the snowfall is not very severe. Once, the incarnation of God Nārāyaṇa Ṛṣi was sitting amongst many devotees in the village known as Kalāpagrāma. Of course, these were not ordinary sages who were sitting with him, and the great sage Nārada also appeared there. After offering his respects to Nārāyaṇa Ṛṣi, Nārada asked him exactly the same question asked by King Parīkṣit of Śukadeva Gosvāmī. When Nārada asked his question of Nārāyaṇa Ṛṣi, the Ṛṣi also answered by following in the footsteps of his predecessors. He narrated a story of how the same question had been discussed on the planet known as Janaloka. Janaloka is above the Svargaloka planets, such as the moon, Venus, etc. In this planet, great sages and saintly persons live, and they were also discussing the same point regarding the understanding of Brahman and His real identity.

The great sage Nārāyaṇa began to speak. "My dear Nārada," he said, "I will tell you a story which took place long, long ago. There was a great meeting of the denizens of the heavenly planets, and almost all the important *brahmacārīs,* such as the four Kumāras—Sanat, Sanandana, Sanaka and Sanātana Kumāra—attended. Their discussion was on the subject matter of understanding the Absolute Truth, Brahman. You were not present at that meeting because you went to see My expansion Aniruddha, who lives on the island of Śvetadvīpa. In this meeting, all the great sages and *brahmacārīs* very elaborately discussed the point about which you have asked me, and it was very interesting. The discussion was so delicate that even the *Vedas* were unable to answer the intricate questions raised.

Nārāyaṇa Ṛṣi told Nāradajī that the same question which Nāradajī had raised had been discussed in that meeting in Janaloka. This is the way of understanding through the *paramparā,* or disciplic succession. Mahārāja Parikṣit was sent to Śukadeva Gosvāmī; Śukadeva Gosvāmī referred the matter to Nārada, who had in the same way questioned Nārāyaṇa Ṛṣi, who had put the matter to still higher authorities in the planet of Janaloka, where it was discussed among the great Kumāras—Sanat, Sanātana, Sanaka Kumāra and Sanandana. These four *brahmacārīs* are recognized scholars in the *Vedas* and *śāstras.* Their unlimited volumes of knowledge, backed by austerities and penances, are exhibited by their sublime, ideal character. They are very amiable and gentle in behavior, and for them there is no distinction between friends, well-wishers and enemies. Being transcendentally situated, such personalities as the Kumāras are above all material considerations and are always neutral in respect to material dualities. In the discussions held among the four brothers, one of them, namely Sanandana, was selected to speak, and the other brothers became the audience to hear him.

Sanandana said, "After the dissolution of the whole cosmic manifestation, the entire energy and the whole creation in its nucleus form enters into the body of Garbhodakaśāyī Viṣṇu. The Lord at that time remains asleep for a long, long time, and where there is again necessity of creation, the *Vedas* personified assemble around the Lord and begin to glorify Him, describing His wonderful transcendental pastimes. It is exactly like a king: when he is asleep in the morning, the appointed reciters come around his bedroom and begin to sing of his chivalrous activities, and while hearing of his glorious activities, the king gradually awakens.

"The Vedic reciters or the personified *Vedas* sing thus: 'O unconquerable, You are the Supreme Personality. No one is equal to You or greater than You. No one can be more glorious in His activities. All glories unto

You! All glories unto You! By Your own transcendental nature You fully possess all six opulences. As such, You are able to deliver all conditioned souls from the clutches of *māyā*. O Lord, we fervently pray that You kindly do so. All the living entities, being Your parts and parcels, are naturally joyful, eternal and full of knowledge, but due to their own faults they try to imitate You by trying to become the supreme enjoyer; thus they disobey Your supremacy and become offenders. And because of their offenses, Your material energy has taken charge of them; thus, their transcendental qualities of joyfulness, bliss and wisdom have been covered by the clouds of the three material qualities. This cosmic manifestation, made of the three material qualities, is just like a prison house for the conditioned souls. The conditioned souls are struggling very hard to escape from the material bondage, and according to their different conditions of life they have been given different types of engagement. But all engagements are based on Your knowledge. Pious activities can be executed only when inspired by Your mercy. Therefore, without taking shelter at Your lotus feet one cannot surpass the influence of material energy. Actually, we, as personified Vedic knowledge, are always engaged in Your service to help the conditioned soul understand You."

This prayer of the *Vedas* personified illustrates that the *Vedas* are meant for helping the conditioned souls to understand Kṛṣṇa. All the *śrutis* or personified *Vedas* offered glories to the Lord again and again, singing, *"Jaya! Jaya!"* This indicates that the Lord is praised for His glories. Of all His glories the most important is His causeless mercy upon the conditioned souls in reclaiming them from the clutches of *māyā*.

There are unlimited numbers of living entities in different varieties of bodies, some moving and some standing in one place, and the conditioned life of these living entities is due only to their forgetfulness of their eternal relationship with the Supreme Personality of Godhead. When the living entity wants to lord it over the material energy by imitating the position of Kṛṣṇa, he is immediately captured by the material energy and, according to his desire, is offered a variety of 8,400,000 different kinds of bodies. Although undergoing the threefold miseries of material existence, the illusioned living entity falsely thinks himself the master of all he surveys. Under the spell of the material energy, which represents the threefold material qualities, the living entity is so entangled that it is not at all possible for him to become free unless he is graced by the Supreme Lord. The living entity cannot conquer the influence of the material modes of nature by his own endeavor, but because material nature is working under the control of the Supreme Lord, the Lord is beyond its jurisdiction.

Except for Him, all living entities, beginning from Brahmā down to an ant, are conquered by the contact of material nature.

Because He possesses in full the six opulences of wealth, strength, fame, beauty, knowledge and renunciation, the Lord alone is beyond the spell of material nature. Unless the living entity is situated in Kṛṣṇa consciousness, he cannot approach the Supreme Personality of Godhead, yet the Lord, by His omnipotency, can dictate from within as the Supersoul. In the *Bhagavad-gītā,* the Lord advises, "Whatever you do, do for Me; whatever you eat, first of all offer to Me; whatever charity you want to give, first give to Me; and whatever austerities and penances you want to perform, perform for Me." In this way the *karmīs* are directed to gradually develop Kṛṣṇa consciousness. Similarly, Kṛṣṇa directs the philosophers to approach Him gradually by discriminating between Brahman and *māyā.* At last when one is mature in knowledge, he surrenders unto Kṛṣṇa. As Kṛṣṇa says in *Bhagavad-gītā*, "After many, many births, the wise philosopher surrenders unto Me." The *yogīs* are also directed to concentrate their meditation upon Kṛṣṇa within the heart, and by such continued process of Kṛṣṇa consciousness the *yogī* can become free from the clutches of material energy. But, as is stated in *Bhagavad-gītā,* because the devotees are engaged in devotional service with love and affection from the very beginning, the Lord directs them so that they can approach Him without difficulty or deviation. Only by the grace of the Lord can the living entity understand the exact position of Brahman, Paramātmā and Bhagavān.

The statements of the personified *Vedas* give clear evidence that the Vedic literature is presented only for understanding Kṛṣṇa. It is confirmed in the *Bhagavad-gītā* that through all the *Vedas* it is Kṛṣṇa alone who has to be understood. Kṛṣṇa is always enjoying, either in the material world or in the spiritual world; because He is the supreme enjoyer, for Him there is no distinction between the material world and spiritual worlds. The material world is an impediment for the ordinary living entities because they are under its control, but Kṛṣṇa, being the controller of the material world, has nothing to do with the impediments it offers. Therefore, in different parts of the *Upaniṣads,* the *Vedas* declare: "Brahman is eternal, full of all knowledge and all bliss, but the one Supreme Personality of Godhead is existing in the heart of every living entity." Because of His all-pervasiveness, He is able to enter not only into the hearts of the living entities, but even into the atoms also. As the Supersoul, He is the controller of all activities of the living entities. He is living within all of them and witnessing their actions, allowing them to act according to their desires, and also giving them the results of their different activities. He is the living force of all things, but still He is transcendental to the material qualities. He is omnipotent; He is expert in manufacturing everything, and on account of His superior, natural knowledge, He can bring everyone under His control. As such, He is everyone's master. He is sometimes manifest on the surface of the globe, but He is simultaneously within all matter. Desiring to expand Himself in multi-forms, He glanced over the material energy, and thus innumerable living entities became manifest. Everything is created by His superior energy, and everything in His creation appears to be perfectly done without deficiency.

Those who aspire for liberation from this material world must therefore worship the Supreme Personality of Godhead, the ultimate cause of all causes. He is just like the total mass of earth, from which varieties of earthly pots are manufactured: the pots are made of earthly clay, they rest on the earth, and after being destroyed, their elements ultimately merge back into earth. Although the Personality of Godhead is the original cause of all varieties of manifestation, the impersonalists especially stress the Vedic statement, *sarvaṁ khalv idam brahma:* "Everything is Brahman." The impersonalists do not take into account the varieties of manifestation emanating from the supreme cause of Brahman. They simply take into consideration that everything emanates from Brahman and after destruction merges into Brahman and that the intermediate stage of manifestation is also Brahman. Although the Māyāvādīs believe that prior to its manifestation the cosmos was in Brahman, after creation it remains in Brahman and after destruction it merges into Brahman, they do not know what Brahman is. This fact is clearly described in the *Brahma-saṁhitā:* The living entities, space, time, and the material elements like fire, earth, sky, water and mind, constitute the total cosmic manifestation, known as *bhūr bhuvaḥ svaḥ,* which is manifested by Govinda. It flourishes on the strength of Govinda and after annihilation enters into and is conserved in Govinda. Lord Brahmā therefore says, "I worship Lord Govinda, the original personality, the cause of all causes."

The word Brahman indicates the greatest of all and the maintainer of everything. The impersonalists are attracted by the greatness of the sky, but because of their poor fund of knowledge they are not attracted by the greatness of Kṛṣṇa. In our practical life, however, we are attracted by the greatness of a person and not by the greatness of a big mountain. Actually the term *Brahman* can be applied to Kṛṣṇa only; therefore in the *Bhagavad-gītā* Arjuna admitted that Lord Kṛṣṇa is the *Parambrahman,* or the supreme rest of everything.

Kṛṣṇa is the Supreme Brahman because of His unlimited knowledge, unlimited potencies, unlimited strength, unlimited influence, unlimited beauty and unlimited renunciation. Therefore the word *Brahman* can be applied to Kṛṣṇa only. Arjuna affirms that because the impersonal Brahman is the effulgence emanating as rays of Kṛṣṇa's transcendental body, Kṛṣṇa is the Parambrahman. Everything is resting on Brahman, but Brahman itself is resting on Kṛṣṇa. Therefore Kṛṣṇa is the ultimate Brahman or Parambrahman. The material elements are accepted as inferior energies of Kṛṣṇa because by their interaction the cosmic manifestation takes place, rests on Kṛṣṇa, and after dissolution again enters into the body of Kṛṣṇa as His subtle energy. Kṛṣṇa is therefore the cause of both manifestation and dissolution.

Sarvaṁ khalv idaṁ brahma means everything is Kṛṣṇa, and that is the vision of the *mahābhāgavatas.* They see everything in relation to Kṛṣṇa. The impersonalists argue that Kṛṣṇa has transformed Himself into many and that therefore everything is Kṛṣṇa and worship of everything is worship of Him. This false argument is answered by Kṛṣṇa in the *Bhagavad-gītā:* although everything is a transformation of the energy of Kṛṣṇa, He is not present everywhere. He is simultaneously present and not present. By His energy He is present everywhere, but as the energetic He is not present everywhere. This simultaneous presence and non-presence is inconceivable to our present senses. But a clear explanation is given in the beginning of the *Īśopaniṣad,* in which it is stated that the Supreme Lord is so complete that although unlimited energies and their transformations are emanating from Kṛṣṇa, Kṛṣṇa's personality is not in the least bit transformed. Therefore, since Kṛṣṇa is the cause of all causes, intelligent persons should take shelter of His lotus feet.

Kṛṣṇa advises everyone just to surrender unto Him alone, and that is the way of Vedic instruction. Since Kṛṣṇa is the cause of all causes, He is worshiped by all kinds of sages and saints by observance of the regulative principles. When there is a necessity for meditation, great personalities meditate on the transcendental form of Kṛṣṇa within the heart. In this way the minds of great personalities are always engaged in Kṛṣṇa. With minds engaged in Kṛṣṇa, naturally the captivated devotees simply talk of Kṛṣṇa.

Talking of Kṛṣṇa or singing of Kṛṣṇa is called *kīrtana.* Lord Caitanya also recommends *kīrtanīyaḥ sadā hariḥ,* which means always thinking and talking of Kṛṣṇa and nothing else. That is called Kṛṣṇa consciousness. Kṛṣṇa consciousness is so sublime that anyone who takes to this process is elevated to the highest perfection of life—far, far beyond the concept of liberation. In the *Bhagavad-gītā,* therefore, Kṛṣṇa advises everyone to always think of Him, render devotional service to Him, worship Him and offer obeisances to Him. In this way a devotee becomes fully Kṛṣṇa-ized and, being always situated in Kṛṣṇa consciousness, ultimately goes back to Kṛṣṇa.

Although the *Vedas* have recommended worship of different demigods as different parts and parcels of Kṛṣṇa, it is to be understood that such instructions are meant for the less intelligent class of men, who are still attracted by material sense enjoyment. But the person who actually wants perfect fulfillment of the mission of human life should simply worship Lord Kṛṣṇa, and that will simplify the matter and completely guarantee the success of his human life. Although the sky, the water and the land are all part and parcel of the material world, when one stands on the solid land his position is more secure than when he stands in the sky or the water. An intelligent person, therefore, does not stand under the protection of different demigods, although they are part and parcel of Kṛṣṇa. Rather, he stands on the solid ground of Kṛṣṇa consciousness. That makes his position sound and secure.

Impersonalists sometimes give the example that if one stands on a stone or a piece of wood, one certainly stands on the surface of the land, because the stone and wood are both resting on the surface of the earth. But it may be replied that if one stands directly on the surface of the earth, he is more secure than on the wood or stone which are resting on the earth. In other words, taking shelter of Paramātmā or taking shelter of impersonal Brahman is not as secure a course as taking direct shelter of Kṛṣṇa in Kṛṣṇa consciousness. The position of the *jñānis* and *yogīs* is therefore not as secure as the position of the devotees of Kṛṣṇa. Lord Kṛṣṇa has therefore advised in the *Bhagavad-gītā* that only a person who has lost his senses takes to the worship of demigods. And regarding persons who are attached to the impersonal Brahman, the *Śrīmad-Bhāgavatam* says, "My dear Lord, those who are thinking of themselves as liberated by mental speculation are not yet purified of the contamination of material nature because of their inability to find the shelter of Your lotus feet. Although they rise to the transcendental situation of existence in impersonal Brahman, they certainly fall from that exalted position because they have neglected to desire Your lotus feet." Lord Kṛṣṇa therefore advises that the worshipers of the demigods are not very intelligent persons because they derive only temporary, exhaustible results. Their endeavors are those of less intelligent men. But the Lord assures that His devotee has no fear of falling.

The personified *Vedas* continued to pray: "Dear Lord, considering all points of view, if one has to worship someone superior to him, then just out of good behavior one should stick to the worship of Your lotus feet because You are the ultimate controller of creation, maintenance and dissolution. You are the controller of the three worlds, Bhūr, Bhuvar and Svar, You are the controller of the fourteen upper and lower worlds, and You are the controller of the three material qualities. Demigods and persons advanced in spiritual knowledge are always engaged in hearing and chanting about Your transcendental pastimes because this has the specific potency of nullifying the accumulated results of sinful life. Intelligent persons factually take a dip in the ocean of Your nectarean activities and very patiently hear of them. Thus they immediately become freed from the contamination of the material qualities; they do not have to undergo severe penances and austerities for advancement of spiritual life. This chanting and hearing of Your transcendental pastimes is the easiest process for self-realization. Simply by submissive aural reception of the transcendental message, one's heart becomes cleansed of all dirty things. Thus Kṛṣṇa consciousness becomes fixed in the heart of a devotee.

"The great authority Bhīṣmadeva has also given the opinion that this process of chanting and hearing about the Supreme Personality of Godhead is the essence of all Vedic ritualistic performances. Dear Lord, the devotee who wants to elevate himself simply by this process of devotional activities, especially by hearing and chanting, very soon comes out of the clutches of the dualities of material existence. By this simple process of penance and austerity the Supersoul within the devotee's heart becomes very pleased and gives the devotee directions so that he may go back to home, back to Godhead. It is stated in the *Bhagavad-gītā* that one who engages all his activities and senses in the devotional service of the Lord becomes completely pacified because the Supersoul is satisfied with him; thus the devotee becomes transcendental to all kinds of dualities, such as heat and cold, honor and dishonor. Being freed from all dualities, he feels transcendental bliss, and he no longer suffers cares and anxieties due to material existence. *Bhagavad-gītā* confirms that the devotee who is always absorbed in Kṛṣṇa consciousness has no anxieties for his maintenance or protection. Being constantly absorbed in Kṛṣṇa consciousness, he ultimately achieves the highest perfection. While in the material existence, he lives very peacefully and blissfully without any cares and anxieties, and after quitting this body he goes back to home, back to Godhead. The Lord confirms in the *Bhagavad-gītā,* 'My supreme abode is a transcendental place where going no one returns to this material world. Anyone who attains the supreme perfection, being engaged in My personal devotional service in the eternal abode, reaches the highest perfection of human life and doesn't have to come back again to the miserable material world.'

"My dear Lord, it is imperative that the living entities be engaged in Kṛṣṇa consciousness, always rendering devotional service by prescribed methods such as hearing and chanting and executing Your orders. If a person is not engaged in Kṛṣṇa consciousness and devotional service, it is useless for him to exhibit the symptoms of life. Generally it is accepted that if a person is breathing he is alive. But a person without Kṛṣṇa consciousness may be compared to a bellows in a blacksmith's shop. The big bellows is a bag of skin which exhales and inhales air, and a human being who is simply living within the bag of skin and bones without taking to Kṛṣṇa consciousness and loving devotional service is no better than the bellows. Similarly, a nondevotee's long duration of life is compared to the long existence of a tree, his voracious eating capacity is compared to the eating of dogs and hogs, and his enjoyment in sex life is compared to that of hogs and goats.

"The cosmic manifestation has been possible because of the entrance of the Supreme Personality of Godhead as Mahā-Viṣṇu within this material world. The total material energy becomes agitated by the glance of Mahā-Viṣṇu, and only then does the interaction of the three material qualities begin. Therefore it should be concluded that whatever material facilities we are trying to enjoy are available only due to the mercy of the Supreme Personality of Godhead.

"Within the body there are five different departments of existence, known as *annamaya, prāṇamaya, manomaya, vijñānamaya,* and at last *ānandamaya.* In the beginning of life, every living entity is food conscious. A child or an animal is satisfied only by getting nice food. This stage of consciousness, in which the goal is to eat sumptuously, is called *annamaya. Anna* means food. After this one lives in the consciousness of being alive. If one can continue his life without being attacked or destroyed, one thinks himself happy. This stage is called *prāṇamaya,* or consciousness of one's existence. After this stage, when one is situated on the mental platform, that consciousness is called *manomaya.* The material civilization is primarily situated in these three stages, *annamaya, prāṇamaya* and *manomaya.* The first concern of civilized persons is economic development, the next concern is defense against being annihilated, and the next consciousness is mental speculation, the philosophical approach to the values of life.

"If by the evolutionary process of philosophical life one happens to reach to the platform of intellectual life and understands that he is not this material body, but is a spirit soul, then by evolution of spiritual life he comes to the understanding of the Supreme Lord or the Supreme Soul. When one develops his relationship with Him and executes devotional service, that stage of life is called Kṛṣṇa consciousness, the *ānandamaya* stage. *Ānandamaya* is the blissful life of knowledge and eternity. As it is said in the *Vedānta-sūtra, ānandamayo 'bhyāsāt.* The Supreme Brahman and the subordinate Brahman, or the Supreme Personality of Godhead and the living entities, are both joyful by nature. As long as the living entities are situated in the lower four stages of life, *annamaya, prāṇamaya, manomaya* and *vijñānamaya,* they are considered to be in the material condition of life, but as soon as one reaches the stage of *ānandamaya* he becomes a liberated soul. This *ānandamaya* stage is explained in the *Bhagavad-gītā* as the *brahma-bhūta* stage. There it is said that in the *brahma-bhūta* stage of life there is no anxiety and no hankering. This stage begins when one becomes equally disposed toward all living entities, and it then expands to the stage of Kṛṣṇa consciousness in which one always hankers to render service unto the Supreme Personality of Godhead. This hankering for advancement in devotional service is not the same as hankering for sense gratification in material existence. In other words, hankering remains in spiritual life, but it becomes purified. When our senses are purified, they become freed from all material stages, namely *annamaya, prāṇamaya, manomaya* and *vijñānamaya,* and they become situated in the highest stage—*ānandamaya,* or blissful life in Kṛṣṇa consciousness. The Māyāvādī philosophers consider *ānandamaya* to be the state of being merged in the Supreme. To them, *ānandamaya* means that the Supersoul and the individual soul become one. But the real fact is that oneness does not mean merging into the Supreme and losing one's own individual existence. Merging in the spiritual existence is the living entity's realization of qualitative oneness with the Supreme Lord in His eternity and knowledge aspects. But the actual *ānandamaya* (blissful) stage is obtained when one is engaged in devotional service. That is confirmed in the *Bhagavad-gītā. Mad-bhaktiṁ labhate parām:* the *brahma-bhūta ānandamaya* stage is complete only when there is the exchange of love between the Supreme and the subordinate living entities. Unless one comes to this *ānandamaya* stage of life, his breathing is like the breathing of a bellows in a blacksmith's shop, his duration of life is like that of a tree, and he is no better than the lower animals like the camels, hogs and dogs.

Undoubtedly the eternal living entity cannot be annihilated at any point. But the lower species of life exist in a miserable condition, whereas one who is engaged in devotional service of the Supreme Lord is situated in the pleasurable or *ānandamaya* status of life. The different stages described above are all in relationship with the Supreme Personality of Godhead. Although in all circumstances there exist both the Supreme Personality of Godhead and the living entities, the difference is that the Supreme Personality of Godhead always exists in the *ānandamaya* stage, whereas the subordinate living entities, because of their minute position as fragmental portions of the Supreme Lord, are prone to fall to the other stages of life. Although in all the stages both the Supreme Lord and the living entities exist, the Supreme Personality of Godhead is always transcendental to our concept of life, whether we are in bondage or in liberation. The whole cosmic manifestation becomes possible by the grace of the Supreme Lord, it exists by the grace of the Supreme Lord, and when it is annihilated, it merges into the existence of the Supreme Lord. As such, the Supreme Lord is the supreme existence, the cause of all causes. Therefore the conclusion is that without development of Kṛṣṇa consciousness, one's life is simply a waste of time.

Those who are very materialistic and cannot understand the situation of the spiritual world cannot understand the abode of Kṛṣṇa. For such persons, great sages have recommended the yogic process whereby one gradually rises from meditation on the abdomen, which is called *mūlādhāra* or *maṇipūraka* meditation. *Mūlādhāra* and *maṇipūraka* are technical terms which refer to the intestines within the abdomen. Grossly materialistic persons think that economic development is of foremost importance because they are under the impression that a living entity exists only by eating. Such grossly materialistic persons forget that although we may eat as much as we like, if the food is not digested it produces the troubles of indigestion and acidity. Therefore, in itself, eating is not the cause of the vital energy of life. For digestion of eatables we have to take shelter of another, superior energy, which is mentioned in the *Bhagavad-gītā* as *vaiśvānara.* Lord Kṛṣṇa says in the *Bhagavad-gītā* that He helps the digestion in the form of *vaiśvānara.* The Supreme Personality of Godhead is all-pervasive; therefore, His presence as *vaiśvānara* is not extraordinary.

Kṛṣṇa is actually present everywhere. The Vaiṣṇava, therefore, marks his body with temples of Viṣṇu: he first marks a *tilaka* temple on the abdomen, then on the chest, then between the collarbones, then on the forehead, and gradually he marks the top of the head, the *brahma-randhra.* The thirteen temples of *tilaka* marked on the body of a Vaiṣṇava are known as follows: On the forehead is the temple of Lord Keśava, on the belly is the temple of Lord Nārāyaṇa, on the chest is the temple of Lord Mādhava, and on the throat, between the two collarbones, is the temple of Lord Govinda. On the right side of the waist is the temple of Lord Viṣṇu, on the right arm is the temple of Lord Madhusūdana, and on the right side of the collarbone is the temple of Lord Trivikrama. Similarly, on the left side of the waist is the temple of Lord Vāmanadeva, on the left arm is the temple of Śrīdhara, on the left side of the collarbone is the temple of Hṛṣīkeśa, on the upper back the temple is called Padmanābha, and on the lower back the temple is called Dāmodara. On the top of the head the temple is called Vāsudeva. This is the process of meditation on the Lord's situation in the different parts of the body, but for those who are not Vaiṣṇavas, great sages recommend meditation on the bodily concept of life—meditation on the intestines, on the heart, on the throat, on the eyebrows, on the forehead and then on the top of the head. Some of the sages in the disciplic succession from the great saint Aruṇa meditate on the heart because the Supersoul is also staying within the heart along with the living entity. This is confirmed in *Bhagavad-gītā,* Fifteenth Chapter, wherein the Lord states, "I am situated in everyone's heart."

For the Vaiṣṇava, the protection of the body for the service of the Lord is a part of devotional service, but those who are gross materialists accept the body as the self. They worship the body by the yogic process of meditation on the different bodily parts, such as *maṇipūraka, dahara* and *hṛdaya,* gradually rising to the *brahma-randhra* on the top of the head. The first-class *yogī* who has attained perfection in the practice of the *yoga* system ultimately passes through the *brahma-randhra* to any one of the planets in either the material or spiritual worlds. How a *yogī* can transfer himself to another planet is very vividly described in the Second Canto of *Śrīmad-Bhāgavatam.*

In this regard, Śukadeva Gosvāmī has recommended that the beginners worship the *virāṭa puruṣa,* the gigantic universal form of the Lord. One who cannot believe that the Lord can be worshiped with equal success in the Deity or *arcā* form, or who cannot concentrate on this form, is advised to worship the universal form of the Lord. The lower part of the universe is considered the feet and legs of the Lord's universal form, the middle part of the universe is considered the navel or abdomen of the Lord, the upper planetary systems such as Janaloka and Maharloka are the heart of the Lord, and the topmost planetary system, Brahmaloka, is considered the top of the Lord's head. There are different processes recommended by great sages, according to the position of the worshiper, but the ultimate aim of all meditational and yogic processes is to go back home, back to Godhead. As stated in *Bhagavad-gītā,* anyone who reaches the highest planet, the abode of Kṛṣṇa, or even the Vaikuṇṭha planets, never has to come down again to this miserable material condition of life.

The Vedic recommendation, therefore, is that one make the lotus feet of Viṣṇu the target of all one's efforts. *Tad viṣṇoḥ paramaṁ padaṁ,* Viṣṇuloka or the Viṣṇu planets, are situated above all the material planets. These Vaikuṇṭha planets are known as *sanātana-dhāma,* and they are eternal. They are never annihilated, not even by the annihilation of this material world. The conclusion is that if a human being does not fulfill the mission of his life by worshiping the Supreme Lord and does not go back to Godhead, then it is to be understood that he has been frustrated in fulfilling the main purpose of human life.

The next prayer of the personified *Vedas* to the Lord concerns His entering into different species of life. It is stated in *Bhagavad-gītā,* Fourteenth Chapter, that in every species and form of life the spiritual part and parcel of the Supreme Lord is present. The Lord Himself claims in the *Gītā* that He is the seed-giving father of all forms and species, and therefore they must all be considered sons of the Lord. The entrance of the Supreme Lord into everyone's heart as Paramātmā sometimes bewilders the impersonalists, who think in terms of the equality of the living entities with the Supreme Lord. They think that because the Supreme Lord enters into different bodies along with the individual soul, there is no distinction between the Lord and the individual entities. Their challenge is, "Why should individual souls worship the Paramātmā or Supersoul?" According to them, both the Supersoul and the individual soul are on the same level; they are one, without any difference between them. There is a difference, however, between the Supersoul and the individual soul, and this is explained in *Bhagavad-gītā,* Fifteenth Chapter, wherein the Lord says that although He is situated with the living entity in the same body, He is superior. He is dictating to or giving intelligence to the individual soul from within. It is clearly stated in the *Gītā* that the Lord gives intelligence to the individual soul and that both memory and forgetfulness are due to the influence of the Supersoul. No one can act independently of the sanction of the Supersoul. Therefore, the individual soul acts according to his past *karma,* reminded by the Lord. The nature of the individual soul is forgetfulness, but the presence of the Lord within the heart reminds him of what he wanted to do in his past life. The intelligence of the individual soul is exhibited like fire in wood. Although fire is always fire, it is exhibited in a size proportionate to the size of the wood. Similarly, although the individual soul is qualitatively one with the Supreme Lord, he exhibits himself according to the limitations of his present body.

The Supreme Lord or the Supersoul is said to be *eka-rasa. Eka* means one, and *rasa* means mellow. The transcendental position of the Supreme Lord is that of eternity, bliss and full knowledge. His position of *eka-rasa* does not change in the slightest when He becomes a witness and advisor to the individual soul in each individual body.

The individual soul, beginning from Lord Brahmā down to the ant, exhibits his spiritual potency according to his present body. The demigods are in the same category with the individual souls in the bodies of the human beings or in the bodies of lower animals. Intelligent persons, therefore, do not worship different demigods, who are simply infinitesimal representatives of Kṛṣṇa manifesting in conditioned bodies. The individual soul can exhibit his power and potencies only in proportion to the shape and constitution of the body. The Supreme Personality of Godhead, however, can exhibit His full potencies in any shape or form without any change. The Māyāvādī philosophers' thesis that God and the individual soul are one and the same cannot be accepted because the individual soul has to develop his power and potencies according to the development of different types of bodies. The individual soul in the body of a baby cannot show the full power and potency of a grown man, but the Supreme Personality of Godhead Kṛṣṇa, even when lying on the lap of His mother as a baby, could exhibit His full potency and power by killing Pūtanā and other demons who tried to attack Him. Therefore the spiritual potency of the Supreme Personality of Godhead is said to be *eka-rasa*, or without change. Therefore the Supreme Personality of Godhead is the only worshipable object, and this is perfectly known to persons who are uncontaminated by the force of material nature. In other words, only the liberated souls can worship the Supreme Personality of Godhead. Less intelligent Māyāvādīs take to the worship of demigods, thinking that the demigods and the Supreme Personality of Godhead are on the same level.

The personified *Vedas* continued to offer their obeisances. "Dear Lord," they prayed, "after many, many births, those who have actually become wise take to the worship of Your lotus feet in complete knowledge." This is also confirmed in the *Bhagavad-gītā*, wherein the Lord says that after many, many births, a great soul or *mahātmā* surrenders unto the Lord, knowing well that Vāsudeva, Kṛṣṇa, is the cause of all causes. The *Vedas* continued: "As has already been explained, since our mind, intelligence and senses have been given to us by God, when these instruments are actually purified there is no alternative than to engage them all in the devotional service of the Lord. A living entity's entrapment in different species of life is due to the misapplication of his mind, intelligence and senses in material activities. Various kinds of bodies are awarded as the result of a living entity's actions, and they are created by the material nature according to the living entity's desire. Because a living entity desires and deserves a particular kind of body, it is given to him by the material nature under the order of the Supreme Lord.

In the *Śrīmad-Bhāgavatam,* Third Canto, it is explained that under the control of superior authority a living entity is put within the semina of a male and injected into the womb of a particular female in order to develop a particular type of body. A living entity utilizes his senses, intelligence, mind, etc., in a specific way of his own choosing and thus develops a particular type of body within which he becomes encaged. In this way the living entity becomes situated in different species of life, either in a demigod, human or animal body, according to different situations and circumstances.

It is explained in the Vedic literatures that the living entities entrapped in different species of life are part and parcel of the Supreme Lord. The Māyāvādī philosophers mistake the living entity for the Paramātmā, who is actually sitting with the living entity as a friend. Because the Paramātmā, the localized aspect of the Supreme Personality of Godhead, and the individual living entity are both within the body, a misunderstanding sometimes takes place that there is no difference between the two. But there is a definite difference between the individual soul and the Supersoul, and it is explained in the *Varāha Purāṇa* as follows. The Supreme Lord has two kinds of parts and parcels: the living entity is called *vibhinnāṁśa,* and the Paramātmā or the plenary expansion of the Supreme Lord is called *svāṁśa.* The *svāṁśa* plenary expansion of the Supreme Personality is as powerful as the Supreme Personality of Godhead Himself. There is not even the slightest difference between the potency of the Supreme Person and that of His plenary expansion as Paramātmā, but the *vibhinnāṁśa* parts and parcels possess only a minute portion of the potencies of the Lord. The *Nārāyaṇa-Pañcarātra* states that the living entities who are the marginal potency of the Supreme Lord are undoubtedly of the same quality of spiritual existence as the Lord Himself, but they are prone to be tinged with the material qualities. Because he is prone to be subjected to the influence of material qualities, the minute living entity is called *jīva.* Sometimes the Supreme Personality of Godhead is also known as Śiva, the all-auspicious. So the difference between Śiva and *jīva* is that the all-auspicious Personality of Godhead is never affected by the material qualities, whereas the minute portions of the Supreme Personality of Godhead are prone to be affected by the qualities of material nature.

The Supersoul within the body of a particular living entity, although a plenary portion of the Lord, is worshipable by the individual living entity. Great sages have therefore concluded that the process of meditation is designed so that the individual living entity may concentrate his attention on the lotus feet of the Supersoul form (Viṣṇu). That is the real form of *samādhi.* The living entity cannot become liberated from material entanglement by his own effort. He must therefore take to the devotional service of the lotus feet of the Supreme Lord, or the Supersoul within himself. Śrīdhara Svāmī, the great commentator on *Śrīmad-Bhāgavatam,* has composed a nice verse in this regard, the purport of which is as follows: "My dear Lord, I am eternally Your part and parcel, but I have been entrapped by the material potencies, which are also an emanation from You. As the cause of all causes, You have entered my body as the Supersoul, and I have the prerogative to enjoy the supreme blissful life of knowledge along with You. Therefore, my dear Lord, please order me to render You loving service so that I can again be brought to my original position of transcendental bliss."

Great personalities understand that a living entity entangled in this material world cannot become freed by his own efforts. With firm faith and devotion, such great personalities engage themselves in rendering transcendental loving service to the Lord. That is the verdict of the personified *Vedas.*

The personified *Vedas* continued: "Dear Lord, it is very difficult to achieve perfect knowledge of the Absolute Truth. Your Lordship is so kind to the fallen souls that You appear in different incarnations and execute different activities. You appear even as a historical personality of this material world, and Your pastimes are very nicely described in the Vedic literatures. Such pastimes are as attractive as the ocean of transcendental bliss. People in general have a natural inclination to read narrations in which ordinary *jīvas* are glorified, but when they become attracted by the Vedic literatures which delineate Your eternal pastimes, they actually dip into the ocean of transcendental bliss. As a fatigued man feels refreshed by dipping into a reservoir of water, so the conditioned soul who is very much disgusted with material activities becomes refreshed and forgets all the fatigue of material activities simply by dipping into the transcendental ocean of Your pastimes. And eventually he merges in the ocean of transcendental bliss. The most intelligent devotees, therefore, do not take to any means of self-realization except devotional service and constant engagement in the nine different processes of devotional life, especially hearing and chanting. When hearing and chanting about Your transcendental pastimes, Your devotees do not care even for the transcendental bliss derived from liberation or from merging into the existence of the Supreme. Such devotees are not interested even in so-called liberation, and certainly they have no interest in material activities for elevation to the heavenly planets for sense gratification. Pure devotees seek only the association of *paramahaṁsas,* or great liberated devotees, so that they can continually hear and chant about Your glories. For this purpose the pure devotees are prepared to sacrifice all comforts of life, even giving up the material comforts of family life and so-called society, friendship and love. Those who have tasted the nectar of devotion by relishing the transcendental vibration of chanting Your glories, Hare Kṛṣṇa, Hare Kṛṣṇa, Kṛṣṇa Kṛṣṇa, Hare Hare/ Hare Rāma, Hare Rāma, Rāma Rāma, Hare Hare, do not care for any other spiritual bliss or for material comforts, which appear to the pure devotee to be less important than the straw in the street."

The personified *Vedas* continued: "Dear Lord, when a person is able to purify his mind, senses and intelligence by engaging himself in devotional service in full Kṛṣṇa consciousness, his mind becomes his friend. Otherwise, his mind is always his enemy. When the mind is engaged in devotional service of the Lord, it becomes the intimate friend of the living entity because the mind can then think of the Supreme Lord always. Your Lordship is eternally dear to the living entity, so when the mind is engaged in thought of You, one immediately feels the great satisfaction for which he has been hankering life after life. When one's mind is thus fixed on the lotus feet of the Supreme Personality of Godhead, one does not take to any kind of inferior worship or inferior process of self-realization. By attempting to worship a demigod or by taking to any other process of self-realization, the living entity becomes a victim of the cycle of birth and death, and no one can estimate how much the living entity becomes degraded by entering the abominable species of life such as the cats and dogs."

Śrī Narottama dāsa Ṭhākur has sung that persons who do not take to devotional service of the Lord but are attracted to the process of philosophical speculation and fruitive activities drink the poisonous results of such actions. Such persons are forced to take birth in different species of life and are forced to adopt obnoxious practices like meat-eating and intoxication. Materialistic persons generally worship the transient material body and forget the welfare of the spirit soul within the body. Some take shelter of materialistic science to improve bodily comforts, and some take to the worship of demigods in order to be promoted to the heavenly planets. Their goal in life is to make the material body comfortable while forgetting the interest of the spirit soul. Such persons are described in the Vedic literature as suicidal because attachment for the material body and its comforts forces the living entity to wander through the process of birth and death perpetually and suffer the material pangs as a matter of course. The human form of life is a chance for one to understand his position, and the most intelligent person takes to devotional service just to engage his mind, senses and body in the service of the Lord without deviation.

The personified *Vedas* continued: "Dear Lord, there are many mystic *yogīs* who are very learned and deliberate in achieving the highest perfection of life. They engage themselves in the yogic process of controlling the life-air within the body. Concentrating the mind upon the form of Viṣṇu and controlling the senses very rigidly, they practice the *yoga* system, but even after much laborious austerity, penance, and regulation, they achieve the same destination as persons who are inimical toward You. In other words, both the *yogīs* and great, wise philosophical speculators ultimately attain the impersonal Brahman effulgence, which is also automatically attained by the demons who are regular enemies of the Lord. Demons like Kaṁsa, Śiśupāla and Dantavakra also attain the Brahman effulgence because they constantly meditate upon the Supreme Personality of Godhead. Women such as the *gopīs* were attached to Kṛṣṇa and captivated by His beauty, and their mental concentration on Kṛṣṇa was provoked by lust. They wanted to be embraced by the arms of Kṛṣṇa, which resemble the beautiful round shape of a snake. Similarly, there are the Vedic hymns, and we also simply concentrate our minds on the lotus feet of Your Lordship. Women like the *gopīs* concentrate upon You dictated by lust, and we concentrate upon Your lotus feet to go back home, back to Godhead. Your enemies also concentrate upon You, thinking always how to kill You, and the *yogīs* undertake great penances and austerities just to attain Your impersonal effulgence. All these different persons, although concentrating their minds in different ways, achieve spiritual perfection according to their different perspectives because You are equal to all Your devotees."

Śrīdhara Svāmī has composed a nice verse in this regard: "My dear Lord, to be engaged always in thinking of Your lotus feet is very difficult. It is possible by great devotees who have already achieved love for You and who are engaged in transcendental loving service. My dear Lord, I wish that my mind also may be engaged somehow or other on Your lotus feet, at least for some time."

The attainment of spiritual perfection by different spiritualists is explained in the *Bhagavad-gītā*, wherein the Lord says that He grants the perfection the devotee desires in proportion to the devotee's surrender unto Him. The impersonalists, *yogīs* and the enemies of the Lord enter into the Lord's transcendental effulgence, but the personalists who are following in the footsteps of the inhabitants of Vṛndāvana or strictly following the path of devotional service are elevated to the personal abode of Kṛṣṇa, Goloka Vṛndāvana, or to the Vaikuṇṭha planets. Both the impersonalists and the personalists enter into the spiritual realm or the spiritual sky, but the impersonalists are given their place in the impersonal Brahman effulgence, whereas the personalists are given a position in the Vaikuṇṭha planets or in the Vṛndāvana planet, according to their desire to serve the Lord in different mellows.

The personified *Vedas* stated that persons who are born after the creation of this material world cannot understand the existence of the Supreme Personality of Godhead by manipulating their material knowledge. Just as a person born in a particular family cannot understand the position of his great-grandfather who lived before the birth of the recent generation, we are unable to understand the Supreme Personality of Godhead, Nārāyaṇa or Kṛṣṇa, who exists eternally in the spiritual world. In the Eighth Chapter of the *Bhagavad-gītā* it is clearly said that the Supreme Person, who lives eternally in the spiritual kingdom of God *(sanātana-dhāma),* can be approached only by devotional service.

As for the material creation, Brahmā is the first created person. Before Brahmā there was no living creature within this material world; it was void and dark until Brahmā was born on the lotus flower sprouted from the abdomen of Garbhodakaśāyī Viṣṇu. Garbhodakaśāyī Viṣṇu is an expansion of Kāraṇodakaśāyī Viṣṇu, Kāraṇodakaśāyī Viṣṇu is an expansion of Saṅkarṣaṇa, and Saṅkarṣaṇa is an expansion of Balarāma. Balarāma is an immediate expansion of Lord Kṛṣṇa. After the creation of Brahmā, the two kinds of demigods were born: demigods like the four brothers Sanaka, Sanātana, Sananda and Sanat-kumāra, who are representatives of renunciation of the world, and demigods like Marīci and their descendants who are meant to enjoy this material world. From these two kinds of demigods were gradually manifested all other living entities, including the human beings. Thus any living creature within this material world, including Brahmā, all the demigods and all the *rākṣasas,* are to be considered modern. This means that they were all recently born. Therefore, just as a person recently born in a family cannot understand the situation of his distant forefather, so anyone within this material world cannot understand the position of the Supreme Lord in the spiritual world because the material world has only recently been created. Although they have a long duration of existence, all the manifestations of the material world, namely, the time elements, the living entities, the *Vedas,* and the gross and subtle elements, are all created at some point. Anything manufactured within this created situation or accepted as a means to understanding the original source of creation is to be considered modern.

Therefore by the process of self-realization or God realization through fruitive activities, philosophical speculation or mystic *yoga,* one cannot actually approach the supreme source of everything. When the creation is completely terminated, when there is no existence of the *Vedas,* no existence of material time, no existence of the gross and subtle material elements, and when all the living entities are in the nonmanifested stage resting within Nārāyaṇa, then all these manufactured processes become null and void and cannot act. Devotional service, however, is eternally going on in the eternal spiritual world. Therefore the only factual process of self-realization or God realization is devotional service, and if one takes to this process he takes to the real process of God realization. Śrīla Śrīdhara Svāmī has therefore composed a verse in this regard which conveys the idea that the supreme source of everything, the Supreme Personality of Godhead, is so great and unlimited that it is not possible for the living entity to understand Him by any material acquisition. Everyone should therefore pray to the Lord to be engaged in His devotional service eternally, so that by the grace of the Lord one can understand the supreme source of creation. The supreme source of creation, the Supreme Lord, reveals Himself only to the devotees. In the Fourth Chapter of *Bhagavad-gītā* the Lord says to Arjuna, "My dear Arjuna, because you are My devotee and because you are My intimate friend I shall therefore reveal to you the process of understanding Me." In other words, the supreme source of creation, the Supreme Personality of Godhead, cannot be understood by our own endeavor. We have to please Him with devotional service, and then He will reveal Himself to us. Then we can understand Him to some extent.

There are different kinds of philosophers who have tried to understand the supreme source by their mental speculation. There are generally six kinds of mental speculators, and they are called *ṣaḍ-darśana.* All these philosophers are impersonalists and are known as Māyāvādīs. Every one of them has tried to establish his own opinion, although they all have later compromised and stated that all opinions lead to the same goal and that every opinion is therefore valid. According to the prayers of the personified *Vedas,* however, none of them are valid because their process of knowledge is created within the temporary material world. They have all missed the real point: the Supreme Personality of Godhead or the Absolute Truth can be understood only by devotional service.

One class of philosophers, known as Mīmāṁsakas, represented by sages such as Jaimini, have concluded that everyone should be engaged in pious activities or prescribed duties and that such activities will lead one to the highest perfection. But this is contradicted in the Ninth Chapter of *Bhagavad-gītā,* where Lord Kṛṣṇa says that by pious activities one may be elevated to the heavenly planets, but as soon as one's accumulation of pious activities is used up, one has to leave the enjoyment of a higher standard of material prosperity in the heavenly planets and immediately come down again to these lower planets, where the duration of life is very short and where the standard of material happiness is of a lower grade. The exact words used in the *Gītā* are *kṣīṇe puṇye martya-lokaṁ viśanti.* Therefore the conclusion of the Mīmāṁsaka philosophers, that pious activities will lead one to the Absolute Truth, is not valid. Although a pure devotee is by nature inclined to pious activities, no one can attain the favor of the Supreme Personality of Godhead by pious activities alone. Pious activities may purify one of the contamination caused by ignorance and passion, but this is automatically attained by a devotee who is constantly engaged in hearing the transcendental message of Godhead in the form of the *Bhagavad-gītā, Śrīmad-Bhāgavatam* or similar scriptures. From the *Bhagavad-gītā* we understand that even a person who is not up to the standard of pious activities but who is absolutely engaged in devotional service is to be considered well situated on the path of spiritual perfection. It is also said in the *Bhagavad-gītā* that a person who is engaged in devotional service with love and faith is guided from within by the Supreme Personality of Godhead. The Lord Himself as Paramātmā, or the spiritual master sitting within one's heart, gives the devotee exact direction by which he can gradually go back to Godhead. The conclusion of the Mīmāṁsaka philosophers is not actually the truth which can lead one to real understanding.

Similarly, there are Sāṅkhya philosophers, metaphysicians or material scientists who study this cosmic manifestation by their invented scientific method and who do not recognize the supreme authority of God as the creator of the cosmic manifestation. Rather, they wrongly conclude that the reaction of material elements is the original cause of creation. The *Bhagavad-gītā,* however, does not accept this theory. It is clearly said therein that behind the cosmic activities is the direction of the Supreme Personality of Godhead. This fact is corroborated by the Vedic injunction *asad vā idam agra āsīt,* which means that the origin of the creation existed before the cosmic manifestation. Therefore, the material elements cannot be the cause of material creation. Although the material elements are accepted as material causes, the ultimate cause is the Supreme Personality of Godhead Himself. The *Bhagavad-gītā* says, therefore, that material nature works under the direction of Kṛṣṇa.

The conclusion of the atheistic Sāṅkhya philosophy is that because the effects of the material worlds are temporary or illusory, the cause is therefore also illusory. The Sāṅkhya philosophers are in favor of voidism, but the actual fact is that the original cause is the Supreme Personality of Godhead and this cosmic manifestation is the temporary manifestation of His material energy. When this temporary manifestation is annihilated, its cause, the eternal existence of the spiritual world, continues as it is, and therefore the spiritual world is called *sanātana-dhāma,* the eternal abode. The conclusion of the Sāṅkhya philosopher is therefore not valid.

Then there are the philosophers headed by Gautama and Kaṇāda. They have very minutely studied the cause and effect of the material elements and have ultimately come to the conclusion that atomic combination is the original cause of creation. Present material scientists also follow in the footsteps of Gautama and Kaṇāda, who propounded this theory of *paramānuvāda.* This theory, however, cannot be supported because the original cause of everything is not inert atoms. This is confirmed in *Bhagavad-gītā* and *Śrīmad-Bhāgavatam* as well as in the *Vedas,* wherein it is stated *eko nārāyaṇa āsīt,* only Nārāyaṇa existed before the creation. The *Śrīmad-Bhāgavatam* and *Vedānta-sūtra* also say that the original cause is sentient and both indirectly and directly cognizant of everything within this creation. In the *Bhagavad-gītā* Kṛṣṇa says, *ahaṁ sarvasya prabhavaḥ:* "I am the original cause of everything," and *mattaḥ sarvaṁ pravartate:* "From Me everything comes into existence." Therefore, atoms may form the basic combinations of material existence, but these atoms are generated from the Supreme Personality of Godhead. Thus the philosophy of Gautama and Kaṇāda cannot be supported.

Similarly, impersonalists headed by Aṣṭāvakra and later on by Śaṅkarācārya accept the impersonal Brahman effulgence as the cause of everything. According to their theory, the material manifestation is temporary and unreal, whereas the impersonal Brahman effulgence is reality. But this theory cannot be supported either, because the Lord Himself says in the *Bhagavad-gītā* that this Brahman effulgence is resting on His personality. It is also confirmed in the *Brahma-saṁhitā* that the Brahman effulgence is the personal bodily rays of Kṛṣṇa. As such, impersonal Brahman cannot be the original cause of the cosmic manifestation. The original cause is the all-perfect sentient Personality of Godhead, Govinda.

The most dangerous theory of the impersonalists is that when God comes as an incarnation He accepts a material body created by the three modes of material nature. This Māyāvādī theory has been condemned by Lord Caitanya as most offensive. He has said that anyone who accepts the transcendental body of the Personality of Godhead to be made of this material nature commits the greatest offense at the lotus feet of Viṣṇu. Similarly, the *Bhagavad-gītā* also states that only the fools and rascals deride the Personality of Godhead when He descends in a human form. Lord Kṛṣṇa, Lord Rāma and Lord Caitanya actually move within human society as human beings.

The personified *Vedas* condemn the impersonal conception as a gross misrepresentation. In the *Brahma-saṁhitā,* the body of the Supreme Personality of Godhead is described as *ānanda-cin-maya-rasa.* The Supreme Personality of Godhead possesses a spiritual body, not a material body. He can enjoy anything through any part of His body, and therefore He is omnipotent. The limbs of a material body can perform only a particular function, just as hands can hold, but they cannot see or hear. Because the body of the Supreme Personality of Godhead is made of *ānanda-cin-maya-rasa* or *sac-cid-ānanda-vigraha,* He can enjoy anything and do everything with any of His limbs. Acceptance of the spiritual body of the Lord as material is dictated by the tendency to make the Supreme Personality of Godhead equal to the conditioned soul. The conditioned soul has a material body. Therefore, if God also has a material body, then the impersonalistic theory that the Supreme Personality of Godhead and the living entities are one and the same can be very easily propagandized.

Factually, when the Supreme Personality of Godhead comes He exhibits different pastimes, and yet there is no difference between His childish body when He is lying on the lap of His mother Yaśodā and His so-called grown up body fighting with the demons. In His childhood body also, He fought with demons such as Pūtanā, Tṛṇāvarta, Aghāsura, etc., with strength equal to that with which He fought in His youth against demons like Dantavakra, Śiśupāla and others. In material life, as soon as a conditioned soul changes his body, he forgets everything of his past body, but from the *Bhagavad-gītā* we understand that Kṛṣṇa, because He has a *sac-cid-ānanda* body, did not forget instructing the sun-god about the *Bhagavad-gītā* millions of years ago. The Lord is therefore known as Puruṣottama because He is transcendental to both material and spiritual existence. That He is the cause of all causes means that He is the cause of the spiritual world and of the material world as well. The Supreme Personality of Godhead is omnipotent and omniscient. Therefore, because a material body can be neither omnipotent nor omniscient, the Lord's body surely is not material. The Māyāvādī theory that the Personality of Godhead comes within this material world with a material body cannot be supported by any means.

It can be concluded that all the theories of the material philosophers are generated from the temporary illusory existence, like the conclusions in a dream. Such conclusions certainly cannot lead us to the Absolute Truth. The Absolute Truth can only be realized through devotional service. As the Lord says in the *Bhagavad-gītā, bhaktyā mām abhijānāti,* "Only by devotional service can one understand Me." Śrīla Śrīdhara Svāmī has composed a nice verse in this regard, which states: "My dear Lord, let others be engaged in false argument and dry speculation, theorizing upon their great philosophical theses. Let them loiter in the darkness of ignorance and illusion, falsely enjoying as if very learned scholars, although they are without knowledge of the Supreme Personality of Godhead. As far as I am concerned, I wish to be liberated simply by chanting the holy names of the all-beautiful Supreme Personality of Godhead—Mādhava, Vāmana, Trinayana, Saṅkarṣaṇa, Śrīpati and Govinda. Simply by chanting His transcendental names, let me become free from the contamination of this material existence."

In this way the personified *Vedas* said, "My dear Lord, when a living entity, by Your grace only, comes to the right conclusion about Your exalted transcendental position, at that time he no longer bothers with the different theories manufactured by the mental speculators or so-called philosophers. This is a reference to the speculative theories of Gautama, Kaṇāda, Patañjali and Kapila (Nirīśvara). There are actually two Kapilas: one Kapila, the son of Kardama Muni, is an incarnation of God, and the other is an atheist of the modern age. The atheistic Kapila is often misrepresented to be the Supreme Personality of Godhead who appeared as the son of Kardama Muni during the time of Svāyambhuva Manu. Lord Kapila, the incarnation of Godhead, appeared long long ago; the modern age is the age of Vaivasvata Manu, whereas He appeared during the time of Svāyambhuva Manu.

According to Māyāvādī philosophy, this manifested world or the material world is *mithyā* or *māyā,* false. Their preaching principle is *brahma-satya jagat-mithyā.* According to them, only the Brahman effulgence is true, and the cosmic manifestation is illusory or false. But according to Vaiṣṇava philosophy, this cosmic manifestation is caused by the Supreme Personality of Godhead. In the *Bhagavad-gītā* the Lord says that He enters within this material world by one of His plenary portions, and thus the creation takes place. From the *Vedas* also, we can understand that this *asat* or temporary cosmic manifestation is also an emanation from the Supreme *sat* or fact. From the *Vedānta-sūtra* also it is understood that everything has emanated from the Supreme Brahman. As such the Vaiṣṇavas do not take this cosmic manifestation to be false. The Vaiṣṇava philosopher sees everything in this material world in relationship with the Supreme Lord.

This conception of the material world is very nicely explained by Śrīla Rūpa Gosvāmī, who said that renunciation of this material world as illusory or false without knowledge that the material world is also the manifestation of the Supreme Lord is of no practical value. The Vaiṣṇavas, however, are free of attachment to this world because generally the material world is accepted as an object of sense gratification. The Vaiṣṇavas are not in favor of sense gratification; therefore, they are not attached to material activities. The Vaiṣṇava accepts this material world according to the regulative principles of the Vedic injunctions. Since the Supreme Personality of Godhead is the original cause of everything, the Vaiṣṇava sees everything in relationship with Kṛṣṇa, even in this material world. By such advanced knowledge, everything becomes spiritualized. In other words, everything in the material world is already spiritual, but due to our lack of knowledge we see things as material.

The personified *Vedas* presented the example that those who are seeking after gold do not reject gold earrings, gold bangles or anything else made of gold simply because they are shaped differently from the original gold. All living entities are part and parcel of the Supreme Lord and are qualitatively one, but they are now differently shaped in 8,400,000 species of life, just like many different ornaments which have been manufactured from the same source of gold. As one who is interested in gold accepts all the differently shaped gold ornaments, so a Vaiṣṇava, knowing well that all living entities are of the same quality as the Supreme Personality of Godhead, accepts all living entities as eternal servants of God. As a Vaiṣṇava, then, one has ample opportunity to serve the Supreme Personality of Godhead simply by reclaiming these conditioned, misled living entities, training them in Kṛṣṇa consciousness and leading them back to home, back to Godhead. The fact is that the minds of the living entities are now agitated by the three material qualities, and the living entities are therefore transmigrating, as if in dreams, from one body to another. When their consciousness is changed into Kṛṣṇa consciousness, however, they immediately fix Kṛṣṇa within their hearts, and thus their path for liberation becomes clear.

In all the *Vedas* the Supreme Personality of Godhead and the living entities are stated to be of the same quality—*caitanya,* or spiritual. This is also confirmed in the *Padma Purāṇa,* wherein it is said that there are two kinds of spiritual entities; one is called the *jīva,* and the other is called the Supreme Lord. Beginning from Lord Brahmā down to the ant, all living entities are *jīvas,* whereas the Lord is the Supreme four-handed Viṣṇu or Janāradana. The word *ātmā* can be applied only to the Supreme Personality of Godhead, but because the living entities are His parts and parcels, sometimes the word *ātmā* is applied to them also. The living entities are therefore called *jivātmā,* and the Supreme Lord is called *Paramātmā.* Both the *Paramātmā* and *jivātmā* are within this material world, and therefore this material world has a purpose other than sense gratification. The conception of a life of sense gratification is illusion but the conception of service by the *jivātmā* to the *Paramātmā,* even in this material world, is not at all illusory. A Kṛṣṇa conscious person is fully aware of this fact, and thus he does not take this material world to be false, but acts in the reality of transcendental service. The devotee therefore sees everything in this material world as an opportunity to serve the Lord. He does not reject anything as material, but dovetails everything in the service of the Lord. Thus a devotee is always in the transcendental position, and everything that he uses becomes spiritually purified by being used in the service of the Lord.

Śrīdhara Svāmi has composed a nice verse in this regard: "I worship the Supreme Personality of Godhead who is always manifested as reality even within this material world, which is considered by some to be false." The conception of the falsity of this material world is due to lack of knowledge, but a person advanced in Kṛṣṇa consciousness sees the Supreme Personality of Godhead in everything. This is actually realization of the Vedic aphorism, *sarvaṁ khalv idaṁ brahma:* "Everything is Brahman."

The personified *Vedas* continued: "Dear Lord, less intelligent men take to other ways of self-realization, but actually there is no chance to become purified from material contamination or to stop the repeated cycle of birth and death unless one is a thoroughly pure devotee. Our dear Lord, everything is resting on Your different potencies; and everyone is supported by You, as is stated in the *Vedas (eko bahūnāṁ yo vidadhāti kāmān).* Therefore Your Lordship is the supporter and maintainer of all living entities—demigods, human beings and animals. Everyone is supported by You, and You are also situated in everyone's heart. In other words, You are the root of the whole creation. Therefore those who are engaged in Your devotional service without deviation always worship You. Such devotees actually pour water on the root of the universal tree. By devotional service, therefore, one satisfies not only the Personality of Godhead but also all others, because everyone is maintained and supported by Him. Because he understands the all-pervasive feature of the Supreme Personality of Godhead, a devotee is the most practical philanthropist and altruist. Such pure devotees, thoroughly engaged in Kṛṣṇa consciousness, very easily overcome the cycle of birth and death, and they as much as jump over the head of death."

A devotee is never afraid of death or of changing his body; his consciousness is transformed into Kṛṣṇa consciousness, and even if he does not go back to Godhead, even if he transmigrates to another material body, he has nothing to fear. A vivid example is Bharata Mahārāja. Although in his next life he became a deer, in the life after that he became completely free from all material contamination and was elevated to the kingdom of God. The *Bhagavad-gītā* affirms, therefore, that a devotee is never vanquished. A devotee's path to the spiritual kingdom, back home, back to Godhead, is guaranteed. Even though a devotee slips in one birth, the continuation of his Kṛṣṇa consciousness elevates him further and further until he goes back to Godhead. Not only does a pure devotee purify his own personal existence, but whoever becomes his disciple also ultimately becomes purified and able to enter the kingdom of God without difficulty. Not only can a pure devotee easily surpass death, but by his grace his followers also can do so without difficulty. The power of devotional service is so great that a pure devotee can electrify another person by his transcendental instruction on crossing over the ocean of nescience.

The instructions of a pure devotee to his disciple are also very simple. No one feels any difficulty in following in the footsteps of a pure devotee. Anyone who follows in disciplic succession from recognized devotees of the Lord, such as Lord Brahmā, Lord Śiva, the Kumāras, Manu, Kapila, King Prahlāda, King Janaka, Śukadeva Gosvāmī, Yamarāja, etc., very easily finds the door of liberation open. On the other hand, those who are not devotees but are engaged in uncertain processes of self-realization, such as *jñāna, yoga* and *karma,* are understood to be still contaminated. Such contaminated persons, although apparently advanced in self-realization, cannot even liberate themselves, not to speak of others who follow them. Such nondevotees are compared to chained animals, for they are not able to go beyond the jurisdiction of the formalities of a certain type of faith. In the *Bhagavad-gītā* they are condemned as *veda-vādah.* They cannot understand that the *Vedas* deal with activities of the material modes of nature—goodness, passion and ignorance.

Lord Kṛṣṇa advised Arjuna that one has to go beyond the jurisdiction of the duties prescribed in the *Vedas* and take to Kṛṣṇa consciousness, devotional service. It is said in the *Bhagavad-gītā, nistraiguṇyo bhavārjuna,* "My dear Arjuna, just try to become transcendental to the Vedic rituals." This transcendental position beyond the Vedic ritualistic performances is devotional service. In the *Bhagavad-gītā* the Lord clearly says that persons who are engaged in His devotional service without adulteration are situated in Brahman. Actual Brahman realization means Kṛṣṇa consciousness and engagement in devotional service. The devotees are therefore real *brahma-cārīs* because their activities are always in Kṛṣṇa consciousness, devotional service.

The Kṛṣṇa consciousness movement is therefore a supreme call to all kinds of religionists asking them with great authority to join this movement by which one can learn how to love God and thus surpass all formulas and formalities of scriptural injunction. A person who cannot overcome the jurisdiction of stereotyped religious principles is compared to an animal chained up by his master. The purpose of all religion is to understand God and develop one's dormant love of Godhead. If one simply sticks to the religious formulas and formalities and does not become elevated to the position of love of God, he is considered to be a chained animal. In other words, if one is not in Kṛṣṇa consciousness, he is not eligible for liberation from the contamination of material existence.

Śrila Śrīdhara Svāmī has composed a nice verse which says, "Let others engage in severe austerities, let others fall to the land from the tops of hills and give up their lives, let others travel to many holy places of pilgrimage for salvation, or let them be engaged in deep study of philosophy and Vedic literatures; let the mystic *yogīs* engage in their meditational service, and let the different sects engage in unnecessary arguing as to which is the best. But it is a fact that unless one is Kṛṣṇa conscious, unless one is engaged in devotional service, and unless one has the mercy of the Supreme Personality of Godhead, he cannot cross over this material ocean." An intelligent person, therefore, gives up all stereotyped ideas and joins the Kṛṣṇa consciousness movement for factual liberation.

The personified *Vedas* continued their prayers. "Our dear Lord, Your impersonal feature is explained in the *Vedas:* You have no hands, but You can accept all sacrifices which are offered to You; You have no legs, but You can walk more swiftly than anyone. Although You have no eyes, You can see whatever happens in the past, present and future. Although You have no ears, You can hear everything that is said. Although You have no mind, You know everyone and everyone's activities, past, present and future, and yet no one knows who You are. You know everyone, but no one knows You; therefore, You are the oldest and supreme personality."

Similarly, in another part of the *Vedas* it is said, "You have nothing to do. You are so perfect in Your knowledge and potency that everything becomes manifest simply by Your will. There is no one equal to or greater than You, and everyone is acting as Your eternal servant." Thus the Vedic statements describe that the Absolute has no legs, no hands, no eyes, no ears and no mind, and yet He can act through His potencies and fulfill the needs of all living entities. As stated in the *Bhagavad-gītā,* His hands and legs are everywhere; He is all-pervasive. The hands, legs, ears and eyes of all living entities are acting and moving by the direction of the Supersoul sitting within the living entity's heart. Unless the Supersoul is present, it is not possible for the hands and legs to be active. The Supreme Personality of Godhead is so great, independent and perfect, however, that even without having any eyes, legs and ears, He is not dependent on others for His activities. On the contrary, others are dependent on Him for the activities of their different sense organs. Unless the living entity is inspired and directed by the Supersoul, he cannot act.

The fact is that ultimately the Absolute Truth is the Supreme Person. But because He is acting through His different potencies which are impossible for the gross materialists to see, the materialists accept Him as impersonal. For example, one can observe the personal artistic work in a painting of a flower, and one can understand that the color adjustment, the shape, etc., have demanded the minute attention of the artist. The artist's work is clearly exhibited in a painting of different blooming flowers. But the gross materialist, without seeing the hand of God in such artistic manifestations as the actual flowers blooming in nature, concludes that the Absolute Truth is impersonal. Actually, the Absolute is personal, but He is independent. He does not require to personally take a brush and colors to paint the flowers, but His potencies are acting so wonderfully that it appears as if flowers have come into being without the aid of an artist. The impersonal view of the Absolute Truth is accepted by less intelligent men because unless one is engaged in the service of the Lord, he cannot understand how the Supreme is acting—he cannot even know His name. Everything about His activities and personal features is revealed to the devotee only through his loving service attitude.

In the *Bhagavad-gītā* it is clearly said, ***bhoktāraṁ yajña tapasām:*** the Lord is the enjoyer of all kinds of sacrifices and of the results of all austerities. Then again the Lord says, *sarva-loka-maheśvaram:* "I am the proprietor of all planets." So that is the position of the Supreme Personality of Godhead. Although He is present in Vṛndāvana and enjoys transcendental pleasure in the company of His eternal associates, the *gopīs* and the cowherd boys, His potencies are acting under His direction all over the creation. They do not disturb His eternal pastimes.

Through devotional service only can one understand how the Supreme Personality of Godhead, by His inconceivable potencies, simultaneously acts impersonally and as a person. He is acting just like the supreme emperor, and many thousands of kings and chiefs are working under Him. The Supreme Personality of Godhead is the supreme independent controlling person, and all the demigods—including Lord Brahmā, Lord Śiva, Indra the king of heaven, the king of the moon planet, and the king of the sun planet—are working under His direction. It is confirmed in the *Vedas* that the sun is shining, the air is blowing, and fire is distributing heat out of fear of the Supreme Personality of Godhead. The material nature is producing all kinds of movable and immovable objects within the material world, but none of them can independently act or create without the direction of the Supreme Lord. All of them are acting as tributaries, just like subordinate kings who offer their annual taxes to the emperor.

The Vedic injunction states that every living entity lives by eating the remnants of foodstuffs offered to the Personality of Godhead. In great sacrifices the injunction is that Nārāyaṇa should be present as the supreme predominating Deity of the sacrifice, and after the sacrifice is performed, the remnants of foodstuffs are distributed amongst the demigods. This is called *yajña-bhāga.* Every demigod has an allotment of *yajña-bhāga* which he accepts as *prasādam.* The conclusion is that the demigods are not independently powerful; they are posted as different executives under the order of the Supreme Personality of Godhead, and they are eating *prasādam* or the remnants of sacrifices. They are executing the order of the Supreme Lord exactly according to His plan. The Supreme Personality of Godhead is in the background, and His orders are carried out by others. It only appears that He is impersonal. In our grossly materialistic way, we cannot conceive how the Supreme Person is above the impersonal activities of material nature. Therefore the Lord explains in the *Bhagavad-gītā* that there is nothing superior to Himself and that the impersonal Brahman is subordinately situated as a manifestation of His personal rays. Śrīpāda Śrīla Śrīdhara Svāmī has therefore composed a nice verse in this regard: "Let me offer my respectful obeisances unto the Supreme Personality of Godhead, who has no material senses but through whose direction and will all the material senses are working. He is the supreme potency of all material senses or sense organs. He is omnipotent, and He is the supreme performer of everything. Therefore He is worshipable by everyone. Unto that Supreme Person do I offer my respectful obeisances."

Kṛṣṇa Himself declares in the *Bhagavad-gītā* that He is Puruṣottama, which means the Supreme Personality. *Puruṣa* means person, and *uttama* means supreme or transcendental. Also in *Bhagavad-gītā* the Lord declares that because He is transcendental to all sentient and insentient beings, He is therefore known as the *puruṣottama.* In another place the Lord says that as the air is situated in the all-pervading sky, so everyone is situated in Him, and everyone is acting under His direction.

The *Vedas* personified continued. "Our dear Lord," they prayed, "You are equal to all, with no partiality toward a particular type of living entity. As Your parts and parcels, all living entities enjoy or suffer in different conditions of life. They are just like the sparks of a fire. Just as sparks dance on a blazing fire, so all living entities are dancing on Your support. You are providing them with everything they desire, and yet You are not responsible for their position of enjoyment or suffering. There are different types of living entities—demigods, human beings, animals, trees, birds, beasts, germs, worms, insects and aquatics—and all are enjoying or suffering in life by resting on You. The living entities are of two kinds: one class is called ever-liberated, *nitya-mukta,* and the other class is called *nitya-baddha.* The *nitya-mukta* living entities are in the spiritual kingdom, and the *nitya-baddha* are in the material world.

"In the spiritual world both the Lord and the living entities are manifest in their original status, like live sparks in a blazing fire. But in the material world, although the Lord is all-pervasive in His impersonal feature, the living entities have forgotten their Kṛṣṇa consciousness, just as sparks sometimes fall from a blazing fire and lose their original brilliant condition. Some sparks fall onto dry grass and thus ignite another big fire. This is a reference to the pure devotees who take compassion on the poor and innocent living entities. The pure devotee enlightens Kṛṣṇa consciousness in the hearts of the conditioned souls, and thus the blazing fire of the spiritual world becomes manifest even within this material world. Some sparks fall onto water; they immediately lose their original brilliance and become almost extinct. This is comparable to the living entities who take their birth in the midst of gross materialists, in which case their original Kṛṣṇa consciousness becomes almost extinct. Some sparks fall to the ground and remain midway between the blazing and extinct conditions. Thus some living entities are without Kṛṣṇa consciousness, some are between having and not having Kṛṣṇa consciousness, and some are actually situated in Kṛṣṇa consciousness. The demigods in the higher planets, beginning from Lord Brahmā, Indra, Candra, the sun-god, the moon-god, and various other demigods, are all Kṛṣṇa conscious. Human society is between the demigods and the animals, and thus some are more or less Kṛṣṇa conscious, and some are completely forgetful of Kṛṣṇa consciousness. The third-grade living entities, namely the animals, beasts, plants, trees and aquatics, have completely forgotten Kṛṣṇa consciousness. This example stated in the *Vedas* of the sparks of a blazing fire is very appropriate for understanding the condition of different types of living entities. But above all other living entities is the Supreme Personality of Godhead, Kṛṣṇa or Puruṣottama, who is always liberated from all material conditions.

"The question may be raised as to why the living entities have fallen by chance into different conditions of life. To answer this question, we first have to understand that there cannot be any influence of chance for the living entities; chance is for nonliving entities. According to the Vedic literatures, living entities have knowledge, and thus they are called *caitanya,* which means in knowledge. Their situation in different conditions of life, therefore, is not accidental. It is by their choice because they have knowledge. In the *Bhagavad-gītā* the Lord says, 'Give up everything and just surrender unto Me.' This process of realizing the Supreme Personality of Godhead is open for everyone, but still it is the choice of the particular living entity whether to accept or reject this proposal. In the last portion of the *Bhagavad-gītā,* Lord Kṛṣṇa very plainly said to Arjuna, 'My dear Arjuna, now I have spoken everything to You. Everything now depends on whether you choose to accept it.' Similarly, the living entities who have come down to this material world have made their own choice to enjoy this material world. It is not that Kṛṣṇa sent them into this material world. The material world is created for the enjoyment of living entities who wanted to give up the eternal service of the Lord to become the supreme enjoyer themselves. According to Vaiṣṇava philosophy, when a living entity desires to gratify his senses and forgets the service of the Lord, he is given a place in the material world to act freely according to his desire, and therefore he creates a condition of life in which he either enjoys or suffers. We should know definitely that both the Lord and the living entities are eternally cognizant. There is no birth and death for either the Lord or the living entities. When creation takes place, it does not mean that the living entities are created. The Lord creates this material world to give the conditioned souls a chance to elevate themselves to the higher platform of Kṛṣṇa consciousness. If the conditioned soul does not take advantage of this opportunity, then after the dissolution of this material world, he enters into the body of Nārāyaṇa and remains there in deep sleep until the time of another creation.

"In this connection the example of the rainy season is very appropriate. Seasonal rainfall may be taken as the agent for creation because after the rainfall the wet fields are favorable for growing different types of vegetation. Similarly, as soon as there is creation by the Lord's glancing over the material nature, immediately the living entities spring up in their different living conditions, just as different types of vegetation grow after a rainfall. The rainfall is one, but the creation of the different vegetables is varied. The rain falls equally on the whole field, but the different vegetables sprout up in different shapes and different forms according to the seeds planted. Similarly, the seeds of our desires are varied. Every living entity has a different type of desire, and that desire is the seed which causes his growth in a certain type of body. This is explained by Rūpa Gosvāmī by the word *pāpa-bīja. Pāpa* means sinful. All our material desires are to be taken as *pāpa-bīja,* or the seeds of sinful desires. *Bhagavad-gītā* explains that our sinful desire is that we do not surrender unto the Supreme Lord. The Lord therefore says in *Bhagavad-gītā,* 'I shall give you protection from the resultant actions of sinful desires.' These sinful desires are manifested in different types of bodies; therefore, no one can accuse the Supreme Lord of partiality in His giving one type of body to a certain type of living entity and another type of body to another living entity. All the bodies of the 8,400,000 species come according to the mental condition of the individual living entities. The Supreme Personality of Godhead, Puruṣottama, only gives them a chance to act according to their desires. Therefore, the living entities are acting, taking advantage of the facility given by the Lord.

"At the same time, they are born from the transcendental body of the Lord. This relationship between the Lord and the living entities is explained in the Vedic literatures, wherein it is said that the Supreme Lord maintains all His children, giving them whatever they want. Similarly, in the *Bhagavad-gītā,* the Lord says, 'I am the seed-giving father of all living entities.' It is very simple to understand that the father gives birth to the children, but the children act according to their own desires. Therefore the father is never responsible for the different futures of his children. Each child can take advantage of the father's property and instruction, but even though the inheritance and instruction may be the same for all the children, out of their different desires, each child creates a different life and thereby suffers or enjoys.

"Similarly, the *Bhagavad-gītā's* instructions are equal for everyone; everyone should surrender unto the Supreme Lord, and He will take charge of them and protect them from sinful reactions. The facilities of living in the creation of the Lord are equally offered to all living entities. Whatever there is, either on the land, on water or in the sky, is equally given to all living entities. Since they are all sons of the Supreme Lord, everyone can enjoy the material facilities given by the Lord, but unfortunate living entities create unfavorable conditions of life by fighting among themselves. The responsibility for this fighting and creating favorable and unfavorable situations of life lies with the living entities, not with the Supreme Personality of Godhead. Therefore, if the living entities take advantage of the Lord's instructions as given in the *Bhagavad-gītā* and develop Kṛṣṇa consciousness, then their lives become sublime, and they can go back to Godhead.

"One may argue that because this material world is created by the Lord, He is therefore responsible for its condition. Certainly He is indirectly responsible for the creation and maintenance of this material world, but He is never responsible for the different conditions of the living entities. The Lord's creation of this material world is compared to the cloud's creation of vegetation. In the rainy season the cloud creates different varieties of vegetables. The cloud pours water on the surface of the earth, but it never touches the earth directly. Similarly, the Lord creates this material world simply by glancing over the material energy. This is confirmed in the *Vedas:* He threw His glance over the material nature, and thus there was creation. In the *Bhagavad-gītā* it is also confirmed that simply by His transcendental glance over the material nature, He creates different varieties of entities, both movable and immovable, living and dead.

"The creation of the material world can therefore be taken as one of the pastimes of the Lord; it is called one of the pastimes of the Lord because He creates this material world whenever He desires. This desire of the Supreme Personality of Godhead is also extreme mercy on His part because it gives another chance to the conditioned souls to develop their original consciousness and thus go back to Godhead. Therefore no one can blame the Supreme Lord for creating this material world.

"From the subject matter under discussion, we can gain a clear understanding of the difference between the impersonalists and the personalists. The impersonal conception recommends merging in the existence of the Supreme, and the voidist philosophy recommends making all material varieties void. Both these philosophies are known as Māyāvāda. Certainly the cosmic manifestation comes to a close and becomes void when the living entities merge into the body of Nārāyaṇa to rest until another creation, and this may be called an impersonal condition, but these conditions are never eternal. The cessation of the variegatedness of the material world and the merging of the living entities into the body of the Supreme are not permanent because the creation will take place again, and the living entities who merge into the body of the Supreme without having developed their Kṛṣṇa consciousness will again appear in this material world when there is another creation. The *Bhagavad-gītā* confirms the fact that this material world is created and annihilated. This is going on perpetually, and conditioned souls who are without Kṛṣṇa consciousness come back again and again whenever the material creation is manifest. If such conditioned souls take advantage of this opportunity and develop Kṛṣṇa consciousness under the direct instruction of the Lord, then they are transferred to the spiritual world and do not have to come back again to the material creation. It is said, therefore, that the voidists and the impersonalists are not very intelligent because they do not take shelter under the lotus feet of the Lord. Because they are less intelligent, these voidists and impersonalists take to different types of austerities, either to attain the stage of *nirvāṇa,* which means finishing the material conditions of life, or to attain oneness by merging into the body of the Lord. All of them again fall down because they neglect the lotus feet of the Lord."

In the *Caitanya-caritāmṛta,* the author, Kṛṣṇadāsa Kavirāja Gosvāmī, after studying all the Vedic literature and hearing from all authorities, has given his opinion that Kṛṣṇa is the only supreme master and that all living entities are His eternal servants. His statement is confirmed in the prayers by the personified *Vedas.* The conclusion is, therefore, that everyone is under the control of the Supreme Personality of Godhead, everyone is serving under the supreme direction of the Lord, and everyone is afraid of the Supreme Personality of Godhead. It is out of fear of Him that activities are being rightly executed. Everyone's position is to be subordinate to the Supreme Lord, yet the Lord has no partiality in His view of the living entities. He is just like the unlimited sky; as the sparks of a fire dance in the fire, similarly, all living entities are like birds flying in the unlimited sky. Some of them are flying very high, some are flying at a lesser altitude, and some are flying at a still lesser altitude. The different birds are flying in different positions according to their respective abilities to fly, but the sky has nothing to do with this ability. In the *Bhagavad-gītā* also, the Lord confirms that He awards different positions to different living entities according to their proportionate surrender. This proportionate reward by the Personality of Godhead to the living entities is not partiality. Therefore, in spite of the living entities' being situated in different positions, in different spheres, and in different species of life, all of them are always under the control of the Supreme Personality of Godhead, and yet He is never responsible for their different living conditions. It is foolish and artificial, therefore, to think oneself equal to the Supreme Lord, and it is still more foolish to think that one has not seen God. Everyone is seeing

God in His different aspects; the only difference is that the theist sees God as the Supreme Personality, the most beloved, Kṛṣṇa, and the atheist sees the Absolute Truth as ultimate death.

The personified *Vedas* continued to pray. "Our dear Lord, from all Vedic information it is understood that You are the supreme controller, and all living entities are controlled. Both the Lord and the living entities are called *nitya,* eternal, and so are qualitatively one, yet the singular *nitya,* or the Supreme Lord, is the controller, whereas the plural *nityas* are controlled. The individual controlled living entity resides within the body, and the supreme controller, as Supersoul, is also present there, but the Supersoul is controlling the individual soul. That is the verdict of the *Vedas.* If the individual soul were not controlled by the Supersoul, then how could one explain the Vedic version that a living entity transmigrates from one body to another, enjoying and suffering the effects of his past deeds? Sometimes he is promoted to a higher standard of life, and sometimes he is degraded to a lower standard of life. Thus the conditioned souls are not only under the control of the Supreme Lord, but they are also conditioned by the control of the material nature. This relationship of the living entities to the Supreme Lord as the controlled and the controller definitely proves that although the Supersoul is all-pervasive, the individual living entities are never all-pervasive. If the individual souls were all-pervasive, there would be no question of their being controlled. The theory that the Supersoul and the individual soul are equal is therefore a polluted conclusion, and no sensible person accepts it; rather, one should try to understand the distinctions between the supreme eternal and the subordinate eternals."

The personified *Vedas* therefore concluded, "O Lord, both You and the limited *dhruvas,* the living entities, are eternal. The form of the unlimited eternal is sometimes calculated as the universal form, and in the Vedic literatures like the *Upaniṣads,* the form of the limited eternal is vividly described. It is said therein that the original spiritual form of the living entity is one ten-thousandth the size of the tip of a hair. It is stated that the spirit is greater than the greatest and smaller than the smallest. The individual living entities, who are eternally part and parcel of God, are smaller than the smallest. With our material senses, we can perceive neither the Supreme, who is greater than the greatest, nor the individual soul, who is smaller than the smallest. We have to understand both the greatest and the smallest from the authoritative sources of Vedic literature. Vedic literature states that the Supersoul is sitting within the body of a living entity and is as big as a thumb. Therefore the argument may be put forward, how can something the size of a thumb be accommodated within the heart of an ant? The answer is that this thumb measurement of the Supersoul is imagined in proportion to the body of the living entity. In all circumstances, therefore, the Supersoul and the individual living entity cannot be taken as one, although both of them enter within the material body of a living entity. The Supersoul living within the heart is for directing or controlling the individual living entity. Although both are *dhruva,* or eternal, the living entity is always under the direction of the Supreme.

"It may be argued that because the living entities are born of the material nature, they are all equal and independent. In the Vedic literature, however, it is said that the Supreme Personality of Godhead impregnates the material nature with the living entities, and then they come out. Therefore, the appearance of the individual living entities is not factually due to material nature alone, just as a child produced by a woman is not her independent production. A woman is first impregnated by a man, and then a child is produced. As such, the child produced by the woman is part and parcel of the man. Similarly, the living entities are apparently produced by the material nature, but not independently. It is due to the impregnation of material nature by the supreme father that the living entities are present. Therefore the argument that the individual living entities are not part and parcel of the Supreme cannot stand. For example, the different parts and parcels of the body cannot be taken as equal to the whole; rather, the whole body is the controller of the different limbs. Similarly, the parts and parcels of the supreme whole are always dependent and are always controlled by the source of the parts and parcels. It is confirmed in the *Bhagavad-gītā* that the living entities are part and parcel of Kṛṣṇa: *mamaivāṁśo.* No sane man, therefore, will accept the theory that the Supersoul and the individual soul are of the same category. They are equal in quality, but quantitatively the Supersoul is always the Supreme, and the individual soul is always subordinate to the Supersoul. That is the conclusion of the *Vedas.*"

Two significant words used in this connection are *yanmaya* and *cinmaya.* In Sanskrit grammar, the word *mayat* is used in the sense of transformation, and also in the sense of sufficiency. The Māyāvādī philosophers interpret that *yanmaya* or *cinmaya* indicates that the living entity is always equal to the Supreme. But one has to consider whether this affix, *mayat,* is used for sufficiency or for transformation. The living entity never possesses anything exactly in the same proportion as the Supreme Personality of Godhead. Therefore, this *mayat* affix cannot be used to mean that the individual living entity is self-sufficient. The individual living entity never has sufficient knowledge; otherwise, how could he have come under the control of *maya,* or the material energy? The word sufficient can be accepted, therefore, only in proportion to the magnitude of the living entity. The spiritual oneness of the Supreme Lord and the living entities is never to be accepted as homogeneity. Each and every living entity is individual. If homogeneous oneness is accepted, then by the liberation of one individual soul, all other individual souls would have been liberated immediately. But the fact is that every individual soul is differently enjoying and suffering in the material world.

The word *mayat* is also used in the sense of transformation, or sometimes it is used to mean by-product. The impersonalist theory is that Brahman Himself has accepted different types of bodies and that this is His *līlā* or pastime. There are, however, many hundreds and thousands of species of life in different standards of living conditions, such as human beings, demigods, animals, birds and beasts, and if all of them were expansions of the Supreme Absolute Truth, then there would be no question of liberation because Brahman is already liberated. Another interpretation put forward by the Māyāvādīs is that in every millennium different types of bodies are manifested, and when the millennium is closed, all the different bodies or expansions of Brahman automatically become one, ending all different manifestations. Then in the next millennium, according to this theory, Brahman again expands in different bodily forms. If we accept this theory, then Brahman becomes subject to change. But this cannot be accepted. From *Vedānta-sūtra* we understand that Brahman is by nature joyful. He cannot, therefore, change Himself into a body which is subject to painful conditions. Actually, the living entities who are part and parcel of Brahman are infinitesimal particles prone to be covered by the illusory energy. As explained before, the particles of Brahman are like sparks blissfully dancing within a fire, but there is a chance of their falling from the fire to smoke, although smoke is another condition of fire. This material world is just like smoke, and the spiritual world is just like a blazing fire. The innumerable living entities are prone to fall down to the material world from the spiritual world when influenced by illusory energy, and it is also possible for the living entity to become liberated again when by cultivation of real knowledge he becomes completely freed from the contamination of the material world.

The theory of the *asuras* is that the living entities are born of material nature, or *prakṛti,* in touch with the *puruṣa.* This theory also cannot be accepted because both the material nature and the Supreme Personality of Godhead are eternally existing. Neither the material nature nor the Supreme Personality of Godhead can be born. The Supreme Lord is known as *aja,* or unborn. Similarly, the material nature is also called *ajā.* Both these terms, *aja* and *ajā,* mean unborn. Because both the material nature and the Supreme Lord are unborn, it is not possible that they can beget the living entities. As water in contact with air sometimes presents innumerable bubbles, so a combination of material nature and the Supreme Person causes the appearence of the living entities within this material world. As bubbles in the water appear in different shapes, similarly the living entities also appear in the material world in different shapes and conditions, influenced by the modes of material nature. As such, it is not improper to conclude that the living entities appearing within this material world in different shapes, such as human beings, demigods, animals, birds, beasts, etc., all get their respective bodies due to different desires. No one can say when such desires were awakened in them, and therefore it is said, *anādi-karma:* the cause of such material existence is untraceable. No one knows when material life began, but it is a fact that it does have a point of beginning because originally every living entity is a spiritual spark. As sparks falling onto the ground from a fire have a beginning, similarly the living entities coming to this material world have a beginning, but no one can say when. Even during the time of dissolution, these living entities remain merged in the spiritual existence of the Lord, as if in deep sleep, but their original desires to lord it over the material nature do not subside. Again, when there is cosmic manifestation, they come out to fulfill the same desires, and therefore they appear in different species of life.

This merging into the Supreme at the time of dissolution is compared to honey. In the honeycomb, the taste of different flowers and fruits are conserved. When one drinks honey, one cannot distinguish what sort of honey has been collected from what sort of flower, but the palatable taste of the honey presupposes that the honey is not homogeneous, but is a combination of different tastes. Another example is that although different rivers ultimately mix with the water of the sea, that does not mean that the individual identities of the rivers are thereby lost. Although the water of the Ganges and the Yamunā mixes with the water of the sea, the River Ganges and River Yamunā still continue to exist independently. The merging of different living entities into Brahman at the time of dissolution involves the dissolution of different types of bodies, but the living entities, along with their different tastes, remain individually submerged in Brahman until another manifestation of the material world. As the salty taste of sea water and the sweet taste of Ganges water are different, and this difference continually exists, so the difference between the Supreme Lord and the living entities continually exists, even though it appears that at the time of dissolution they merge. The conclusion is, therefore, that even when the living entities become free from all contamination of material conditions, they merge into the spiritual kingdom, but still their individual tastes in relationship with the Supreme Lord continue to exist.

The personified *Vedas* continued: "Our dear Lord, it is our conclusion that all living entities are attracted by Your material energy, and only due to their mistakenly identifying themselves as products of the material nature are they transmigrating from one kind of body to another in forgetfulness of their eternal relationship with You. Because of ignorance, these living entities are misidentifying themselves in different species of life, and especially when they are elevated to the human form of life, they identify with a particular class of men, or a particular nation or race or so-called religion, forgetting their real identity as eternal servants of Your Lordship. Due to this faulty conception of life, they are undergoing repeated birth and death. Out of many millions of them, if one becomes intelligent enough, by association with pure devotees, he comes to the understanding of Kṛṣṇa consciousness and comes out of the jurisdiction of the material misconception."

In the *Caitanya-caritāmṛta* it is confirmed by Lord Caitanya that the living entities are wandering within this universe in different species of life, but if one of them becomes intelligent enough, by the mercy of the spiritual master and the Supreme Personality of Godhead, Kṛṣṇa, then he begins his devotional life in Kṛṣṇa consciousness. It is said, *hariṁ vinā na mṛtim taranti:* without the help of the Supreme Personality of Godhead, one cannot get out of the clutches of repeated birth and death. In other words, only the Supreme Lord, the Personality of Godhead, can relieve the conditioned souls from the cycle of repeated birth and death.

The personified *Vedas* continued: "The influence of time—past, present and future—and the material miseries, such as excessive heat, excessive cold, birth, death, old age, disease, are all simply the movement of Your eyebrows. Everything is working under Your direction. It is said in the *Bhagavad-gītā* that all material activity is going on under the direction of the Supreme Personality of Godhead, Kṛṣṇa. All the conditions of material existence are opposing elements for persons who are not surrendered unto You. But for those who are surrendered souls and are in full Kṛṣṇa consciousness, these things cannot be a source of fearfulness. When Lord Nṛsiṁhadeva appeared, Prahlāda Mahārāja was never afraid of Him, whereas his atheist father was immediately faced with death personified and was killed. Therefore, although Lord Nṛsiṁhadeva appears as death for an atheist like Hiraṇyakaśipu, He is always kind and is the reservoir of all pleasure to the devotees like Prahlāda. A pure devotee is not, therefore, afraid of birth, death, old age and disease.

Śrīpāda Śrīdhara Svāmī has composed a nice verse, the purport of which is as follows: "My dear Lord, I am a living entity perpetually disturbed by the conditions of material existence. I have been cracked into different pieces by the smashing wheel of material existence, and because of my various sinful activities while existing in this material world, I am burning in the blazing fire of material reaction. Somehow or other, my dear Lord, I have come to take shelter under Your lotus feet. Please accept me and give me protection." Śrīla Narottama dāsa Ṭhākur also prays like this: "My dear Lord, O son of Nanda Mahārāja, associated with the daughter of Vṛṣabhānu, I have come to take shelter under Your lotus feet after suffering greatly in the material condition of life, and I am praying that You please be merciful upon me. Please do not kick me away; I have no other shelter but You."

The conclusion is that any process of self-realization or God realization other than *bhakti-yoga,* or devotional service, is extremely difficult. Taking shelter of devotional service to the Lord in full Kṛṣṇa consciousness is therefore the only way to become free from the contamination of material conditional life, especially in this age. Those who are not in Kṛṣṇa consciousness are simply wasting their time, and they have no tangible proof of spiritual life.

It is said by Lord Rāmacandra, "I always give confidence and security to anyone who surrenders unto Me and decides definitely that He is My eternal servant because that is My natural inclination." Similarly, Lord Kṛṣṇa says in the *Bhagavad-gītā,* "The influence of the material nature is insurmountable, but anyone who surrenders unto Me can verily overcome the influence of material nature." The devotees are not at all interested in arguing with the nondevotees to nullify their theories. Rather than wasting their time, they always engage themselves in the transcendental loving service of the Lord in full Kṛṣṇa consciousness.

The personified *Vedas* continued: "Our dear Lord, although great mystic *yogīs* may have full control over the elephant of the mind and the hurricane of the senses, unless they take shelter of a bona fide spiritual master, they fall victims to the material influence and never become successful in their attempts at self-realization. Such unguided persons are compared to merchants going to sea on a ship without a captain. By his personal attempts, therefore, no one can get free from the clutches of material nature. One has to accept a bona fide spiritual master and work according to his direction. Then it is possible to cross over the nescience of material conditions. Śrīpāda Śrīdhara Svāmī has composed a nice verse in this connection, in which he says, "O all-merciful spiritual master, representative of the Supreme Personality of Godhead, when will my mind be completely surrendered unto your lotus feet? At that time, only by your mercy, I shall be able to get relief from all obstacles to spiritual life, and I shall be situated in blissful life."

Actually, ecstatic *samādhi* or absorption in the Supreme Personality of Godhead can be achieved by constant engagement in His service, and this constant engagement in devotional service can be performed only when one is working under the direction of a bona fide spiritual master. The *Vedas* therefore instruct that in order to know the science of devotional service, one has to submit himself unto the bona fide spiritual master. The bona fide spiritual master is he who knows the science of devotional service in disciplic succession. This disciplic succession is called *śrotriyam.* The prime symptom of one who has become a spiritual master in disciplic succession is that he is one hundred percent fixed in *bhakti-yoga.* Sometimes people neglect to accept a spiritual master, and instead they endeavor for self-realization by mystic *yoga* practice, but there are many instances of failure, even by great *yogīs* like Viśvāmitra. Arjuna said in the *Bhagavad-gītā* that controlling the mind is as impractical as stopping the blowing of a hurricane. Sometimes the mind is compared to a maddened elephant. Without following the direction of a spiritual master one cannot control the mind and the senses. In other words, if one practices *yoga* mysticism and does not accept a bona fide spiritual master, he will surely fail. He will simply waste his valuable time. The Vedic injunction is that no one can have full knowledge without being under the guidance of an *ācārya. Ācāryavān puruṣo veda:* one who has accepted an *ācārya* knows what is what. The Absolute Truth cannot be understood by arguments. One who has attained the perfect brahminical stage naturally becomes renounced; he does not strive for material gain because by spiritual knowledge he has come to the conclusion that in this world there is no insufficiency. Everything is sufficiently provided by the Supreme Personality of Godhead. A real *brāhmana,* therefore, does not endeavor for material perfection; rather, he approaches a bona fide spiritual master to accept orders from him. A spiritual master's qualification is that he is *brahmaniṣṭham,* which means that he has given up all other activities and has dedicated his life to working only for the Supreme Personality of Godhead, Kṛṣṇa. When a bona fide student approaches a bona fide spiritual master, he submissively prays to the spiritual master, "My dear Lord, kindly accept me as your student and train me in such a way that I will be able to give up all other kinds of processes for self-realization and simply engage in Kṛṣṇa consciousness, devotional service."

The devotee engaged by the direction of the spiritual master in the transcendental loving service of the Lord contemplates as follows: "My dear Lord, You are the reservoir of pleasure. Since You are present, what is the use of the transient pleasure derived from society, friendship and love? Persons who are unaware of the supreme reservoir of pleasure falsely engage in deriving pleasure from sense gratification, but this is transient and illusory." In this connection, Vidyāpati, a great Vaiṣṇava devotee and poet, says, "My dear Lord, undoubtedly there is some pleasure in the midst of society, friendship and love, although it is materially conceived, but such pleasure cannot satisfy my heart, which is like a desert." In a desert there is need of an ocean of water. But if only a drop of water is poured on the desert, what is the value of such water? Similarly, our material hearts are full of multi-desires, which cannot be fulfilled within the material society of friendship and love. When our hearts begin to derive pleasure from the supreme reservoir of pleasure, then we can be satisfied. That transcendental satisfaction is only possible in devotional service, in full Kṛṣṇa consciousness.

The personified *Vedas* continued: "Our dear Lord, You are *sac-cid-ānanda-vigraha,* the ever-blissful form of knowledge, and because the living entities are parts and parcels of Your personality, their natural state of existence is to be fully conscious of You. In this material world, anyone who has developed such Kṛṣṇa consciousness is no longer interested in the materialistic way of life. A Kṛṣṇa conscious being becomes disinterested in family life or opulent living conditions, and he requires only a little concession for his bodily needs. In other words, he is no longer interested in sense gratification. The perfection of human life is based on knowledge and renunciation, but it is very difficult to attempt to reach the stage of knowledge and renunciation while in family life. Kṛṣṇa conscious persons therefore take shelter of the association of devotees or sanctified places of pilgrimage. Such persons are aware of the relationship between the Supersoul and the individual living entities, and they are never in the bodily concept of life. Because they always carry You in full consciousness within their hearts, they are so purified that any place they go becomes a holy place of pilgrimage, and the water which washes their feet is able to deliver many sinful persons hovering within this material world."

When Prahlāda Mahārāja was asked by his atheistic father to describe something very good which he had learned, he replied to his father that for a materialistic person who is always full of anxieties due to being engaged in temporary and relative truths, the best course is to give up the blind well of family life and go to the forest to take shelter of the Supreme Lord. Those who are actually pure devotees are celebrated as *mahātmās,* or great sages, personalities perfect in knowledge. They always think of the Supreme Lord and His lotus feet, and thus they become automatically liberated. Devotees who are always situated in that position become electrified by the inconceivable potencies of the Lord, and thus they themselves become the source of liberation for their followers and devotees. A Kṛṣṇa conscious person is fully electrified spiritually, and therefore anyone who touches or takes shelter of such a pure devotee becomes similarly electrified with spiritual potencies. Such devotees are never puffed up with material opulences. Generally, the material opulences are good parentage, education, beauty and riches, but although a devotee of the Lord may possess all four of these material opulences, he is never carried away by the pride of possessing such distinctions. Great devotees of the Lord travel all over the world from one place of pilgrimage to another, and on their way they meet many conditioned souls and deliver them by their association and distribution of transcendental knowledge. They reside in places like Vṛndāvana, Mathurā, Dvārakā, Jagannātha Purī and Navadvīpa because only devotees assemble in such places. In this way they take advantage of saintly association, and by such association the devotees advance more and more in Kṛṣṇa consciousness. Such advancement is not possible in ordinary household life which is devoid of Kṛṣṇa consciousness.

The personified *Vedas* continue: "Our dear Lord, there are two classes of transcendentalists, the impersonalists and the personalists. The opinion of the impersonalists is that this material manifestation is false and that only the Absolute Truth is factual. The view of the personalist, however, is that the material world, although very temporary, is nevertheless not false, but is factual. Such transcendentalists have different arguments to establish the validity of their philosophies. Factually, the material world is simultaneously both truth and untruth. It is truth because everything is an expansion of the Supreme Absolute Truth, and it is untruth because the existence of the material world is temporary; it is created, and it is annihilated. Because of its different conditions of existence, the cosmic manifestation has no fixed position. Those who advocate acceptance of this material world as false are generally known by the maxim *brahma satya jagan mithyā.* They put forward the argument that everything in the material world is prepared from matter. For example, there are many things made of clay, such as earthen pots, dishes and balls. After their annihilation, these things may become transformed into many other material objects, but in all cases, their existence as clay continues. An earthen water jug, after being broken, may be transformed into a bowl or dish, but either as a dish, bowl or water jug, the earth itself continues to exist. Therefore, the forms of a water jug, bowl or dish are false, but their existence as earth is real. This is the impersonalists' version. This cosmic manifestation is certainly produced from the Absolute Truth, but because its existence is temporary, it is therefore false; the impersonalists' understanding is that the Absolute Truth, which is always present, is the only truth. In the opinion of other transcendentalists, however, this material world, being produced of the Absolute Truth, is also truth. The impersonalists' counter-argument is that the material world is not factual because sometimes it is found that matter is produced from spirit soul, and sometimes spirit soul is produced from matter. Such philosophers push forward the argument that although cow dung is dead matter, sometimes it is found that scorpions come out of cow dung. Similarly, dead matter like nails and hair comes out of the living body. Therefore, things produced of of a certain thing are not always the same. On the strength of this argument, Māyāvādī philosophers establish that although this cosmic manifestation is certainly an emanation from the Absolute Truth, the cosmic manifestation does not necessarily have truth in it. According to this view, the Absolute Truth, Brahman, should therefore be accepted as truth, whereas the cosmic manifestation, although a product of the Absolute Truth, cannot be taken as truth.

The view of the Māyāvādī philosopher, however, is stated in the *Bhagavad-gītā* to be the view of the *asuras,* or demons. The Lord says in *Bhagavad-gītā, asatyam apratiṣṭham te jagad āhur anīśvaram.* The *asuras'* view of this cosmic manifestation is that the whole creation is false. The *asuras* think that the mere interaction of matter is the source of the creation, and there is no controller or God. But actually that is not the fact. From the Seventh Chapter of the *Bhagavad-gītā,* we understand that the five gross elements—earth, water, air, fire and sky—plus the subtle elements—mind, intelligence and false ego—are the eight separated energies of the Supreme Lord. Beyond this inferior material energy, there is a spiritual energy, which is known as the living entities. The living entities are also accepted as the superior energy of the Lord The whole cosmic manifestation is a combination of the inferior and superior energies, and the source of the energies is the Supreme Personality of Godhead. The Supreme Personality of Godhead has many different types of energies.

That is confirmed in the *Vedas: parāsya śaktir vividhaiva śrūyate* the transcendental energies of the Lord are variegated, and because such varieties have emanated from the Supreme Lord, they cannot be false. The Lord is ever-existing, and the energies are ever-existing. Some of the energy is temporary—sometimes manifested and sometimes unmanifested—but that does not mean that it is false. The example may be given that when a person is angry he does things which are different from his normal condition of life, but that the mood of anger only appears and disappears does not mean that the energy of anger is false. As such, the argument of the Māyāvādī philosophers that this world is false is not accepted by the Vaiṣṇava philosophers. It is confirmed by the Lord Himself that the view that there is no supreme cause of this material manifestation, that there is no God, and that everything is only the creation of the interaction of matter is a view of the *asuras.*

The Māyāvādī philosopher sometimes puts forward the argument of the snake and the rope. In the dark of evening, a curled up rope is sometimes, due to ignorance, taken for a snake. But mistaking the rope as a snake does not mean that the rope or the snake is false, and therefore this example, used by the Māyāvādīs to illustrate the falsity of this material world, is not valid. When a thing is taken as fact but actually has no existence at all, it is called false. But if something is mistaken for something else, that does not mean that it is false. The Vaiṣṇava philosophers use a very appropriate example comparing this material world to an earthen pot. When we see an earthen pot, it does not at once disappear and turn into something else. It may be temporary, but the earthen pot is taken into use for bringing water, and we continue to see it as an earthen pot. Therefore, although the earthen pot is temporary and is different from the original earth, still we cannot say that it is false. We should therefore conclude that the entire earth and the earthen pot are both truths because one is the product of the other. We understand from *Bhagavad-gītā* that after the dissolution of this cosmic manifestation, the energy enters into the Supreme Personality of Godhead. The Supreme Personality of Godhead is ever-existing with His varied energies. Because the material creation is an emanation from Him, we cannot say that this cosmic manifestation is a product of something void. Kṛṣṇa is not void. Whenever we speak of Kṛṣṇa, He is present with His form, quality, name, entourage and paraphernalia. Therefore, Kṛṣṇa is not impersonal. The original cause of everything is neither void nor impersonal, but is the Supreme Person. Demons may say that this material creation is *anīśvara,* without a controller or God, but such arguments ultimately cannot stand.

The example given by the Māyāvādī philosophers that inanimate matter like nails and hair comes out from the living body is not a very sound argument. Nails and hair are undoubtedly inanimate, but they come not from the animate living being, but from the inanimate material body. Similarly, the argument that the scorpion comes from cow dung, meaning that a living entity comes from matter, is also not sound. The scorpion which comes out of the cow dung is certainly a living entity, but the living entity does not come out of the cow dung. Only the living entity's material body, or the body of the scorpion, comes out of the cow dung. The sparks of the living entity, as we understand from *Bhagavad-gītā*, are impregnated within material nature, and then they come out. The body of the living entity in different forms is supplied by material nature, but the living entity himself is begotten by the Supreme Lord. The father and the mother give the body which is necessary for the living entity under certain conditions. The living entity transmigrates from one body to another according to his different desires. The desires in the subtle form of intelligence, mind and false ego accompany the living entity from body to body, and by superior arrangement a living entity is put into the womb of a certain type of material body, and then he develops a similar body. Therefore, the spirit soul is not produced from matter, but it takes on a particular type of body under superior arrangement. To our present experience, this material world is a combination of matter and spirit. The spirit is moving the matter. The spirit soul (the living entity) and matter are different energies of the Supreme Lord. Since both the energies are products of the supreme eternal or the supreme truth, they are therefore factual; they are not false. Because the living entity is part and parcel of the Supreme, he is existing eternally. Therefore, there cannot be any question of birth or death. So-called birth and death occur because of the material body. The Vedic version ***sarvaṁ khalv idaṁ brahma*** means that since both the energies have emanated from the Supreme Brahman, everything that we experience is not different from Brahman.

There are many arguments about the existence of this material world, but the Vaiṣṇava philosophical conclusion is the best. The example of the earthen pot is very suitable: the form of the earthen pot may be temporary, but it has a specific purpose. The purpose of the earthen pot is to carry water from one place to another. Similarly, this material body, although temporary, has a special use. The living entity is given a chance from the beginning of the creation to evolve different kinds of material bodies according to the reserve desires he has accumulated from time immemorial. The human form of body is a special chance in which the developed form of consciousness can be utilized.

Sometimes the Māyāvadī philosophers push forward the argument that if this material world is truth, then why are householders advised to give up their connection with this material world and take *sannyāsa*? But the Vaiṣṇava philosopher's view of *sannyāsa* is not that because the world is false, one must therefore give up material activities. The purpose of Vaiṣṇava *sannyāsa* is to utilize things as they are intended. Śrīla Rūpa Gosvāmī has given two formulas for our dealing with this material world. When a Vaiṣṇava renounces this materialistic way of life and takes to *sannyāsa,* it is not on the conception of the falsity of the material world, but to devote himself fully to engaging everything in the service of the Lord. Śrīla Rūpa Gosvāmī therefore gives this formula: one should be unattached to the material world because material attachment is meaningless. The entire material world, the entire cosmic manifestation, belongs to God, Kṛṣṇa. Therefore, everything should be utilized for Kṛṣṇa, and the devotee should remain unattached to material things. This is the purpose of Vaiṣṇava *sannyāsa.* A materialist sticks to the world for sense gratification, but a Vaiṣṇava *sannyāsī,* although not accepting anything for his personal sense gratification, knows the art of utilizing everything for the service of the Lord. Śrīla Rūpa Gosvāmī has therefore criticized the Māyāvādī *sannyāsīs* because they do not know that everything has a utilization for the service of the Lord. On the contrary, they take the world to be false and thus falsely think of being liberated from the contamination of the material world. Since everything is an expansion of the energy of the Supreme Lord, the expansions are as real as the Supreme Lord is.

That the cosmic world is only temporarily manifested does not mean that it is false or that the source of its manifestation is false. Since the source of its manifestation is truth, the manifestation is also truth, but one must know how to utilize it. The same example can be cited: the temporary earthen pot is produced from the whole earth, but when it is utilized for a proper purpose, the earthen pot is not false. The Vaiṣṇava philosophers know how to utilize the temporary construction of this material world, just as a sane man knows how to utilize the temporary construction of the earthen pot. When the earthen pot is utilized for a wrong purpose, that is false. Similarly, this human form of body, or this material world, when utilized for false sense gratification, is false. But if this human form of body and the material creation are utilized for the service of the Supreme Lord, their activities are never false. It is therefore confirmed in the *Bhagavad-gītā* that a little service attitude in utilizing this body and the material world for the service of the Lord can deliver a person from the gravest danger of life. When they are properly utilized, neither the superior nor inferior energies emanating from the Supreme Personality of Godhead are false. As far as fruitive activities are concerned, they are mainly based on the platform of sense gratification. Therefore an advanced Kṛṣṇa conscious person does not take to them. The result of fruitive activities can elevate one to the higher planetary system, but as it is said in the *Bhagavad-gītā,* foolish persons, after exhausting the results of their pious activities in the heavenly kingdom, come back again to this lower planetary system and then again try to go to the higher planetary system. Their only profit is to take the trouble of going and coming back, just as at present many material scientists are spoiling their time by trying to go to the moon planet and again come back. Those who are engaged in such activities are described by the *Vedas* personified as *andha-paramparā,* or blind followers of the Vedic ritualistic ceremonies. Although such ceremonies are certainly mentioned in the *Vedas,* they are not meant for the intelligent class of men. Men who are too much attached to material enjoyment are captivated by the prospect of being elevated to the higher planetary systems, and so they take to such ritualistic activities. But a person who is intelligent, or who has taken shelter of a bona fide spiritual master to see things as they are, does not take to fruitive activities, but engages himself in the transcendental loving service of the Lord.

Persons who are not devotees take to the Vedic ritualistic ceremonies for materialistic reasons, and then they are bewildered. A vivid example can be given: an intelligent person possessing millions of dollars in currency notes does not hold the money without using it, even though he knows perfectly well that the currency notes in themselves are nothing but paper. When one has one million dollars in currency notes, he is actually holding only a huge bunch of papers, but if he utilizes it for a purpose, then he benefits. Similarly, although this material world may be false, just like the paper, it has its proper beneficial utilization. Because the currency notes, although paper, are issued by the government, they therefore have full value. Similarly, this material world may be false or temporary, but because it is an emanation from the Supreme Lord, it has its full value. The Vaiṣṇava philosopher acknowledges the full value of this material world and knows how to properly utilize it, whereas the Māyāvādī philosopher, mistaking the currency note for false paper, gives it up and cannot utilize the money. Śrīla Rūpa Gosvāmī therefore declares that if one rejects this material world as false, not considering the importance of this material world as a means to serve the Supreme Personality of Godhead, such renunciation has very little value. A person who knows the intrinsic value of this material world for the service of the Lord, who is not attached to the material world, and who renounces the material world by not accepting it for sense gratification is situated in real renunciation. This material world is an expansion of the material energy of the Lord. Therefore it is real. It is not false, as it is sometimes concluded from the example of the snake and the rope.

The personified *Vedas* continued: "The cosmic manifestation, because of the flickering nature of its impermanent existence, appears to less intelligent men to be false." The Māyāvādī philosophers take advantage of the flickering nature of this cosmic manifestation to prove their thesis that this world is false. According to the Vedic version, before the creation this world had no existence, and after dissolution the world will no longer by manifested. Voidists also take advantage of this Vedic version and conclude that the cause of this material world is void. But Vedic injunction does not say that it is void. The Vedic injunction defines the source of creation and dissolution as *yato vā imāni bhūtāni jāyante,* "He from whom this cosmic manifestation has emanated and in whom, after annihilation, everything will merge." The same is explained in the *Vedānta-sūtra* and in the first verse of the First Chapter of *Śrīmad-Bhāgavatam* by the word *janmādyasya,* He from whom all things emanate. All these Vedic injunctions indicate that the cosmic manifestation is due to the Supreme Absolute Personality of Godhead, and when it is dissolved it merges into Him. The same is confirmed in the *Bhagavad-gītā:* this cosmic manifestation is coming into existence and again dissolving, and after dissolution it merges into the existence of the Supreme Lord. This statement definitely confirms that the particular energy known as *bahiraṅgā-māyā,* or the external energy, although of flickering nature, is the energy of the Supreme Lord, and as such it cannot be false. It simply appears to be false. The Māyāvādī philosophers conclude that because the material nature has no existence in the beginning and is nonexistent after dissolution, it is therefore false. But by the example of the earthen pots and dishes the Vedic version is presented: although the existence of the particular by-products of the Absolute Truth are temporary, the energy of the Supreme Lord is permanent. The earthen pot or water jug may be broken or transformed into another shape, such as that of a dish or bowl, but the ingredient, or the material basis, namely the earth, continues to be the same. The basic principle of this cosmic manifestation is always the same, Brahman, or the Absolute Truth; therefore, the Māyāvādī philosophers' theory that it is false is certainly only mental concoction. That the cosmic manifestation is flickering and temporary does not mean that it is false. The definition of falsity is that which never had any existence but is existing only in name. For instance, the eggs of a horse or the flower of the sky or the horn of a rabbit are phenomena which exist only in name. There are no horse's eggs, there is no rabbit's horn, nor are there flowers growing in the sky. There are many things which exist in name or imagination but actually have no factual manifestation. Such things can be called false. But the Vaiṣṇava cannot take this material world to be false simply because its temporary nature is manifesting and again dissolving.

The personified *Vedas* continued to say that the Supersoul and the individual soul, or Paramātmā and *jīvātmā,* cannot be equal in any circumstance, although both of them are sitting within the same body, like two birds sitting in the same tree. As declared in the *Vedas,* these two birds, although sitting as friends, are not equal. One is simply a witness. This bird is Paramātmā, or the Supersoul. And the other bird is eating the fruit of the tree. That is *jīvātmā.* When there is cosmic manifestation, the *jīvātmā,* or the individual soul, appears in the creation in different forms, according to his previous fruitive activities, and due to his long forgetfulness of real existence, he identifies himself with a particular form awarded to him by the laws of material nature. After assuming a material form, he becomes subjected to the three material modes of nature and acts accordingly to continue his existence in the material world. While enwrapped in such ignorance, his natural opulences, although existing in minute quantity, are almost extinct. The opulences of the Supersoul, or the Supreme Personality of Godhead, however, are not diminished, although He appears within this material world. He maintains all opulences and perfections in full and yet keeps Himself apart from all the tribulations of this material world. The conditioned soul becomes entrapped in the material world, whereas the Supersoul, or the Supreme Personality of Godhead, leaves it without affection, just as a snake sheds his skin. The distinction between the Supersoul and the conditioned individual soul is that the Supersoul, or the Supreme Personality of Godhead, maintains His natural opulences, known as *ṣaḍ-aiśvarya, aṣṭa-siddhi and aṣṭa-guṇa.*

Because of their poor fund of knowledge, the Māyāvādī philosophers forget the fact that Kṛṣṇa is always full of six opulences, eight transcendental qualities and eight kinds of perfection. The six opulences are that no one is greater than Kṛṣṇa in wealth, in strength, in beauty, in fame, in knowledge and in renunciation. The first of Kṛṣṇa's eight transcendental qualities is that He is always untouched by the contamination of material existence. This is also mentioned in the *Īśopaniṣad: apāpa-viddham:* just as the sun is never polluted by any contamination, the Supreme Lord is never polluted by any sinful activities. Similarly, although Kṛṣṇa's actions might sometimes seem to be impious, He is never polluted by such actions. The second transcendental quality is that Kṛṣṇa never dies. In the *Bhagavad-gītā,* Fourth Chapter, He informs Arjuna that both He and Arjuna had many appearances in this material world, but He alone remembers all such activities—past, present and future. This means that He never dies. Forgetfulness is due to death. As we die, we change our bodies. That is forgetfulness. Kṛṣṇa, however, is never forgetful. He can remember everything that has happened in the past. Otherwise, how could He remember that He first taught the *Bhagavad-gītā yoga* system to the sun-god, Vivasvān? Therefore, He never dies. Nor does He ever become an old man. Although Kṛṣṇa was a great-grandfather when He appeared on the Battlefield of Kurukṣetra, He did not appear as an old man. Kṛṣṇa cannot be polluted by any sinful activities, Kṛṣṇa never dies, Kṛṣṇa never becomes old, Kṛṣṇa never becomes subjected to any lamentation, Kṛṣṇa is never hungry, and He is never thirsty. Whatever He desires is perfectly lawful, and whatever He decides cannot be changed by anyone. These are the transcendental qualities of Kṛṣṇa. Besides that, Kṛṣṇa is known as Yogeśvara. He has all the opulences or facilities of mystic powers, such as *aṇima-siddhi,* the power to become smaller than the smallest. It is stated in the *Brahma-saṁhitā* that Kṛṣṇa has entered even within the atom, *aṇḍāntarastha-paramāṇu-cayāntarastham.* Similarly, Kṛṣṇa, as Garbhodakaśāyī Viṣṇu, is within the gigantic universe, and He is lying in the Causal Ocean as Mahā-Viṣṇu in a body so gigantic that when He exhales, millions and trillions of universes emanate from His body. This is called *mahima-siddhi.* Kṛṣṇa also has the perfection of *laghimā:* He can become the lightest. It is stated in the *Bhagavad-gītā* that it is because Kṛṣṇa enters within this universe and within the atoms that all the planets are floating in the air. That is the explanation of weightlessness. Kṛṣṇa also has the perfection of *prāpti:* He can get whatever He likes. Similarly, He has the facility of *īśitā,* controlling power. He is called the supreme controller, Parameśvara. In addition, Kṛṣṇa can bring anyone under His influence. This is called *vaśitā.*

Kṛṣṇa is endowed with all opulences, transcendental qualities and mystic powers. No ordinary living being can be compared to Him. Therefore, the Māyāvādīs' theory that the Supersoul and the individual soul are equal is only a misconception. The conclusion is, therefore, that Kṛṣṇa is worshipable and that all other living entities are simply His servants. This understanding is called self-realization. Any other realization of one's self beyond this relationship of eternal servitorship of Kṛṣṇa is impelled by *māyā.* It is said that the last snare of *māyā* is to dictate to the living entity to try to become equal to the Supreme Personality of Godhead. The Māyāvādī philosopher claims to be equal to God, but he cannot reply to the question of why he has fallen into material entanglement. If He is the Supreme God, then how is it that he has been overtaken by impious activities and thereby subjected to the tribulations of the law of *karma?* When the Māyāvādīs are asked about this, they cannot properly answer. The speculation that one is equal to the Supreme Personality of Godhead is another symptom of sinful life. One cannot take to Kṛṣṇa consciousness unless he is completely freed from all sinful activities. The very fact that the Māyāvādī claims to become one with the Supreme Lord means that he is not yet freed from the reactions of sinful activities. *Śrīmad-Bhāgavatam* says that such persons are *aviśuddha-buddhayā,* which means that they falsely think themselves liberated, although at the same time they think themselves equal with the Absolute Truth. Their intelligence is not purified.

The personified *Vedas* said that if the *yogīs* and the *jñānīs* do not free themselves from sinful desires, then their particular process of self-realization will never be successful. "My dear Lord," the personified *Vedas* continued, "if saintly persons do not take care to eradicate completely the roots of sinful desires, they cannot experience the Supersoul, although He is sitting side by side with the individual soul. *Samādhi,* or meditation, means that one has to find the Supersoul within himself. One who is not free from sinful reactions cannot see the Supersoul. If a person has a jeweled locket in his necklace but forgets the jewel, it is almost as though he does not possess it. Similarly, if an individual soul meditates but does not actually perceive the presence of the Supersoul within himself, he has not realized the Supersoul. Persons who have taken to the path of self-realization must therefore be very careful to be uncontaminated by the influence of *māyā.* Śrīla Rūpa Gosvāmī says that a devotee should be completely free from all sorts of material desires. A devotee should not be affected by the resultant actions of *karma* and *jñāna.* One simply has to understand Kṛṣṇa and carry out His desires. That is the pure devotional stage. Mystic *yogīs* who still have contaminated desires for sense gratification never become successful in their attempt, nor can they realize the Supersoul within the individual self. As such, the so-called *yogīs* and *jñānīs* who are simply wasting their time in different types of sense gratification, either by mental speculation or by exhibition of limited mystic powers, will never become liberated from conditional life and will continue to go through repeated births and deaths. For such persons, both this life and the next life become sources of tribulation. Such sinful persons are already suffering tribulation in this life, and because they are not perfect in self-realization, they will be plagued with further tribulation in the next life. Despite all endeavors to attain perfection, such *yogīs,* contaminated by desires for sense gratification, will continue to suffer in this life and in the next.

Śrīla Viśvanātha Cakravartī Ṭhākur remarks in this connection that if *sannyāsīs* and persons in the renounced order of life who have left their homes for self-realization do not engage themselves in the devotional service of the Lord but become attracted by philanthropic work, such as opening educational institutions, hospitals, or even monastaries, churches or temples of demigods, they find only trouble from such engagements, not only in this life but in the next. *Sannyāsīs* who do not take advantage of this life to realize Kṛṣṇa simply waste their time and energy in activities outside the jurisdiction of the renounced order of life. A devotee's attempt to engage his energies in such activities as constructing a Viṣṇu temple is, however, never wasted. Such engagements are called *Kṛṣṇārthe akhila-ceṣṭā,* variegated activities performed to please Kṛṣṇa. A philanthropist's opening a school building and a devotee's constructing a temple are not on the same level. Although a philanthropist's opening an educational institution may be pious activity, it comes under the laws of *karma,* whereas constructing a temple for Viṣṇu is devotional service.

Devotional service is never within the jurisdiction of the law of *karma.* It is stated in the *Bhagavad-gītā* that devotees transcend the reaction of the three modes of material nature and stand on the platform of Brahman realization: *brahma-bhūyāya kalpate.* The *Bhagavad-gītā* says, *sa guṇān samatītyaitān brahma-bhūyāya kalpate:* devotees of the Personality of Godhead transcend all the reactions of the three modes of material nature and are situated on the transcendental Brahman platform. The devotees are liberated both in this life and in the next life. Any work done in this material world for Yajña or Viṣṇu or Kṛṣṇa is considered to be liberated work, but without connection with Acyuta, the infallible Supreme Personality of Godhead, there is no possibility of stopping the resultant actions of the law of *karma.* The life of Kṛṣṇa consciousness is the life of liberation. The conclusion is that a devotee, by the grace of the Lord, is liberated, both in this life and the next, whereas *karmīs, jñānīs* and *yogīs* are never liberated, either in this life or in the next.

The personified *Vedas* continued: "Dear Lord, anyone who, by Your grace, has understood the glories of Your lotus feet is callous to material happiness and distress. The material pangs are inevitable as long as we are existing within the material world, but a devotee does not divert his attention to such actions and reactions, which are the result of pious and impious activities. Nor is a devotee very much disturbed or pleased by praise or condemnation by the people in general. A devotee is sometimes greatly praised by the people in general because of his transcendental activities, and sometimes he is criticized, even though there is no reason for adverse criticism. The pure devotee is always callous to praise or condemnation by the ordinary people. Actually, the devotee's activities are on the transcendental plane. He is not interested in the praise or condemnation of people engaged in material activities. If the devotee can thus maintain his transcendental position, then his liberation in this life and in the next life is guaranteed by the Supreme Personality of Godhead. A devotee's transcendental position within this material world is maintained in the association of pure devotees, simply by hearing the glorious activities enacted by the Lord in different ages and in different incarnations."

The Kṛṣṇa consciousness movement is based on this principle. Śrīla Narottama dāsa Ṭhākur has sung, "My dear Lord, let me be engaged in Your transcendental loving service, as indicated by the previous *ācāryas,* and let me live in the association of pure devotees. That is my desire, life after life." In other words, a devotee does not much care whether or not he is liberated, but he is anxious only for devotional service. Devotional service means that one does not do anything independently of the sanction of the *ācāryas.* The actions of the Kṛṣṇa consciousness movement are directed by the previous *ācāryas,* headed by Śrīla Rūpa Gosvāmī; in the association of devotees following these principles, a devotee is able to perfectly maintain his transcendental position.

In the *Bhagavad-gītā,* the Lord says that a devotee who knows Him perfectly is very dear to Him. Four kinds of pious men take to devotional service. If a man is pious, then in his distressed condition he approaches the Lord for mitigation of his distress. If a pious man is in need of material help, he also prays to the Lord for such help. If a pious man is actually inquisitive about the science of God, he also approaches the Supreme Personality of Godhead, Kṛṣṇa. Similarly, a pious man who is simply anxious to know the science of Kṛṣṇa also approaches the Supreme Lord. Out of these four classes of men, the last is praised by Kṛṣṇa Himself in the *Bhagavad-gītā.* A person who tries to understand Kṛṣṇa with full knowledge and devotion by following in the footsteps of previous *ācāryas* conversant with the scientific knowledge of the Supreme Lord is praiseworthy. Such a devotee can understand that all conditions of life, favorable and unfavorable, are created by the supreme will of the Lord. And when he has fully surrendered unto the lotus feet of the Supreme Lord, he does not care whether his condition of life is favorable or unfavorable. A devotee takes even an unfavorable condition to be the special favor of the Personality of Godhead. Actually, there are no unfavorable conditions for a devotee. He sees everything coming by the will of the Lord as favorable, and in any condition of life he is simply enthusiastic to discharge his devotional service. This devotional attitude is explained in the *Bhagavad-gītā:* a devotee is never distressed in reverse conditions of life, nor is he overjoyed in favorable conditions. In the higher stages of devotional service, a devotee is not even concerned with the list of do's and do not's. Such a position can be maintained only by following in the footsteps of the *ācāryas.* Because a pure devotee follows in the footsteps of the *ācāryas,* any action he performs to discharge devotional service is to be understood to be on the transcendental platform. Lord Kṛṣṇa therefore instructs us that an *ācārya* is above criticism. A neophyte devotee should not consider himself to be on the same plane as the *ācārya.* It should be accepted that the *ācāryas* are on the same platform as the Supreme Personality of Godhead, and as such, neither Kṛṣṇa nor His representative *ācārya* should be subject to any adverse criticism by the neophyte devotees.

The personified *Vedas* thus worshiped the Supreme Personality of Godhead in different ways. Offering worship to the Supreme Lord by praying means remembering His transcendental qualities, pastimes and activities. But the Lord's pastimes and qualities are unlimited. It is not possible for us to remember all the qualities of the Lord. Therefore, the personified *Vedas* worshiped to the best of their ability, and at the end they spoke as follows.

"Our dear Lord, although Lord Brahmā, the predominating deity of the highest planet, Brahmaloka, and King Indra, the predominating demigod of the heavenly planet, as well as the predominating deities of the sun planet, the moon planet, etc., are all very confidential directors of this material world, they have very little knowledge about You. And what to speak of ordinary human beings and mental speculators? It is not possible for anyone to enumerate the unlimited transcendental qualities of Your Lordship. No one, including the mental speculators and the demigods in higher planetary systems, is actually able to estimate the length and breadth of Your form and characteristics. We think that even Your Lordship does not have complete knowledge of Your transcendental qualities. The reason is that You are unlimited. Although it is not befitting in Your case to say that You do not know Yourself, it is nevertheless practical to understand that because You have unlimited qualities and energies and because Your knowledge is also unlimited, there is unlimited competition between Your knowledge and Your expansion of energies."

The idea is that because God and His knowledge are both unlimited, as soon as God is cognizant of some of His energies, He perceives that He has still more energies. In this way, both His energies and His knowledge increase. Because both of them are unlimited, there is no end to the energies and no end to the knowledge with which to understand the energies. God is undoubtedly omniscient, but the personified *Vedas* say that even God Himself does not know the full extent of His energies. This does not mean that God is not omniscient. When an actual fact is unknown to a certain person, this is called ignorance or lack of knowledge. This is not applicable to God, however, because He knows Himself perfectly, but still His energies and activities increase. Therefore He also increases His knowledge to understand it. Both are increasing unlimitedly, and there is no end to it. In that sense it can be said that even God Himself does not know the limit of His energies and qualities.

How God is unlimited in His expansion of energies and activities can be roughly calculated by any sane and sober living entity. It is said in the Vedic literature that innumerable universes issue forth when Mahā-Viṣṇu exhales in His *yoga-nidrā,* and innumerable universes enter His body when He again inhales. We have to imagine that these universes, which, according to our limited knowledge, are expanded unlimitedly, are so great that the gross ingredients, the five elements of the cosmic manifestation, namely earth, water, fire, air and sky, are not only within the universe, but are covering the universe in seven layers, each layer ten times bigger than the previous one. In this way, each and every universe is very securely packed, and there are numberless universes. All these universes are floating within the innumerable pores of the transcendental body of Mahā-Viṣṇu. It is stated that just as the atoms and particles of dust are floating within the air along with the birds and their number cannot be calculated, so innumerable universes are floating within the pores of the transcendental body of the Lord. For this reason, the *Vedas* say that God is beyond the capacity of our knowledge. *Abāṅmanasagocara:* to understand the length and breadth of God is beyond the jurisdiction of our mental speculation. Therefore, a person who is actually learned and sane does not claim to be God, but tries to understand God, making distinctions between spirit and matter. By such careful discrimination, one can clearly understand that the Supreme Soul is transcendental to both the superior and inferior energies, although He has a direct connection with both. In the *Bhagavad-gītā,* Lord Kṛṣṇa explains that although everything is resting on His energy, He is different or separate from the energy.

Nature and the living entities are sometimes designated as *prakṛti* and *puruṣa* respectively. The whole cosmic manifestation is an amalgamation of the *prakṛti* and *puruṣa.* Nature is the ingredient cause, and the living entities are the effective cause. These two causes combine together, and the effect is this cosmic manifestation. When one is fortunate enough to come to the right conclusion about this cosmic manifestation and everything which is going on within it, he knows it to be caused directly and indirectly by the Supreme Personality of Godhead Himself. It is concluded in the *Brahma-saṁhitā,* therefore, *īśvaraḥ paramaḥ kṛṣṇaḥ sac-cid-ānanda-vigrahaḥ anādir ādir govindaḥ sarva-kāraṇa-kāraṇam.*

After much deliberation and consideration, when one has attained the perfection of knowledge, he comes to the conclusion that Kṛṣṇá, or God, is the original cause of all causes. Instead of speculating about the measurement of God—whether He is so long or so wide—or philosophizing, one should come to the conclusion of *Brahma-saṁhitā: sarva-kāraṇa-kāraṇam:* "Kṛṣṇa, or God, is the cause of all causes." That is the perfection of knowledge.

Thus the *Veda-stuti,* or the prayers offered by the personified *Vedas* to the Garbhodakaśāyī Viṣṇu, were first narrated in disciplic succession by Sanandana to his brothers, all of whom were born of Brahmā. In the beginning the four Kumāras were the first-born of Brahmā; therefore they are known as *pūrva-jāta.* It is stated in the *Bhagavad-gītā* that the *paramparā* system, or the disciplic succession, begins with Kṛṣṇa Himself. Similarly, here, in the prayers of the personified *Vedas,* it is to be understood that the *paramparā* system begins with the Personality of Godhead Nārāyaṇa Ṛṣi. We should remember that this *Veda-stuti* is being narrated by Kumāra Sanandana, and the narration is being repeated by Nārāyaṇa Ṛṣi in Bodi Āśrama Nārāyaṇa Ṛṣi is the incarnation of Kṛṣṇa for showing us the path of self-realization by undergoing severe austerities. In this age Lord Caitanya demonstrated the path of pure devotional service by putting Himself in the role of a pure devotee. Similarly, in the past Lord Nārāyaṇa Ṛṣi was an incarnation of Kṛṣṇa who performed severe austerities in the Himalayan ranges. Śrī Nārada Muni was hearing from Him. So in the statement given by Nārāyaṇa Ṛṣi to Nārada Muni, as it was narrated by Kumāra Sanandana in the form of *Veda-stuti,* it is understood that God is the one supreme and that all others are His servants.

In the *Caitanya-caritāmṛta* it is stated, *ekalā īśvara kṛṣṇa:* "Kṛṣṇa is the only Supreme God." *Āra sava bhṛtya:* "All others are His servants." *Yāre yaiche nācāya, se taiche kare nṛtya:* "The Supreme Lord, as He desires, is engaging all living entities in different activities, and thus they are exhib-

iting their different talents and tendencies." This *Veda-stuti* is thus the original instruction regarding the relationship existing between the living entity
their different talents and tendencies." This *Veda-stuti* is thus the original instruction regarding the relationship existing between the living entity and the Supreme Personality of Godhead. The highest platform of realization for the living entity is the attainment of this devotional life. One cannot be engaged in devotional life or Kṛṣṇa consciousness unless he is fully free from material contamination. Nārāyaṇa Ṛṣi informed Nārada Muni that the essence of all *Vedas* and Vedic literatures (namely, the four *Vedas,* the *Upaniṣads,* the *Purāṇas*) teaches the rendering of transcendental loving service to the Lord. In this connection Nārāyaṇa Ṛṣi has used one particular word—*rasa.* In devotional service this *rasa* is the via media or the basic principle for exchanging a relationship between the Lord and the living entity. A *rasa* is also described in the *Vedas* as *īśāvāsya:* "The Supreme Lord is the reservoir of all pleasure." All the Vedic literatures, the *Purāṇas,* the *Vedas,* the *Upaniṣads,* the *Vedānta-sūtras,* etc., are teaching the living entities how to attain the stage of *rasa.* The *Bhāgavatam* also says that the statements in the *Mahāpurāṇa (Śrīmad-Bhāgavatam)* contain the essence of *rasas* in all Vedic literatures. *Nigama-kalpa-taror galitaṁ phalaṁ.* The *Bhāgavatam* is the essence of the ripened fruit in the tree of the Vedic literature.

We understand that with the breathing of the Supreme Personality of Godhead there issued forth the four *Vedas,* namely the *Ṛg-veda,* the *Sāma-veda, Yajur-veda,* and the *Atharva-veda,* and the histories like the *Mahābhārata* and all the *Purāṇas,* which are also considered to be the history of the world. The Vedic histories like the *Purāṇas* and *Mahābhārata* are called the fifth *Veda.*

The verses of *Veda-stuti* are to be considered the essence of all Vedic knowledge. The four Kumāras and all other authorized sages know perfectly that devotional service in Kṛṣṇa consciousness is the essence of all Vedic literatures, and they are preaching this in different planets, traveling in outer space. It is stated herein that such sages, including Nārada Muni, hardly ever travel on land; they are perpetually traveling in space.

Sages like Nārada and the Kumāras travel throughout the universe in order to educate the conditioned souls and show them that their business in the world is not that of sense gratification, but of reinstating themselves again in their original position of devotional service to the Supreme Personality of Godhead. It is stated in several places that the living entities are like sparks of the fire, and the Supreme Personality of Godhead is like the fire itself. Somehow or other when the sparks fall out of the fire they lose their natural illumination; thus it is ascertained that the living entities come into this material world exactly as sparks fall from a great fire. The living entity wants to imitate Kṛṣṇa and tries to lord it over material nature; thus he forgets his original position, and his illuminating power, his spiritual identity, is extinguished. However, if a living entity takes to Kṛṣṇa consciousness, he is reinstated in his original position. Sages and saints like Nārada and the Kumāras are traveling all over the universe educating people and encouraging their disciples to preach this process of devotional service so that all the conditioned souls may be able to revive their original consciousness, or Kṛṣṇa consciousness, and thus gain relief from the miserable conditions of material life.

Śrī Nārada Muni is *naiṣṭika-brahmacārī.* There are four types of *brahmacārī,* and the first is called *sāvitra,* which refers to a *brahmacārī* who, after initiation and the sacred thread ceremony, must observe at least three days celibacy. The next is called *prājāpatya,* which refers to a *brahmacārī* who strictly observes celibacy for at least one year after initiation. The next is called *brāhma-brahmacārī,* which refers to a *brahmacārī* who observes celibacy from the time of initiation up to the time of the completion of his study of Vedic literature. The next stage is called *naiṣṭika,* which refers to a *brahmacārī* who is celibate throughout his whole life. Out of these, the first three are *upqrvma,* which means that the *brahmacārī* can marry later on after the *brahmacārī* period is over. The *naiṣṭika-brahmacārī* is completely reluctant to have any sex life; therefore the Kumāras and Nārada are known as *naiṣṭika-brahmacārīs.* The *brahmacārī* system of life is especially advantageous in that it increases the power of memory and determination. It is specifically mentioned in this connection that because Nārada was *naiṣṭika-brahmacārī* he could remember whatever he heard from his spiritual master and would never forget it. One who can remember everything perpetually is called *śruta-dhara.* A *śruta-dhara brahmacārī* can repeat all that he has heard verbatim without notes and without reference to books. The great sage Nārada has this qualification, and therefore, taking instruction from Nārāyaṇa Ṛṣi, he is engaged in propagating the philosophy of devotional service all over the world. Because such great sages can remember everything, they are very much thoughtful, self-realized and completely fixed in the service of the Lord. Thus the great sage Nārada, after hearing from his spiritual master Nārāyaṇa Ṛṣi, became completely realized. He became established in the truth, and he became so happy that he offered the following prayers to Nārāyaṇa Ṛṣi.

A *naiṣṭhika-brahmacārī* is also called *vīra-vrata.* Nārada Muni addressed Nārāyaṇa Ṛṣi as an incarnation of Kṛṣṇa, and he specifically addressed him as the supreme well-wisher of the conditioned souls. It is stated in the *Bhagavad-gītā* that Lord Kṛṣṇa descends in every millennium just to give protection to His devotees and to annihilate the nondevotees. Nārāyaṇa Ṛṣi, also being an incarnation of Kṛṣṇa, is also addressed as the well-wisher of the conditioned souls. As is stated in the *Bhagavad-gītā,* everyone should know that there is no well-wisher like Kṛṣṇa. Everyone should understand that Lord Kṛṣṇa is the well-wisher of everyone and should take shelter of Kṛṣṇa. In this way one can become completely confident and satisfied knowing that he has someone who is able to give him all protection. Kṛṣṇa Himself, His incarnations and His plenary expansions are all supreme well-wishers of the conditioned souls, but Kṛṣṇa is the well-wisher even for the demons, for He gave salvation to all demons who came to kill Him at Vṛndāvana; therefore Kṛṣṇa's welfare activities are absolute, for even though He annihilates a demon or gives protection to a devotee, His activities are one and the same. It is said that the demon Pūtanā was elevated to the same position as Kṛṣṇa's mother. When Kṛṣṇa kills a demon it should be known that the demon is supremely benefitted by this; however, a pure devotee is always protected by the Lord.

Nārada Muni, after offering respects to his spiritual master, went to the *āśrama* of Vyāsadeva and narrated the entire story to his disciple. Thus Nārada Muni, being properly received by Vyāsadeva in his *āśrama* and seated very comfortably, began to narrate what he had heard from Nārāyaṇa Ṛṣi. In this way Śukadeva Gosvāmī informed Mahārāja Parīkṣit of the answers to his questions regarding the essence of Vedic knowledge and regarding what is considered to be the ultimate goal in the *Vedas.* The supreme goal in life is to seek the transcendental blessings of the Supreme Personality of Godhead and thus become engaged in the loving service of the Lord. One should follow in the footsteps of Śukadeva Gosvāmī and all the Vaiṣṇavas in the disciplic succession and should pay respectful obeisances unto Lord Kṛṣṇa, the Supreme Personality of Godhead Hari. The four sects of Vaiṣṇava disciplic succession, namely the Madhva-sampradāya, the Rāmānuja-sampradāya, the Viṣṇusvāmī-sampradāya, and the Nimbārka-sampradāya, in pursuance of all Vedic conclusions, agree that one should surrender unto the Supreme Personality of Godhead.

The Vedic literatures are divided into two parts: the *śrutis* and the *smṛtis.* The *śrutis* are the four *Vedas: Ṛk, Sāma, Atharva* and *Yajus,* and the *Upaniṣads,* and the *smṛtis* are the *Purāṇas* like *Mahābhārata,* which includes *Bhagavad-gītā.* The conclusion of all these is that one should know Śrī Kṛṣṇa as the Supreme Personality of Godhead. He is the Parampuruṣa, or the Supreme Personality of Godhead under whose superintendence material nature works, being created, maintained and destroyed. After the creation, the Supreme Lord incarnates into three, Brahmā, Viṣṇu and Lord Śiva. All of these take charge of the three qualities of material nature, but the ultimate direction is in the hand of Lord Viṣṇu. The complete activities of material nature under the three modes are being conducted under the direction of the Supreme Personality of Godhead, Kṛṣṇa. This is confirmed in the *Bhagavad-gītā, nyadarśana,* and in the *Vedas: sa aikṣata.*

The atheistic Sāṅkhyaite philosophers offer their arguments that this material cosmic manifestation is due to *prakṛti* and *puruṣa.* They argue that nature and material energy constitute the material cause and the effective cause. But Kṛṣṇa is the cause of all causes. He is the cause of all material and effective causes. *Prakṛti* and *puruṣa* are not the ultimate cause. Superficially it appears that a child is born due to the combination of the father and mother, but the ultimate cause of both the father and the mother is Kṛṣṇa. He is therefore the original cause, or the cause of all causes, as is confirmed in the *Brahma-saṁhitā.*

In the material nature, both the Supreme Lord and the living entities enter. The Supreme Lord Kṛṣṇa, by one of His plenary expansions, manifests as the Kṣīrodakaśāyī Viṣṇu and the Mahā-Viṣṇu, the gigantic Viṣṇu form lying in the Causal Ocean. Then from that gigantic form of the Mahā-Viṣṇu, the Garbhodakaśāyī Viṣṇu expands in every universe. From Him, Brahmā, Viṣṇu and Śiva expand. Viṣṇu enters into the hearts of all living entities, as well as into all material elements, including the atom. The *Brahma-saṁhitā* says: *aṇḍāntarastha-paramāṇu-cayāntarastham.* He is within this universe and also within every atom.

The living entity has a small material body taken from various species and forms, and similarly the whole universe is but the material body of the Supreme Personality of Godhead. This body is described in the *śāstras* as *virāṭa rūpa.* As the individual living entity maintains his particular body, the Supreme Personality of Godhead maintains the whole cosmic creation and everything within it. As soon as the individual living entity leaves the material body, the body is immediately annihilated, and similarly as soon as Lord Viṣṇu leaves the cosmic manifestation, everything is annihilated. Only when the individual living entity surrenders unto the Supreme Personality of Godhead is his liberation from material existence assured. This is confirmed in the *Bhagavad-gītā: mām eva ye prapadyante māyām etāṁ taranti te.* Surrendering unto the Supreme Personality of Godhead is therefore the cause of liberation and nothing else. How the living entity becomes liberated from the modes of material nature after surrendering unto the Supreme Personality of Godhead is illustrated by a sleeping man within a room. When a man is sleeping, everyone sees that he is present within the room, but actually the man himself is not within that body, for while sleeping a man forgets his bodily existence, although others may see that his body is present. Similarly, a liberated person engaged in devotional service of the Lord may be seen by others to be engaged in the household duties of the material world, but since his consciousness is fixed in Kṛṣṇa he does not live within this world. His engagements are different, exactly as the sleeping man's engagements are different from his bodily engagements. It is confirmed in the *Bhagavad-gītā* that a devotee engaged full time in the transcendental loving service of the Lord has already surpassed the influence of the three modes of material nature. He is already situated on the Brahman platform of spiritual realization, although he appears to be living with the body or within the material world.

Śrīla Rūpa Gosvāmī stated in this connection in his *Bhakti-rasāmṛta-sindhu* that the person whose only desire is to serve the Supreme Personality of Godhead may be situated in any condition in the material world, but he is to be understood as *jīvanmukta,* that is to say he is to be considered liberated while living within the body or the material world. The conclusion, therefore, is that a person fully engaged in Kṛṣṇa consciousness is a liberated person. Such a person has actually nothing to do with the material world. Those who are not in Kṛṣṇa consciousness are called *karmīs* and *jñānīs,* and they hover on the bodily and mental platform and thus are not liberated. This situation is called *kaivalya-nirasta-yoni.* A person situated on the transcendental platform becomes freed from the repetition of birth and death. This is also confirmed in *Bhagavad-gītā,* Fourth Chapter. Simply by knowing the transcendental nature of the Supreme Personality of Godhead Kṛṣṇa, one becomes free from the chains of the repetition of birth and death, and after quitting his present body he goes back home, back to Godhead. This is the conclusion of all the *Vedas.* Thus one should surrender unto the lotus feet of Lord Kṛṣṇa after understanding the prayers offered by the personified *Vedas.*

Thus ends the Bhaktivedanta purport of the Third Volume, Eighteenth Chapter, of* Kṛṣṇa, *"Prayers by the Personified Vedas."

19 / Deliverance of Lord Śiva

As a great devotee of Kṛṣṇa, King Parīkṣit was already liberated, but for clarification he was asking various questions of Śukadeva Gosvāmī. In the previous chapter, King Parīkṣit's question was, "What is the ultimate goal of the *Vedas?*" And Śukadeva Gosvāmī explained the matter, giving authoritative descriptions from the disciplic succession, beginning with Sanandana down to Nārāyaṇa Ṛṣi, Nārada, Vyāsadeva, and then he himself. The conclusion was that devotional service, or *bhakti,* is the ultimate goal of the *Vedas.* A neophyte devotee may question, "If the ultimate goal of life, or the conclusion of the *Vedas,* is to elevate oneself to the platform of devotional service, then why is it observed that a devotee of Lord Viṣṇu is generally not very prosperous materially, whereas a devotee of Lord Śiva is found to be very opulent?" In order to clarify this matter, Parīkṣit Mahārāja asked Śukadeva Gosvāmī: "My dear Śukadeva Gosvāmī, it is generally found that those who engage in the worship of Lord Śiva, whether in human, demoniac, or demigod society, become very opulent materially, although Lord Śiva himself lives just like a poverty-stricken person. On the other hand, the devotees of Lord Viṣṇu, who is the controller of the goddess of fortune, do not appear to be very prosperous, and sometimes they are even found to be living without any material opulence at all. Lord Śiva lives underneath a tree or in the snow of the Himalayan Mountains. He does not even construct a house for himself, but still the worshipers of Lord Śiva are very rich. Kṛṣṇa, or Lord Viṣṇu, however, lives very opulently, whether in Vaikuṇṭha or in this material world, but His devotees appear to be poverty-stricken. Why is this so?"

Mahārāja Parīkṣit's question is very intelligent. The two classes of devotees, namely the devotees of Lord Śiva and the devotees of Lord Viṣṇu, are always in disagreement. Even today in India these two classes of devotees still criticize each other, and especially in South India, the followers of Rāmānujācārya and the followers of Śaṅkarācārya hold occasional meetings for understanding the Vedic conclusion. Generally, the followers of Rāmānujācārya come out victorious in such meetings. So Parīkṣit Mahārāja wanted to clarify the situation by asking this question of Śukadeva Gosvāmī. That Lord Śiva lives as a poor man although his devotees appear to be very opulent, whereas Lord Kṛṣṇa or Lord Viṣṇu is always opulent, and yet His devotees appear to be poverty-stricken, is a situation which appears contradictory and puzzling to a discriminating person.

Śukadeva Gosvāmī began to reply to King Parīkṣit's inquiry about the apparent contradictions regarding the worship of Lord Śiva and that of Lord Viṣṇu. Lord Śiva is the master of the material energy. The material energy is represented by goddess Durgā, and Lord Śiva happens to be her husband. Since goddess Durgā is completely under the subjugation of Lord Śiva, it is to be understood that Lord Śiva is the master of this material energy. The material energy is manifested in three qualities, namely goodness, passion and ignorance, and therefore Lord Śiva is the master of these three qualities. Although he is in association with these qualities for the benefit of the conditioned soul, Lord Śiva is the director and is not affected. Although the conditioned soul is affected by the three qualities, Lord Śiva, because he is the master of these qualities, is not affected by them.

From the statements of Śukadeva Gosvāmī we can understand that the effects of worshiping different demigods are not, as some less intelligent persons suppose, the same as the effects of worshiping Lord Viṣṇu. He clearly states that by worshiping Lord Śiva one achieves one reward, whereas by worshiping Lord Viṣṇu one achieves a different reward. This is also confirmed in the *Bhagavad-gītā:* those who worship the different demigods achieve the desired results which the respective demigods can reward. Similarly, those who worship the material energy receive the suitable reward for such activities, and those who worship the *pitās* receive similar results. But those who are engaged in devotional service or worship of the Supreme Lord, Viṣṇu or Kṛṣṇa, go to the Vaikuṇṭha planets or Kṛṣṇaloka. One cannot approach the transcendental region or *paravyoma,* the spiritual sky, by worshiping Lord Śiva or Brahmā or any other demigod.

Since this material world is a product of the three qualities of material nature, all varieties of manifestations come from those three qualities. With the aid of materialistic science, modern civilization has created many machines and comforts of life, and yet they are only varieties of the interactions of the three material qualities. Although the devotees of Lord

Śiva are able to obtain many material acquisitions, we should know that they are simply collecting products manufactured by the three qualities. The three qualities are again subdivided into sixteen, namely the ten senses (five working senses and the five knowledge-acquiring senses), the mind, and the five elements (earth, water, air, fire and sky). These sixteen items are further extensions of the three qualities. Material happiness or opulence means gratification of the senses, specifically the genitals, the tongue and the mind. By exercising our minds we create many pleasurable things just for enjoyment by the genitals and the tongue. The opulence of a person within this material world is estimated in terms of his exercise of the genitals and the tongue, or in other words, how well he is able to utilize his sexual capacities and how well he is able to satisfy his fastidious taste by eating palatable dishes. Material advancement of civilization necessitates creating objects of enjoyment by mental concoction just to become happy on the basis of these two principles: pleasures for the genitals and pleasures for the tongue. Herein lies the answer to King Parīkṣit's question to Sukadeva Gosvāmī as to why the worshipers of Lord Śiva are so opulent.

The devotees of Lord Śiva are only opulent in terms of the material qualities. Factually, such so-called advancement of civilization is the cause of entanglement in material existence. It is actually not advancement, but degradation. The conclusion is that because Lord Śiva is the master of the three qualities, his devotees are given things manufactured by the interaction of these qualities for satisfaction of the senses. In the *Bhagavad-gītā*, however, we get instruction from Lord Kṛṣṇa that one has to transcend the qualitative existence. *Nistraiguṇyo bhavārjuna:* the mission of human life is to become transcendental to the three qualities. Unless one is *nistraiguṇya,* he cannot get free from material entanglement. In other words, favors received from Lord Śiva are not actually beneficial to the conditioned souls, although apparently such facilities seem to be opulent.

Śukadeva Gosvāmī continued: "The Supreme Personality of Godhead Hari is transcendental to the three qualities of material nature." It is stated in the *Bhagavad-gītā* that anyone who surrenders unto Him surpasses the control of the three qualities of material nature. Therefore, since Hari's devotees are transcendental to the control of the three material qualities, certainly He Himself is transcendental. It is stated, therefore, in the *Śrīmad-Bhāgavatam* that Hari, or Kṛṣṇa, is the original Supreme Personality. There are two kinds of *prakṛtis,* or potencies, namely the internal potency and the external potency, and Kṛṣṇa is the overlord of both these *prakṛtis* or potencies. He is *sarva-dṛk,* or the overseer of all the actions of the internal and external potencies, and He is also described as *upadraṣṭa,* the supreme advisor. Because He is the supreme advisor, He is above all the demigods, who merely follow the directions of the supreme advisor. As such, if one directly follows the instructions of the Supreme Lord, as inculcated in the *Bhagavad-gītā* and the *Śrīmad-Bhāgavatam,* then gradually one becomes *nirguṇa,* or above the interaction of the material qualities. To be *nirguṇa* means to be bereft of material opulences because, as we have explained, material opulence means an increase of the actions and reactions of the three material qualities. By worshiping the Supreme Personality of Godhead, instead of being puffed up with material opulences one becomes enriched with spiritual advancement of knowledge in Kṛṣṇa consciousness. To become *nirguṇa* means to achieve eternal peace, fearlessness, religiousness, knowledge and renunciation. All these are symptoms of becoming free from the contamination of the material qualities.

Śukadeva Gosvāmī, in answering Parīkṣit Mahārāja's question, went on to cite an historical instance regarding Parīkṣit Mahārāja's grandfather, King Yudhiṣṭhira. He said that after finishing the *aśvamedha* sacrifice in the great sacrificial arena, King Yudhiṣṭhira, in the presence of great authorities, enquired on that very same point: how is it that the devotees of Lord Śiva become materially opulent, whereas the devotees of Lord Viṣṇu do not? Śukadeva Gosvāmī specifically referred to King Yudhiṣṭhira as "your grandfather" so that Mahārāja Parīkṣit would be encouraged to think that he was related to Kṛṣṇa and that his grandfathers were intimately connected with the Supreme Personality of Godhead.

Although Kṛṣṇa is always very satisfied by nature, when this question was asked by Mahārāja Yudhiṣṭhira He became even more satisfied because these questions and their answers would bear a great meaning for the entire Kṛṣṇa conscious society. Whenever Lord Kṛṣṇa speaks about something to a specific devotee, it is not only meant for that devotee, but for the entire human society. Instructions by the Supreme Personality of Godhead are important even to the demigods, headed by Lord Brahmā, Lord Śiva and others, and anyone who does not take advantage of the instructions of the Supreme Personality of Godhead, who descends within this world for the benefit of all living entities, is certainly very unfortunate.

Lord Kṛṣṇa answered the question of Mahārāja Yudhiṣṭhira as follows: "If I especially favor a devotee and especially wish to care for him, the first thing I do is take away his riches." When the devotee becomes a penniless pauper or is put into a comparatively poverty-stricken position, his relatives and family members no longer take interest in him, and in most cases they give up their connection with him. The devotee then becomes doubly unhappy. First of all he becomes unhappy because his riches have been taken away by Kṛṣṇa, and he is made even more unhappy when his relatives desert him because of his poverty-stricken position. We should note, however, that when a devotee falls into a miserable condition in this way, it is not due to past impious activities, known as *karma-phala;* the poverty-stricken position of the devotee is a creation of the Personality of Godhead. Similarly, when a devotee becomes materially opulent, that is also not due to his pious activities. In either case, whether the devotee becomes poorer or richer, the arrangement is made by the Supreme Personality of Godhead. This arrangement is especially made by Kṛṣṇa for His devotee just to make him completely dependent upon Him and to free him from all material obligations. He can then concentrate his energies, mind and body—everything—for the service of the Lord, and that is pure devotional service. In the *Nārada-pañcarātra* it is therefore explained, *sarvopādhi-vinirmuktam,* which means "being freed from all designations." Works performed for family, society, community, nation, or humanity are all designated: "I belong to this society," "I belong to this community," "I belong to this nation," "I belong to this species of life." Such identities are all merely designations. When, by the grace of the Lord, a devotee becomes freed from all designation, his devotional service is actually *naiṣkarma. Jñānīs* are very much attracted by the position of *naiṣkarma,* in which one's actions no longer have material effect. When the devotee's actions are freed from effects, they are no longer in the category of *karma-phalam,* or fruitive activities. As explained before by the personified *Vedas,* the unhappiness and distress of a devotee are produced by the Personality of Godhead for the devotee, and the devotee therefore does not care whether he is in happiness or in distress. He goes on with his duties in executing devotional service. Although his behavior seems to be subject to the action and reaction of fruitive activities, he is actually freed from the results of action.

It may be questioned why a devotee is put into such tribulation by the Personality of Godhead. The answer is that this kind of arrangement by the Lord is just like the father's sometimes becoming unkind to his sons. Because the devotee is a surrendered soul and is taken charge of by the Supreme Lord, whenever the Lord puts him into any condition of life—either in distress or happiness—it is to be understood that behind this arrangement there is a large plan designed by the Personality of Godhead. For example, Lord Kṛṣṇa put the Pāṇḍavas into a distressed condition so acute that even Grandfather Bhīṣma could not comprehend how such distress could occur. He lamented that although the whole Pāṇḍava family was headed by King Yudhiṣṭhira, the most pious king, and protected by the two great warriors Bhīma and Arjuna, and although, above all, the Pāṇḍavas were all intimate friends and relatives of Lord Kṛṣṇa, they still had to undergo such tribulations. Later on, however, it was proved that this was planned by the Supreme Personality of Godhead Kṛṣṇa as part of His great mission to annihilate the miscreants and protect the devotees.

Another question may be raised: Since a devotee is put into different kinds of happy and distressful conditions by the arrangement of the Personality of Godhead, and a common man is put into such conditions as a result of his past deeds, then what is the difference? How is the devotee any better than the ordinary *karmī*? The answer is that the *karmīs* and the devotees are not on the same level. In whatever condition of life the *karmī* may be, he continues in the cycle of birth and death because the seed of *karma,* or fruitive activity, is there, and it fructifies whenever there is opportunity. By the law of *karma* a common man is perpetually entangled in repeated birth and death, whereas a devotee's distress and happiness, not being under the laws of *karma,* are part of a temporary arrangement by the Supreme Lord which does not entangle the devotee. Such an arrangement is made by the Lord only to serve a temporary purpose. If a *karmī* performs auspicious acts, he is elevated to the heavenly planets, and if he acts impiously, he is put into a hellish condition of life. But whether a devotee acts in a so-called pious or in an impious manner, he is neither elevated nor degraded, but is transferred to the spiritual kingdom. Therefore a devotee's happiness and distress and a *karmī's* happiness and distress are not on the same level. This fact is corroborated by a speech by Yamarāja to his servants in connection with the liberation of Ajāmila. Yamarāja advised his followers that persons who have never uttered the holy name of the Lord nor remembered the form, quality and pastimes of the Lord should be approached by his watchguards. Yamarāja also advised his servants never to approach the devotees. On the contrary, he instructed his messengers that if they meet a devotee they should offer their respectful obeisances. So there is no question of a devotee's being promoted or degraded within this material world. As there is a gulf of difference between the punishment awarded by the mother and the punishment awarded by an enemy, so a devotee's distressed condition is not the same as the distressed condition of a common *karmī.*

Here another question may be raised. If God is all-powerful, why should He try to reform His devotee by putting him into distress? The answer is that when the Supreme Personality of Godhead puts His devotee into a condition of distress, it is not without purpose. Sometimes the purpose is that in distress a devotee's feelings of attachment to Kṛṣṇa are magnified.

For example, when Kṛṣṇa, before leaving the capital of the Pāṇḍavas for His home, was asking for permission to leave, Kuntīdevī said, "My dear Kṛṣṇa, in our distressed condition You are always present with us. Now, because we have been elevated to a royal position, You are leaving us. I would therefore prefer to live in distress than to lose You." When a devotee is put into a situation of distress, his devotional activities are accelerated. Therefore, to show special favor to a devotee, the Lord sometimes puts him into distress. Besides that, it is stated that the sweetness of happiness is sweeter to those who have tasted bitterness. The Supreme Lord descends to this material world just to protect His devotees from distress. In other words, if devotees were not in a distressed condition, the Lord would not have come down. As for His killing the demons or the miscreants, this can be easily done by His various energies, just as many *asuras* are killed by His external energy, goddess Durgā. Therefore the Lord does not need to come down personally to kill such demons, but when His devotee is in distress He must come. Lord Nṛsiṁhadeva appeared not to kill Hiraṇyakaśipu but to see Prahlāda and to give him blessings. In other words, because Prahlāda Mahārāja was put into very great distress, the Lord appeared.

When, after the dense, dark night, there is finally sunrise in the morning, it is very pleasant. When there is scorching heat, cold water is very pleasant. And when there is freezing winter, hot water is very pleasant. Similarly, when a devotee, after experiencing the condition of the material world, relishes the spiritual happiness awarded by the Lord, his position becomes still more pleasant and enjoyable.

The Lord continued: "When My devotee is bereft of all material riches and is deserted by his relatives, friends and family members, because he has no one to look after him, he completely takes shelter of the lotus feet of the Lord." Śrīla Narottamadāsa Ṭhākur has sung in this connection, "My dear Lord Kṛṣṇa, O son of Nanda Mahārāja, You are now standing before me along with Śrīmatī Rādhārāṇī, the daughter of King Vṛṣabhānu. I am now surrendering unto You. Please accept me. Please do not kick me away. I have no shelter other than You."

When a devotee is thus put into so-called miserable conditions and is bereft of riches and family, he tries to revive his original position of material opulence. But although he tries again and again, Kṛṣṇa again and again takes away all his resources. Thus he finally becomes disappointed in material activities, and in that stage of frustration in all endeavors, he can fully surrender unto the Supreme Personality of Godhead. Such persons are advised by the Lord from within to associate with devotees. By associating with devotees they naturally become inclined to render service to the Personality of Godhead, and they immediately get all facilities from the Lord to advance in Kṛṣṇa consciousness. The non-devotees, however, are very careful about preserving their material condition of life. Generally, therefore, such nondevotees do not come to worship the Supreme Personality of Godhead, but worship Lord Śiva or other demigods for immediate material profit. In the *Bhagavad-gītā* it is said, therefore, *kāṇkṣantaḥ karmaṇāṁ siddhiṁ yajanta iha devatāḥ:* the *karmīs,* in order to achieve success within this material world, worship the various demigods. It is also stated by Lord Kṛṣṇa that those who worship the demigods are not mature in their intelligence. The devotees of the Supreme Personality of Godhead, therefore, because of their strong attachment for Him, do not foolishly go to the demigods.

Lord Kṛṣṇa said to King Yudhiṣṭhira: "My devotee is not deterred by any adverse conditions of life; he always remains firm and steady. Therefore I give Myself to him, and I favor him so he can achieve the highest success in life." The mercy bestowed upon the tried devotee by the Supreme Personality is described as *Brahman,* which indicates that the greatness of that mercy can be compared only to the all-pervasive greatness. *Brahman* means unlimitedly great and unlimitedly expanding. That mercy is also described as *parama,* for it has no comparison within this material world, and it is also called *sūkṣmam,* very fine. The Lord's mercy upon the tried devotee is not only great and unlimitedly expansive, but it is of the finest quality of transcendental love between the devotee and the Lord. Such mercy is further described as *cinmātram,* completely spiritual. The use of the word *mātram* indicates absolute spirituality, with no tinge of material qualities. That mercy is also called *sat,* eternal, and *anantakam,* unlimited. Since the devotee of the Lord is awarded such unlimited spiritual benefit, why should he worship the demigods? A devotee of Kṛṣṇa does not worship Lord Śiva or Brahmā or any other subordinate demigod. He completely devotes himself to the transcendental loving service of the Supreme Personality of Godhead.

Śukadeva Gosvāmī continued: "The demigods, headed by Lord Brahmā and Lord Śiva and including Lord Indra, Candra, Varuṇa and others, are apt to become very quickly satisfied and very quickly angered by the good and ill behavior of their devotees. But this is not so with the Supreme Personality of Godhead, Viṣṇu," This means that any living entity within this material world, including the demigods, is conducted by the three modes of material nature, and therefore the qualities of ignorance and passion are very prominent within the material world. Those devotees who take blessings from the demigods are also infected with the material qualities, especially passion and ignorance. Lord Śrī Kṛṣṇa has therefore stated in the *Bhagavad-gītā* that to take blessings from the demigods is less intelligent because when one takes benedictions from the demigods, the results of such benedictions are temporary. It is easy to get material opulence by worshiping the demigods, but the result is sometimes disastrous. As such, the benedictions derived from demigods are appreciated by the less intelligent class of men. Persons who derive benedictions from the demigods gradually become puffed up with material opulence and neglectful of their benefactors.

Śukadeva Gosvāmī addressed King Parīkṣit thus: "My dear King, Lord Brahmā, Lord Viṣṇu, and Lord Śiva, the principal trio of the material creation, are able to bless or to curse anyone. Of this trio, Lord Brahmā and Lord Śiva become very easily satisfied, and at the same time they become very easily angered. When they are satisfied they give benedictions without any consideration, and when they are angry, they curse the devotee without any consideration. But Lord Viṣṇu is not like that. Lord Viṣṇu is very considerate. Whenever a devotee wants something from Lord Viṣṇu, Lord Viṣṇu first of all considers whether such a benediction will ultimately be good for the devotee. Lord Viṣṇu never bestows any benediction which will ultimately prove disastrous to the devotee, He is, by His transcendental nature, always merciful; therefore, before giving any benediction, He considers whether it will prove beneficial for the devotee. Since the Supreme Personality of Godhead is always merciful, even when it appears that He has killed a demon, or even when He apparently becomes angry toward a devotee, His actions are always auspicious. The Supreme Personality of Godhead is therefore known as all-good. Whatever He does is good.

As for the benedictions given by demigods like Lord Śiva, there is the following historical incident cited by great sages. Once, Lord Śiva, after giving benediction to a demon named Vṛkāsura, the son of Śakuni, was himself entrapped in a very dangerous position. Vṛkāsura was searching after a benediction and was trying to decide which of the three presiding deities to worship in order to get it. In the meantime he happened to meet the great sage Nārada and consulted with him as to whom he should approach to achieve quick results from his austerity. He inquired, "Of the three deities, namely Lord Brahmā, Lord Viṣṇu and Lord Śiva, who is most quickly satisfied?" Nārada could understand the plan of the demon, and he advised him, "You had better worship Lord Śiva; then you will quickly get the desired result. Lord Śiva is very quickly satisfied and very quickly dissatisfied also. So you try to satisfy Lord Śiva." Nārada also cited instances wherein demons like Rāvaṇa and Bāṇāsura were enriched with great opulences simply by satisfying Lord Śiva with prayers. Because the great sage Nārada was aware of the nature of the demon Vṛkāsura, he did not advise him to approach Viṣṇu or Lord Brahmā. Persons such as Vṛkāsura who are situated in the material mode of ignorance, cannot stick to the worship of Viṣṇu.

After receiving instruction from Nārada, the demon Vṛkāsura went to Kedāranātha. The pilgrimage site of Kedāranātha still exists near Kashmere. It is almost always covered by snow, but for part of the year, during the month of July, it is possible to see the deity, and devotees go there to offer their respects. Kedāranātha is for the devotees of Lord Śiva. According to the Vedic principle, when something is offered to the deities to eat, it is offered in a fire. Therefore a fire sacrifice is necessary in all sorts of ceremonies. It is specifically stated in the ***śāstras*** that gods are to be offered something to eat through the fire. The demon Vṛkāsura therefore went to Kedāranātha and ignited a sacrificial fire to please Lord Śiva.

After igniting the fire in the name of Śiva, he began to offer his own flesh, by cutting it from his body so as to please Lord Śiva. Here is an instance of worship in the mode of ignorance. In the *Bhagavad-gītā*, different types of sacrifice are mentioned. Some sacrifices are in the mode of goodness, some are in the mode of passion, and some are in the mode of ignorance. There are different kinds of *tapasya* and worship because there are different kinds of people within this world. But the ultimate *tapasya,* Kṛṣṇa consciousness, is the topmost *yoga* and the topmost sacrifice. As confirmed in the *Bhagavad-gītā,* the topmost *yoga* is to think always of Lord Kṛṣṇa within the heart, and the topmost sacrifice is to perform the ***saṅkīrtana-yajña.***

In the *Bhagavad-gītā* it is stated that the worshipers of the demigods have lost their intelligence. As will be revealed later in this chapter, Vṛkāsura wanted to satisfy Lord Śiva for a third-class materialistic objective, which was temporary and without real benefit. The ***asuras*** or persons within the mode of ignorance will accept such benedictions from the demigods. In complete contrast to this sacrifice in the modes of ignorance, the *arcanā-viddhi* process for worshiping Lord Viṣṇu or Kṛṣṇa is very simple. Lord Kṛṣṇa says in the *Bhagavad-gītā* that He accepts from His devotee even a little fruit, a flower or some water, which can be gathered by any person, poor or rich. Of course, those who are rich are not expected to offer only a little water, a little piece of fruit or a little leaf to the Lord. A rich man should offer according to his position, but if the devotee happens to be a very poor man the Lord will accept even the most meager offering. The worship of Lord Viṣṇu or Kṛṣṇa is very simple, and it can be executed by anyone in this world. But worship in the mode of ignorance, as exhibited by Vṛkāsura, is not only very difficult and painful, but it is also a useless waste of time. Therefore *Bhagavad-gītā* says that the worshipers of the demigods are bereft of intelligence; their process of worship is very difficult, and at the same time the result obtained is flickering and temporary.

Although Vṛkāsura continued his sacrifice for six days, he was nevertheless unable to personally see Lord Śiva, which was his objective; he wanted to see him face to face and ask him for a benediction. Here is another contrast between a demon and a devotee. A devotee is confident that whatever he offers to the Deity in full devotional service is accepted by the Lord, but a demon wants to see his worshipable deity face to face so that he can directly take the benediction. A devotee, however, does not worship Viṣṇu or Lord Kṛṣṇa for any benediction. Therefore a devotee is called *akāma,* free of desire, and a nondevotee is called *sarva-kāma,* or desirous of everything. On the seventh day, the demon Vṛkāsura decided that he should cut off his head and offer it to satisfy Lord Śiva. Thus he took bath in the nearby lake, and without drying his body and hair, he prepared to cut off his head. According to the Vedic system, an animal which is to be offered as a sacrifice has to be bathed first, and while the animal is wet he is sacrificed. When the demon was thus preparing to cut off his head, Lord Śiva became very compassionate. This compassion, however, is a symptom of the quality of goodness. Lord Śiva is called *triliṅga.* Therefore his manifestation of the nature of compassion is a sign of the quality of goodness. This compassion, however, is present in every living entity. The compassion of Lord Śiva was aroused because the demon was offering his flesh to the sacrificial fire. This is natural compassion. Even if a common man sees someone preparing to commit suicide, it is his duty to try to save him. He does so automatically. There is no need to appeal to him. Therefore when Lord Śiva appeared from the fire to check the demon from suicide, it was not as a very great favor to him.

The demon was saved from committing suicide by the touch of Lord Śiva; his bodily injuries immediately healed, and his body became as it was before. Then Lord Śiva told the demon, "My dear Vṛkāsura, you do not need to cut off your head. You can ask from me any benediction you like, and I shall fulfill your desire. I do not know why you wanted to cut off your head to satisfy me. I become satisfied even by an offering of a little water." Actually, according to the Vedic process, the Śiva *liṅga* in the temple or the form of Lord Śiva in the temple is worshiped simply by offering Ganges water because it is said that Lord Śiva is greatly satisfied when Ganges water is poured upon his head. Generally, devotees offer Ganges water and the leaves of the *bilva* tree, which are especially meant for offering to Lord Śiva and the goddess Durgā. The fruit of this tree also is offered to Lord Śiva. Lord Śiva assured Vṛkāsura that he becomes satisfied by a very simple process of worship. Why then was he so anxious to cut off his head, and why was he taking so much pain by cutting his body to pieces and offering it in the fire? There was no need of such severe penances. Anyway, out of compassion and sympathy, Lord Śiva prepared to give him any benediction he liked.

When the demon was offered this facility by Lord Śiva, he asked for a very fearful and abominable benediction. The demon was very sinful, and sinful persons do not know what sort of benediction should be asked from the deity. Therefore he asked Lord Śiva to be benedicted with such power that as soon as he would touch anyone's head, immediately it would crack, and the man would die. The demons are described in the *Bhagavad-gītā* as *duṣkṛtinas,* or miscreants. *Kṛtī* means very meritorious, but when *duṣ,* is added, it means abominable. Instead of surrendering unto the Supreme Personality of Godhead, the *duṣkṛtinas* worship different demigods in order to derive abominable material benefits. Sometimes such demons as material scientists discover lethal weapons. They cannot show their meritorious power by discovering something which can save man from death, but instead they discover weapons which accelerate the process of death. Because Lord Śiva is powerful enough to give any benediction, the demon could have asked of him something beneficial for human society, but for his personal interest he asked that anyone whose head would be touched by his hand would at once die.

Lord Śiva could understand the motive of the demon, and he was very sorry that he had assured him whatever benediction he liked. He would not withdraw his promise, but he was very sorry in his heart that he was to offer him a benediction so dangerous to human society. The demons are described as *duṣkṛtinas,* miscreants, because although they have brain power and merit, the merit and brain power are used for abominable activities. Sometimes, for example, the materialistic demons discover a lethal weapon. The scientific research for such a discovery certainly requires a very good brain, but instead of discovering something beneficial to human society, they discover something to accelerate the death which is already assured to every man. Similarly, Vṛkāsura, instead of asking Lord Śiva for something beneficial to human society, asked for something very dangerous to human society. Therefore Lord Śiva felt sorry within himself. Devotees of the Personality of Godhead, however, never ask any benediction from Lord Viṣṇu or Kṛṣṇa, and even if they ask something from the Lord, it is not at all dangerous for human society. That is the difference between the demons and the devotees, or the worshipers of Lord Śiva and the worshipers of Lord Viṣṇu.

While Śukadeva Gosvāmī was narrating the history of Vṛkāsura, he addressed Mahārāja Parīkṣit as *Bhārata,* referring to King Parīkṣit's birth in a family of devotees. Mahārāja Parīkṣit was saved by Lord Kṛṣṇa while he was in his mother's womb. Similarly, he could have asked Lord Kṛṣṇa to save him from the curse of the *brāhmaṇa,* but he did not do so. The demon, however, wanted to become immortal by killing everyone with the touch of his hand. Lord Śiva could understand this, but because he had promised, he gave him the benediction.

The demon, however, being very sinful, immediately decided that he would use the benediction to kill Lord Śiva and take away Gaurī (Pārvatī) for his personal enjoyment. He immediately decided to place his hand on the head of Lord Śiva. Thus Lord Śiva was put into an awkward position because he was endangered by his own benediction to a demon. This is also another instance of a materialistic devotee's misusing the power derived from the demigods.

Without further deliberation, the demon Vṛkāsura immediately approached Lord Śiva to place his hand on Lord Śiva's head. Lord Śiva was so afraid of him that his body trembled, and he began to flee from the land to the sky and from the sky to other planets until he reached the limits of the universe, above the higher planetary systems. Lord Śiva fled from one place to another, but the demon Vṛkāsura continued to chase him. The predominating deities of other planets, such as Brahmā, Indra and Candra, could not find any way to save Lord Śiva from the impending danger. Wherever Lord Śiva went, they remained silent.

At last Lord Śiva approached Lord Viṣṇu, who is situated within this universe in the planet known as Śvetadvīpa. Śvetadvīpa is the local Vaikuṇṭha planet beyond the jurisdiction of the influence of external energy. Lord Viṣṇu in His all-pervasive feature remains everywhere, but wherever He remains personally is the Vaikuṇṭha atmosphere. In the *Bhagavad-gītā* it is stated that the Lord remains within the heart of all living entities. As such, the Lord remains within the heart of many low-born living entities, but that does not mean that He is low-born. Wherever He remains is transformed into Vaikuṇṭha. So the planet within this universe known as Śvetadvīpa is also Vaikuṇṭhaloka. It is said in the *śāstras* that residential quarters within the forest are in the mode of goodness, residential quarters in big cities, towns and villages are in the mode of passion, and residential quarters in an atmosphere wherein indulgence in the four sinful activities of illicit sex, intoxication, meat-eating and gambling predominate are in the mode of ignorance. But residential quarters in a temple of Viṣṇu, the Supreme Lord, are in Vaikuṇṭha. It doesn't matter where the temple is situated, but the temple itself, wherever it may be, is Vaikuṇṭha. Similarly, the Śvetadvīpa planet, although within the material jurisdiction, is Vaikuṇṭha.

Lord Śiva finally entered Śvetadvīpa Vaikuṇṭha. In Śvetadvīpa there are great saintly persons who are completely freed from the envious nature of the material world and are beyond the jurisdiction of the four principles of material activities, namely, religiousness, economic development, sense gratification and liberation. Anyone who enters into that Vaikuṇṭha planet never comes back again to this material world. Lord Nārāyaṇa is celebrated as a lover of His devotees, and as soon as He understood that Lord Śiva was in great danger, He appeared as a *brahmacārī* and personally approached Lord Śiva to receive him from a distant place. The Lord appeared as a perfect *brahmacārī*, with a belt around His waist, sacred thread, deerskin, a *brahmacārī* stick and *raudra* beads. (*Raudra* beads are different from *tulasī* beads. *Raudra* beads are used by the devotees of Lord Śiva.) Dressed as a *brahmacārī*, Lord Nārāyaṇa stood before Lord Śiva. The shining effulgence emanating from His body attracted not only Lord Śiva but also the demon Vṛkāsura.

Lord Nārāyaṇa offered his respects and obeisances unto Vṛkāsura, just to attract his sympathy and attention. Thus checking the demon, the Lord addressed him as follows: "My dear son of Śakuni, you appear to be very tired, as if coming from a very distant place. What is your purpose? Why have you come so far? I see that you are very tired and fatigued, so I request you to take a little rest. You should not unnecessarily tire your body. Everyone greatly values his body because with this body only can one fulfill all the desires of one's mind. We should not, therefore, unnecessarily give trouble to this body."

The *brahmacārī* addressed Vṛkāsura as the son of Śakuni just to convince him that He was known to his father, Śakuni. Vṛkāsura then took the *brahmacārī* to be someone known to his family, and therefore the *brahmacārī's* sympathetic words appealed to him. Before the demon could argue that he had no time to take rest, the Lord began to inform him about the importance of the body, and the demon was convinced. Any man, especially a demon, takes his body to be very important. Thus Vṛkāsura became convinced about the importance of his body.

Then, just to pacify the demon, the *brahmacārī* told him, "My dear lord, if you think that you can disclose the mission for which you have taken the trouble to come here, maybe I shall be able to help you so that your purpose will be easily served." Indirectly, the Lord informed him that because the Lord is the Supreme Brahman, certainly He would be able to adjust the awkward situation created by Lord Śiva.

The demon was greatly pacified by the sweet words of Lord Nārāyaṇa in the form of a *brahmacārī*, and at last he disclosed all that had happened in regard to the benediction offered by Lord Śiva. The Lord replied to the demon as follows: "I myself cannot believe that Lord Śiva has in truth given you such a benediction. As far as I know, Lord Śiva is not in a sane mental condition. He had a quarrel with his father-in-law Dakṣa, and he has been cursed to become a *piśāca* (ghost). Thus he has become the leader of the ghosts and hobgoblins. Therefore I cannot put any faith in his words. But if you have faith still in the words of Lord Śiva, my dear king of the demons, then why don't you make an experiment by putting your hand on your head? If the benediction proves false, then you can immediately kill this liar, Lord Śiva, so that in the future he will not dare to give out false benedictions."

In this way, by Lord Nārāyaṇa's sweet words and by the expansion of His superior illusion, the demon became bewildered, and he actually forgot the power of Lord Śiva and his benediction. He was thus very easily persuaded to put his hand on his own head. As soon as the demon did that, his head cracked, as if struck by thunder, and he immediately died. The demigods from heaven began to shower flowers on Lord Nārāyaṇa, praising Him with all glories and all thanksgiving, and they offered their obeisances to the Lord. On the death of Vṛkāsura, all the denizens in the higher planetary systems, namely, the demigods, the *pitās*, the Gandharvas and the inhabitants of Janaloka, began to shower flowers on the Personality of Godhead.

Thus Lord Viṣṇu in the form of a *brahmacārī* released Lord Śiva from the impending danger and saved the whole situation. Lord Nārāyaṇa then informed Lord Śiva that this demon, Vṛkāsura, was killed as the result of his sinful activities. He was especially sinful and offensive because he wanted to experiment on his own master, Lord Śiva. Lord Nārāyaṇa then told Lord Śiva, "My dear lord, a person who commits an offense to great souls cannot continue to exist. He becomes vanquished by his own sinful activities, and this is certainly true of this demon, who has committed such an offensive act against you."

Thus, by the grace of the Supreme Personality of Godhead Nārāyaṇa, who is transcendental to all material qualities, Lord Śiva was saved from being killed by a demon. Anyone who hears this history with faith and devotion certainly becomes liberated from material entanglement as well as from the clutches of his enemies.

Thus ends the Bhaktivedanta purport of the Third Volume, Nineteenth Chapter, of Kṛṣṇa, *"Deliverance of Lord Śiva."*

20 / The Superexcellent Power of Kṛṣṇa

Long, long ago, there was an assembly of great sages on the bank of the River Sarasvatī, and they performed a great sacrifice of the name *Satrayajña.* In such assemblies, the great sages present usually discuss Vedic subject matters and philosophical topics, and in this particular meeting the following question was raised: The three predominating deities of this material world, namely, Lord Brahmā, Lord Viṣṇu and Lord Śiva, are directing all the affairs of the this cosmos, but who among them is the Supreme? After much discussion on this question, the great sage named Bhṛgu, who is the son of Lord Brahmā, was deputed to test all three predominating deities and report to the assembly as to who is the greatest.

Being thus deputed, the great sage Bhṛgumuni first of all went to his father's residence in Brahmaloka. The three deities are the controllers of the three material qualities, namely the qualities of goodness, passion and ignorance. The plan decided upon by the sages was for Bhṛgu to test which of the predominating deities possesses the quality of goodness in full. Therefore, when Bhṛgumuni reached his father, Lord Brahmā, because he wanted to test whether he had the quality of goodness, he purposely did not offer his respects to his father either by offering obeisances or by offering prayers. It is the duty of a son or a disciple to offer respects and recite suitable prayers when he approaches his father or spiritual master. But Bhṛgumuni purposefully failed to offer respects, just to see Lord Brahmā's reaction to this negligence. Lord Brahmā was very angry at his son's impudency, and he showed signs which definitely proved this to be so. He was even prepared to condemn Bhṛgu by cursing him, but because Bhṛgu was his son, Lord Brahmā controlled his anger with his great intelligence. This means that although the quality of passion was prominent in Lord Brahmā, he had the power to control it. Lord Brahmā's anger and his controlling his anger are likened to fire and water. Water is produced from fire, but at the same time, fire can be extinguished with water. Similarly, although Lord Brahmā was very angry due to his quality of passion, he could still control his passion because Bhṛgumuni was his son.

After testing Lord Brahmā, Bhṛgumuni went directly to the planet Kailāsa, where Lord Śiva resides. Bhṛgumuni happened to be Lord Śiva's brother. Therefore, as soon as Bhṛgumuni approached, Lord Śiva became very glad and personally rose to embrace him. But when Lord Śiva approached, Bhṛgumuni refused to embrace him. "My dear brother," he said, "you are always very impure. Because you smear your body with ashes, you are therefore not very clean. Please do not touch me." When Bhṛgumuni refused to embrace his brother, saying that Lord Śiva was very impure, the latter became very angry with him. It is said that an offense can be committed either with the body, with the mind or by speech. Bhṛgumuni's first offense, committed towards Lord Brahmā, was an offense with the mind. His second offense, committed towards Lord Śiva by insulting him, criticizing him for unclean habits, was an offense by speech. Because the quality of ignorance is prominent in Lord Śiva, when he heard Bhṛgu's insult, his eyes immediately became red with anger. With uncontrollable rage, he took up his trident and prepared to kill Bhṛgumuni. At that time, Lord Śiva's wife, Pārvatī, was present. Her personality is a mixture of the three qualities, and therefore she is called Triguṇamayī. In this case, she saved the situation by evoking Lord Śiva's quality of goodness. She fell down at the feet of her husband, and with her sweet words she talked him out of killing Bhṛgumuni.

After being saved from the anger of Lord Śiva, Bhṛgumuni went directly to the planet Śvetadvīpa, where Lord Viṣṇu was lying on a bed of flowers, accompanied by His wife, the goddess of fortune, who was engaged in massaging His lotus feet. There Bhṛgumuni purposely committed the greatest sin by offending Lord Viṣṇu by his bodily activities. The first offense committed by Bhṛgumuni was mental, the second offense was vocal, and the third offense was corporal. These different offenses are progressively greater in degree. An offense committed within the mind is a positive offense, the same offense, committed verbally is comparatively more grave, and when committed by bodily action it is superlative in offensiveness. So Bhṛgumuni committed the greatest offense by touching the chest of the Lord with his foot in the presence of the goddess of fortune. Of course, Lord Viṣṇu is all-merciful. He did not become angry at the activities of Bhṛgumuni because Bhṛgumuni was a great *brāhmaṇa.* A *brāhmaṇa* is to be excused even if he sometimes commits an offense, and Lord Viṣṇu set the example. Yet it is said that from the time of this incident, the goddess of fortune, Lakṣmī, has not been very favorably disposed towards the *brāhmaṇas,* and therefore because the goddess of fortune witholds her benedictions from them, the *brāhmaṇas* are generally very poor. Bhṛgumuni's touching the chest of Lord Viṣṇu with his foot was certainly a great offense, but Lord Viṣṇu is so great that He did not care. The so-called *brāhmaṇas* of the Kali-yuga are sometimes very proud that they can touch the chest of Lord Viṣṇu with their feet. But when Bhṛgumuni touched the chest of Lord Viṣṇu with his feet, it was different because although it was the greatest offense, Lord Viṣṇu, being greatly magnanimous, did not take it very seriously.

Instead of being angry or cursing Bhṛgumuni, Lord Viṣṇu immediately got up from His bed along with His wife, the goddess of fortune, and offered respectful obeisances to the *brāhmaṇa.* He addressed Bhṛgumuni as follows: "My dear *brāhmaṇa,* it is a great blessing for Me that you have come here. Please, therefore, sit down on this cushion for a few minutes. My dear *brāhmaṇa,* I am very sorry that when you first entered I could not receive you properly. It was a great offense on My part, and I beg you to pardon Me. You are so pure and great that the water which washes your feet can purify even the places of pilgrimage. Therefore, I request you to purify the Vaikuṇṭha planet where I live with My associates. My dear father, O great sage, I know that your feet are very soft, like a lotus flower, and that My chest is as hard as a thunderbolt. I am therefore afraid that you may have felt some pain by touching My chest with your feet. Let Me therefore touch your feet to relieve the pain you have suffered." Lord Viṣṇu then began to massage the feet of Bhṛgumuni.

The Lord continued to address Bhṛgumuni. "My dear lord," He said, "My chest has now become sanctified because of the touch of your feet, and I am now assured that the goddess of fortune, Lakṣmī, will be very glad to live there perpetually." Another name for Lakṣmī is Cañcalā. She does not stay in one place for a long time. Therefore, we see that a rich man's family sometimes becomes poor after a few generations, and sometimes we see that a poor man's family becomes very rich. Lakṣmī, the goddess of fortune, is Cañcalā in this material world, whereas in the Vaikuṇṭha planets she eternally lives at the lotus feet of the Lord. Because Lakṣmī is famous as Cañcalā, Lord Nārāyaṇa indicated that she might not have been living perpetually by His chest, but because His chest had been touched by the feet of Bhṛgumuni, it was now sanctified, and there was no chance that the goddess of fortune would leave. Bhṛgumuni, however, could understand his position and that of the Lord, and he was struck with wonder at the behavior of the Supreme Personality of Godhead. Because of his gratitude, his voice choked up, and he was not able to reply to the words of the Lord. Tears glided from his eyes, and he could not say anything. He simply stood silently before the Lord.

After testing Lord Brahmā, Lord Śiva and Lord Viṣṇu, Bhṛgumuni returned to the assembly of great sages on the bank of the River Sarasvatī and described his experience. After hearing him with great attention, the sages concluded that of all the predominating deities, certainly Viṣṇu is situated in the mode of goodness in the highest degree. In the *Śrīmad-Bhāgavatam,* these great sages are described as *brahma-vādinām. Brahma-vādinām* means those who talk about the Absolute Truth but have not yet come to a conclusion. Generally *brahma-vādi* refers to the impersonalists or to those who are students of the *Vedas.* It is to be understood, therefore, that all the gathered sages were serious students of Vedic literature, but had not come to definite conclusions as to who is the Supreme Absolute Personality of Godhead.

After hearing of Bhṛgumuni's experience in meeting all three predominating deities, Lord Śiva, Lord Brahmā, and Lord Viṣṇu, the sages concluded that Lord Viṣṇu is the Supreme Truth, the Personality of Godhead. It is said in the *Śrīmad-Bhāgavatam* that after hearing the details from Bhṛgumuni, the sages were astonished because although Lord Brahmā and Lord Śiva were immediately agitated, Lord Viṣṇu, in spite of being kicked by Bhṛgumuni, was not agitated in the least. The example is given that small lamps may become agitated by a little breeze, but the greatest lamp or the greatest illuminating source, the sun, is never moved, even by the greatest hurricane. One's greatness has to be estimated by one's ability to tolerate provoking situations. The sages gathered on the bank of the River Sarasvatī concluded that if anyone wants actual peace and freedom from all fearfulness, he should take shelter of the lotus feet of Viṣṇu. If Lord Brahmā and Lord Śiva lost their peaceful attitude upon a slight provocation, how could they maintain the peace and tranquility of their devotees? As for Lord Viṣṇu, however, it is stated in the *Bhagavad-gītā* that anyone who accepts Lord Viṣṇu or Kṛṣṇa as the supreme friend attains the highest perfection of peaceful life.

The sages thus concluded that by following the principles of *vaiṣṇava-dharma,* one becomes actually perfect. But if one follows all the religious principles of a particular sect and does not become advanced in understanding the Supreme Personality of Godhead, Viṣṇu, all such labor of love is fruitless. To execute religious principles means to come to the platform of perfect knowledge. If one comes to the platform of perfect knowledge, then he will be disinterested in material affairs. Perfect knowledge means to know one's own self and to know the Supreme Self. The Supreme Self and the individual self, although one in quality, are different in quantity. This analytical understanding of knowledge is perfect. Simply to understand, "I am not matter; I am spirit," is not perfect knowledge. The real religious principle is devotional service, or *bhakti.* This is confirmed in the *Bhagavad-gītā.* Lord Kṛṣṇa says, "Give up all other religious principles and simply surrender unto Me." Therefore, the term *dharma* applies only to the *vaiṣṇava-dharma* or *bhagavad-dharma,* following which all other good qualities and advancements in life are automatically achieved.

The highest perfectional knowledge is to know the Supreme Lord. He cannot be understood by any process of religion other than devotional service; therefore, the immediate result of perfect knowledge is achieved by executing devotional service. After attainment of knowledge, one becomes disinterested in the material world. This is not because of dry philosophical speculation. The devotees become disinterested in the material world, not simply because of theoretical understanding, but practical experience. When a devotee realizes the effect of association with the Supreme Lord, he naturally hates the association of so-called society, friendship and love. This detachment is not dry, but is due to achieving a higher status of life by relishing transcendental mellows. It is further stated in the *Śrīmad-Bhāgavatam* that after attainment of such knowledge and detachment from material sense gratification, one's advancement in the eight opulences attained by mystic *yoga* practice, namely the *aṇimā, laghimā* and *prāpti siddhis,* etc., are also achieved without separate effort. The perfect example is Mahārāja Ambarīṣa. He was not a mystic *yogī* but was a great devotee, yet in a disagreement with Mahārāja Ambarīṣa, the great mystic Durvāsā was defeated in the presence of his devotional attitude. In other words, a devotee does not need to practice the mystic *yoga* system to achieve power. The power is behind him by the grace of the Lord, just as when a small child is surrendered to a powerful father, all the powers of the father are behind him.

When a person becomes famous as a devotee of the Lord, his reputation is never to be extinguished. Lord Caitanya, when discoursing with Rāmānanda Rāya, questioned, "What is the greatest fame?" Rāmānanda Rāya replied that to be known as a pure devotee of Lord Kṛṣṇa is the perfect fame. The conclusion, therefore, is that Viṣṇu-*dharma,* or the religion of devotional service unto the Supreme Personality of Godhead, is meant for persons who are thoughtful. By proper utilization of thoughtfulness, one comes to the stage of thinking of the Supreme Personality of Godhead. By thinking of the Supreme Personality of Godhead, one becomes free from the contamination of the faulty association of the material world, and thus one becomes peaceful. The world is in a disturbed condition because of a scarcity of such peaceful devotees in human society. Unless one is a devotee, one cannot be equal to all living entities. A devotee is equally disposed towards the animals, the human beings and all living entities because he sees every living entity as a part and parcel of the Supreme Lord. In the *Īśopaniṣad* it is clearly stated that one who has come to the stage of seeing all living beings equally does not hate anyone or favor anyone. The devotee does not hanker to possess more than he requires. Devotees are therefore *akiñcana;* in any condition of life a devotee is satisfied. It is said that a devotee is evenminded whether he is in hell or in heaven. A devotee is callous to all subjects other than his engagement in devotional service. This mode of life is the highest perfectional stage, from which one can be elevated to the spiritual world, back home, back to Godhead. The devotees of the Supreme Personality of Godhead are especially attracted by the highest material quality, goodness, and the qualified *brāhmaṇa* is the symbolic representation of this goodness. Therefore, a devotee is attached to the brahminical stage of life. He is not very much interested in passion or ignorance, although these qualities also emanate from the Supreme Lord, Viṣṇu. In the *Śrīmad-Bhāgavatam* the devotees are described as *nipuṇa-buddhayaḥ,* which means that they are the most intelligent class of men. Uninfluenced by attachment or hatred, the devotee lives very peacefully and is not agitated by the influence of passion and ignorance.

It may be questioned here why a devotee should be attached to the quality of goodness in the material world if he is transcendental to all material qualities. The answer is that there are different kinds of people existing in the modes of material nature. Those who are in the mode of ignorance are called *rākṣasas,* those in the mode of passion are called *asuras,* and those in the mode of goodness are called *suras,* or demigods. Under the direction of the Supreme Lord, these three classes of men are created by material nature, but those who are in the mode of goodness have a greater chance to be elevated to the spiritual world, back home, back to Godhead.

Thus all the sages who assembled on the bank of the River Sarasvatī to try to determine who is the supreme predominating Deity became freed from all doubts about Viṣṇu worship. All of them thereafter engaged in devotional service, and thus they achieved the desired result and went back to Godhead.

Those who are actually anxious to become liberated from material entanglement would do better to accept at once the conclusion given by

Śrī Śukadeva Gosvāmī in the beginning of the *Śrīmad-Bhāgavatam.* It is said there that hearing the *Śrīmad-Bhāgavatam* is extremely conducive to liberation because it is spoken by Śukadeva Gosvāmī. The same fact is again confirmed by Sūta Gosvāmī: if anyone who is travelling aimlessly within this material world cares to hear the nectarean words spoken by Śukadeva Gosvāmī, certainly he will come to the right conclusion; simply by discharging devotional service to the Supreme Personality of Godhead he will be able to stop the fatigue of migrating from one material body to another perpetually. In other words, by proper hearing one will become fixed in loving devotional service to Viṣṇu. He will certainly be able to get relief from this material journey of life, and the process is very simple. One has to give aural reception to the sweet words spoken by Śukadeva Gosvāmī in the form of *Śrīmad-Bhāgavatam.*

Another conclusion is that we should never consider the demigods, even Lord Śiva and Lord Brahmā, to be on an equal level with Lord Viṣṇu. If we do this, then according to *Padma Purāṇa,* we immediately become atheists. In the Vedic literature known as *Harivaṁśa* it is also stated that only the Supreme Personality of Godhead, Viṣṇu, is to be worshiped. The Hare Kṛṣṇa *mahāmantra,* or any such Viṣṇu *mantra,* is always to be chanted. In the Second Canto of *Śrīmad-Bhāgavatam,* Lord Brahmā says, "Both Lord Śiva and myself are engaged by the Supreme Personality of Godhead to act in different capacities under His direction." In the *Caitanya-caritāmṛta* it is also stated that the only master is Kṛṣṇa, and everyone in all categories of life are servants of Kṛṣṇa only.

In the *Bhagavad-gītā* it is confirmed by the Lord that there is no truth superior to Kṛṣṇa. Śukadeva Gosvāmī also, in order to draw attention to the fact that among all *Viṣṇu-tattva* forms, Lord Kṛṣṇa is one hundred percent the Supreme Personality of Godhead, narrated the story of an incident which took place when Lord Kṛṣṇa was present.

Once upon a time, a *brāhmaṇa's* wife gave birth to a child. Unfortunately, however, just after being born and touching the ground, the child immediately died. The *brāhmaṇa* father took the dead child and went directly to Dvārakā to the palace of the king. The *brāhmaṇa* was very upset because of the untimely death of the child in the presence of his young father and mother. Thus his mind became very disturbed. Formerly, when there were responsible kings, up to the time of Dvāpara-yuga, when Lord Kṛṣṇa was present, the king was liable to be blamed for the untimely death of a child in the presence of his parents. Similarly, such responsibility was there during the time of Lord Rāmacandra. As we have explained in the First Canto of *Śrīmad-Bhāgavatam,* the king was so responsible for the comforts of the citizens that he was to see that there was not even excessive heat or cold. Although there was no fault on the part of the king, the *brāhmaṇa* whose child had died immediately went to the palace door and began to accuse the king as follows.

"The present king, Ugrasena, is envious of the *brāhmaṇas!*" The exact word used in this connection is *brāhma-dviṣaḥ*. One who is envious of the *Vedas* or one who is envious of a qualified *brāhmaṇa* or the *brāhmana* caste is called *brahma-dvit*. So the King was accused of being *brahma-dvit*. He was also accused of being *śaṭha-dhī*, falsely intelligent. The executive head of a state must be very intelligent to see to the comforts of the citizens, but, according to the *brāhmaṇa* the king was not at all intelligent, although he was occupying the royal throne. Therefore he also called him *lubdha*, which means greedy. In other words, a king or an executive head of state should not occupy the exalted post of presidency or kingship if he is greedy and self-interested. But it is natural that an executive head becomes self-interested when he is attached to material enjoyment. Therefore, another word used here is *viṣayātmanaḥ*.

The *brāhmaṇa* also accused the king of being *kṣatra-bandhu*, which refers to a person born in the family of *kṣatriyas* or the royal order who is without the qualifications of a royal personality. A king should protect brahminical culture and should be very alert to the welfare of his citizens; he should not be greedy due to attachment to material enjoyment. If a person with no qualifications represents himself as a *kṣatriya* of the royal order, he is not called a *kṣatriya*, but a *kṣatra-bandhu*. Similarly, if a person is born of a *brāhmaṇa* father but has no brahminical qualification, he is called *brahma-bandhu*, or *dvija-bandhu*. This means that a *brāhmaṇa* or a *kṣatriya* is not accepted simply by birth. One has to qualify himself for the particular position; only then is he accepted as a *brāhmaṇa* or a *kṣatriya*.

Thus the *brāhmaṇa* accused the king that his newly born baby was dead due to the disqualifications of the king. The *brāhmaṇa* took it most unnaturally, and therefore he held the king to be responsible. We also find in Vedic history that if a *kṣatriya* king were irresponsible, sometimes a consulting board of *brāhmaṇas* maintained by the monarchy would dethrone him. Considering all these points, it appears that the post of monarch in the Vedic civilization is a very responsible one.

The *brāhmaṇa* therefore said, "No one should offer respects or worship to a king whose only business is envy. Such a king spends his time either hunting and killing animals in the forest or killing citizens for criminal acts. He has no self-control and possesses bad character. If such a king is worshiped or honored by the citizens, the citizens will never be happy. They will always remain poor, full of anxieties and aggrievement, and always unhappy." Although in modern politics the post of monarch is abolished, the president is not held responsible for the comforts of the citizens. In this age of Kali, the executive head of a state somehow or other gets votes and is elected to an exalted post, but the condition of the citizens continues to be full of anxiety, distress, unhappiness, and dissatisfaction.

The *brāhmaṇa's* second child was also born dead, and the third also. He had nine children, and each of them was born dead, and each time he came to the gate of the palace to accuse the King. When the *brāhmaṇa* came to accuse the King of Dvārakā for the ninth time, Arjuna happened to be present with Kṛṣṇa. On hearing that a *brāhmaṇa* was accusing the King of not properly protecting him, Arjuna became inquisitive and approached the *brāhmaṇa.* He said, "My dear *brāhmaṇa,* why do you say that there are no proper *kṣatriyas* to protect the citizens of your country? Is there not even someone who can pretend to be a *kṣatriya,* who can carry a bow and arrow at least to make a show of protection? Do you think that all the royal personalities in this country simply engage in performing sacrifices with the *brāhmaṇas* but have no chivalrous power?" Thus Arjuna indicated that *kṣatriyas* should not sit back comfortably and engage only in performing Vedic rituals. Rather, they must be very chivalrous in protecting the citizens. *Brāhmaṇas,* being engaged in spiritual activities, are not expected to do anything which requires physical endeavor. Therefore, they need to be protected by the *kṣatriyas* so that they will not be disturbed in the execution of their higher occupational duties.

"If the *brāhmaṇas* feel unwanted separation from their wives and children," Arjuna continued, "and the *kṣatriya* kings do not take care of them, then such *kṣatriyas* are to be considered no more than stage players. In dramatical performances in the theater, an actor may play the part of a king, but no one expects any benefits from such a make-believe king. Similarly, if the king or the executive head of a state cannot give protection to the head of the social structure, he is considered merely a bluffer. Such executive heads simply live for their own livelihood while occupying exalted posts as chiefs of state. My lord, I promise that I shall give protection to your children, and if I am unable to do so, then I shall enter into blazing fire so that the sinful contamination which has infected me will be counteracted."

Upon hearing Arjuna speak in this way, the *brāhmaṇa* replied, "My dear Arjuna, Lord Balarāma is present, but He could not give protection to my children. Lord Kṛṣṇa is also present, but He also could not give them protection. There are also many other heroes, such as Pradyumna and Aniruddha, carrying bows and arrows, but they could not protect my children." The *brāhmaṇa* directly hinted that Arjuna could not do that which was impossible for the Supreme Personality of Godhead. He felt that Arjuna was promising something beyond his power. The *brāhmaṇa* said, "I consider your promise to be like that of an inexperienced child. I cannot put my faith in your promise."

Arjuna then understood that the *brāhmaṇa* had lost all faith in the *kṣatriya* kings. Therefore, to encourage him, Arjuna spoke as if criticizing even his friend, Lord Kṛṣṇa. While Lord Kṛṣṇa and others were listening, he specifically attacked Kṛṣṇa by saying, "My dear *brāhmaṇa,* I am neither Saṅkarṣaṇa nor Kṛṣṇa nor one of Kṛṣṇa's sons like Pradyumna or Aniruddha. My name is Arjuna, and I carry the bow known as Gāṇḍīva. You cannot insult me because I have satisfied even Lord Śiva by my prowess when we were both hunting in the forest. I had a fight with Lord Śiva, who appeared before me as a hunter, and when I satisfied him by my prowess, he gave me the weapon known as *paśupatāstra.* Do not doubt my chivalry. I shall bring back your sons even if I have to fight with death personified." When the *brāhmaṇa* was assured by Arjuna in such exalted words, he somehow or other was convinced, and thus he returned home.

When the *brāhmaṇa's* wife was to give birth to another child, the *brāhmaṇa* began to chant, "My dear Arjuna, please come now and save my child." After hearing him, Arjuna immediately prepared himself by touching sanctified water and uttering holy *mantras* to protect his bows and arrows from danger. He specifically took the arrow which was presented to him by Lord Śiva, and while going out, he began to remember Lord Śiva and his great favor. In this way, he appeared in front of the maternity home, equipped with his bow, known as Gāṇḍīva, and with various other weapons.

It appears that Arjuna did not leave Dvārakā because he had to fulfill his promise to the *brāhmaṇa.* He was called at night when the *brāhmaṇa's* wife was to give birth to the child. While going to the maternity home to attend to the delivery case of the *brāhmaṇa's* wife, Arjuna remembered Lord Śiva, and not his friend Kṛṣṇa; he thought that since Kṛṣṇa could not give protection to the *brāhmaṇa,* it was better to take shelter of Lord Śiva. This is another instance of how a person takes shelter of the demigods. This is explained in the *Bhagavad-gītā: kāmais tais tair hṛta-jñānāḥ:* a person who loses his intelligence because of greediness and lust forgets the Supreme Personality of Godhead and takes shelter of the demigods. Of course, Arjuna was not an ordinary living entity, but because of his friendly dealings with Kṛṣṇa, he thought that Kṛṣṇa was unable to give protection to the *brāhmaṇa* and that he would do better to remember Lord Śiva. Later on it was proved that Arjuna's taking shelter of Lord Śiva instead of Kṛṣṇa was not at all successful. Arjuna, however, did his best by chanting different *mantras,* and he took up his bow to guard the maternity home from all directions.

The *brāhmaṇa's* wife delivered a male child, and as usual the child began to cry. But suddenly, within a few minutes, both the child and Arjuna's arrows disappeared in the sky. It appeared that the *brāhmaṇa's* house was near Kṛṣṇa's residence and that Lord Kṛṣṇa was enjoying everything that was taking place apparently in defiance of His authority. It was He who played the trick of taking away the *brāhmana's* baby as well as the arrows, including the one given by Lord Śiva, of which Arjuna was so proud. *Tad bhavati alpamedhasām:* less intelligent men take shelter of the demigods due to bewilderment and are satisfied with the benefits they award.

In the presence of Lord Kṛṣṇa and others, the *brāhmaṇa* began to accuse Arjuna: "Everyone see my foolishness! I put my faith in the words of Arjuna, who is impotent and who is expert only in false promises. How foolish I was to believe Arjuna. He promised to protect my child when even Pradyumna, Aniruddha, Lord Balarāma and Lord Kṛṣṇa failed. If such great personalities could not protect my child, then who can do so? I therefore condemn Arjuna for his false promise, and I also condemn his celebrated bow Gāṇḍīva and his impudency in declaring himself greater than Lord Balarāma, Lord Kṛṣṇa, Pradyumna and Aniruddha. No one can save my child, for he has already been transferred to another planet. Due to sheer foolishness only, Arjuna thought that he could bring back my child from another planet."

Thus condemned by the *brāhmaṇa,* Arjuna empowered himself with a mystic *yoga* perfection so that he could travel to any planet to find the *brāhmaṇa's* baby. It seems that Arjuna had mastered the mystic yogic power by which *yogīs* can travel to any planet they desire. He first of all went to the planet known as Yamaloka, where the superintendent of death, Yamarāja, lives. There he searched for the *brāhmaṇa's* baby, but he was unable to find him. He then immediately went to the planet where the King of heaven, Indra, lives. When he was unable to find the baby there, he went to the planets of the fire demigods, Nairṛti, and then to the moon planet. Then he went to Vāyu and to Varuṇaloka. When he was unable to find the baby in those planets, he went down to the Rasātala planet, the lowest of the planetary systems. After traveling to all these different planets, he finally went to Brahmaloka, where even the mystic *yogīs* cannot go. By the grace of Lord Kṛṣṇa, Arjuna had that power, and he went above the heavenly planets to Brahmaloka. When he was unable to find the baby even after searching all possible planets, he then attempted to throw himself into a fire, as he had promised the *brāhmaṇa* if unable to bring back his baby. Lord Kṛṣṇa, however, was very kind toward Arjuna because Arjuna happened to be the most intimate friend of the Lord. Lord Kṛṣṇa persuaded Arjuna not to enter the fire in disgrace. Kṛṣṇa indicated that since Arjuna was His friend, if he were to enter the fire in hopelessness, indirectly it would be a blemish on Him. Lord Kṛṣṇa therefore checked Arjuna, assuring him that He would find the baby. He told Arjuna, "Do not foolishly commit suicide."

After addressing Arjuna in this way, Lord Kṛṣṇa called for His transcendental chariot. He mounted it along with Arjuna and began to proceed north. Lord Kṛṣṇa, the all-powerful Personality of Godhead, could have brought the child back without effort, but we should always remember that He was playing the part of a human being. As a human being has to endeavor to achieve certain results, so Lord Kṛṣṇa, like an ordinary human being, or like His friend Arjuna, left Dvārakā to bring back the *brāhmaṇa's* baby. By appearing in human society and exhibiting His pastimes as a human being, Kṛṣṇa definitely showed that there was not a single personality greater than He. "God is great." That is the definition of the Supreme Personality of Godhead. So at least within this material world, while He was present, Kṛṣṇa proved that there was no greater personality within the universe.

Seated on His chariot with Arjuna, Kṛṣṇa began to proceed north, crossing over many planetary systems. These are described in the *Śrīmad-Bhāgavatam* as *sapta-dvīpa. Dvīpa* means island. All these planets are sometimes described in the Vedic literature as *dvīpas.* The planet on which we are living is called Jambūdvīpa. Outer space is taken as a great ocean of air, and within that great ocean of air there are many islands, which are the different planets. In each and every planet there are oceans also. In some of the planets, the oceans are of salt water, and in some of them there are oceans of milk. In others there are oceans of liquor, and in others there are oceans of ghee or oil. There are different kinds of mountains also. Each and every planet has a different type of atmosphere.

Kṛṣṇa passed over all these planets and reached the covering of the universe. This covering is described in the *Śrīmad-Bhāgavatam* as great darkness. This material world as a whole is described as dark. In the open space there is sunlight, and therefore it is illuminated, but in the covering, because of the absence of sunlight, it is naturally dark. When Kṛṣṇa approached the covering layer of this universe, the four horses which were drawing His chariot—Śaibya, Sugrīva, Meghapuṣpa and Balāhaka—all appeared to hesitate to enter the darkness. This hesitation is also a part of the pastimes of Lord Kṛṣṇa because the horses of Kṛṣṇa are not ordinary. It is not possible for ordinary horses to go all over the universe and then enter into its outer covering layers. As Kṛṣṇa is transcendental, similarly His chariot and His horses and everything about Him are also transcendental, beyond the qualities of this material world. We should always remember that Kṛṣṇa was playing the part of an ordinary human being, and His horses also, by the will of Kṛṣṇa, played the parts of ordinary horses in hesitating to enter the darkness.

Kṛṣṇa is known as Yogeśvara, as is stated in the last portion of *Bhagavad-gītā. Yogeśvara Hari:* all mystic powers are under His control. In our experience, we can see many human beings who have yogic mystic power. Sometimes they perform very wonderful acts, but Kṛṣṇa is understood to be the master of all mystic power. Therefore, when He saw that His horses were hesitant to proceed into the darkness, He immediately released His disc, known as the Sudarśana cakra, which illuminated the sky a thousand times brighter than sunlight. The darkness of the covering of the universe is also a creation of Kṛṣṇa's, and the Sudarśana cakra is Kṛṣṇa's constant companion. Thus the darkness was penetrated by His keeping the Sudarśana cakra in front. *Śrīmad-Bhāgavatam* states that the Sudarśana cakra penetrated the darkness just as an arrow released from the Śārṅga bow of Lord Rāmacandra penetrated the army of Rāvaṇa. *Su* means very nice, and *darśana* means observation; by the grace of Lord Kṛṣṇa's disc, Sudarśana, everything can be seen very nicely, and nothing can remain in darkness. Thus Lord Kṛṣṇa and Arjuna crossed over the great region of darkness covering the material universes.

Arjuna then saw the effulgence of light known as the *brahmajyoti.* The *brahmajyoti* is situated outside the covering of the material universes, and because it cannot be seen with our present eyes, this *brahmajyoti* is sometimes called *avyakta.* This spiritual effulgence is the ultimate destination of the impersonalists known as Vedāntists. The *brahmajyoti* is also described as *anantapāram,* unlimited and unfathomed. When Lord Kṛṣṇa and Arjuna reached this region of the *brahmajyoti,* Arjuna could not tolerate the glaring effulgence, and he closed his eyes. Lord Kṛṣṇa's and Arjuna's reaching the *brahmajyoti* region is described in *Harivaṁśa.* In that portion of the Vedic literature, Kṛṣṇa informed Arjuna, "My dear Arjuna, the glaring effulgence, the transcendental light which you are seeing, is My bodily rays. O chief of the descendants of Bharata, this *brahmajyoti* is Myself." As the sun disc and the sunshine cannot be separated, similarly Kṛṣṇa and His bodily rays, the *brahmajyoti,* cannot be separated. Thus Kṛṣṇa claimed that the *brahmajyoti* is He Himself. This is clearly stated in the *Harivaṁśa* when Kṛṣṇa says, *"ahaṁ saḥ."* The *brahmajyoti* is a combination of the minute particles known as spiritual sparks, or the living entities known as *citkana.* The Vedic word *so'ham,* or "I am the *brahmajyoti,"* can also be applied to the living entities, who can also claim to belong to the *brahmajyoti.* In the *Harivaṁśa,* Kṛṣṇa further explains, "This *brahmajyoti* is an expansion of My spiritual energy."

Kṛṣṇa told Arjuna, "The *brahmajyoti* is beyond the region of My external energy, known as *māyā-śakti."* When one is situated within this material world, it is not possible for him to experience this Brahman effulgence. Therefore, in the material world this effulgence is not manifested, whereas in the spiritual world, it is manifested. That is the purport of the words *vyakta-avyakta.* In the *Bhagavad-gītā* it is said *avyakto-'vyaktāt sanātanaḥ:* both these energies are eternally manifested.

After this, Lord Kṛṣṇa and Arjuna entered a vast extensive spiritual water. This spiritual water is called the Kāraṇārṇava Ocean or Virajā which means that this ocean is the origin of the creation of the material world. In the *Mṛtyuñjaya Tantra,* a Vedic literature, there is a vivid description of this Kāraṇa Ocean, or Virajā. It is stated there that the highest planetary system within the material world is Satyaloka, or Brahmaloka. Beyond that there are Rudraloka and Mahā-Viṣṇuloka. Regarding this Mahā-Viṣṇuloka, it is stated in the *Brahma-saṁhitā, yaḥ kāraṇārṇava-jale bhajati sma yoga:* "Lord Mahā-Viṣṇu is lying in the Kāraṇa Ocean. When He exhales, innumerable universes come into existence, and when He inhales, innumerable universes enter within Him." In this way, the material creation is generated and again withdrawn. When Lord Kṛṣṇa and Arjuna entered the water, it appeared that there was a strong hurricane of transcendental effulgence brewing, and the water of the Kāraṇa Ocean was greatly agitated. By the grace of Lord Kṛṣṇa, Arjuna had the unique experience of being able to see the very beautiful Kāraṇa Ocean.

Accompanied by Kṛṣṇa, Arjuna saw a large palace within the water. There were many thousands of pillars and columns made of valuable jewels, and the glaring effulgence of those columns was so beautiful that Arjuna became charmed by it. Within that palace, Arjuna and Kṛṣṇa saw the gigantic form of Anantadeva, who is also known as Śeṣa. Lord Anantadeva or Śeṣanāga was in the form of a great serpent with thousands of hoods, and each one of them was decorated with valuable, effulgent jewels, which were beautifully dazzling. Each of Anantadeva's hoods had two eyes which appeared to be very fearful. His body was as white as the mountaintop of Kailāsa, which is always covered by snow. His neck was bluish, as were His tongues. Thus Arjuna saw the Śeṣanāga form, and he also saw that on the very soft, white body of Śeṣanāga, Lord Mahā-Viṣṇu was lying very comfortably. He appeared to be all-pervading and very powerful, and Arjuna could understand that the Supreme Personality of Godhead in that form is known as Puruṣottama. He is known as Puruṣottama, the best, or the Supreme Personality of Godhead, because from this form emanates another form of Viṣṇu, which is known as Garbhodakaśāyī Viṣṇu within the material world. The Mahā-Viṣṇu form of the Lord, *Puruṣottama,* is beyond the material world. He is also known as *Uttama. Tama* means darkness, and *ut* means above, transcendental; therefore, *Uttama* means above the darkest region of the material world. Arjuna saw that the bodily color of Puruṣottama, Mahā-Viṣṇu, was as dark as a new cloud in the rainy season; He was dressed in very nice yellow clothing. His face was always beautifully smiling, and His eyes, which were like lotus petals, were very attractive. Lord Mahā-Viṣṇu's helmet was bedecked with valuable jewels, and His beautiful earrings enhanced the beauty of the curling hair on His head. Lord Mahā-Viṣṇu had eight arms, all very long, reaching to His knees. His neck was decorated with the Kaustubha jewel, and His chest was marked with the symbol of *śrīvatsa,* which means the resting place of the goddess of fortune. The Lord wore a garland of lotus flowers down to His knees. This long garland is known as a *vaijayantī* garland.

The Lord was surrounded by His personal associates Nanda and Sunanda, and the personified Sudarśana disc was also standing by Him. As is stated in the *Vedas,* the Lord has innumerable energies, and they were also standing there personified. The most important among them were as follows: *puṣṭi,* the energy for nourishment, *śrī,* the energy of beauty, *kīrti,* the energy of reputation, and *ajā,* the energy of material creation. All these energies are invested in the administrators of the material world, namely Lord Brahmā, Lord Śiva and Lord Viṣṇu, and in the kings of the heavenly planets, Indra, Candra, Varuṇa and the sun-god. In other words, all these demigods, being empowered by the Lord with certain energies, engage in the transcendental loving service of the Supreme Personality of Godhead. The Mahā-Viṣṇu feature is an expansion of Kṛṣṇa's body. It is also confirmed in the *Brahma-saṁhitā* that Mahā-Viṣṇu is a portion of a plenary expansion of Kṛṣṇa. All such expansions are nondifferent from the Personality of Godhead, but since Kṛṣṇa appeared within this material world to manifest His pastimes as a human being, He and Arjuna immediately offered their respects to Lord Mahā-Viṣṇu by bowing down before Him. It is stated in the *Śrīmad-Bhāgavatam* that Lord Kṛṣṇa offered respect to Mahā-Viṣṇu; this means that He offered obeisances unto Him only because Lord Mahā-Viṣṇu is nondifferent from He Himself. This offering of obeisances by Kṛṣṇa to Mahā-Viṣṇu is not, however, the form of worship known as *ahaṅgraha-upāsanā,* which is sometimes recommended for persons who are trying to elevate themselves to the spiritual world by performing the sacrifice of knowledge. This is also stated in the *Bhagavad-gītā: jñāna-yajñena cāpy ante yajanto mām upāsate.*

Although there was no necessity for Kṛṣṇa to offer obeisances, because He is the master teacher, He taught Arjuna just how respect should be offered to Lord Mahā-Viṣṇu. Arjuna, however, became very much afraid upon seeing the gigantic form of everything, distinct from the material experience. Seeing Kṛṣṇa offering obeisances to Lord Mahā-Viṣṇu, he immediately followed Him and stood before the Lord with folded hands. After this, the gigantic form of Mahā-Viṣṇu, greatly pleased, smiled pleasingly and spoke as follows.

"My dear Kṛṣṇa and Arjuna, I was very anxious to see you both, and therefore I arranged to take away the babies of the *brāhmaṇa* and keep them here. I have been expecting to see you both at this palace. You have appeared in the material world as My incarnations in order to minimize the force of the demoniac persons who burden the world. Now after killing all these unwanted demons, you will please again come back to Me. Both of you are incarnations of the great sage Nara-Nārāyaṇa. Although you are both complete in yourselves, to protect the devotees and to annihilate the demons and especially to establish religious principles in the world so that peace and tranquility may continue, you are teaching the basic principles of factual religion so that the people of the world may follow you and thereby be peaceful and prosperous."

Both Lord Kṛṣṇa and Arjuna then offered their obeisances to Lord Mahā-Viṣṇu, and taking back the *brāhmaṇa's* children, they returned to Dvārakā via the same route by which they had entered the spiritual world. All the children of the *brāhmaṇa* had duly grown up. After returning to Dvārakā, Lord Kṛṣṇa and Arjuna delivered to the *brāhmaṇa* all of his sons.

Arjuna, however, was struck with great wonder after visiting the transcendental world by the grace of Lord Kṛṣṇa. And by the grace of Kṛṣṇa he could understand that whatever opulence there may be within this material world is an emanation from Him. Any opulent position a person may have within this material world is due to Kṛṣṇa's mercy. One should therefore always be in Kṛṣṇa consciousness, in complete gratefulness to Lord Kṛṣṇa, because whatever one may possess is all His mercy.

Arjuna's wonderful experience due to the mercy of Kṛṣṇa is one of the many thousands of pastimes performed by Lord Kṛṣṇa during His stay in this material world. They were all unique and have no parallel in the history of the world. All these pastimes prove fully that Kṛṣṇa is the Supreme Personality of Godhead, yet while He was present within this material world, He played just like an ordinary man possessing many worldly duties. He played the part of an ideal householder, and although He possessed 16,000 wives, 16,000 palaces and 160,000 children, He also performed many sacrifices, just to teach the royal order how to live in the material world for the welfare of humanity. As the ideal Supreme Personality, He fulfilled the desires of everyone, from the *brāhmaṇas*, the highest persons in human society, down to the ordinary living entities, including the lowest of men. Just as King Indra is in charge of distributing rain all over the world to satisfy everyone in due course, so Lord Kṛṣṇa satisfies everyone by pouring down His causeless mercy. His mission was to give protection to the devotees and to kill the demoniac kings; therefore, He killed many hundreds and thousands of demons. Some of them He killed personally, and some of them were killed by Arjuna, who was deputed by Kṛṣṇa. In this way He established many pious kings such as Yudhiṣṭhira at the helm of world affairs. Thus, by His divine arrangement He created the good government of King Yudhiṣṭhira, and there ensued peace and tranquility.

Thus ends the Bhaktivedanta purport of the Third Volume, Twentieth Chapter, of Kṛṣṇa, *"The Superexcellent Power of Kṛṣṇa."*

21/ Summary Description of Lord Kṛṣṇa's Pastimes

After returning from the spiritual kingdom, which he was able to visit personally along with Kṛṣṇa, Arjuna was very much astonished. He thought to himself that although he was only an ordinary living entity, by the grace of Kṛṣṇa it had been possible for him to see personally the spiritual world. Not only had he seen the spiritual world, but he had also personally seen the original Mahā-Viṣṇu, the cause of the material creation. It is said that Kṛṣṇa never goes out of Vṛndāva *Vṛndāvanaṁ parityajya na pādam ekaṁ gacchati.* Kṛṣṇa is supreme in Mathurā, He is more supreme in Dvārakā, and He is most supreme in Vṛndāvana. Kṛṣṇa's pastimes in Dvārakā are displayed by His Vāsudeva portion, yet there is no difference between the Vāsudeva portion manifested in Mathurā and Dvārakā and the original manifestation of Kṛṣṇa at Vṛndāvana. In the beginning of this book we have discussed that when Kṛṣṇa appears, all His incarnations, plenary portions and portions of the plenary portions come with Him. Thus some of His different pastimes are manifested not by the original Kṛṣṇa Himself but by His different portions and plenary portions of incarnation. Arjuna was therefore puzzled about how Kṛṣṇa went to see the Kāraṇārṇavaśāyī Viṣṇu in the spiritual world. This iṣ fully discussed in the commentaries of Śrīla Viśvanātha Cakravartī Ṭhākur.

It is understood from the speech of Mahā-Viṣṇu that He was very anxious to see Kṛṣṇa. It may be said, however, that since Mahā-Viṣṇu took away the *brāhmaṇa's* sons, He certainly must have gone to Dvārakā to do so. Therefore, why did He not see Kṛṣṇa there? A possible answer is that Kṛṣṇa cannot be seen even by the Mahā-Viṣṇu who is lying in the Causal Ocean of the spiritual world, unless Kṛṣṇa gives His permission. Thus Mahā-Viṣṇu took away the *brāhmaṇa's* sons one after another just after their births so that Kṛṣṇa would come personally to retrieve them and then Mahā-Viṣṇu would be able to see Him there. If that is so, the next question is this: Why would Mahā-Viṣṇu come to Dvārakā personally if He were not able to see Kṛṣṇa? Why did He not send some of His associates to take away the sons of the *brāhmaṇa?* A possible answer is that it is very difficult to put any of the citizens of Dvārakā into trouble in the presence of Kṛṣṇa. Therefore, it was not possible for any of Mahā-Viṣṇu's associates to take away the *brāhmaṇa's* sons, and thus He personally came to take them.

Another question may also be raised: The Lord is known as *brahmaṇya-deva,* the worshipable Deity of the *brāhmaṇas,* so why was He inclined to put a *brāhmaṇa* into such a terrible condition of lamentation over one son after another until the ninth son was taken away? The answer is that Lord Mahā-Viṣṇu was so anxious to see Kṛṣṇa that He did not hesitate even to give trouble to a *brāhmaṇa.* Although giving trouble to a *brāhmaṇa* is a forbidden act, Lord Viṣṇu was prepared to do anything in order to see Kṛṣṇa—He was so anxious to see Him. After losing each of his sons, the *brāhmaṇa* would come to the gate of the palace and accuse the King of not being able to give the *brāhmaṇas* protection and of thus being unfit to sit on the royal throne. It was Mahā-Viṣṇu's plan that the *brāhmaṇa* would accuse the *kṣatriyas* and Kṛṣṇa, and Kṛṣṇa would be obliged to come see Him to take back the *brāhmaṇa's* sons.

Still another question may be raised: If Mahā-Viṣṇu cannot see Kṛṣṇa, then how was Kṛṣṇa obliged to come before Him after all to take back the sons of the *brāhmaṇa?* The answer is that Lord Kṛṣṇa went to see Lord Mahā-Viṣṇu not exactly to take away the sons of the *brāhmaṇa* but only for Arjuna's sake. His friendship with Arjuna was so intimate that when Arjuna prepared himself to die by entering the fire, Kṛṣṇa wanted to give him complete protection. Arjuna, however, would not desist from entering the fire unless the sons of the *brāhmaṇa* were brought back. Therefore Kṛṣṇa promised him, "I will bring back the *brāhmaṇa's* sons. Do not try to commit suicide."

If Lord Kṛṣṇa were going to see Lord Viṣṇu only to reclaim the sons of the *brāhmaṇa,* then He would not have waited until the ninth son was taken. But when the ninth son was taken away by Lord Mahā-Viṣṇu and Arjuna was therefore ready to enter the fire because his promise was going to prove false, that serious situation made Lord Kṛṣṇa decide to go with Arjuna to see Mahā-Viṣṇu. It is said that Arjuna is an empowered incarnation of Nara-Nārāyaṇa. He is even sometimes called Nara-Nārāyaṇa. The Nara-Nārāyaṇa incarnation is also one of Lord Viṣṇu's plenary expansions. Therefore, when Kṛṣṇa and Arjuna went to see Lord Viṣṇu, it is to be understood that Arjuna visited in His Nara-Nārāyaṇa capacity, just as

Kṛṣṇa, when He displayed His pastimes in Dvārakā, acted in His Vāsudeva capacity.

After visiting the spiritual world, Arjuna concluded that whatever opulence anyone can show within the material or spiritual worlds is all a gift of Lord Kṛṣṇa. Lord Kṛṣṇa is manifested in various forms, as *Viṣṇu-tattva* and *jīva-tattva,* or, in other words, as *sāṁśa* and *vibhinnāṁśa. Viṣṇu-tattva* is known as *sāṁśa,* and *jīva-tattva* is known as *vibhinnāṁśa.* He can, therefore, display Himself by His different transcendental pastimes, either in the portion of *sāṁśa* or *vibhinnāṁśa,* as He likes, but still He remains the original Supreme Personality of Godhead.

The concluding portion of Kṛṣṇa's pastimes is found in the Ninetieth Chapter of the Tenth Canto of *Śrīmad-Bhāgavatam,* and in this chapter Śukadeva Gosvāmī wanted to explain how Kṛṣṇa lived happily at Dvārakā with all opulences. Kṛṣṇa's opulence of strength has already been displayed in His different pastimes, and now it will be shown how His residence at Dvārakā displayed His opulences of wealth and beauty. In this material world, which is only a perverted reflection of the spiritual world, the opulences of wealth and beauty are considered to be the highest of all opulences. Therefore, while Kṛṣṇa stayed on this planet as the Supreme Personality of Godhead, His opulences of wealth and beauty had no comparison within the three worlds. Kṛṣṇa enjoyed sixteen thousand beautiful wives, and it is most significant that He lived at Dvārakā as the only husband of these hundreds and thousands of beautiful women. It is specifically stated in this connection that He was the only husband of sixteen thousand wives. It is, of course, not unheard of in the history of the world that a powerful king would keep many hundreds of queens, but although such a king might be the only husband of so many wives, he could not enjoy all of them at one time. Kṛṣṇa, however, enjoyed all of His sixteen thousand wives simultaneously.

Although it may be said that *yogīs* also can expand their bodies into many forms, the *yogīs'* expansion and Lord Kṛṣṇa's expansion are not one and the same. Kṛṣṇa is therefore sometimes called *yogeśvara,* the master of all *yogīs.* In the Vedic literature we find that the *yogī* Saubhari Muni expanded himself into eight. But that expansion was like a television expansion. The television image is manifested in millions of expansions, but those expansions cannot act differently; they are simply reflections of the original and can only act exactly as the original does. Kṛṣṇa's expansion is not material like the expansion of the television or the *yogī.* When Nārada visited the different palaces of Kṛṣṇa, he saw that Kṛṣṇa, in His different expansions, was variously engaged in each and every palace of the queens.

It is also said that Kṛṣṇa lived at Dvārakā as the husband of the goddess of fortune. Queen Rukmiṇī is the goddess of fortune, and all the other queens are her expansions. So Kṛṣṇa, the chief of the Vṛṣṇi dynasty, enjoyed with the goddess of fortune in full opulence. The queens of Kṛṣṇa are described as permanently youthful and beautiful. Although Kṛṣṇa had grandchildren and great-grandchildren, neither Kṛṣṇa nor His queens looked older than sixteen or twenty years of age. The young queens were so beautiful that when they moved they appeared like lightning moving in the sky. They were always dressed with exalted ornaments and garments and were always engaged in sportive activities like dancing, singing or playing ball on the roofs of the palaces. The dancing and tennis playing of girls in the material world appear to be perverted reflections of the original pastimes of the original Personality of Godhead, Kṛṣṇa, and His wives.

The roads and streets of the city of Dvārakā were always crowded with elephants, horses, chariots and infantry soldiers. When elephants are engaged in service, they are given liquor to drink, and it is said that the elephants in Dvārakā were given so much liquor that they would sprinkle a great quantity of it on the road and still would walk on the streets intoxicated. The infantry soldiers passing on the streets were profusely decorated with golden ornaments, and horses and golden chariots plied along the streets. In all directions of Dvārakā City, wherever one would turn his eyes he would find green parks and gardens, and each of them was filled with trees and plants laden with fruits and flowers. Because there were so many nice trees of fruits and flowers, all the sweetly chirping birds and the buzzing bumblebees joined together to make sweet vibrations. The city of Dvārakā thus fully displayed all opulences. The heroes in the dynasty of Yadu used to think themselves the most fortunate residents of the city, and actually they enjoyed all transcendental facilities.

All the sixteen thousand palaces of Kṛṣṇa's queens were situated in this beautiful city of Dvārakā, and Lord Kṛṣṇa, the supreme eternal enjoyer of all these facilities, expanded Himself into sixteen thousand forms and simultaneously engaged in different family affairs in those sixteen thousand palaces. In each and every one of the palaces there were nicely decorated gardens and lakes. The crystal clear water of the lakes contained many blooming lotus flowers of different colors like blue, yellow, white and red, and the saffron powder from the lotus flowers was blown all around by the breeze. All the lakes were full of beautiful swans, ducks and cranes, crying occasionally with melodious sounds. Lord Śrī Kṛṣṇa sometimes entered those lakes, or sometimes the rivers, with His wives and enjoyed swimming pastimes with them in full jubilation. Sometimes the wives of Lord Kṛṣṇa, who were all goddesses of fortune, would embrace the Lord in the midst of the water while swimming or taking bath, and the red vermilion of *kuṅkuma* decorating the beauty of their breasts would adorn the chest of the Lord with a reddish color.

The impersonalists would not dare to believe that in the spiritual world there are such varieties of enjoyment, but in order to demonstrate the factual, ever-blissful enjoyment in the spiritual world, Lord Kṛṣṇa descended on this planet and showed that the spiritual world is not devoid of such pleasurable facilities of life. The only difference is that in the spiritual world such facilities are eternal, never-ending occurrences, whereas in the material world they are simply impermanent perverted reflections. When Lord Kṛṣṇa was engaged in such enjoyment, the Gandharvas and professional musicians would glorify Him with melodious musical concerts, accompanied by *mṛdaṅgas,* drums, kettledrums, stringed instruments and brass bugles, and the whole atmosphere would change into a greatly festive celebration. In a festive mood, the wives of the Lord would sometimes sprinkle water on the Lord's body with a syringe-like instrument, and the Lord would similarly wet the bodies of the queens. When Kṛṣṇa and the queens engaged themselves in these pastimes, it seemed as if the heavenly King, Yakṣarāja, were engaged in such pastimes with his many wives. (Yakṣarāja is also known as Kuvera and is considered to be the treasurer of the heavenly kingdom.) When the wives of Lord Kṛṣṇa thus became wet, their breasts and thighs would increase in beauty a thousand times, and their long hair would fall down to decorate those parts of their bodies. The beautiful flowers which were placed in their hair would fall, and the queens, being seemingly harassed by the Lord's throwing water at them, would approach Him on the plea of snatching the syringe-like instrument, and this attempt would create a situation wherein the Lord could embrace them as they willingly approached Him. Upon being embraced, the wives of the Lord would feel on their mouths a clear indication of conjugal love, and this would create an atmosphere of spiritual bliss. When the garland on the neck of the Lord then touched the breasts of the queens, their whole bodies became covered with saffron yellow. Being engaged in their celestial pastimes, the queens forgot themselves, and their loosened hair appeared like the beautiful waves of a river. When the queens sprinkled water on the body of Kṛṣṇa or He sprinkled water on the bodies of the queens, the whole situation appeared just like an elephant enjoying in a lake along with many she-elephants.

After enjoying fully amongst themselves, the queens and Lord Kṛṣṇa would come out of the water, and their wet garments, which were very valuable, would be given up by them to be taken away by the professional singers and dancers. These singers and dancers had no other means of subsistence than the rewards of valuable garments and ornaments left by the queens and kings on such occasions. The whole system of society was so well planned that all the members of society in their different positions as *brāhmaṇas, kṣatriyas, vaiśyas,* and *śūdras* had no difficulty in earning their livelihood. There was no competition among the divisions of society. The original conception of the caste system was so planned that one group of men engaged in a particular type of occupation would not compete with another group of men engaged in a different occupation.

In this way, Lord Kṛṣṇa used to enjoy the company of His sixteen thousand wives. Devotees of the Lord who want to love the Supreme Personality of Godhead in the mellow of conjugal love are elevated to the position of becoming wives of Kṛṣṇa, and Kṛṣṇa also keeps them always attached to Him by His kind behavior. Kṛṣṇa's behavior with His wives, His movements, His talking with them, His smiling, His embracing, and similar other activities just like a loving husband kept them always very much attached to Him. That is the highest perfection of life. If someone remains always attached to Kṛṣṇa, it is to be understood that he is liberated, and his life is successful. With any devotee who loves Kṛṣṇa with his heart and soul, Kṛṣṇa reciprocates in such a way that the devotee cannot remain unattached to Him. The reciprocal dealings of Kṛṣṇa and His devotees are so attractive that a devotee cannot think of any subject matter other than Kṛṣṇa.

For all the queens, Kṛṣṇa only was their worshipable objective. They were always absorbed in thought of Kṛṣṇa, the lotus-eyed and beautifully blackish Personality of Godhead. Sometimes, in thought of Kṛṣṇa, they remained silent, and in great ecstasy of *bhāva* and *anubhāva* they sometimes spoke as if in delirium. Sometimes, even in the presence of Lord Kṛṣṇa, they vividly described the pastimes they had enjoyed in the lake or in the river with Him. Some of such talk may be described here.

One of the queens said to the bird *kurarī,* "My dear *kurarī,* now it is very late at night. Everyone is sleeping. The whole world is now calm and peaceful. At this time, the Supreme Personality of Godhead is sleeping, although His knowledge is undisturbed by any circumstance. Then why are you not sleeping? Why are you lamenting like this throughout the whole night? My dear friend, is it that you are also attracted by the lotus eyes of the Supreme Personality of Godhead and by His sweet smiling and attractive words, exactly as I am? Do those dealings of the Supreme Personality of Godhead pinch your heart as they do mine?

"Hello *cakravākī.* Why have you closed your eyes? Are you searching after your husband, who might have gone to foreign countries? Why are you lamenting so pitiably? Alas, it appears that you are very much aggrieved. Or is it a fact that you also are willing to become an eternal servitor of the Supreme Personality of Godhead? I think that you are anxious to put a garland on the lotus feet of the Lord and then place it on your hair.

"O my dear ocean, why are you roaring all day and night? Don't you like to sleep? I think that you have been attacked by insomnia, or, if I am not wrong, my dear Śyāmasundara has tactfully taken away your gravity and power of forbearance which are your natural qualifications. Is it a fact that for this reason you are suffering from insomnia like me? Yes, I admit that there is no remedy for this disease.

"My dear moon-god, I think that you have been attacked by a severe type of tuberculosis. For this reason, you are becoming thinner and thinner day by day. O my lord, you are now so weak that your thin rays cannot dissipate the darkness of night. Or is it a fact that, just as I have, you also have been stunned by the mysteriously sweet words of my Lord Śyāmasundara. Is it a fact that it is because of this severe anxiety that you are so grave?

"O breeze from the Himalayas, what have I done to you that you are so intent on teasing me by awakening my lust to meet Kṛṣṇa? Do you not know that I have already been injured by the crooked policy of the Personality of Godhead? My dear Himalayan breeze, please know that I have already been stricken. There is no need to injure me more and more.

"My dear beautiful cloud, the color of your beautiful body exactly resembles my dearmost Śyāmasundara's bodily hue. I think, therefore, that you are very much dear to my Lord, the chief of the dynasty of the Yadus, and because you are so dear to Him, you are, exactly as I am, absorbed in meditation. I can appreciate that your heart is full of anxiety for Śyāmasundara. You appear to be excessively eager to see Him, and I see that for this reason only, there are drops of tears gliding down from your eyes, just as there are from mine. My dear black cloud, we must admit frankly that to establish an intimate relationship with Śyāmasundara means to purchase unnecessary anxieties while we are otherwise comfortable at home."

Generally the cuckoo sounds its cooing vibration at the end of night or early in the morning. When the queens heard the cooing of the cuckoo at the end of night, they said, "Dear cuckoo, your voice is very sweet. As soon as you vibrate your sweet voice, we immediately remember Śyāmasundara because your voice exactly resembles His. We must frankly admit that your voice is imbued with nectar, and it is so invigorating that it is competent to bring back life to those who are almost dead in separation from their dearmost friend. So we are very much obliged to you. Please let us know how we can welcome you or how we can do something for you."

The queens continued talking like that, and they addressed the mountain as follows: "Dear mountain, you are very generous. By your gravitation only, the whole crust of this earth is properly maintained, and because you are discharging your duties very faithfully, you do not know how to move. Because you are so grave, you do not move hither and thither, nor do you say anything. Rather, you always appear to be in a thoughtful mood. It may be that you are always thinking of a very grave and important subject matter, but we can guess very clearly what you are thinking of. We are sure that you are thinking of placing the lotus feet of Śyāmasundara on your raised peaks, as we want to place His lotus feet on our raised breasts.

"Dear dry rivers, we know that because this is the summer season, all your beds are dry and you have no water. Because all your water has now been dried up, you are no longer beautified by blooming lotus flowers. At the present moment, you appear to be very lean and thin, so we can understand that your position is exactly like ours. We have lost everything due to being separated from Śyāmasundara, and we no longer hear His pleasing words. Our hearts no longer work properly, and therefore we also have become very lean and thin. We think, therefore, that you are just like us. You have turned lean and thin because you are not getting any water from your husband, the ocean, through the clouds." The example given herewith by the queens is very appropriate. The river beds become dry when the ocean no longer supplies water through the clouds. The ocean is supposed to be the husband of the river and therefore is supposed to support her. Unless a woman is supported by the husband with the necessities of life, she also becomes as dry as a dry river.

One queen addressed a swan as follows. "My dear swan, please come here, come here. You are welcome. Please sit down and take some milk. My dear swan, can you tell me if you have any message from Śyāmasundara? I take you to be a messenger from Him. If you have any such news, please tell me. Our Śyāmasundara is always very independent. He never comes under the control of anyone. We have all failed to control Him, and therefore we ask you, is He keeping Himself well? I may inform you that Śyāmasundara is very fickle. His friendship is always temporary; it breaks even by slight agitation. But would you kindly explain why He is so unkind to me? Formerly He said that I alone am His dearmost wife. Does He remember this assurance? Anyway, you are welcome. Please sit down. But I cannot accept your entreaty to go to Śyāmasundara. When He does not care for me, why should I be mad after Him? I am very sorry to let you know that you have become the messenger of a poor-hearted soul. You are asking me to go to Him, but I am not going. What is that? You talk of His coming to me? Does He desire to come here to fulfill my long expectation for Him? All right. You can bring Him here. But don't bring with Him His most beloved goddess of fortune. Do you think that He cannot be separated from the goddess of fortune even for a moment? Could He not come here alone, without Lakṣmī? His behavior is very displeasing. Does it mean that without Lakṣmī, Śyāmasundara cannot be happy? Can't He be happy with any other wife? Does it mean that the goddess of fortune has the ocean of love for Him, and none of us can compare to her?"

All the wives of Lord Kṛṣṇa were completely absorbed in thought of Him. Kṛṣṇa is known as the *yogeśvara,* the master of all *yogīs,* and all the wives of Kṛṣṇa at Dvārakā used to keep this *yogeśvara* within their hearts. Instead of trying to be master of all yogic mystic powers, it is better if one simply keeps the supreme *yogeśvara,* Kṛṣṇa, within his heart. Thus one's life can become perfect, and one can very easily be transferred to the kingdom of God. It is to be understood that all the queens of Kṛṣṇa who lived with Him at Dvārakā were in their previous lives very greatly exalted devotees who wanted to establish a relationship with Kṛṣṇa in conjugal love. Thus they were given the chance to become His wives and enjoy a constant loving relationship with Him. Ultimately, they were all transferred to the Vaikuṇṭha planets.

The Supreme Absolute Truth Personality of Godhead is never impersonal. All the Vedic literatures glorify the transcendental performance of His various personal activities and pastimes. It is said that in the Vedas and in the *Rāmāyaṇa,* only the activities of the Lord are described. Everywhere in the Vedic literature, His glories are sung. As soon as soft-hearted people such as women hear those transcendental pastimes of Lord Kṛṣṇa, they immediately become attracted to Him. Soft-hearted women and girls are therefore very easily drawn to the Kṛṣṇa consciousness movement. One who is thus drawn to the Kṛṣṇa consciousness movement and tries to keep himself in constant touch with such consciousness certainly gets the supreme salvation, going back to Kṛṣṇa at Goloka Vṛndāvana. If simply by developing Kṛṣṇa consciousness one can be transferred to the spiritual world, one can simply imagine how blissful and blessed were the queens of Lord Kṛṣṇa, who talked with Him personally and who saw Lord Kṛṣṇa eye to eye. No one can properly describe the fortune of the wives of Lord Kṛṣṇa. They took care of Him personally by rendering various transcendental services like bathing Him, feeding Him, pleasing Him and serving Him. Thus no one's austerities can compare to the service of the queens at Dvārakā.

Śukadeva Gosvāmī informed Mahārāja Parīkṣit that for self-realization the austerities and penances performed by the queens at Dvārakā have no comparison. The objective of self-realization is one: Kṛṣṇa. Therefore, although the dealings of the queens with Kṛṣṇa appear just like ordinary dealings between husband and wife, the principal point to be observed is the queens' attachment for Kṛṣṇa. The entire process of austerity and penance is meant to detach one from the material world and to enhance one's attachment to Kṛṣṇa, the Supreme Personality of Godhead. Kṛṣṇa is the shelter of all persons advancing in self-realization. As an ideal householder, He lived with His wives and performed the Vedic rituals just to show less intelligent persons that the Supreme Lord is never impersonal. Kṛṣṇa lived with wife and children in all opulence, exactly like an ordinary conditioned soul, just to exemplify to those souls who are actually conditioned that one may enter into the circle of family life as long as Kṛṣṇa is the center. For example, the members of the Yadu dynasty lived in the family of Kṛṣṇa, and Kṛṣṇa was the center of all their activities.

Renunciation is not as important as enhancing one's attachment to Kṛṣṇa. The Kṛṣṇa consciousness movement is especially meant for this purpose. We are preaching on the principle that it does not matter whether a man is a *sannyāsī* or *gṛhastha.* One simply has to increase his attachment for Kṛṣṇa, and then his life is successful. Following in the footsteps of Lord Śrī Kṛṣṇa, one can live with his family members or within the society or nation, not for the purpose of indulging in sense gratification but to realize Kṛṣṇa by advancing in attachment for Him. There are four principles of elevation from conditional life to the life of liberation, which are technically known as *dharma, artha, kāma* and *mokṣa* (religion, economic development, sense gratification and liberation). If one lives a family life following in the footsteps of Lord Kṛṣṇa's family members, one can achieve all four of these principles of success simultaneously by making Kṛṣṇa the center of all activities.

It is already known to us that Kṛṣṇa had 16,108 wives. All these wives were exalted liberated souls, and among them Queen Rukmiṇī was the chief. After Rukmiṇī there were seven other principal wives, and the names of the sons of these eight principal queens have already been mentioned. Besides these eight queens, Lord Kṛṣṇa had ten sons by each of the other queens. Thus all together Kṛṣṇa's children numbered 16,108 times ten. One should not be astonished to hear that Kṛṣṇa had so many sons. One should always remember that Kṛṣṇa is the Supreme Personality of Godhead and that He has unlimited potencies. He claims all living entities as His sons, so even if He had sixteen million sons attached to Him personally, there would be no cause for astonishment.

Among Kṛṣṇa's greatly powerful sons, eighteen sons were *mahā-rathas.* The *mahā-rathas* could fight alone against many thousands of soldiers, charioteers, cavalry and elephants. The reputations of these eighteen sons are very widespread and are described in almost all the Vedic literatures. The eighteen *mahā-ratha* sons are listed as Pradyumna, Aniruddha, Dīptimān, Bhānu, Sāmba, Madhu, Bṛhadbhānu, Citrabhānu, Vṛka, Aruṇa, Puṣkara, Vedabāhu, Śrutadeva, Sunandana, Citrabāhu, Virūpa, Kavi and Nyagrodha. Of these eighteen *mahā-ratha* sons of Kṛṣṇa, Pradyumna is considered to be the foremost. Pradyumna happened to be the eldest son of Queen Rukmiṇī, and he inherited all the qualities of his great father, Lord Kṛṣṇa. He married the daughter of his maternal uncle, Rukmī, and Aniruddha, the son of Pradyumna, was born from that marriage. Aniruddha was so powerful that he could fight against ten thousand elephants. He married the granddaughter of Rukmī, the brother of his grandmother, Rukmiṇī. Because the relationship between these cousins was distant, such a marriage was not uncommon. Aniruddha's son was Vajra. When the whole Yadu dynasty was destroyed by the curse of a *brāhmaṇa,* only Vajra survived. Vajra had one son whose name was Pratibāhu. The son of Pratibāhu was named Subāhu, the son of Subāhu was named Śāntasena, and the son of Śāntasena was Śatasena.

It is stated by Śukadeva Gosvāmī that all the members of the Yadu dynasty had many children. Just as Kṛṣṇa had many sons, grandsons and great-grandsons, so each one of the kings named herewith also had similar family extensions. Not only did all of them have many children, but all were extraordinarily rich and opulent. None of them were weak or short-lived, and above all, all the members of the Yadu dynasty were staunch devotees of the brahminical culture. It is the duty of the *kṣatriya* kings to maintain the brahminical culture and to protect the qualified *brāhmaṇas,* and all these kings discharged their duties very rightly. The members of the Yadu dynasty were so numerous that it would be very difficult to describe them all even if one had a duration of life of many thousands of years. Śrīla Śukadeva Gosvāmī informed Mahārāja Parīkṣit that he had heard from reliable sources that simply to teach the children of the Yadu dynasty, there were as many as 38,800,000 tutors or *ācāryas.* If so many teachers were needed to educate their children, one can simply imagine how vast was the number of family members. As for their military strength, it is said that King Ugrasena alone had ten quadrillion soldiers as personal bodyguards.

Before the advent of Lord Kṛṣṇa within this universe, there were many battles between the demons and the demigods. Many demons died in the fighting, and they all were given the chance to take birth in high royal families on this earth. Because of their royal exalted posts, all these demons became very much puffed up, and their only business was to harass their subjects. Lord Kṛṣṇa appeared on this planet just at the end of Dvāpara-yuga in order to annihilate all these demonic kings. As it is said in the *Bhagavad-gītā, paritrāṇāya sādhūnāṁ vināśāya ca duṣkṛtām:* The Lord comes to protect the devotees and to annihilate the miscreants. Some of the demigods were also asked to appear on this earth to assist in the transcendental pastimes of Lord Kṛṣṇa. When Kṛṣṇa appeared, He came in the association of His eternal servitors, but the demigods also were requested to come down to assist Him, and thus all of them took their births in the Yadu dynasty. The Yadu dynasty had 101 clans in different parts of the country. All the members of these different clans respected Lord Kṛṣṇa in a manner befitting His divine position, and all of them were His devotees heart and soul. Thus all the members of the Yadu dynasty were very opulent, happy and prosperous, and they had no anxieties. Because of their implicit faith in and devotion to Lord Kṛṣṇa, they were never defeated by any other kings. Their love of Krsna was so intense that in their regular activities—in sitting, sleeping, traveling, talking, sporting, cleansing and bathing—they were simply absorbed in thoughts of Kṛṣṇa and paid no attention to bodily necessities. That is the symptom of a pure devotee of Lord Kṛṣṇa. Just as when a man is fully absorbed in some particular thought, he sometimes forgets his other bodily activities, so the members of the Yadu dynasty acted automatically for their bodily necessities, but their actual attention was always fixed on Kṛṣṇa. Their bodily activities were performed mechanically, but their minds were always absorbed in Kṛṣṇa consciousness.

Śrīla Śukadeva Gosvāmī has concluded the Ninetieth Chapter of the Tenth Canto of *Śrīmad-Bhāgavatam* by pointing out five particular excellences of Lord Kṛṣṇa. The first excellence is that before Lord Kṛṣṇa's appearance in the Yadu family, the River Ganges was known as the purest of all things; even impure things could be purified simply by touching the water of the Ganges. This superexcellent power of the Ganges water was due to its having emanated from the toe of Lord Viṣṇu. But when Lord Kṛṣṇa, the Supreme Viṣṇu, appeared in the family of the Yadu dynasty, He traveled personally throughout the kingdom of the Yadus, and by His intimate association with the Yadu dynasty, the whole family not only became very famous but also became more effective in purifying others than the water of the Ganges.

The next excellence of Lord Kṛṣṇa's appearance was that although apparently He gave protection to the devotees and annihilated the demons, both the devotees and the demons achieved the same result. Lord Kṛṣṇa is the bestower of five kinds of liberation, of which *sāyujya-mukti,* or the liberation of becoming one with the Supreme, was given to the demons like Kaṁsa, whereas the *gopīs* were given the chance to associate with Him personally. The *gopīs* kept their individuality to enjoy the company of Lord Kṛṣṇa, but Kaṁsa was accepted into His impersonal *brahmajyoti.* In other words, both the demons and the *gopīs* were spiritually liberated, but because the demons were enemies and the *gopīs* were friends, the demons were killed and the *gopīs* were protected.

The third excellence of Lord Kṛṣṇa's appearance was that the goddess of fortune, who is worshiped by demigods like Lord Brahmā, Indra and Candra, remained always engaged in the service of the Lord, even though the Lord gave more preference to the *gopīs.* Lakṣmījī, the goddess of fortune, tried her best to be on an equal level with the *gopīs,* but she was not successful. Nevertheless, she remained faithful to Kṛṣṇa, although generally she does not remain at one place even if worshiped by demigods like Lord Brahmā.

The fourth excellence of Lord Kṛṣṇa's appearance concerns the glories of His name. It is stated in the Vedic literature that by chanting the different names of Lord Viṣṇu a thousand times, one may be bestowed with the same benefits as by thrice chanting the holy name of Lord Rāma. And by chanting the holy name of Lord Kṛṣṇa only once, one receives the same benefit. In other words, of all the holy names of the Supreme Personality of Godhead, including Viṣṇu and Rāma, the holy name of Kṛṣṇa is the most powerful. The Vedic literature therefore specifically stresses the chanting of the holy name of Kṛṣṇa: Hare Kṛṣṇa, Hare Kṛṣṇa, Kṛṣṇa Kṛṣṇa, Hare Hare/ Hare Rāma, Hare Rāma, Rāma Rāma, Hare Hare. Lord Caitanya introduced this chanting of the holy name of Kṛṣṇa in this age, thus making liberation more easily obtainable than in other ages. In other words, Lord Kṛṣṇa is more excellent than His other incarnations, although all of them are equally the Supreme Personality of Godhead.

The fifth excellence of Lord Kṛṣṇa's appearance is that He established the most excellent of all religious principles by His one statement in the *Bhagavad-gītā* that simply by surrendering unto Him, one can discharge all the principles of religious rites. In the Vedic literature there are twenty kinds of religious principles mentioned, and each of them is described in different *śāstras*. But Lord Kṛṣṇa is so kind to the fallen conditioned souls of this age that He personally appeared and asked everyone to give up all kinds of religious rites and simply surrender unto Him. It is said that this age of Kali is three-fourths devoid of religious principles. Hardly one fourth of the principles of religion are still observed in this age. But by the mercy of Lord Kṛṣṇa, this vacancy of Kali-yuga has not only been completely filled, but the religious process has been made so easy that simply by rendering transcendental loving service unto Lord Kṛṣṇa by chanting His holy names, Hare Kṛṣṇa, Hare Kṛṣṇa, Kṛṣṇa Kṛṣṇa, Hare Hare/ Hare Rāma, Hare Rāma, Rāma Rāma, Hare Hare, one can achieve the highest result of religion, namely, being transferred to the highest planet within the spiritual world, Goloka Vṛndāvana. One can thus immediately estimate the benefit of Lord Kṛṣṇa's appearance and can understand that His giving relief to the people of the world by His appearance was not at all extraordinary.

Śrīla Śukadeva Gosvāmi thus concludes his description of the super-exalted position of Lord Kṛṣṇa by glorifying Him in the following way: "O Lord Kṛṣṇa, all glories unto You. You are present in everyone's heart as Paramātmā. Therefore You are known as Jananivāsa, one who lives in everyone's heart." As confirmed in the *Bhagavad-gītā, īśvaraḥ sarva-bhūtānāṁ hṛd-deśe 'rjuna tiṣṭhati:* The Supreme Lord in His Paramātma feature lives within everyone's heart. This does not mean, however, that Kṛṣṇa has no separate existence as the Supreme Personality of Godhead. The Māyāvādī philosophers accept the all-pervading feature of Para-brahman, but when Parabrahman, or the Supreme Lord, appears, they think that He appears under the control of material nature. Because Lord Kṛṣṇa appeared as the son of Devakī, the Māyāvādī philosophers accept Kṛṣṇa to be an ordinary living entity who takes birth within this material world. Therefore Śukadeva Gosvāmī warns them that *devakī-janma-vāda,* which means that although Kṛṣṇa is famous as the son of Devakī, actually He is the Supersoul or the all-pervading Supreme Personality of Godhead. The devotees, however, take this word *devakī-janma-vāda* in a different way. The devotees understand that actually Kṛṣṇa was the son of mother Yaśodā. Although Kṛṣṇa first of all appeared as the son of Devakī, He immediately transferred Himself to the lap of mother Yaśodā, and His childhood pastimes were blissfully enjoyed by mother Yaśodā and Nanda Mahārāja. This fact was also admitted by Vasudeva himself when he met Nanda Mahārāja and Yaśodā at Kurukṣetra. He admitted that Kṛṣṇa and Balarāma were actually the sons of mother Yaśodā and Nanda Mahārāja. Vasudeva and Devakī were only Their official father and mother. Their actual father and mother were Nanda and Yaśodā. Therefore Śukadeva Gosvāmī addressed Lord Kṛṣṇa as *devakī-janma-vāda.*

Śukadeva Gosvāmī then glorifies the Lord as one who is honored by the *yadu-vara-pariṣat,* the assembly house of the Yadu dynasty, and as the killer of different kinds of demons. Kṛṣṇa, the Supreme Personality of Godhead, could have killed all the demons by employing His different material energies, but He wanted to kill them personally in order to give them salvation. There was no need of Kṛṣṇa's coming to this material world to kill the demons. Simply by His willing, many hundreds and thousands of demons could have been killed without His personal endeavor. But actually He descended for His pure devotees, to play as a child with mother Yaśodā and Nanda Mahārāja and to give pleasure to the inhabitants of Dvārakā. By killing the demons and by giving protection to the devotees, Lord Kṛṣṇa established the real religious principle, which is simply love of God. By following the factual religious principles of love of God, even the living entities known as *sthira-cara* were also delivered of all material contamination and were transferred to the spiritual kingdom. *Sthira* means the trees and plants, which cannot move, and *cara* means the moving animals, specifically the cows. When Kṛṣṇa was present, He delivered all the trees, monkeys and other plants and animals who happened to see Him and serve Him both in Vṛndāvana and in Dvārakā.

Lord Kṛṣṇa is especially glorified for His giving pleasure to the *gopīs* and the queens of Dvārakā. Śukadeva Gosvāmī glorifies Lord Kṛṣṇa for His enchanting smile, by which He enchanted not only the *gopīs* at Vṛndāvana but also the queens at Dvārakā. The exact word used in this connection is *vardhayan kāmadevam.* In Vṛndāvana as the boy friend of many *gopīs* and in Dvārakā as the husband of many queens, Kṛṣṇa increased their lusty desires to enjoy with Him. For God realization or self-realization, one generally has to undergo severe austerities and penances for many, many thousands of years, and then it may be possible to realize God. But the *gopīs* and the queens of Dvārakā, simply by enhancing their lusty desires to enjoy Kṛṣṇa as their boy friend or husband, received the highest type of salvation.

This behavior of Lord Kṛṣṇa with the *gopīs* and queens is unique in the history of self-realization. Usually people understand that for self-realization one has to go to the forest or to the mountains and undergo severe austerities and penances. But the *gopīs* and the queens, simply by being attached to Kṛṣṇa in conjugal love and enjoying His company in a so-called sensuous life full of luxury and opulence, achieved the highest salvation, which is impossible to be achieved even by great sages and saintly persons. Similarly, the demons such as Kaṁsa, Dantavakra, Śiśupāla, etc., also got the highest benefit of being transferred to the spiritual world.

In the beginning of *Śrīmad-Bhāgavatam,* Śrīla Vyāsadeva offered his respectful obeisances to the Supreme Truth, Vāsudeva, Kṛṣṇa. After that he taught his son, Śukadeva Gosvāmī, to preach *Śrīmad-Bhāgavatam.* It is in this connection that Śukadeva Gosvāmī glorifies the Lord as *jayati.* Following in the footsteps of Śrīla Vyāsadeva, Śukadeva Gosvāmī and all the *ācāryas* in disciplic succession, the whole population of the world should glorify Lord Kṛṣṇa, and for their best interest they should take to this Kṛṣṇa consciousness movement. The process is easy and helpful. It is simply to chant the *mahāmantra,* Hare Kṛṣṇa, Hare Kṛṣṇa, Kṛṣṇa Kṛṣṇa, Hare Hare/Hare Rāma, Hare Rāma, Rāma Rāma, Hare Hare. Lord Caitanya has therefore recommended that one should be callous to the material ups and downs. Material life is temporary, and so the ups and downs of life may come and go. When they come, one should be as tolerant as a tree and as humble and meek as the straw in the street, but certainly he must engage himself in Kṛṣṇa consciousness by chanting Hare Kṛṣṇa, Hare Kṛṣṇa, Kṛṣṇa Kṛṣṇa, Hare Hare.

The Supreme Personality of Godhead, Kṛṣṇa, the Supersoul of all living entities, out of His causeless mercy comes down and manifests His different transcendental pastimes in different incarnations. Hearing the attractive pastimes of Lord Kṛṣṇa's different incarnations is a chance for liberation for the conditioned soul, and the most fascinating and pleasing activities of Lord Kṛṣṇa Himself are still more attractive because Lord Kṛṣṇa personally is all-attractive.

Following in the holy footsteps of Śrīla Śukadeva Gosvāmī, we have tried to present this book *Kṛṣṇa* for being read and heard by the conditioned souls of this age. By hearing the pastimes of Lord Kṛṣṇa, one is sure and certain to get salvation and be transferred back home, back to Godhead. It is recommended by Śukadeva Gosvāmī that as we hear the transcendental pastimes and activities of the Lord, we gradually cut the knots of material contamination. Therefore, regardless of what one is, if one wants the association of Lord Kṛṣṇa in the transcendental kingdom of God for eternity in blissful existence, one must hear about the pastimes of Lord Kṛṣṇa and chant the *mahāmantra,* Hare Kṛṣṇa,

Hare Kṛṣṇa, Kṛṣṇa Kṛṣṇa, Hare Hare/Hare Rāma, Hare Rāma, Rāma Rāma, Hare Hare.

The transcendental pastimes of the Supreme Personality of Godhead Kṛṣṇa are so powerful that simply by hearing, reading and memorizing this book *Kṛṣṇa,* one is sure to be transferred to the spiritual world, which is ordinarily very difficult to achieve. The description of the pastimes of Lord Kṛṣṇa is so attractive that automatically it gives us an impetus to study repeatedly, and the more we study the pastimes of the Lord, the more we become attached to Him. This very attachment to Kṛṣṇa makes one eligible to be transferred to His abode, Goloka Vṛndāvana. As we have learned from the previous chapter, to cross over the material world is to cross over the stringent laws of material nature. The stringent laws of material nature cannot check the progress of one who is attracted by the spiritual nature. This is confirmed in the *Bhagavad-gītā* by the Lord Himself: although the stringent laws of material nature are very difficult to overcome, if anyone surrenders unto the Lord, he can very easily cross over nescience. There is, however, no influence of material nature in the spiritual world. As we have learned from the Second Canto of *Śrīmad-Bhāgavatam,* the ruling power of the demigods and the influence of material nature are conspicuous by their absence in the spiritual world.

Śrīla Śukadeva Gosvāmī has therefore advised Mahārāja Parīkṣit in the beginning of the Second Canto that every conditioned soul should engage himself in hearing and chanting the transcendental pastimes of the Lord. Śrīla Śukadeva Gosvāmī also informed King Parīkṣit that previously many other kings and emperors went to the jungle to prosecute severe austerities and penances in order to go back home, back to Godhead. In India, it is still a practice that many advanced transcendentalists give up their family lives and go to Vṛndāvana to live there alone and completely engage in hearing and chanting of the holy pastimes of the Lord. This system is recommended in the *Śrīmad-Bhāgavatam,* and the six Gosvāmīs of Vṛndāvana followed it, but at the present moment many *karmīs* and pseudo-devotees have overcrowded the holy place of Vṛndāvana just to imitate this process recommended by Śukadeva Gosvāmī. It is said that many kings and emperors formerly went to the forest for this purpose, but Śrīla Bhaktisiddhānta Sarasvatī Ṭhākur Gosvāmī Mahārāja does not recommend that one take up this solitary life in Vṛndāvana prematurely.

One who goes prematurely to Vṛndāvana to live in pursuance of the instructions of Śukadeva Gosvāmī again falls a victim of *māyā,* even while residing in Vṛndāvana. To check such unauthorized residence in Vṛndāvana, Śrīla Bhaktisiddhānta Sarasvatī Ṭhākur has sung a nice song in this connection, the purport of which is as follows: "My dear mind, why are you so proud of being a Vaiṣṇava? Your solitary worship and chanting of the holy name of the Lord are based on a desire for cheap popularity, and therefore your chanting of the holy name is only a pretension. Such an ambition for a cheap reputation can be compared to the stool of a hog because such popularity is another extension of the influence of *māyā.*" One may go to Vṛndāvana for cheap popularity, and instead of being absorbed in Kṛṣṇa consciousness, one may always think of money and women, which are simply temporary sources of happiness. It is better that one engage whatever money and women he may have in his possession in the service of the Lord because sense enjoyment is not for the conditioned soul.

The master of the senses is Hṛṣīkeśa, Lord Kṛṣṇa. Therefore, the senses should always be engaged in His service. As for material reputation, there were many demons like Rāvaṇa who wanted to go against the laws of material nature, but they all failed. One should therefore not take to the demoniac activity of claiming to be a Vaiṣṇava just for false prestige, without performing service to the Lord. But when one engages oneself in the devotional service of the Lord, automatically the Vaiṣṇava reputation comes to him. There is no need to be envious of the devotees who are engaged in preaching the glories of the Lord. We have practical experience of being advised by the so-called *bābājīs* in Vṛndāvana that there is no need to preach and that it is better to live in Vṛndāvana in a solitary place and chant the holy name. Such *bābājīs* do not know that if one is engaged in preaching work or in glorifying the Supreme Personality of Godhead, the good reputation of a preacher automatically follows one. One should not, therefore, prematurely give up the honest life of a householder to lead a life of debauchery in Vṛndāvana. Śrīla Śukadeva Gosvāmī's recommendation to leave home and go to the forest in search of Kṛṣṇa is not for immature persons. Mahārāja Parīkṣit was mature. Even in his householder life, or from the very beginning of his life, he worshiped Lord Kṛṣṇa's *mūrti.* In his childhood he worshiped the Deity of Lord Kṛṣṇa, and later, although he was a householder, he was always detached, and therefore when he got the notice of his death, he immediately gave up all connection with household life and sat down on the bank of the Ganges to hear *Śrīmad-Bhāgavatam* in the association of devotees.

Thus ends the Bhaktivedanta purport of the Third Volume, Twenty-first Chapter, of Kṛṣṇa, *"Summary Description of Lord Kṛṣṇa's Pastimes."*

Glossary

Ācāryas—spiritual masters who teach by their own personal behavior.
Asura—a demon or nondevotee.
Ātmārāma—a self-satisfied sage.
Avatāra—an incarnation of Godhead who descends from the spiritual world.
Bhagavad-gītā—the book which records the spiritual instructions given by Kṛṣṇa to His friend Arjuna on the Battlefield of Kurukṣetra.
Bhakta—devotee.
Bhakti-yoga—the *yoga* of devotional service to the Lord.
Brahmā—the first created living being in the universe.
Brahmacārī—a celibate student under the guidance of a spiritual master.
Brahmajyoti—the impersonal effulgence that emanates from the body of Kṛṣṇa.
Brahman—the impersonal feature of the Absolute Truth.
Brāhmaṇas—the spiritual order of society whose occupation is the cultivation of Vedic knowledge.
Brahma-saṁhitā—a scripture written by Lord Brahmā in which his authoritative prayers to the Lord are recorded.
Caitanya Mahāprabhu—the incarnation of Kṛṣṇa as His own devotee who comes in this age to teach the process of devotional service by chanting the holy name of God.
Cāmara—a yak-tail whisk.
Deva—a demigod or devotee.
Ekādaśī—a day of celebration which occurs twice a month and which is meant for increasing Kṛṣṇa consciousness.
Gandharvas—celestial denizens of the heavenly planets who sing very beautifully.
Garuḍa—the giant bird-carrier of Viṣṇu.
Gopīs—cowherd girls, specifically the transcendental girl friends of Lord Kṛṣṇa.

Gṛhastha—one who is in the householder order of spiritual life.
Guru—spiritual master.
Jaya—victory.
Jñānī—one who engages in mental speculation in pursuit of knowledge.
Kadamba—a tree which bears a round yellow flower and which is generally seen only in the Vṛndāvana area.
Karma—fruitive activities or their reactions.
Karmī—a fruitive worker.
Kaumudī—an especially fragrant flower found on the bank of the Yamunā River.
Kaustubha—a transcendental jewel worn around the neck of the Supreme Personality of Godhead.
Kṛṣṇa-kathā—narrations spoken by or about Kṛṣṇa.
Kṣatriya—the spiritual order of society whose occupation is governmental administration and military protection of the citizens.
Kuṅkuma—a sweetly flavored reddish powder which is thrown upon the bodies of worshipable persons.
Līlā—pastimes.
Māgadhas—professional singers present at sacrifices.
Mahābhāgavata—a highly advanced devotee.
Mahāmantra—the Hare Kṛṣṇa *mantra:* Hare Kṛṣṇa, Hare Kṛṣṇa, Kṛṣṇa Kṛṣṇa, Hare Hare/Hare Rāma, Hare Rāma, Rāma Rāma, Hare Hare.
Mantra—a transcendental sound vibration.
Māyā (Mahāmāyā)—the external energy of the Supreme Lord, which covers the conditioned soul and does not allow him to understand the Supreme Personality of Godhead.
Māyāvāda—the impersonalist or voidist philosophy.
Māyāvādī—one who adheres to the impersonalist or voidist philosophy and does not accept the eternal existence of the transcendental form of the Lord.
Mukti—liberation.
Mukunda—Lord Kṛṣṇa, who awards liberation and whose smiling face is like a *kunda* flower.
Nirguṇa—literally, without qualities (used to describe the Supreme Lord, who has no material qualities).
Pāṇḍavas—the five sons of King Pāṇḍu (Yudhiṣṭhira, Arjuna, Bhīma, Nakula and Sahadeva).
Paramahaṁsa—(literally, the supreme swan) a devotee who can appreciate the spiritual essence of life, just as a swan extracts milk from water.
Paramātmā—the expansion of the Supreme Lord who lives in the hearts of all living entities.

Pārijāta—a type of flower found only on the heavenly planets.

Prakṛta sahajiyā—pseudo-devotees of Kṛṣṇa who fail to understand His absolute, transcendental position.

Prāṇāyāma—the yogic breathing exercises.

Prasadam—food first offered to the Supreme Lord and then distributed.

Rasa—a transcendental mellow relationship between the individual soul and the Supreme Lord.

Rāsa-līlā—Lord Kṛṣṇa's transcendental pastime of dancing with the ***gopīs.***

Samādhi—trance, absorption in meditation upon the Supreme.

Saṅkīrtana yajña—the chanting of the holy names of God, which is the recommended sacrifice for this age.

Sannyāsī—one who is in the renounced order of spiritual life.

Śāstras—revealed scriptures.

Sāyujya-mukti—the liberation of merging into the existence of the Supreme Lord.

Siddhi—a mystic yogic perfection.

Śiva—the demigod in charge of annihilation and the mode of igrorance.

Śrīmad-Bhāgavatam—the authoritative Vedic scripture that deals exclusively with the pastimes of the Personality of Godhead and His devotees.

Sudarśana—the wheel which is the personal weapon of Viṣṇu or Kṛṣṇa.

Śūdra—the spiritual order of society who are not very intelligent and are unqualified for any work other than menial service.

Śyāmasundara—a name of Kṛṣṇa. *Śyāma* means blackish, and *sundara* means very beautiful.

Tapasya—austerity.

Tilaka—a clay mark that decorates the faces of Kṛṣṇa and His devotees.

Tulasī—a great devotee in the form of a plant who is very dear to Lord Kṛṣṇa.

Vaiṣṇava—a devotee of the Supreme Lord Viṣṇu or Kṛṣṇa.

Vaiśya—the agricultural community in Vedic culture, who protect cows and cultivate crops.

Viṣṇu—an all-pervasive, fully empowered expansion of Lord Kṛṣṇa, qualified by full truth, full knowledge and full bliss.

Yajña—sacrifice.

Yoga—the process of linking with the Supreme.

Yogamāyā—the principal internal (spiritual) potency of the Supreme Lord.

Yogī—one who practices *yoga.*

Note on Transliterated Sanskrit Words

The vowels are pronounced almost as in Italian. The sound of the short *a* is like the *u* in b*u*t, the long *ā* is like the *a* in f*a*r and held twice as long as the short *a*, and *e* is like the *a* in ev*a*de. Long *ī* is like the *i* in p*i*que. The vowel *ṛ* is pronounced like the *re* in the English word fib*re*. The *c* is pronounced as in the English word *ch*air, and the aspirated consonants (*ch, jh, dh,* etc.) are pronounced as in staun*ch-h*eart, he*dge-h*og, re*d-h*ot, etc. The two spirants *ś* and *ṣ* are pronounced like the English *sh*; *s* is pronounced as in *s*un.